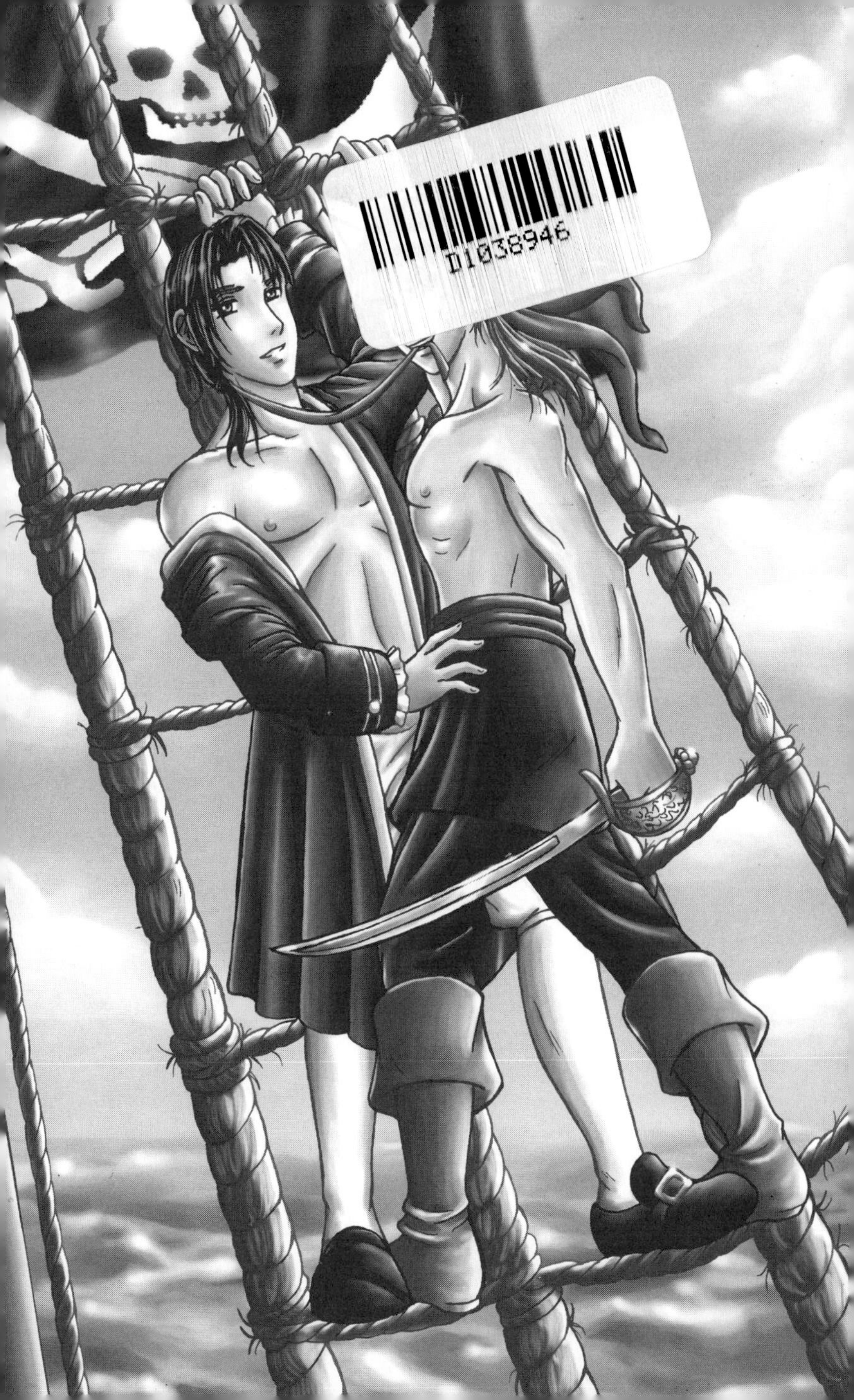

Available Now!

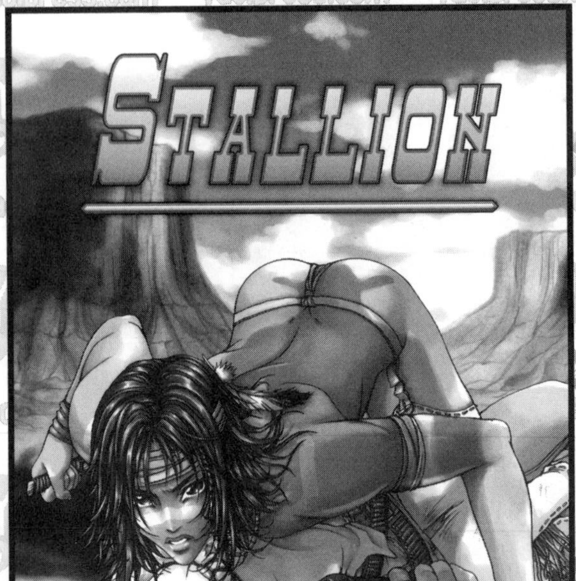
STALLION
By KÔSEN

Stallion
by KÔSEN

Native American Stallion is out for revenge on the cowboy who ruined his life, but has competition from another one of cowboy Bill's victims. Enemies at first, they unite and learn they share a tragic bond due to what they both suffered in the past.

EACH BOOK INCLUDES A SHEET OF COLOR STICKERS!

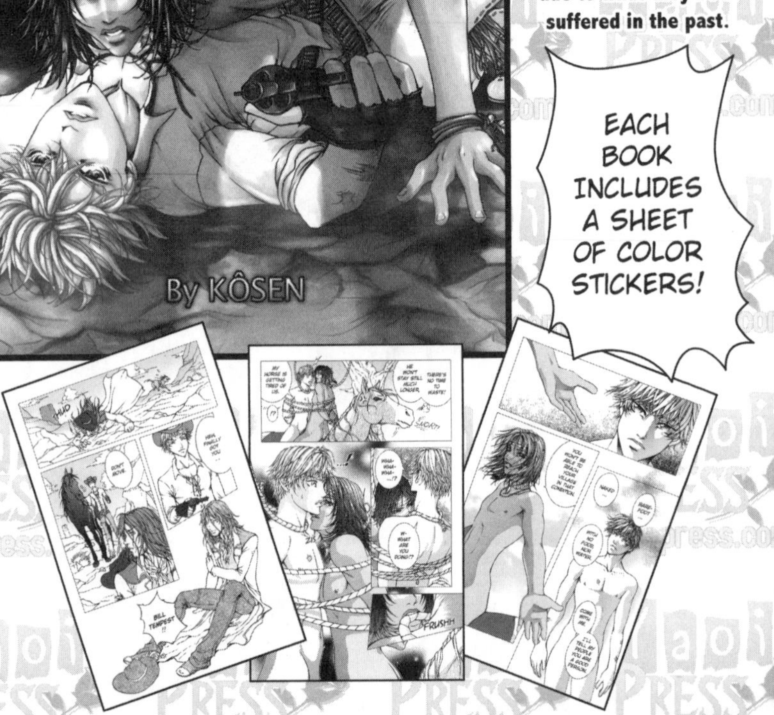
BILL TEMPEST !!
FRUSHH

Coming Sept. 2006!

Yamila Abraham ∗ Studio Kosaru

Winter Demon
by Yamila Abraham and Studio Kosaru

Three fire demons cause the monk Hakuin to seek help from Fuyu, the demon who tormented him the year before. Fuyu will fight the demons, but only if Hakuin becomes his willing slave. Alas, the fire demon leader is too strong...and he's hot for Fuyu.

Treasure

Story and Art by Studio Kawaii, Ana and Mercedes Hidalgo

Small Sacrifice ~ Story by Ashton Kalloway, Art by Studio Kosaru

Edited by Xaviera Pallars and Yamila Abraham.

Printed in the United States of America

ISBN: 1-933664-05-3

ISBN 13: 978-1-933664-05-7

Published by Yaoi Press Ltd. First printing August 2006.

www.yaoipress.com

10 9 8 7 6 5 4 3 2 1

TREASURE

STORY, ART, AND LETTERS
BY STUDIO KAWAII

EDITED BY YAMILA ABRAHAM
XAVIERA PALLARS AND
LAILA REIMOZ

SMALL SACRIFICE

STORY BY KALLOWAY ASHTON
ART BY STUDIO KOSARU
LETTERS BY LAILA REIMOZ
EDITED BY XAVIERA PALLARS

www.yaoipress.com

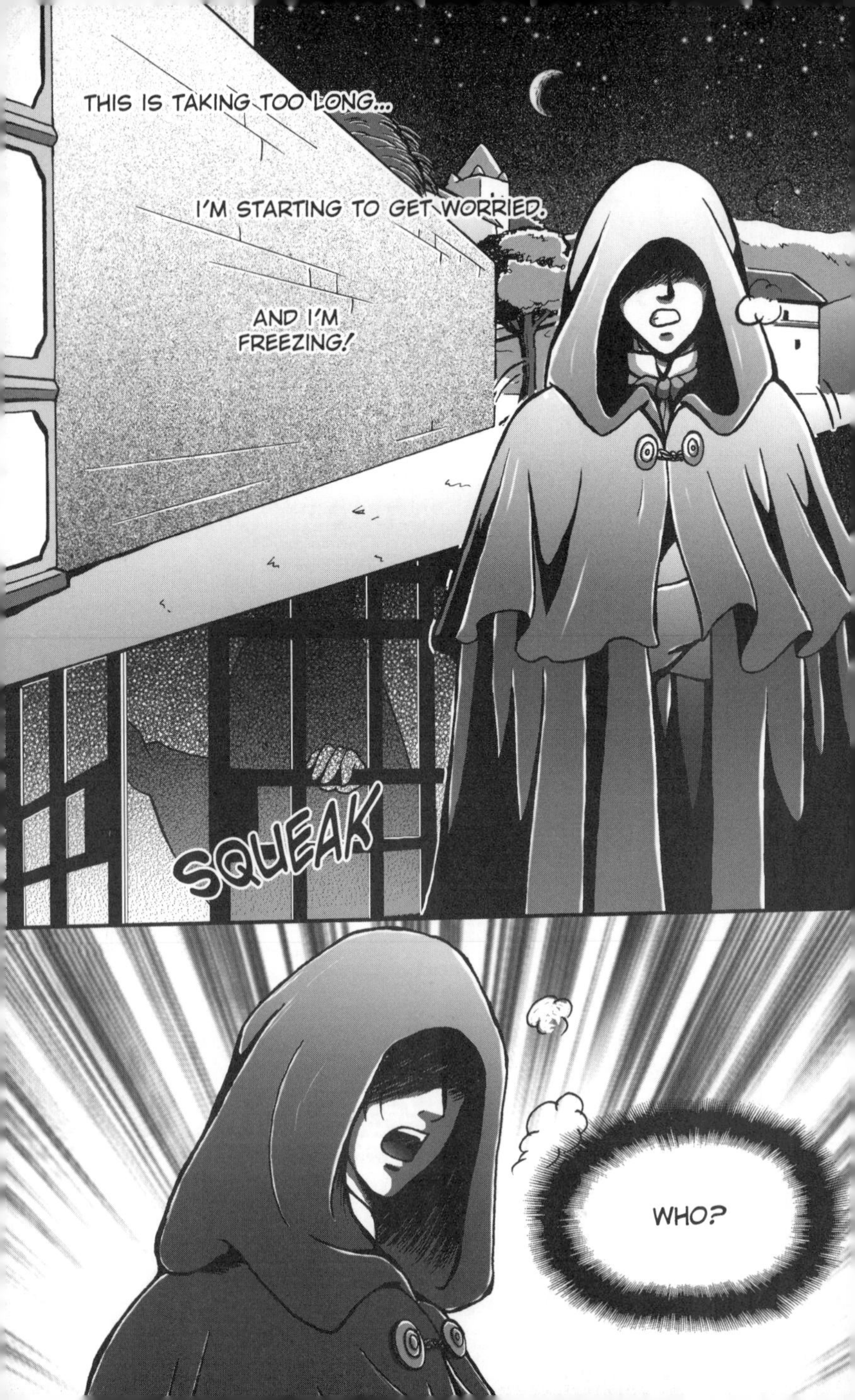
THIS IS TAKING TOO LONG...
I'M STARTING TO GET WORRIED.
AND I'M FREEZING!
SQUEAK
WHO?

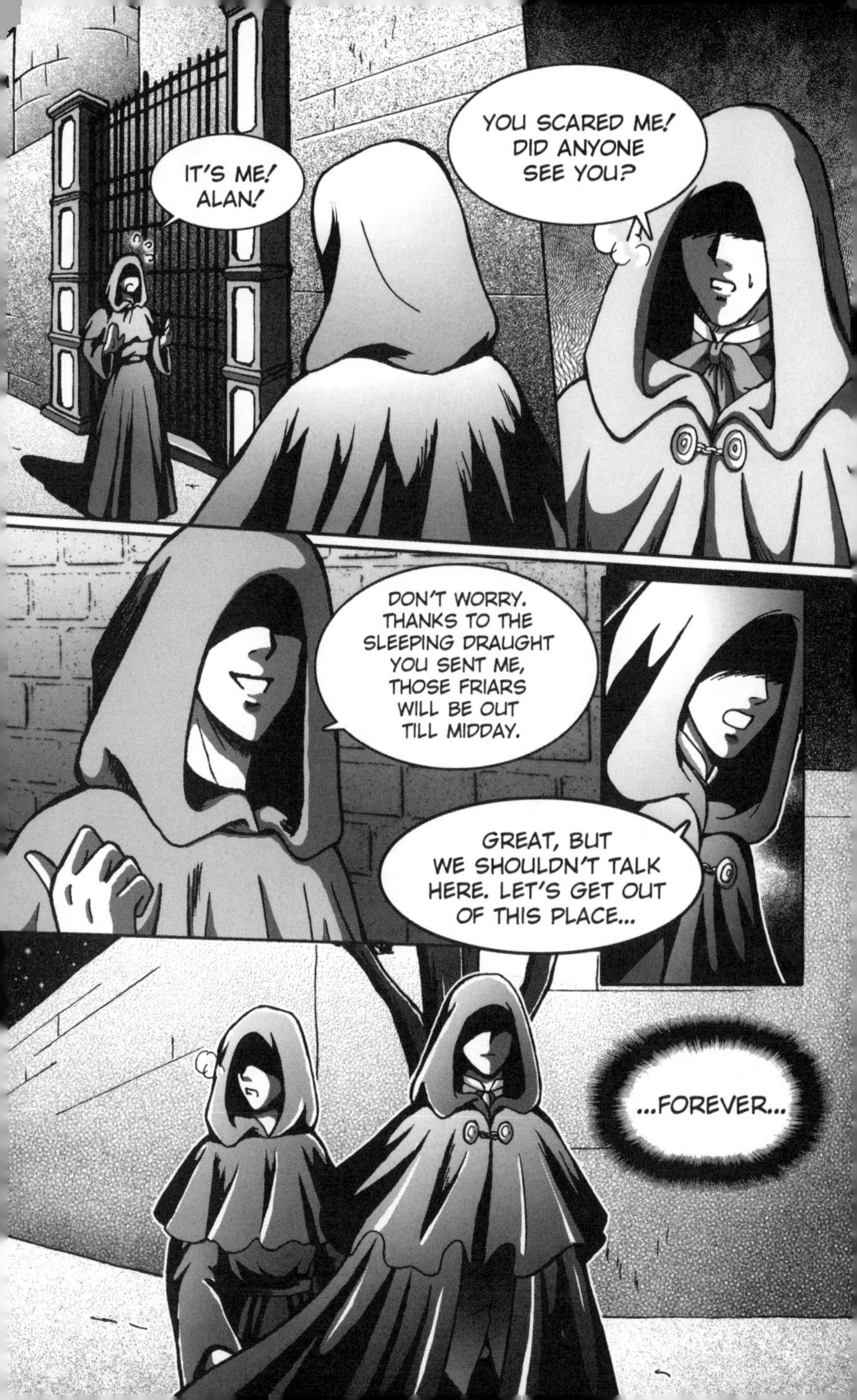
IT'S ME! ALAN!
YOU SCARED ME! DID ANYONE SEE YOU?
DON'T WORRY. THANKS TO THE SLEEPING DRAUGHT YOU SENT ME, THOSE FRIARS WILL BE OUT TILL MIDDAY.
GREAT, BUT WE SHOULDN'T TALK HERE. LET'S GET OUT OF THIS PLACE...
...FOREVER...

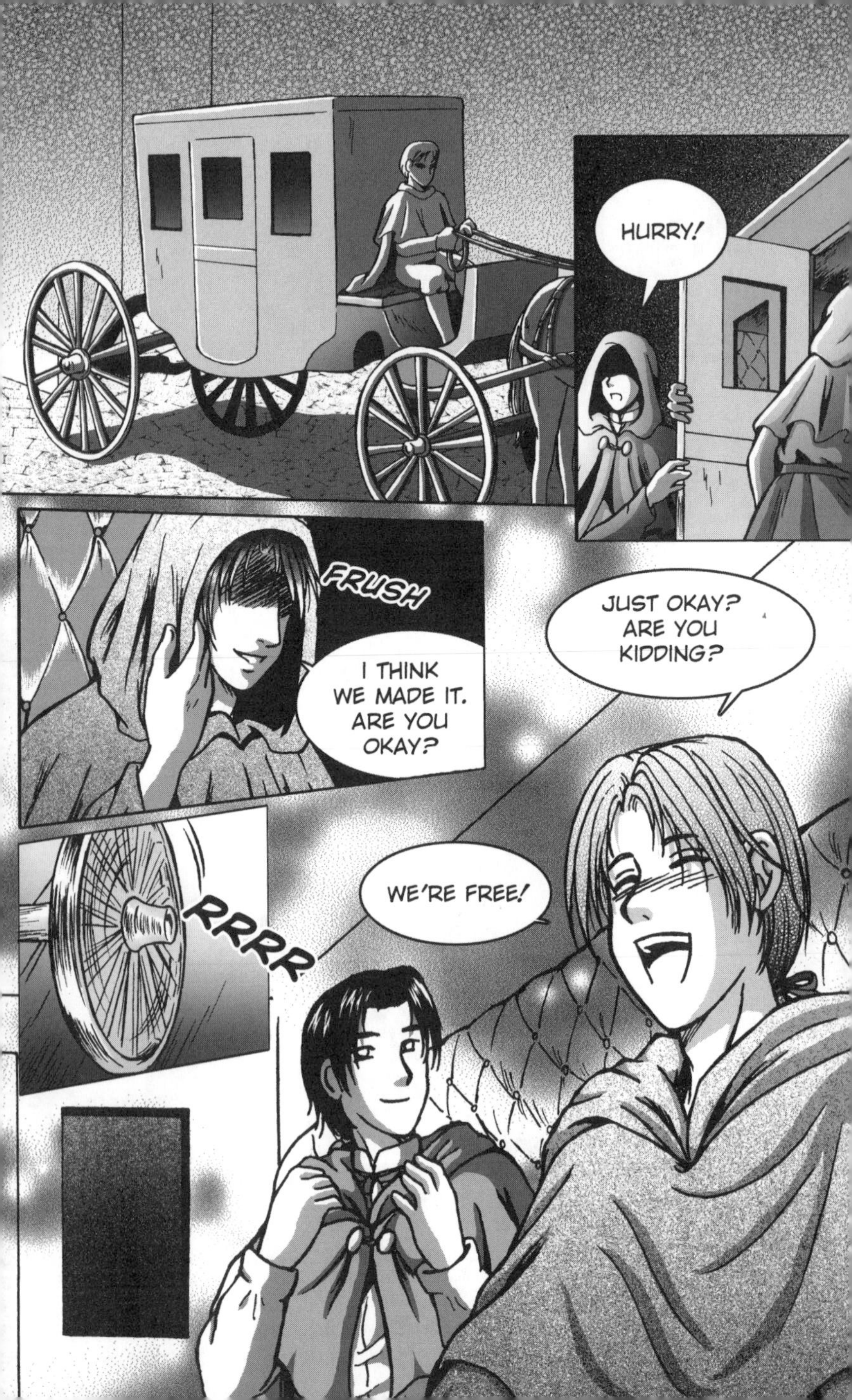
HURRY!
FRUSH
I THINK WE MADE IT. ARE YOU OKAY?
JUST OKAY? ARE YOU KIDDING?
RRRR
WE'RE FREE!

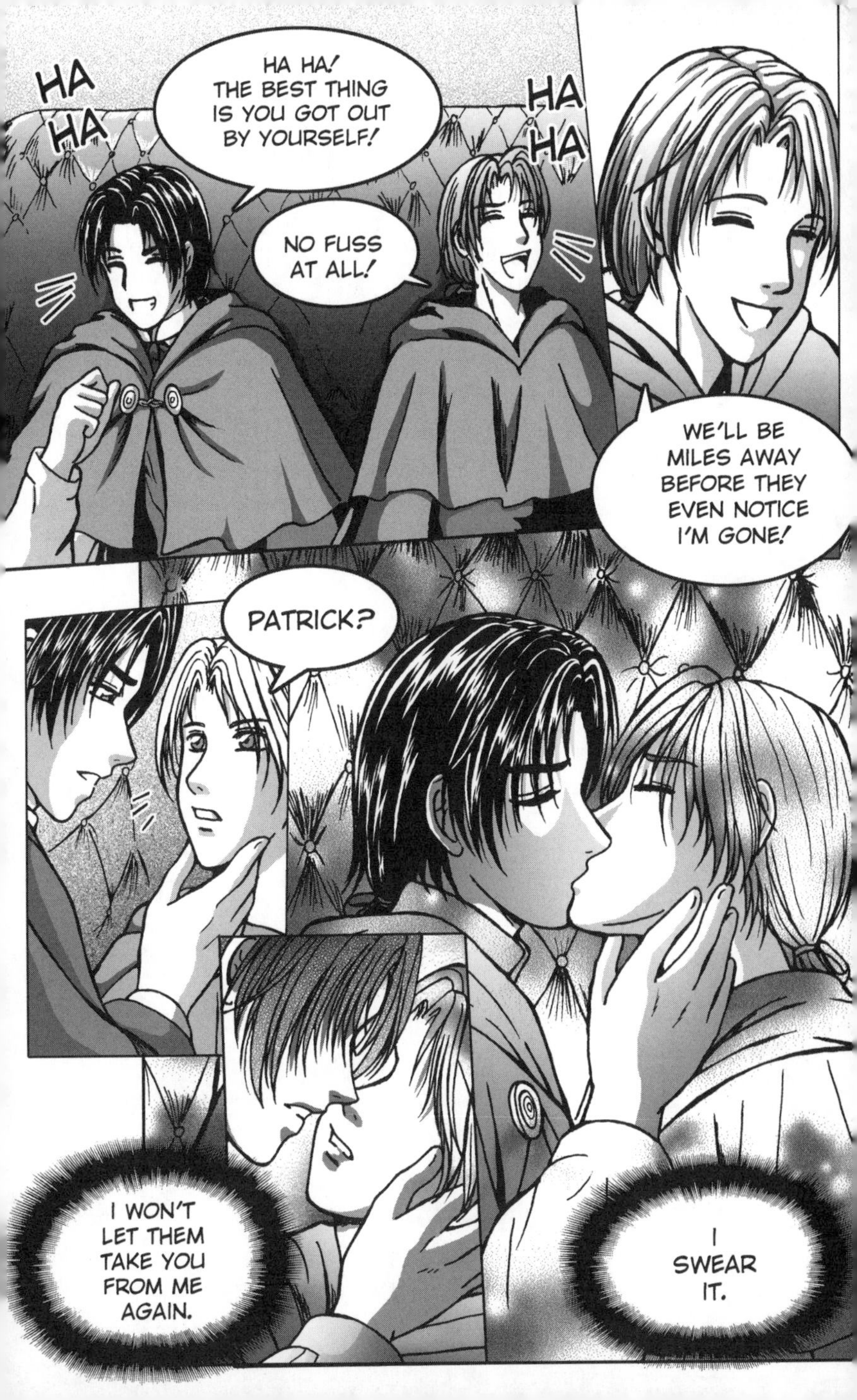
HA HA
HA HA! THE BEST THING IS YOU GOT OUT BY YOURSELF!
HA HA
NO FUSS AT ALL!
WE'LL BE MILES AWAY BEFORE THEY EVEN NOTICE I'M GONE!
PATRICK?
I WON'T LET THEM TAKE YOU FROM ME AGAIN.
I SWEAR IT.

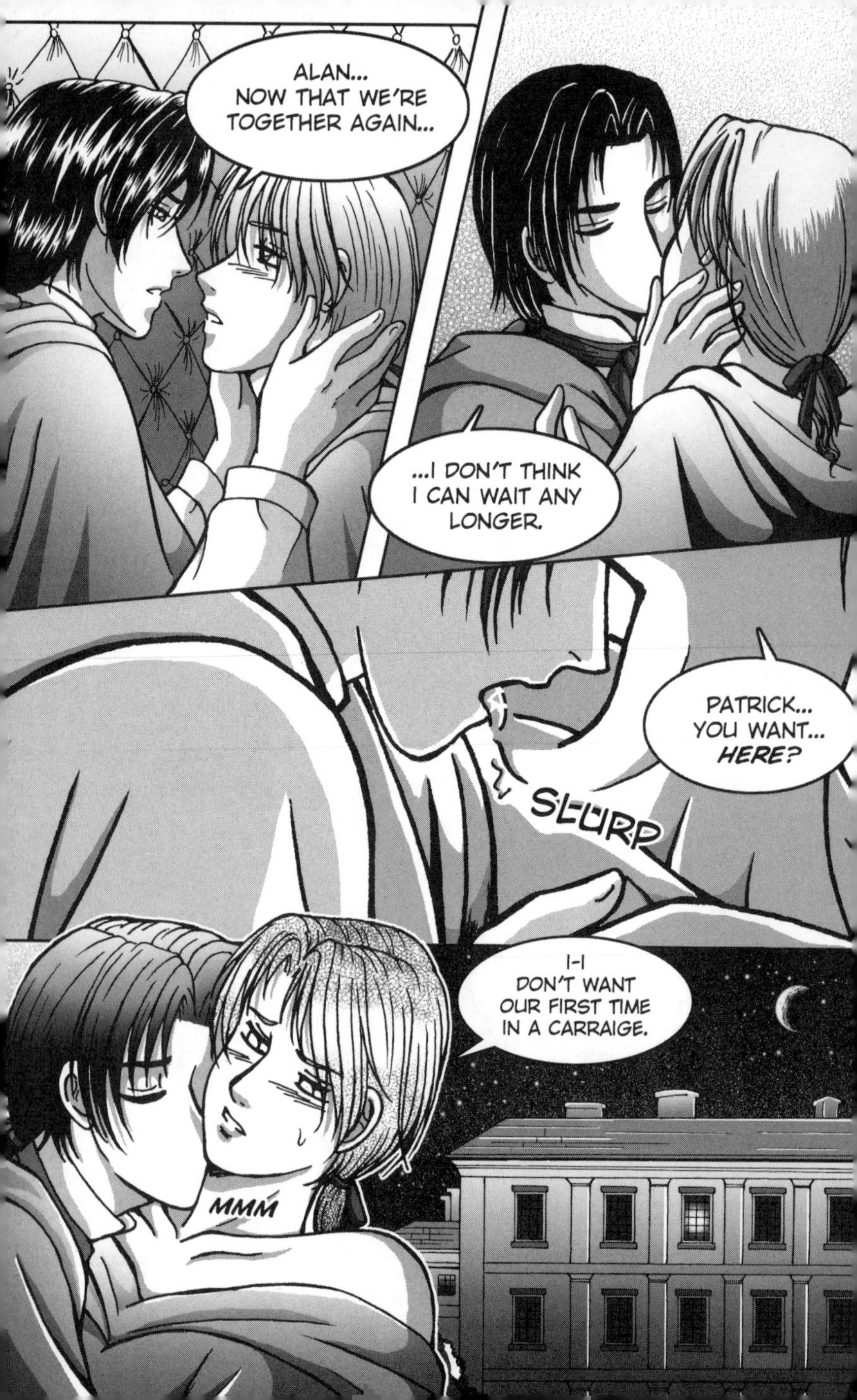
ALAN...
NOW THAT WE'RE
TOGETHER AGAIN...
...I DON'T THINK
I CAN WAIT ANY
LONGER.
PATRICK...
YOU WANT...
HERE?
SLURP
I-I
DON'T WANT
OUR FIRST TIME
IN A CARRAIGE.
MMM

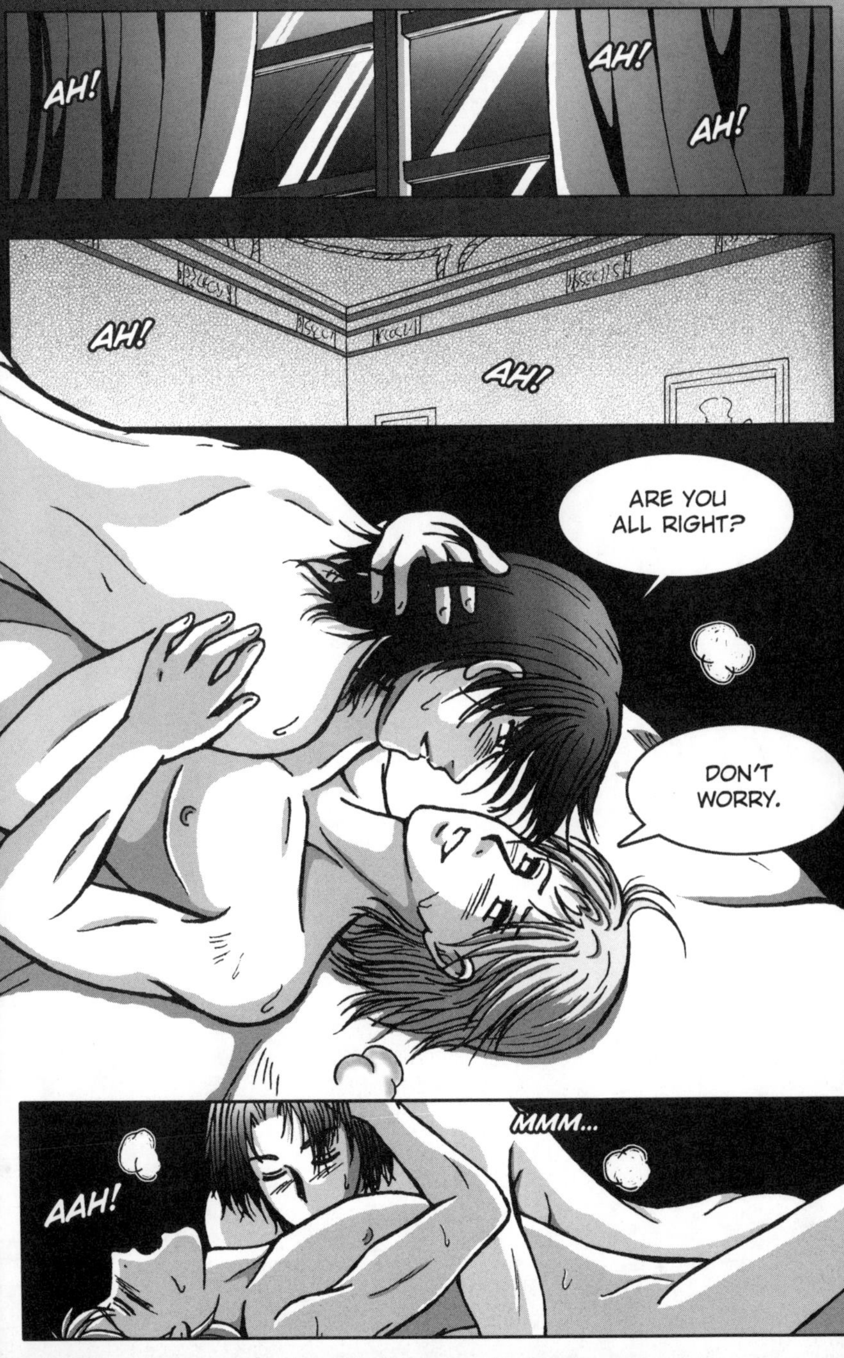
AH!
AH!
AH!
AH!
AH!
ARE YOU ALL RIGHT?
DON'T WORRY.
MMM...
AAH!

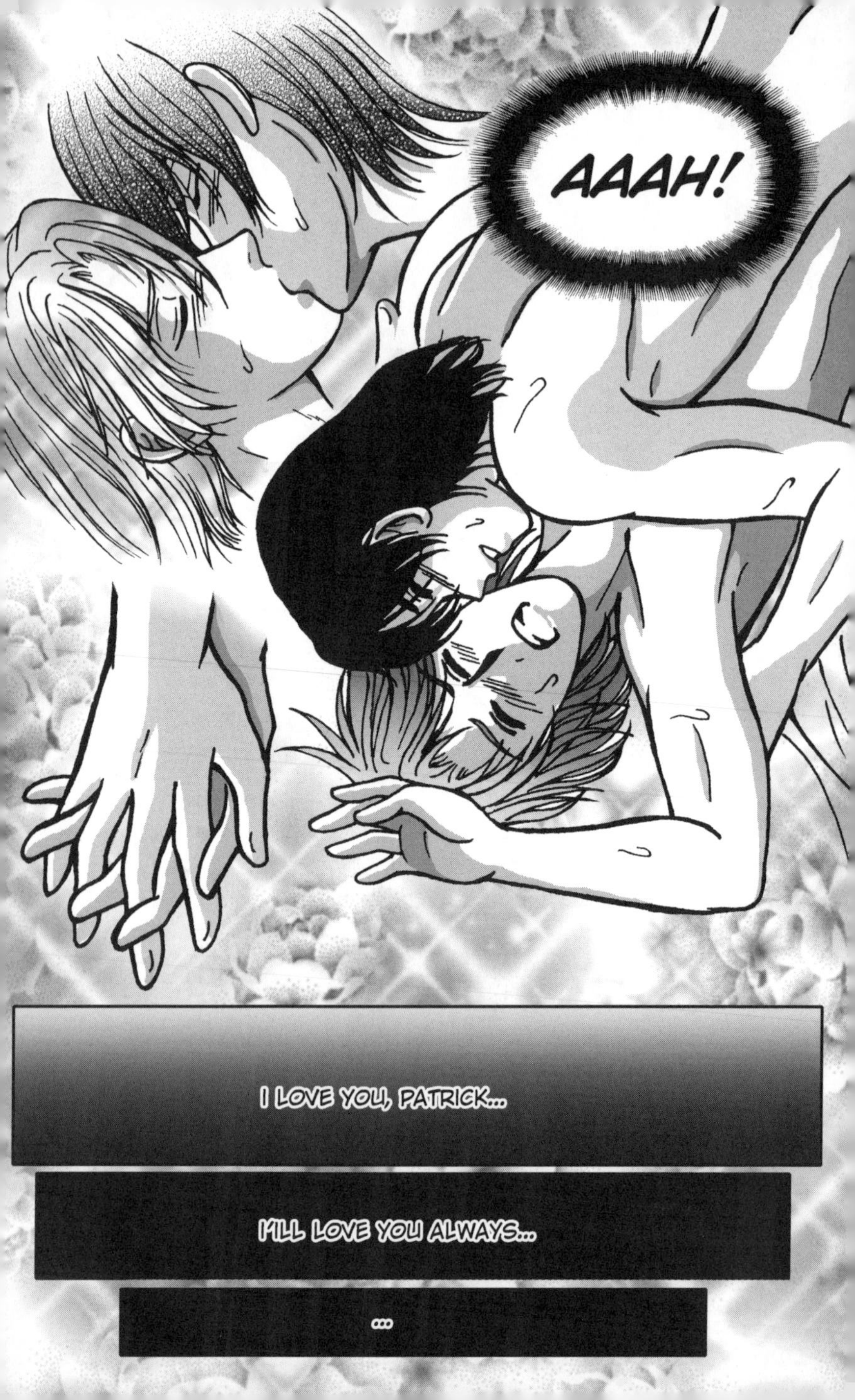
AAAH!
I LOVE YOU, PATRICK...
I'LL LOVE YOU ALWAYS...
...

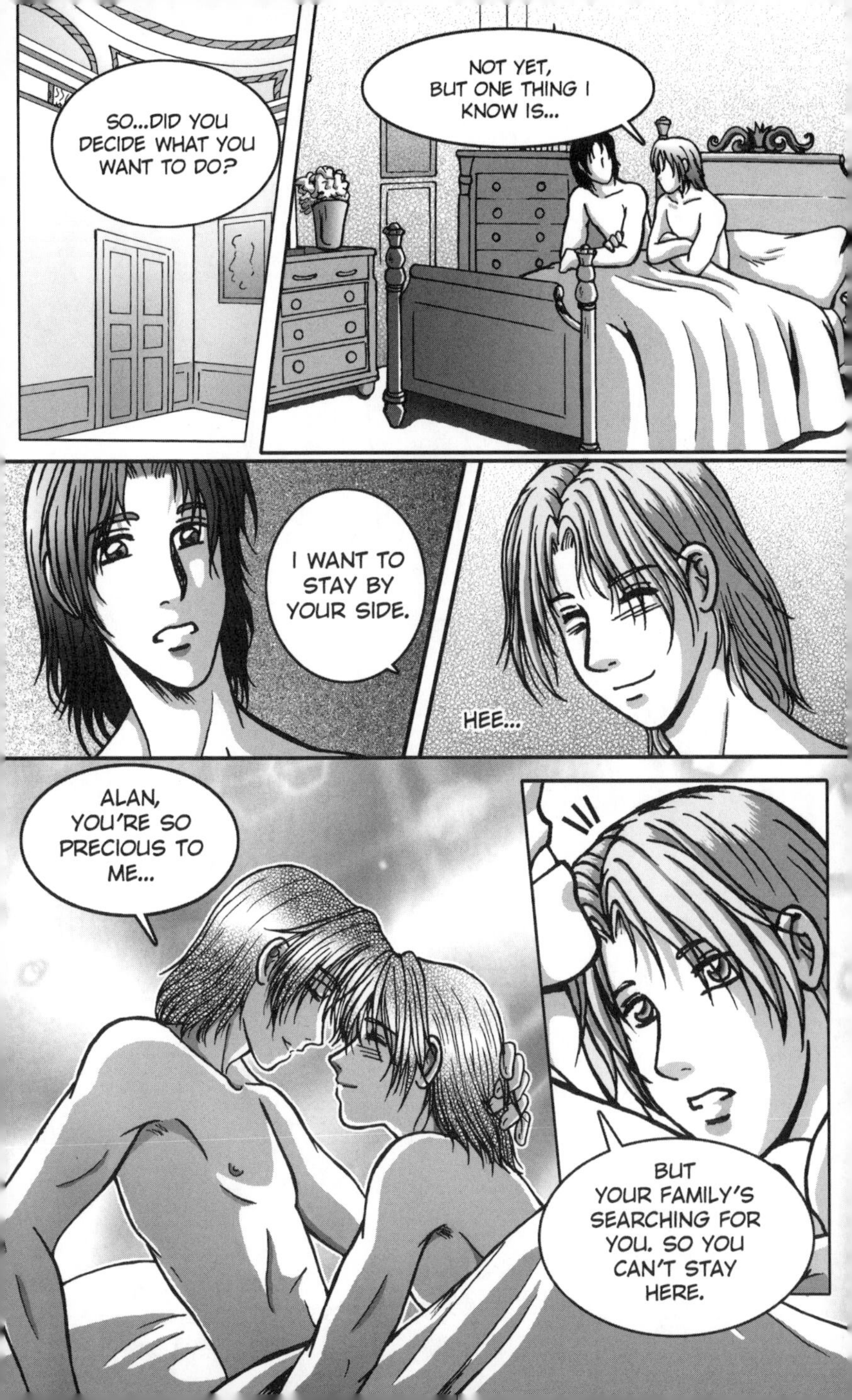

SO...DID YOU DECIDE WHAT YOU WANT TO DO?
NOT YET, BUT ONE THING I KNOW IS...
I WANT TO STAY BY YOUR SIDE.
HEE...
ALAN, YOU'RE SO PRECIOUS TO ME...
BUT YOUR FAMILY'S SEARCHING FOR YOU. SO YOU CAN'T STAY HERE.

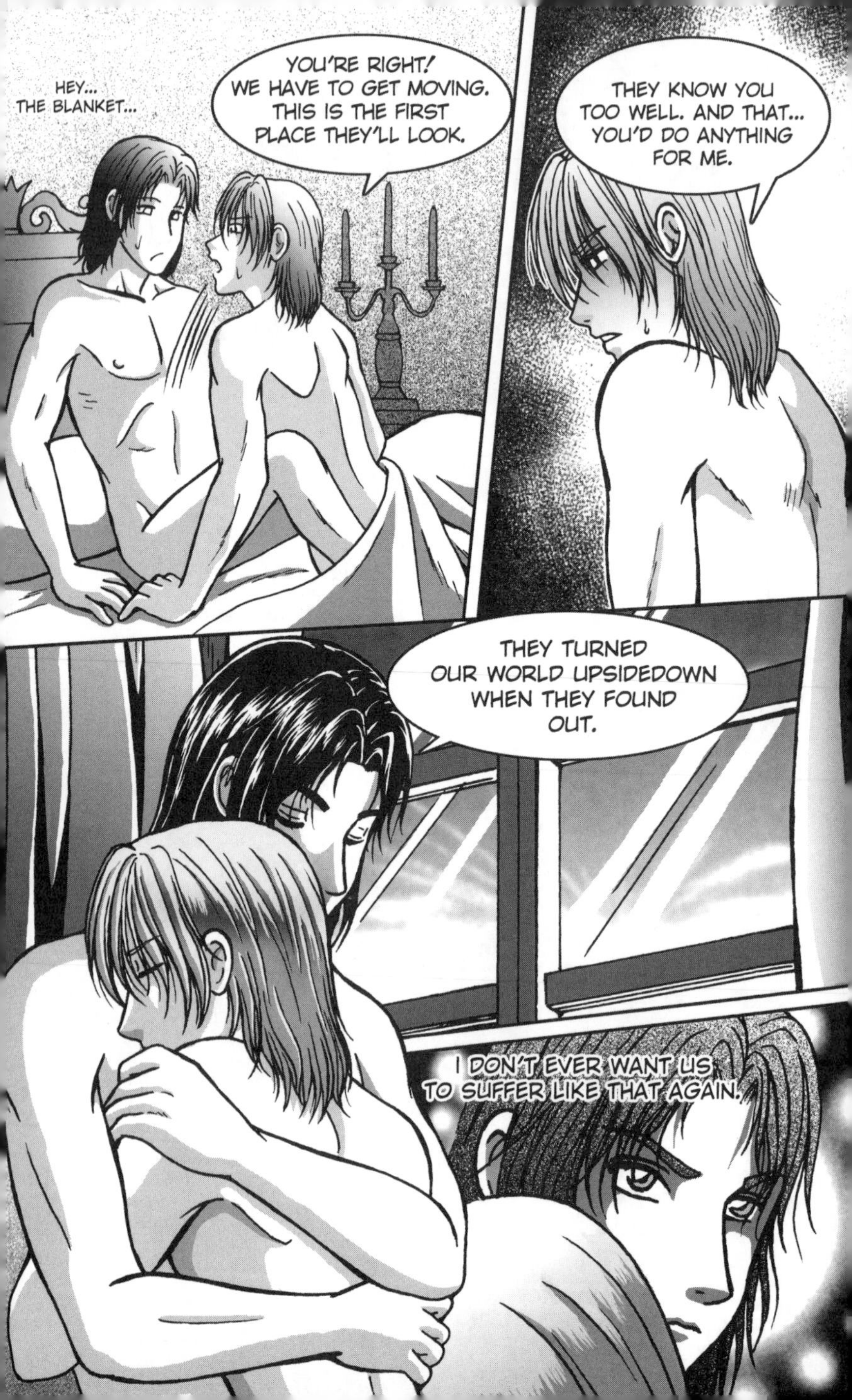
HEY...
THE BLANKET...
YOU'RE RIGHT! WE HAVE TO GET MOVING. THIS IS THE FIRST PLACE THEY'LL LOOK.
THEY KNOW YOU TOO WELL. AND THAT... YOU'D DO ANYTHING FOR ME.
THEY TURNED OUR WORLD UPSIDEDOWN WHEN THEY FOUND OUT.
I DON'T EVER WANT US TO SUFFER LIKE THAT AGAIN.

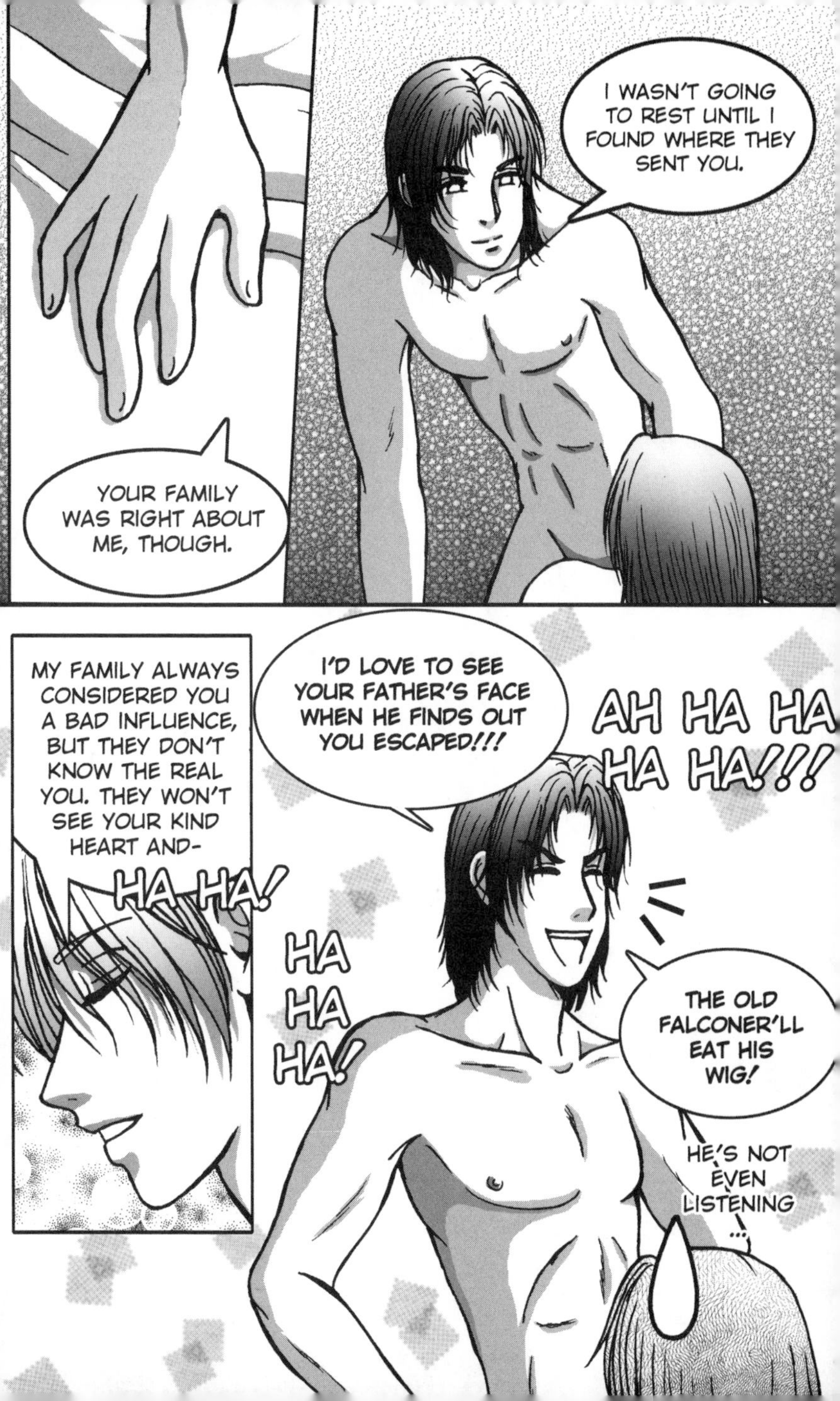
I WASN'T GOING TO REST UNTIL I FOUND WHERE THEY SENT YOU.
YOUR FAMILY WAS RIGHT ABOUT ME, THOUGH.
MY FAMILY ALWAYS CONSIDERED YOU A BAD INFLUENCE, BUT THEY DON'T KNOW THE REAL YOU. THEY WON'T SEE YOUR KIND HEART AND-
I'D LOVE TO SEE YOUR FATHER'S FACE WHEN HE FINDS OUT YOU ESCAPED!!!
AH HA HA HA HA!!!
HA HA!
HA HA HA!
THE OLD FALCONER'LL EAT HIS WIG!
HE'S NOT EVEN LISTENING
...

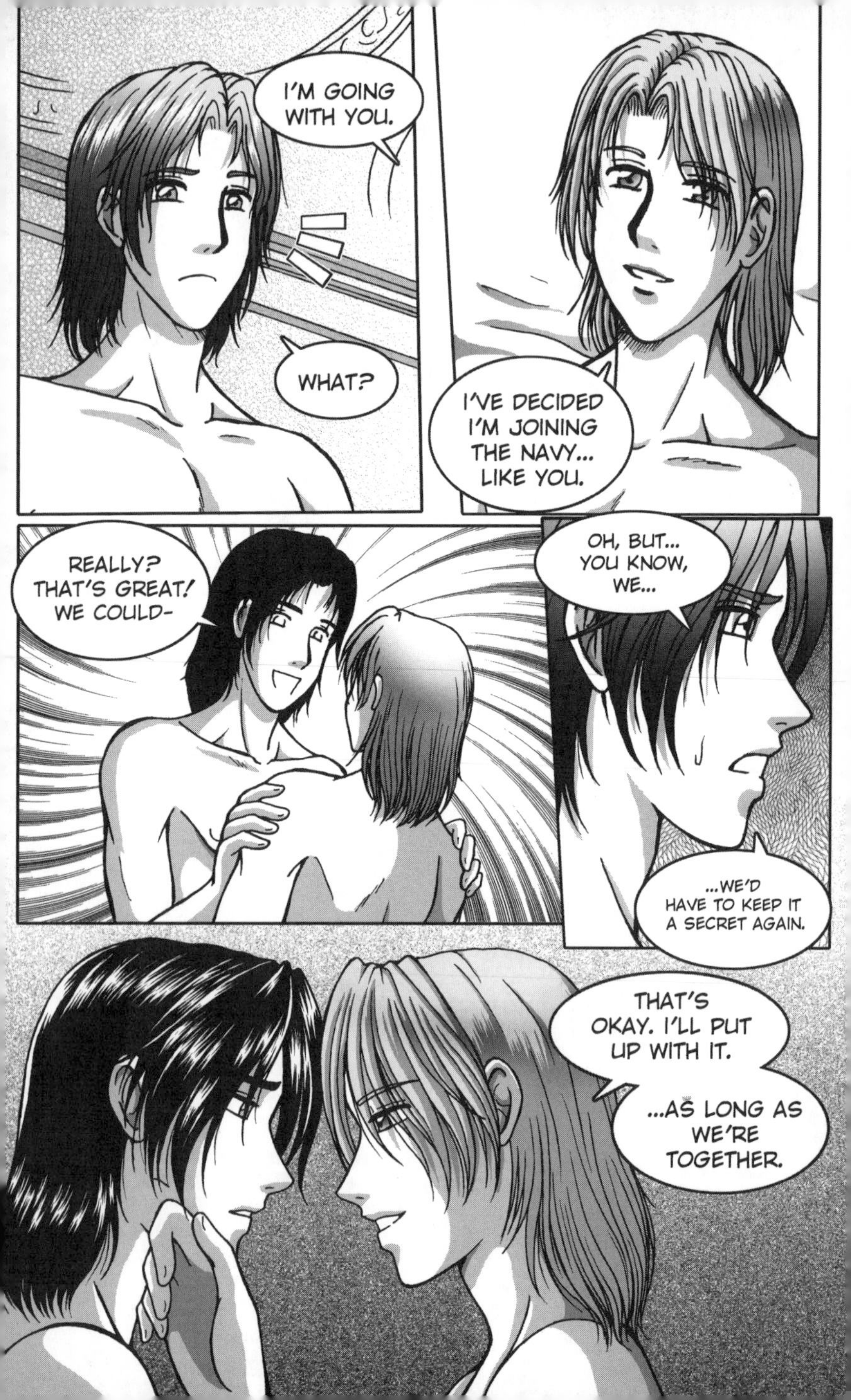
I'M GOING WITH YOU.
WHAT?
I'VE DECIDED I'M JOINING THE NAVY... LIKE YOU.
REALLY? THAT'S GREAT! WE COULD-
OH, BUT... YOU KNOW, WE...
...WE'D HAVE TO KEEP IT A SECRET AGAIN.
THAT'S OKAY. I'LL PUT UP WITH IT.
...AS LONG AS WE'RE TOGETHER.

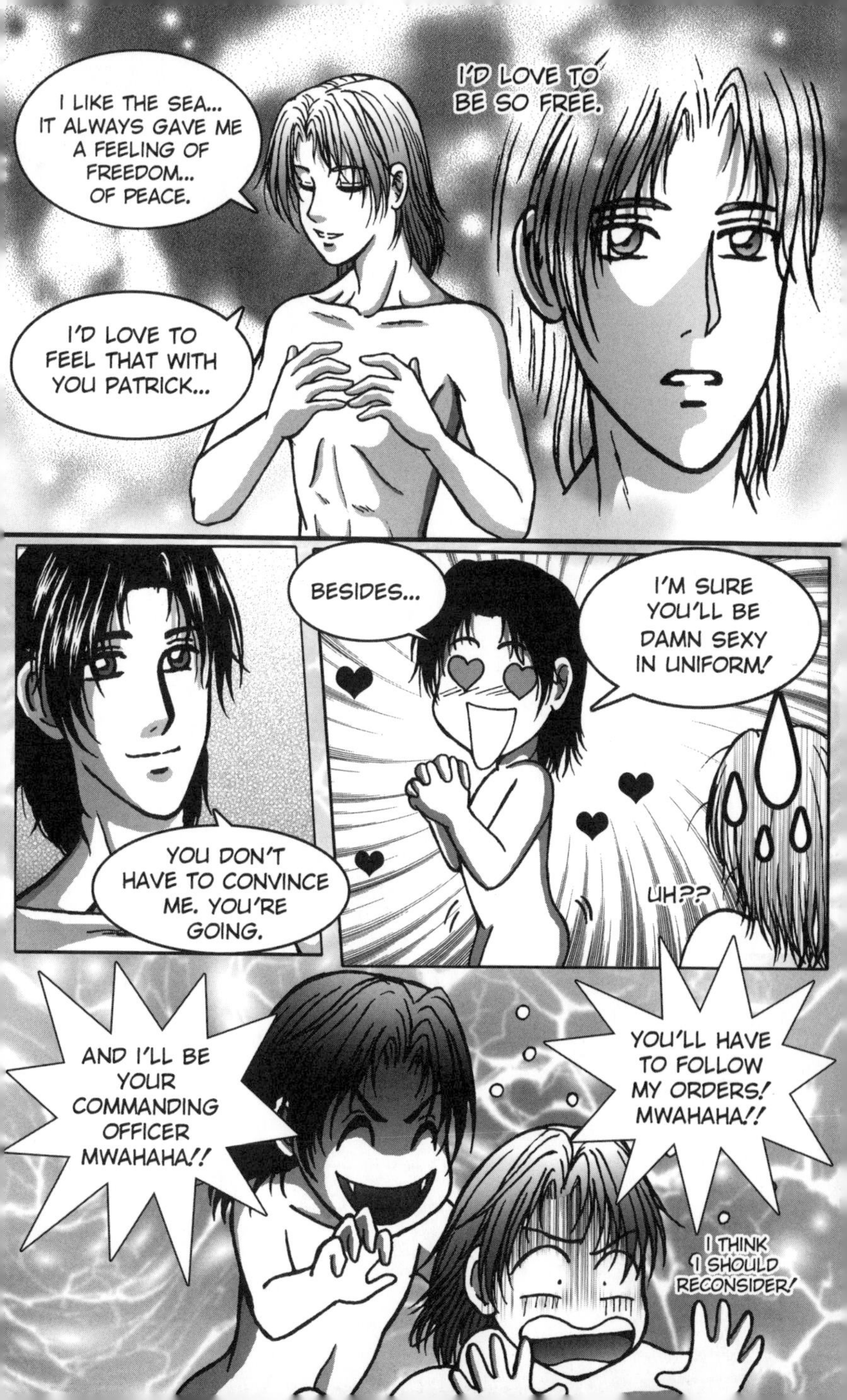
I LIKE THE SEA... IT ALWAYS GAVE ME A FEELING OF FREEDOM... OF PEACE.
I'D LOVE TO BE SO FREE.
I'D LOVE TO FEEL THAT WITH YOU PATRICK...
YOU DON'T HAVE TO CONVINCE ME. YOU'RE GOING.
BESIDES...
I'M SURE YOU'LL BE DAMN SEXY IN UNIFORM!
UH??
AND I'LL BE YOUR COMMANDING OFFICER MWAHAHA!!
YOU'LL HAVE TO FOLLOW MY ORDERS! MWAHAHA!!
I THINK I SHOULD RECONSIDER!

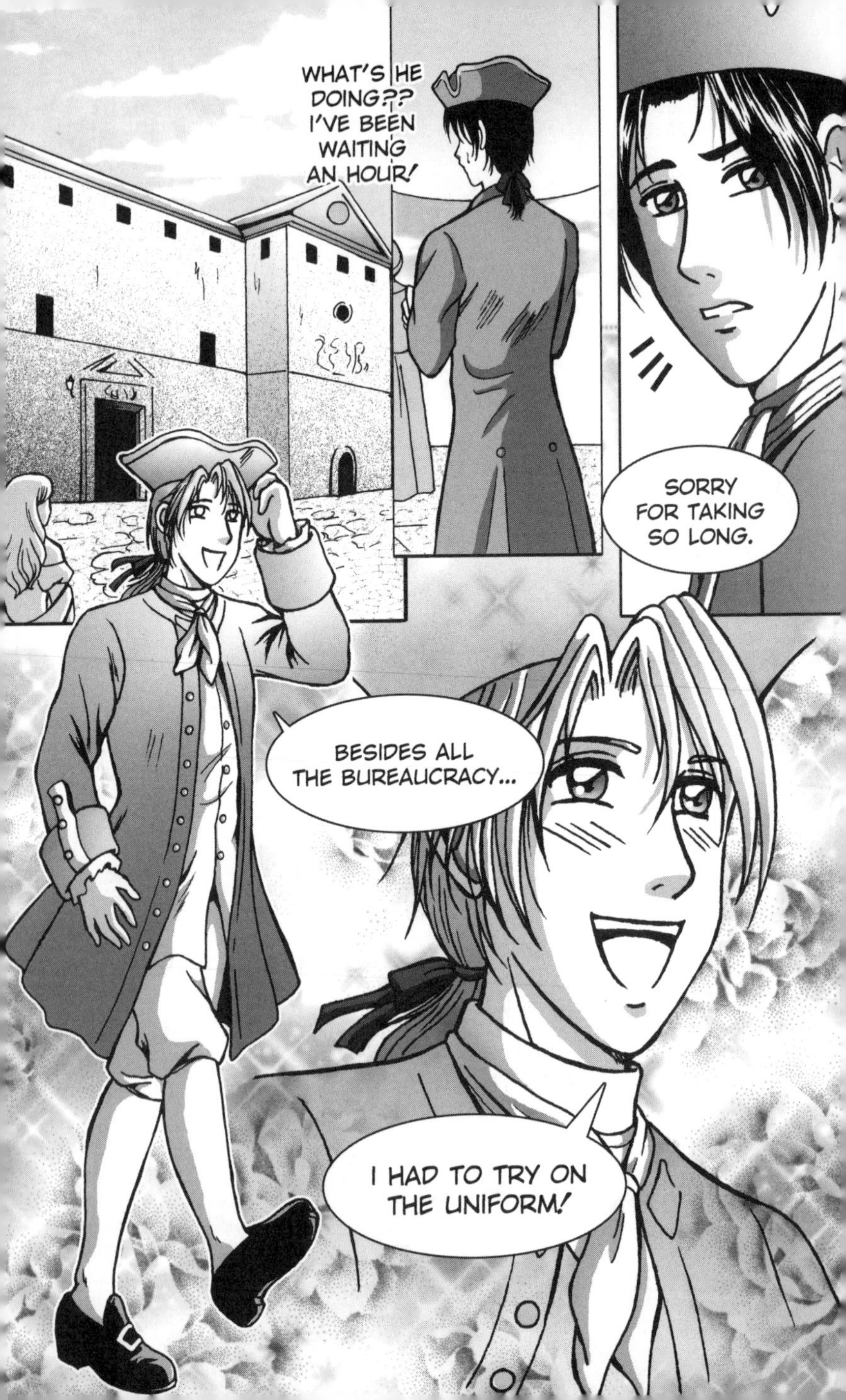
WHAT'S HE DOING?? I'VE BEEN WAITING AN HOUR!
SORRY FOR TAKING SO LONG.
BESIDES ALL THE BUREAUCRACY...
I HAD TO TRY ON THE UNIFORM!

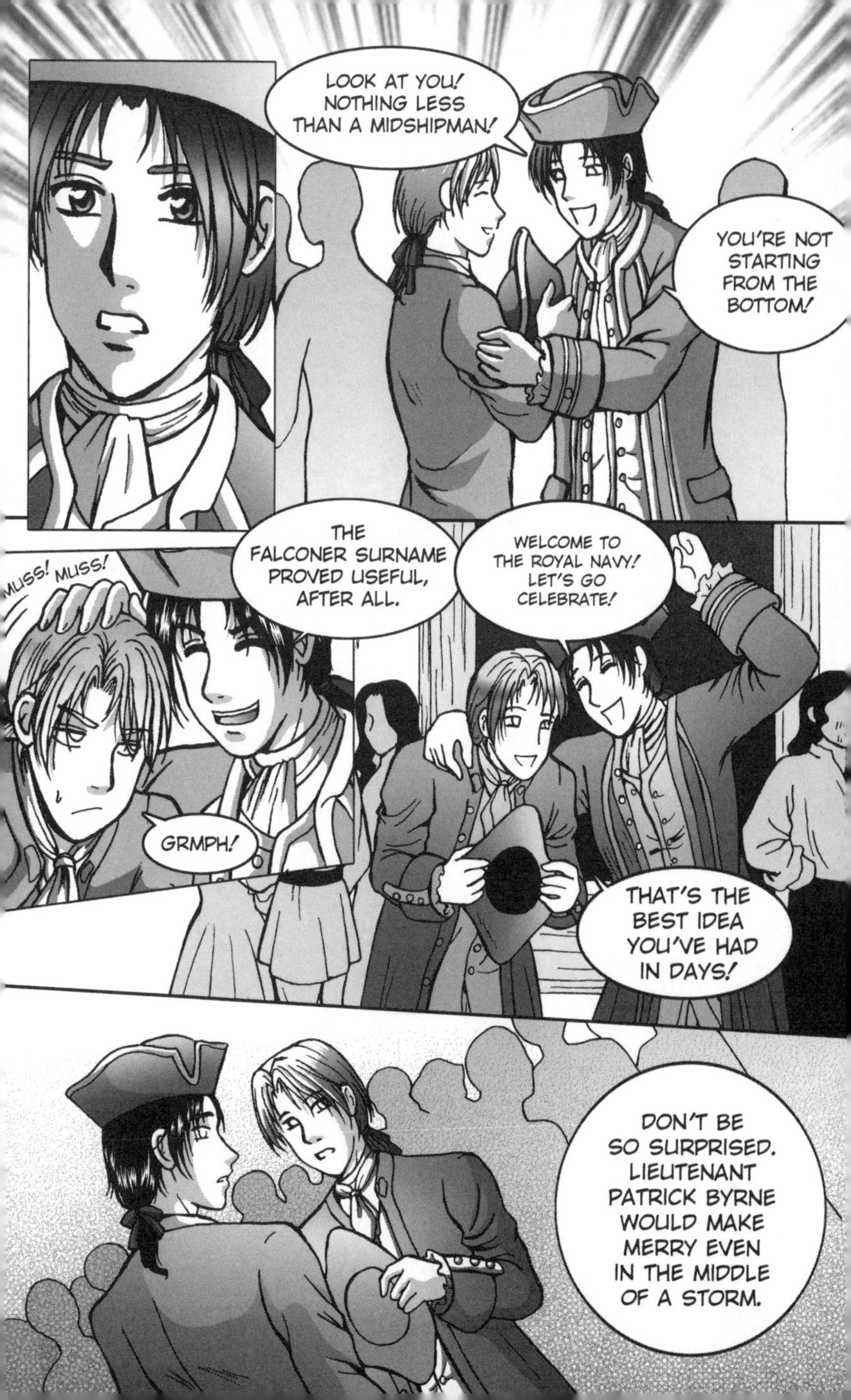
LOOK AT YOU! NOTHING LESS THAN A MIDSHIPMAN!
YOU'RE NOT STARTING FROM THE BOTTOM!
MUSS! MUSS!
THE FALCONER SURNAME PROVED USEFUL, AFTER ALL.
GRMPH!
WELCOME TO THE ROYAL NAVY! LET'S GO CELEBRATE!
THAT'S THE BEST IDEA YOU'VE HAD IN DAYS!
DON'T BE SO SURPRISED. LIEUTENANT PATRICK BYRNE WOULD MAKE MERRY EVEN IN THE MIDDLE OF A STORM.

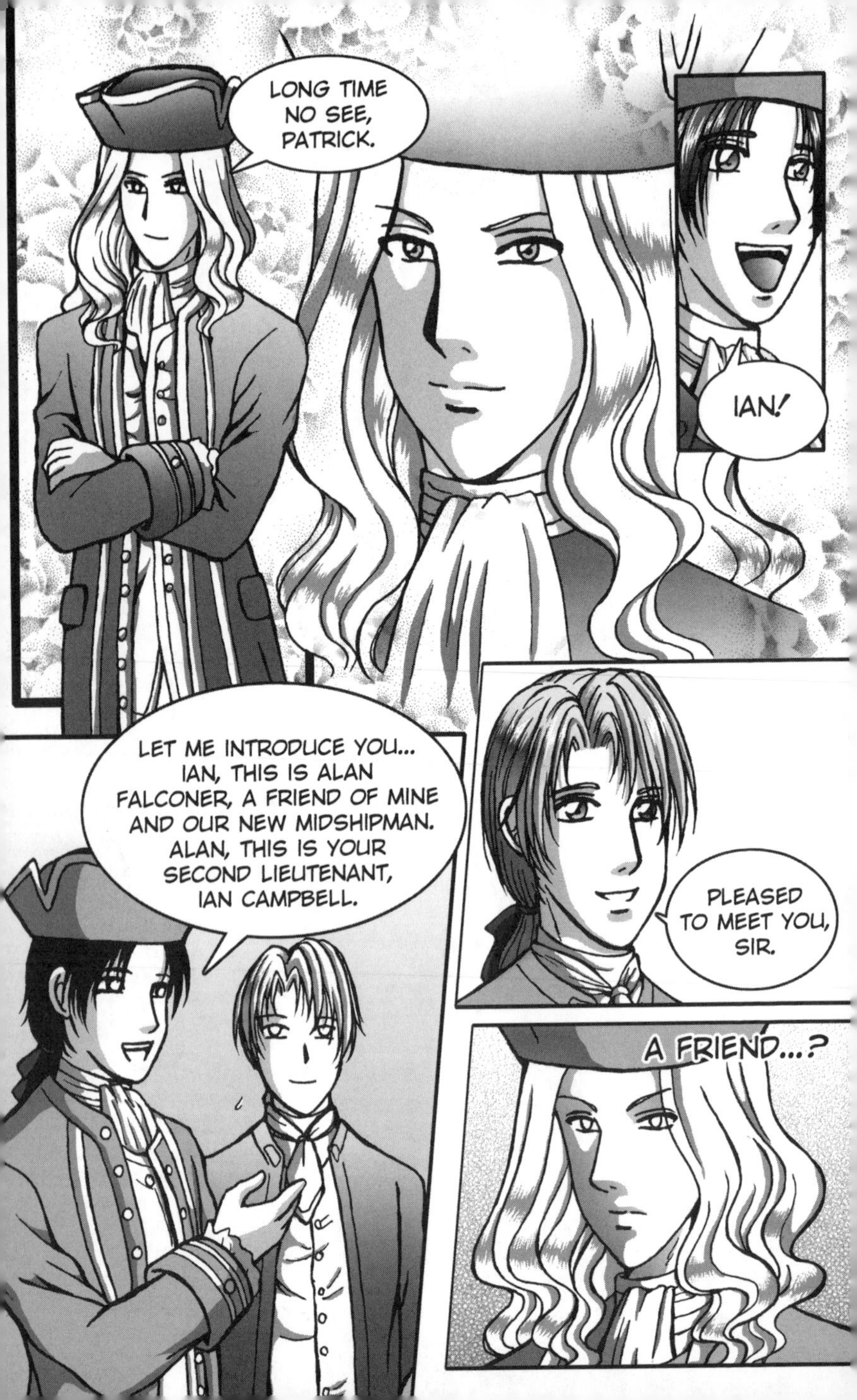
LONG TIME NO SEE, PATRICK.
IAN!
LET ME INTRODUCE YOU... IAN, THIS IS ALAN FALCONER, A FRIEND OF MINE AND OUR NEW MIDSHIPMAN. ALAN, THIS IS YOUR SECOND LIEUTENANT, IAN CAMPBELL.
PLEASED TO MEET YOU, SIR.
A FRIEND...?

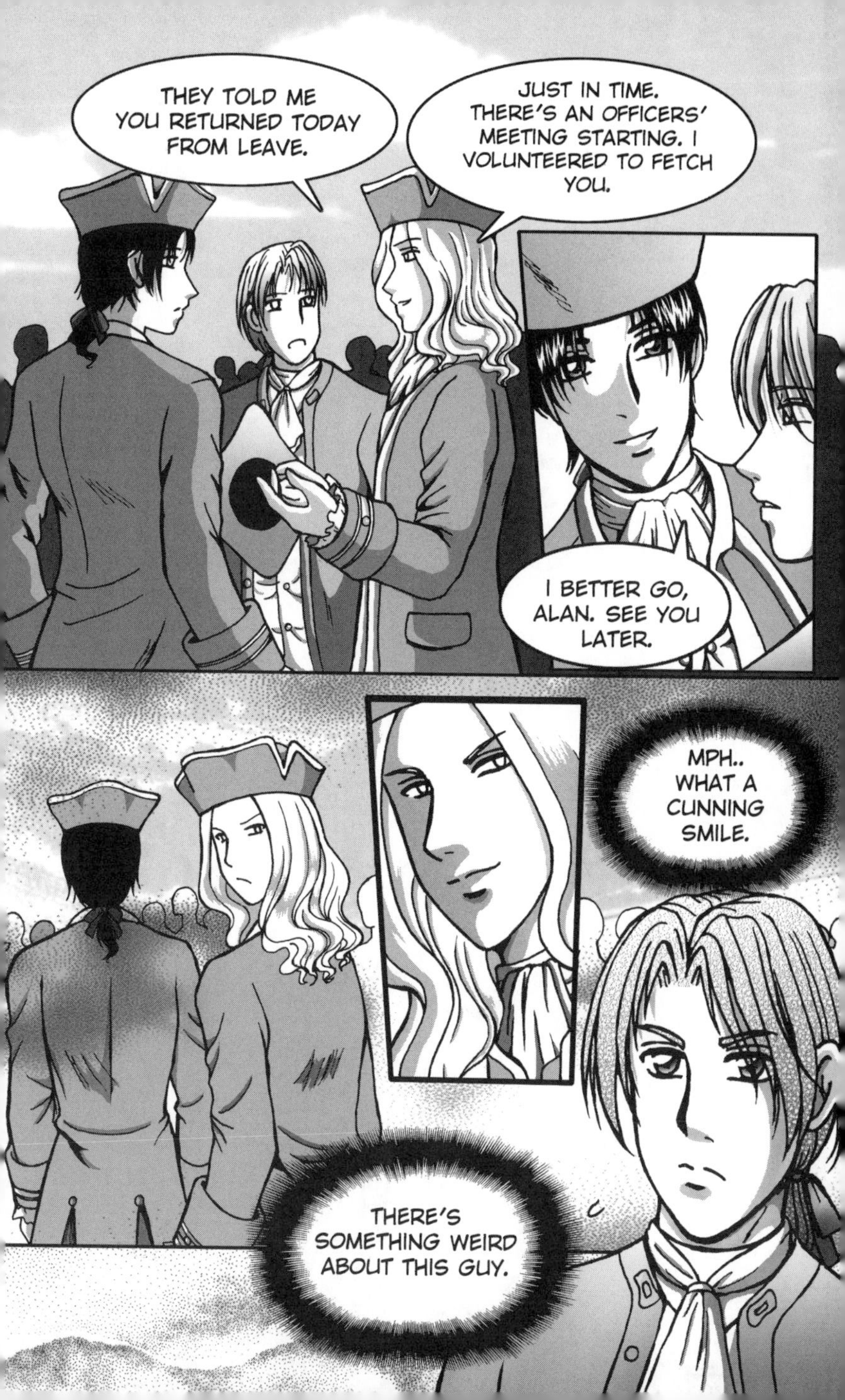
THEY TOLD ME YOU RETURNED TODAY FROM LEAVE.
JUST IN TIME. THERE'S AN OFFICERS' MEETING STARTING. I VOLUNTEERED TO FETCH YOU.
I BETTER GO, ALAN. SEE YOU LATER.
MPH.. WHAT A CUNNING SMILE.
THERE'S SOMETHING WEIRD ABOUT THIS GUY.

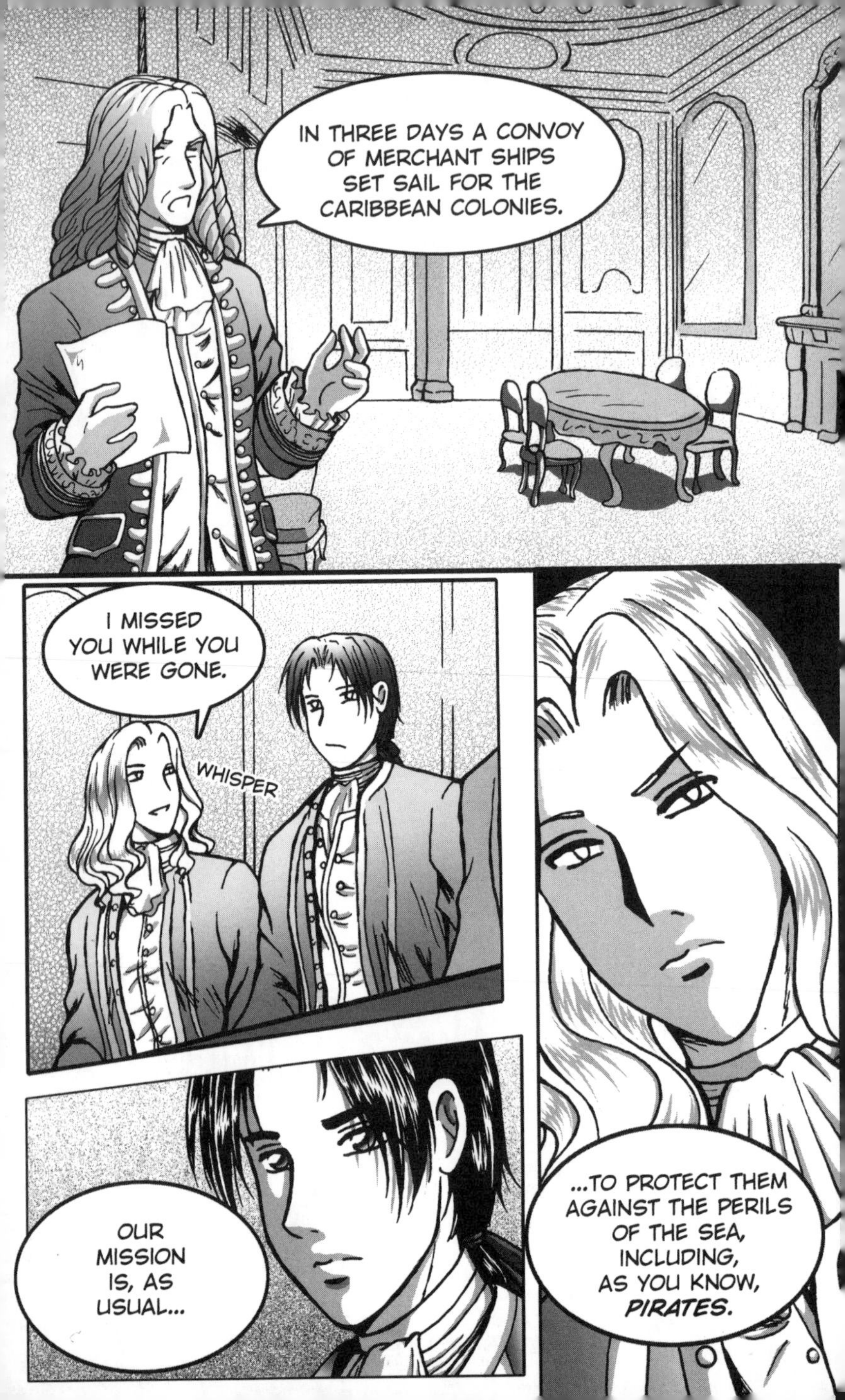
IN THREE DAYS A CONVOY OF MERCHANT SHIPS SET SAIL FOR THE CARIBBEAN COLONIES.
I MISSED YOU WHILE YOU WERE GONE.
WHISPER
OUR MISSION IS, AS USUAL...
...TO PROTECT THEM AGAINST THE PERILS OF THE SEA, INCLUDING, AS YOU KNOW, *PIRATES.*

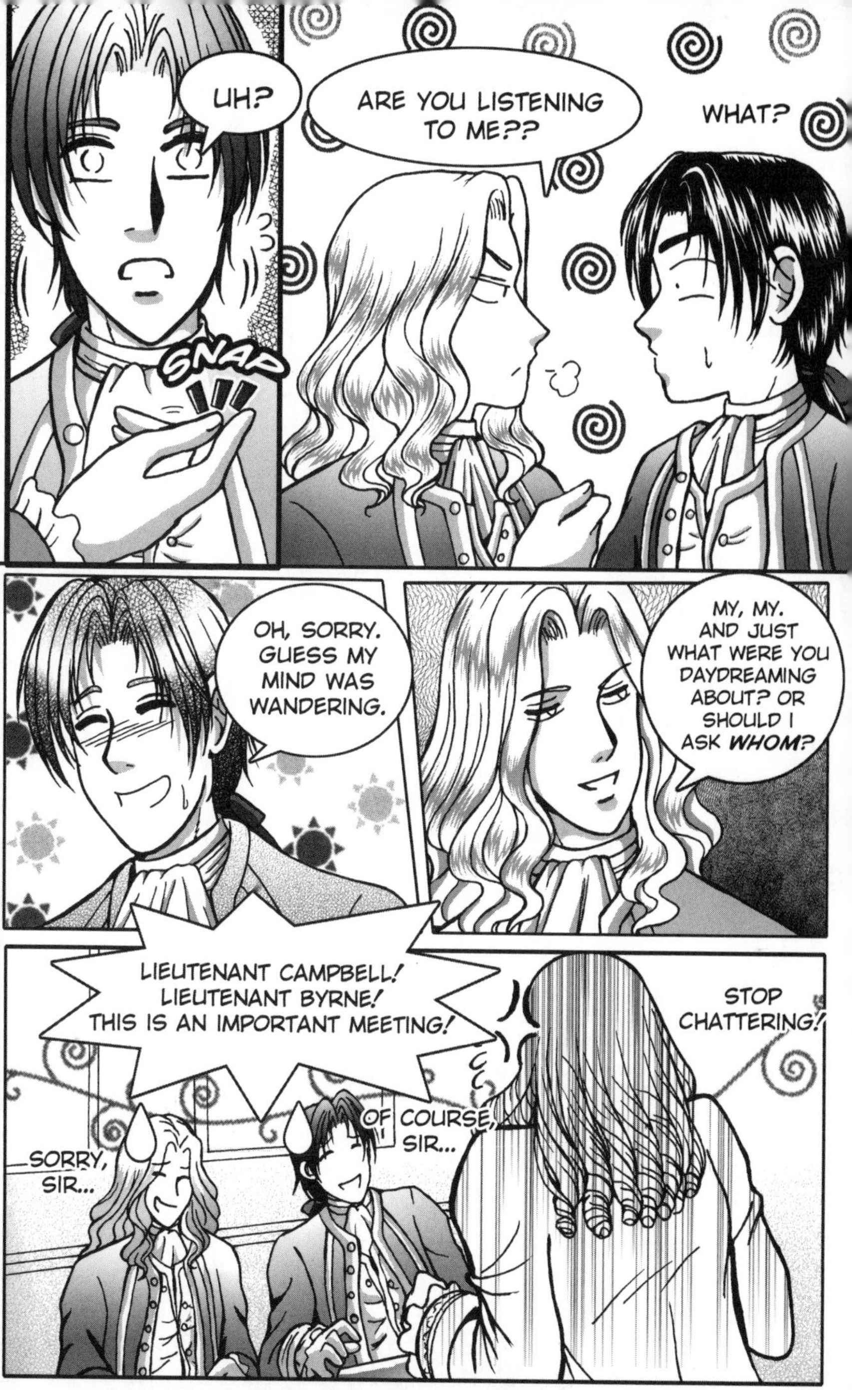
UH?
ARE YOU LISTENING TO ME??
WHAT?
SNAP
OH, SORRY. GUESS MY MIND WAS WANDERING.
MY, MY. AND JUST WHAT WERE YOU DAYDREAMING ABOUT? OR SHOULD I ASK *WHOM*?
LIEUTENANT CAMPBELL! LIEUTENANT BYRNE! THIS IS AN IMPORTANT MEETING!
STOP CHATTERING!
OF COURSE, SIR...
SORRY, SIR...

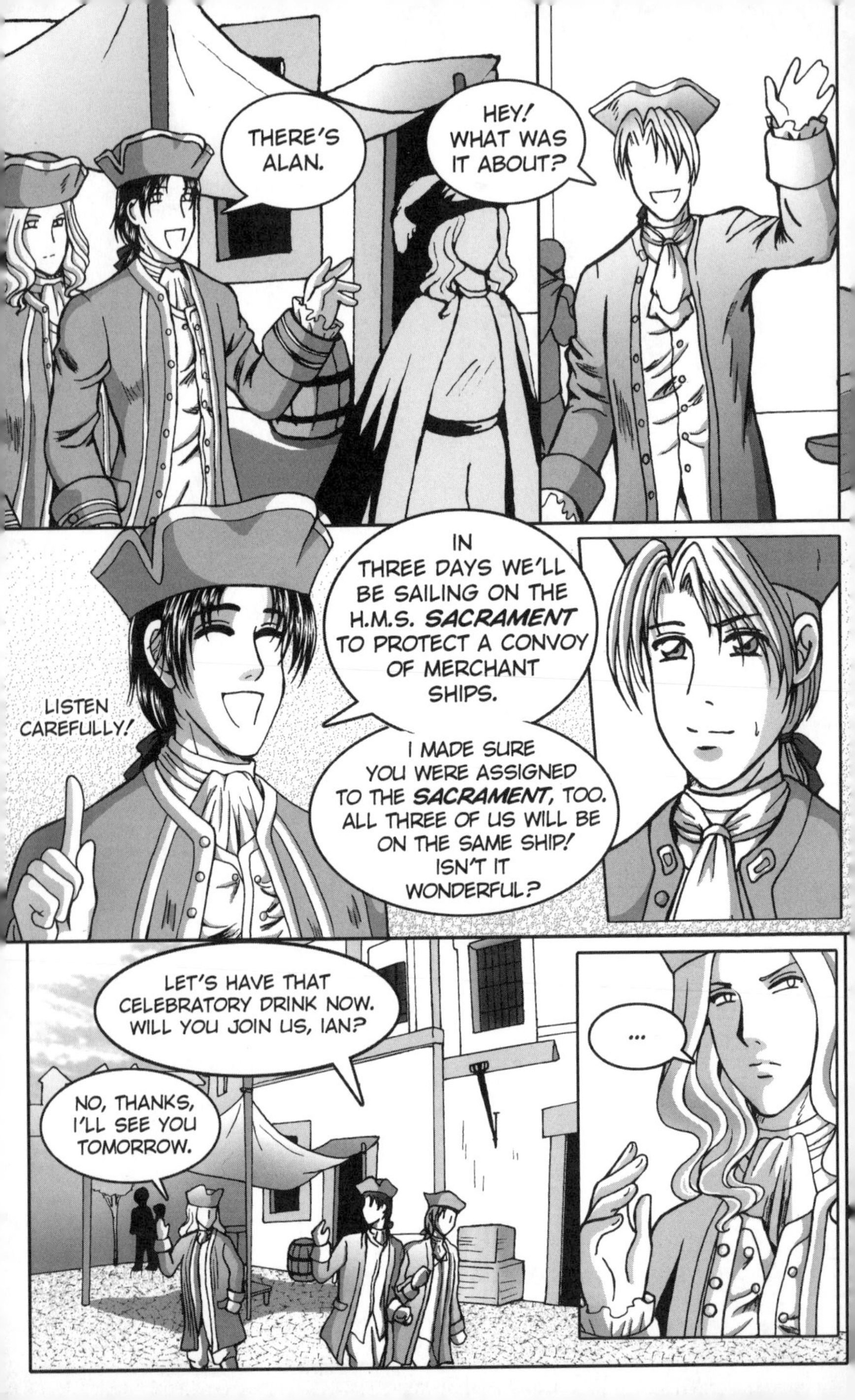
THERE'S ALAN.
HEY! WHAT WAS IT ABOUT?
LISTEN CAREFULLY!
IN THREE DAYS WE'LL BE SAILING ON THE H.M.S. *SACRAMENT* TO PROTECT A CONVOY OF MERCHANT SHIPS.
I MADE SURE YOU WERE ASSIGNED TO THE *SACRAMENT*, TOO. ALL THREE OF US WILL BE ON THE SAME SHIP! ISN'T IT WONDERFUL?
LET'S HAVE THAT CELEBRATORY DRINK NOW. WILL YOU JOIN US, IAN?
NO, THANKS, I'LL SEE YOU TOMORROW.
...

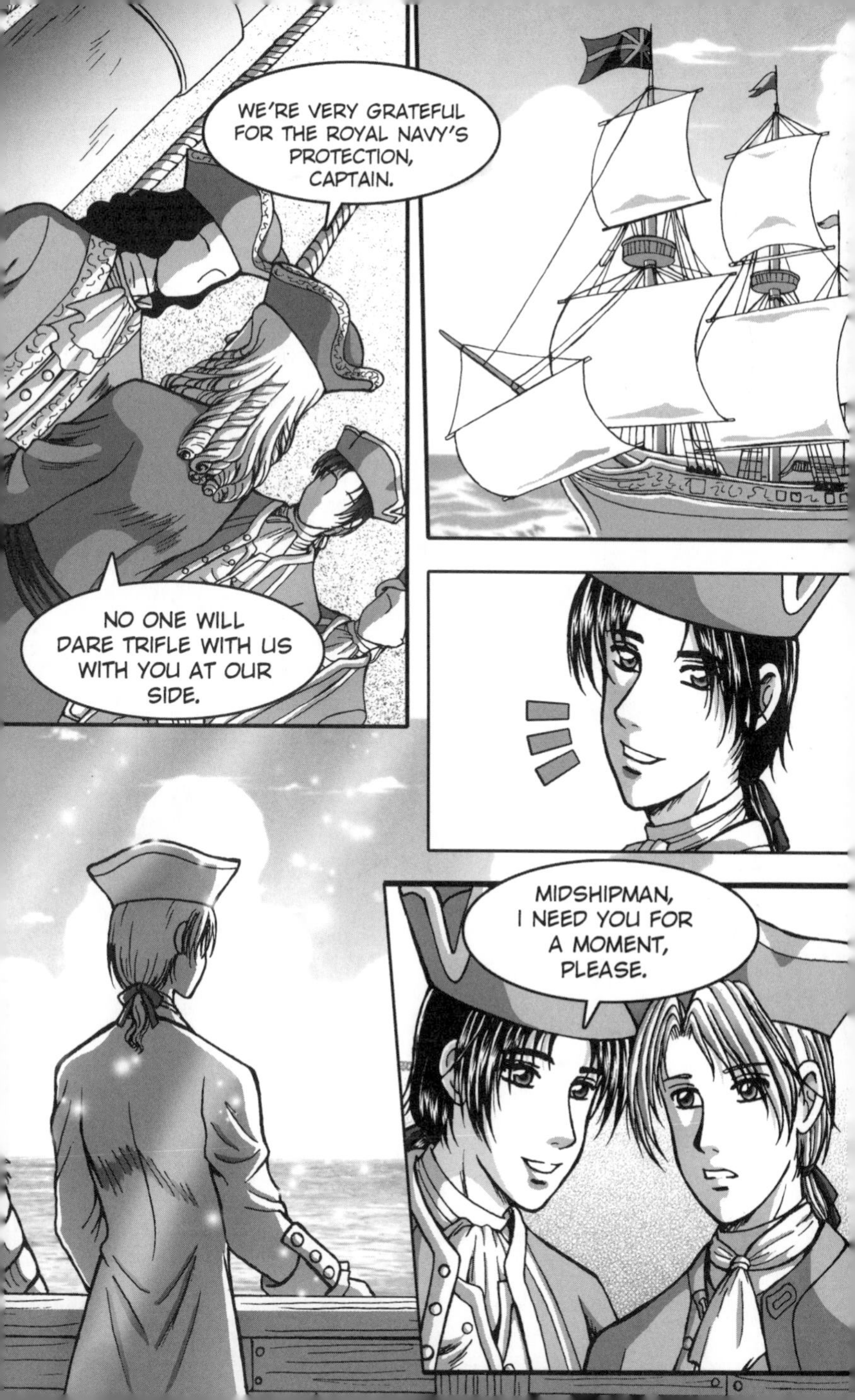
WE'RE VERY GRATEFUL FOR THE ROYAL NAVY'S PROTECTION, CAPTAIN.
NO ONE WILL DARE TRIFLE WITH US WITH YOU AT OUR SIDE.
MIDSHIPMAN, I NEED YOU FOR A MOMENT, PLEASE.

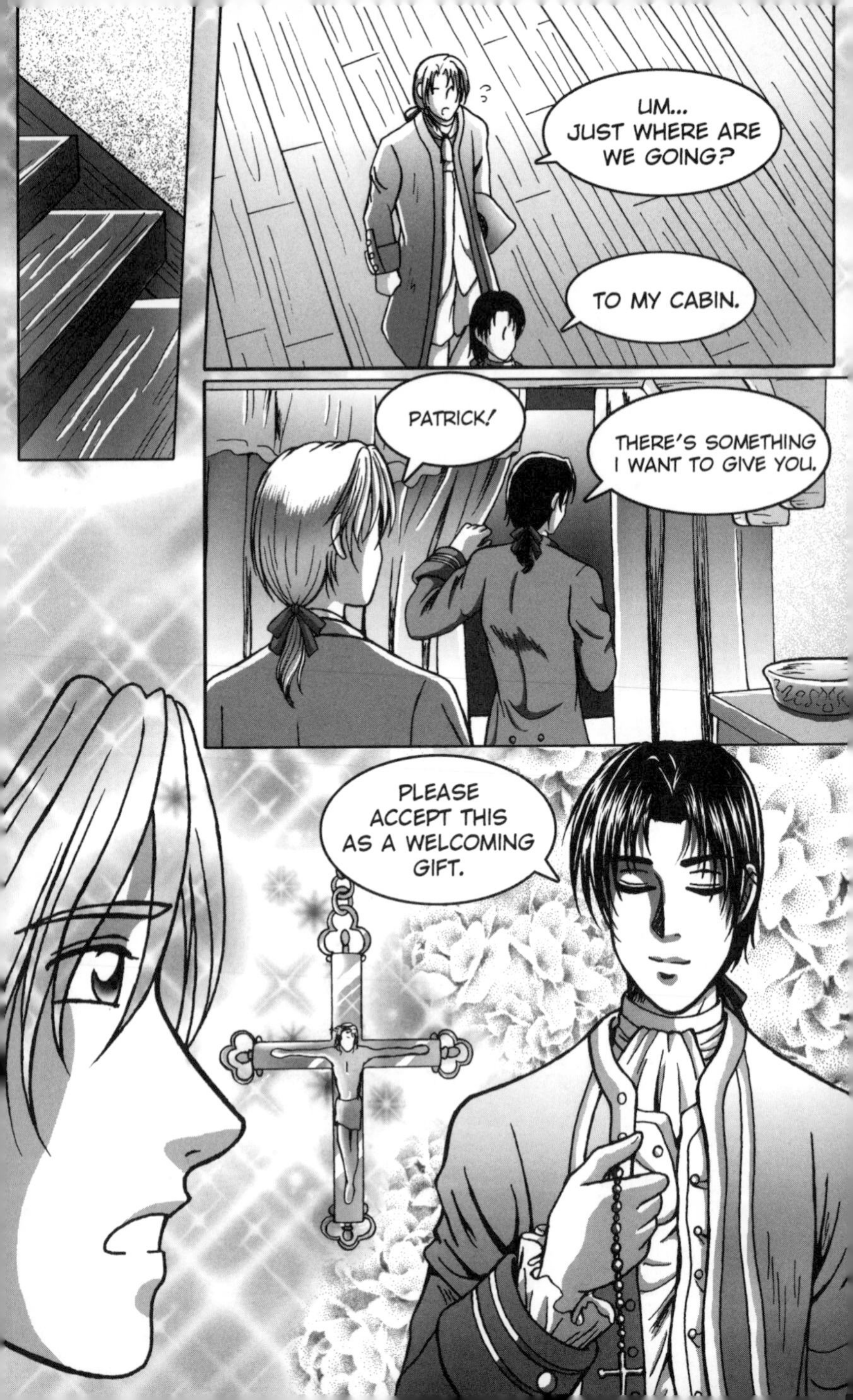
UM...
JUST WHERE ARE WE GOING?
TO MY CABIN.
PATRICK!
THERE'S SOMETHING I WANT TO GIVE YOU.
PLEASE ACCEPT THIS AS A WELCOMING GIFT.

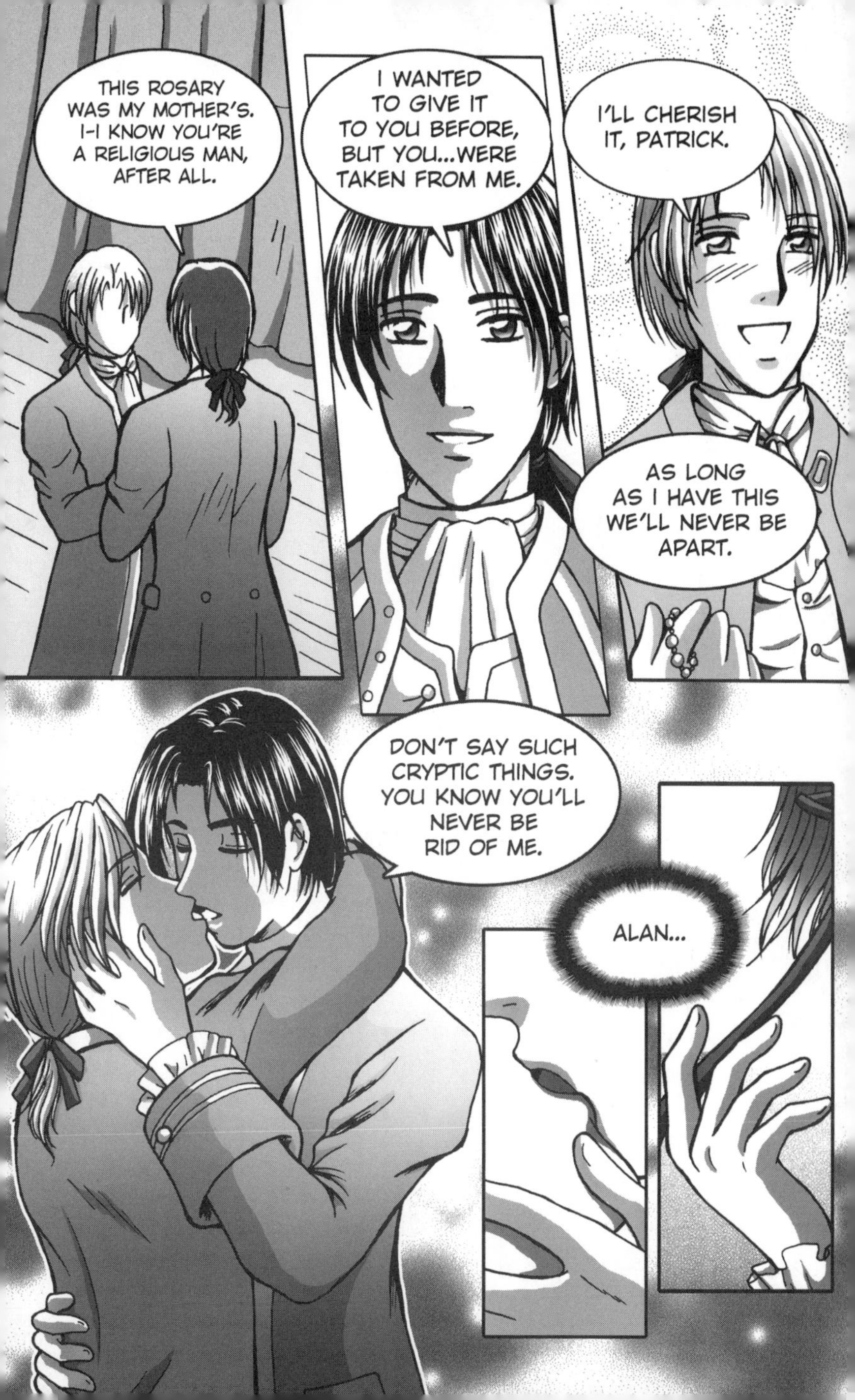
THIS ROSARY WAS MY MOTHER'S. I-I KNOW YOU'RE A RELIGIOUS MAN, AFTER ALL.
I WANTED TO GIVE IT TO YOU BEFORE, BUT YOU...WERE TAKEN FROM ME.
I'LL CHERISH IT, PATRICK.
AS LONG AS I HAVE THIS WE'LL NEVER BE APART.
DON'T SAY SUCH CRYPTIC THINGS. YOU KNOW YOU'LL NEVER BE RID OF ME.
ALAN...

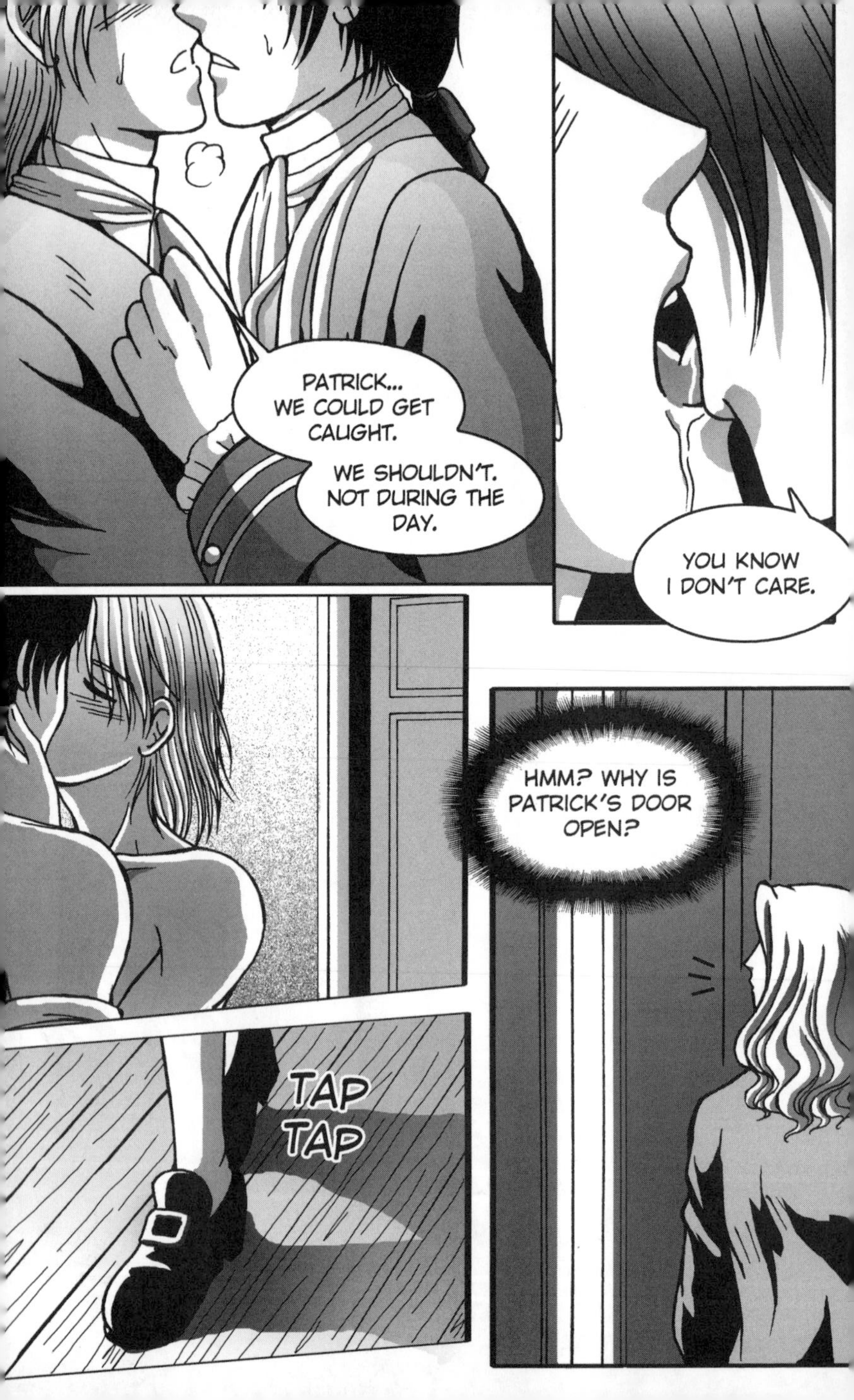
PATRICK... WE COULD GET CAUGHT.
WE SHOULDN'T. NOT DURING THE DAY.
YOU KNOW I DON'T CARE.
TAP TAP
HMM? WHY IS PATRICK'S DOOR OPEN?

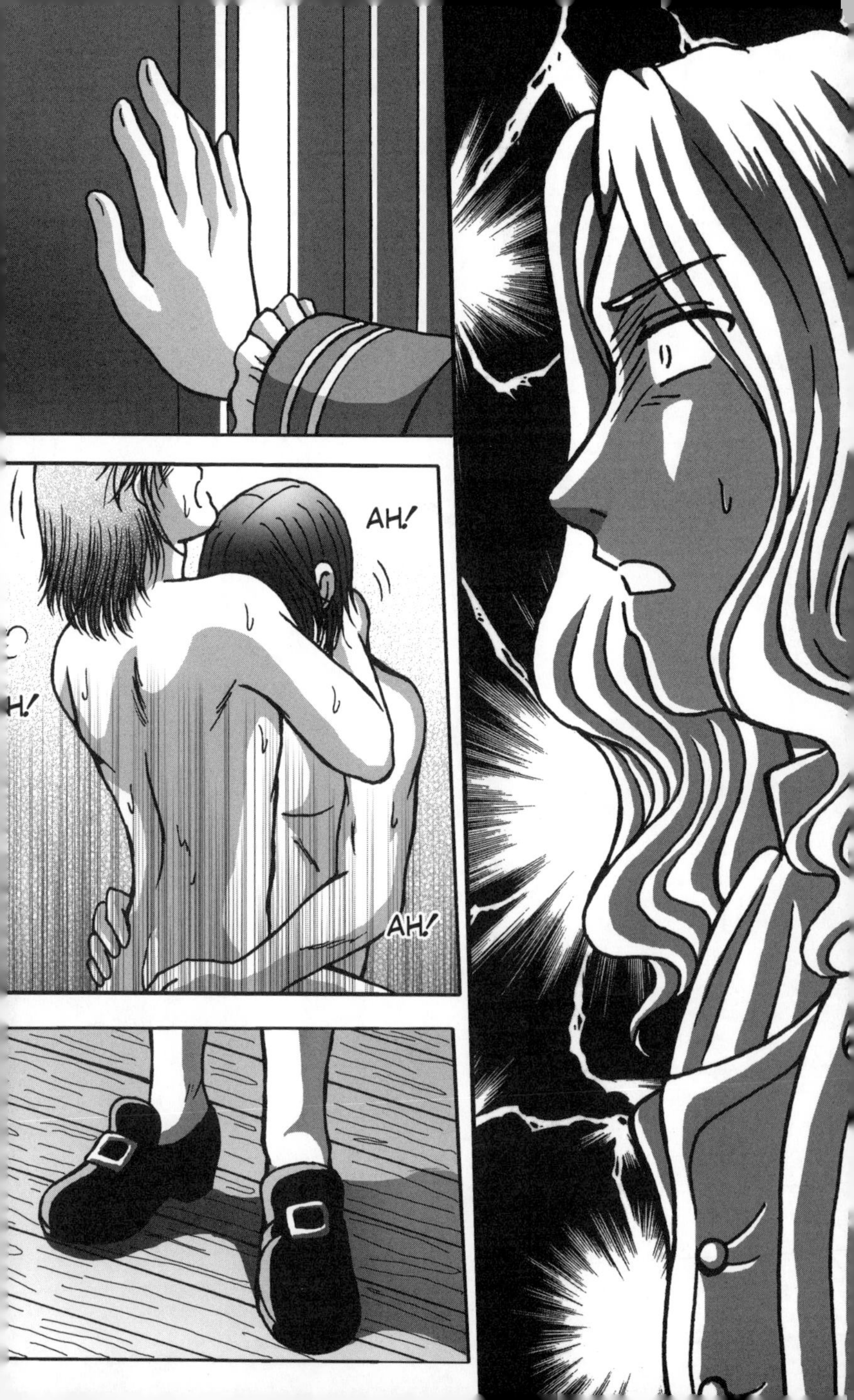
AH!
AH!

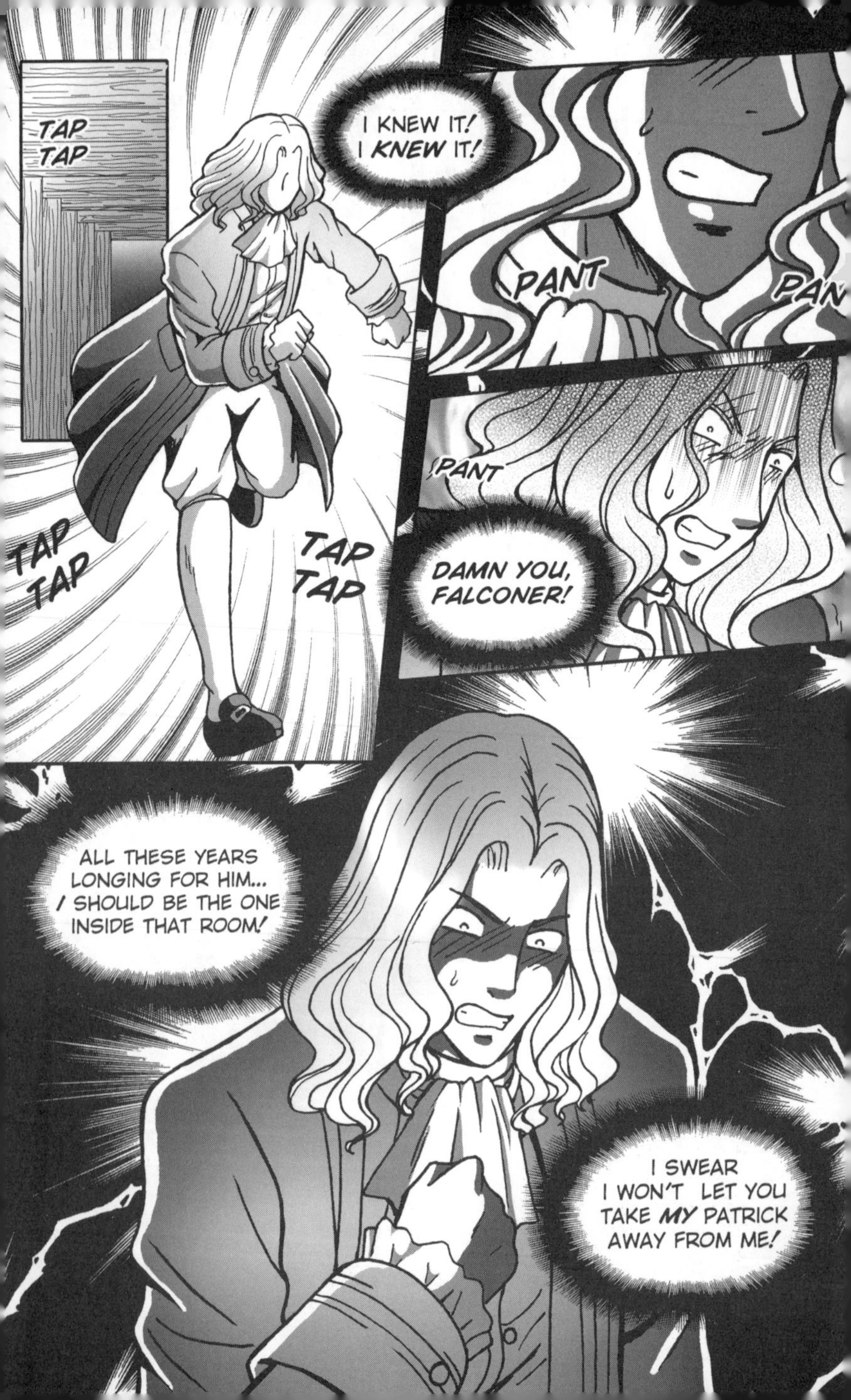
TAP
TAP
TAP
TAP
TAP
TAP
I KNEW IT!
I KNEW IT!
PANT
PAN
PANT
DAMN YOU, FALCONER!
ALL THESE YEARS LONGING FOR HIM... I SHOULD BE THE ONE INSIDE THAT ROOM!
I SWEAR I WON'T LET YOU TAKE MY PATRICK AWAY FROM ME!

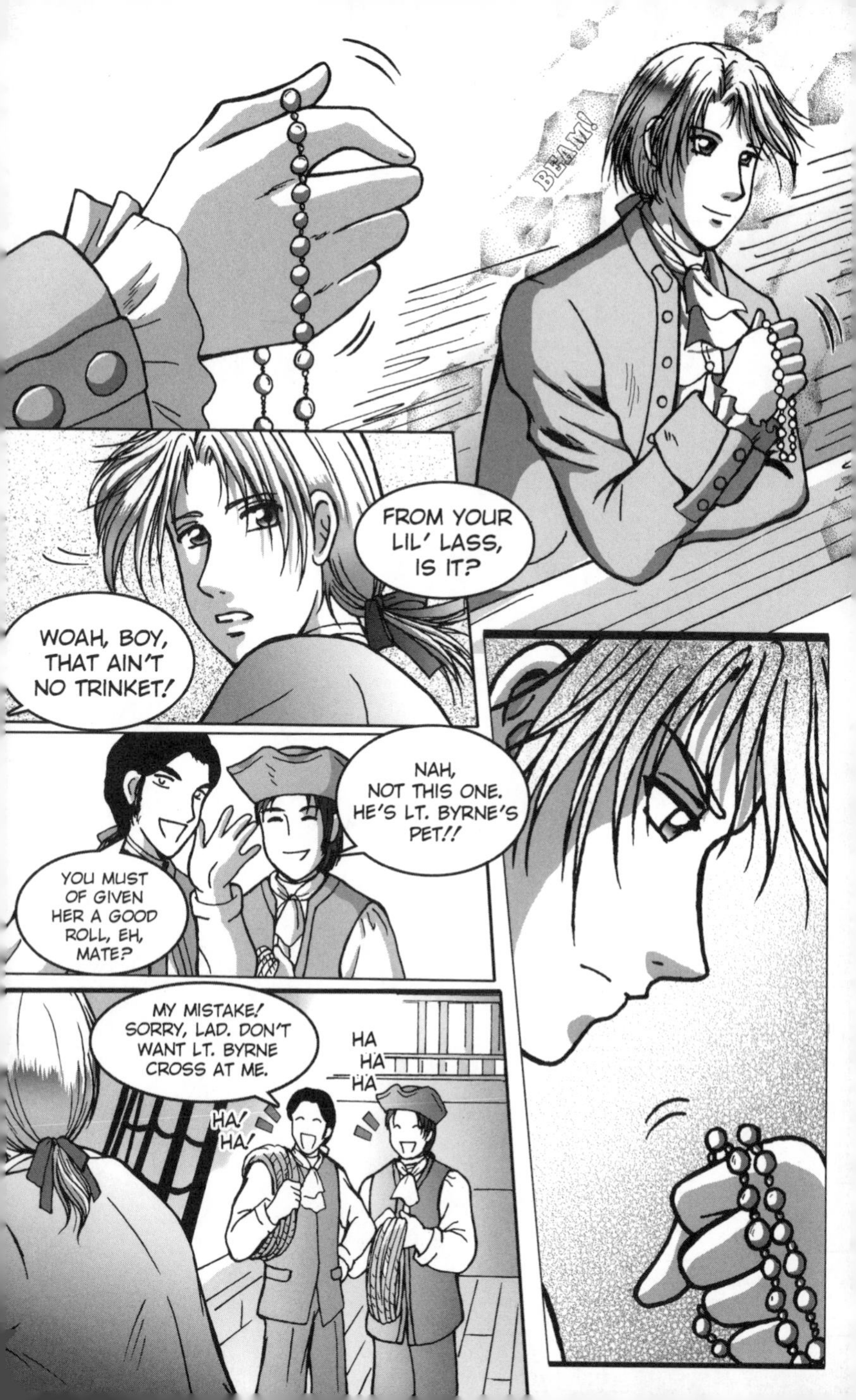
BEAM!
FROM YOUR LIL' LASS, IS IT?
WOAH, BOY, THAT AIN'T NO TRINKET!
YOU MUST OF GIVEN HER A GOOD ROLL, EH, MATE?
NAH, NOT THIS ONE. HE'S LT. BYRNE'S PET!!
MY MISTAKE! SORRY, LAD. DON'T WANT LT. BYRNE CROSS AT ME.
HA HA HA
HA! HA!

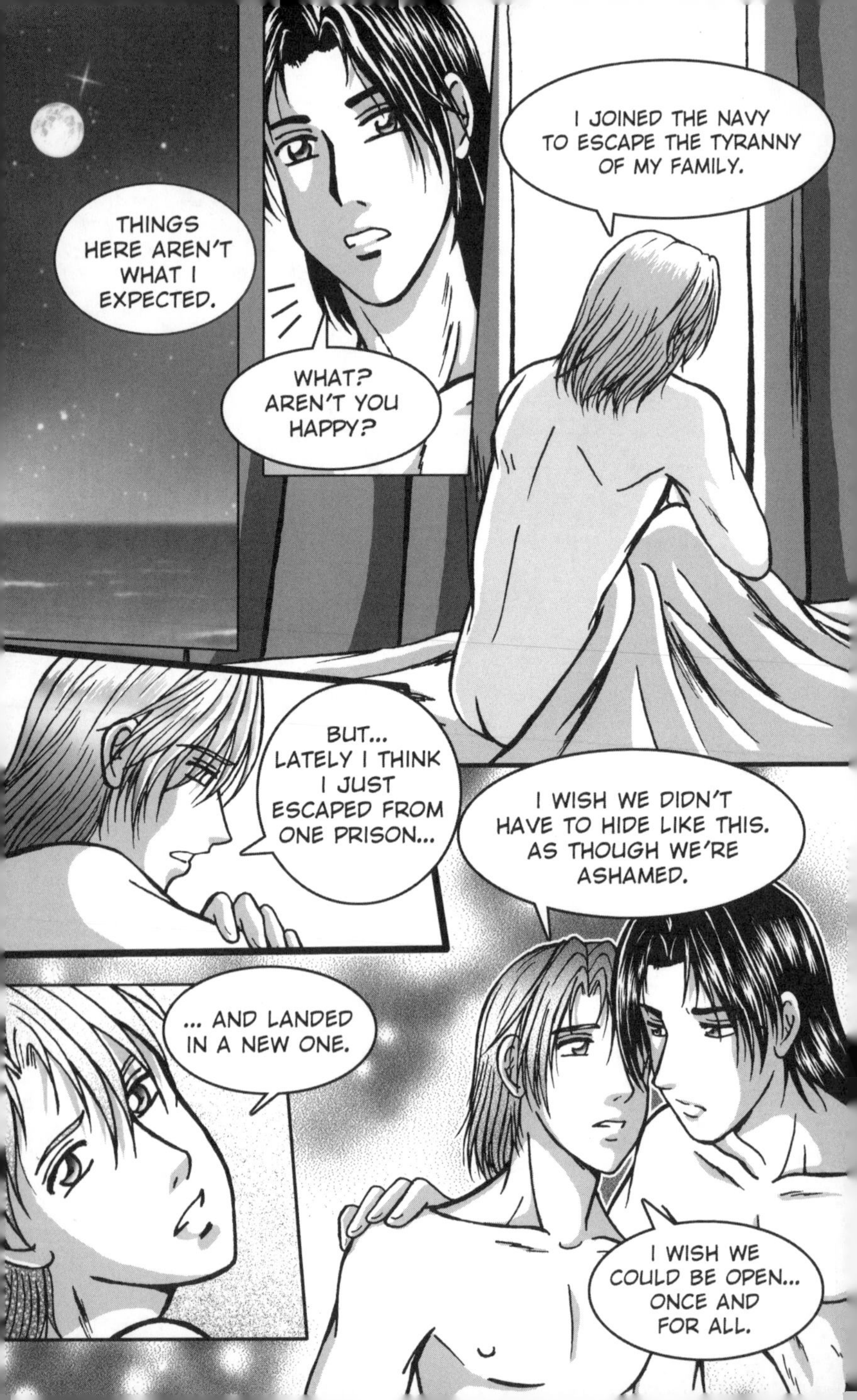
THINGS HERE AREN'T WHAT I EXPECTED.
WHAT? AREN'T YOU HAPPY?
I JOINED THE NAVY TO ESCAPE THE TYRANNY OF MY FAMILY.
BUT... LATELY I THINK I JUST ESCAPED FROM ONE PRISON...
... AND LANDED IN A NEW ONE.
I WISH WE DIDN'T HAVE TO HIDE LIKE THIS. AS THOUGH WE'RE ASHAMED.
I WISH WE COULD BE OPEN... ONCE AND FOR ALL.

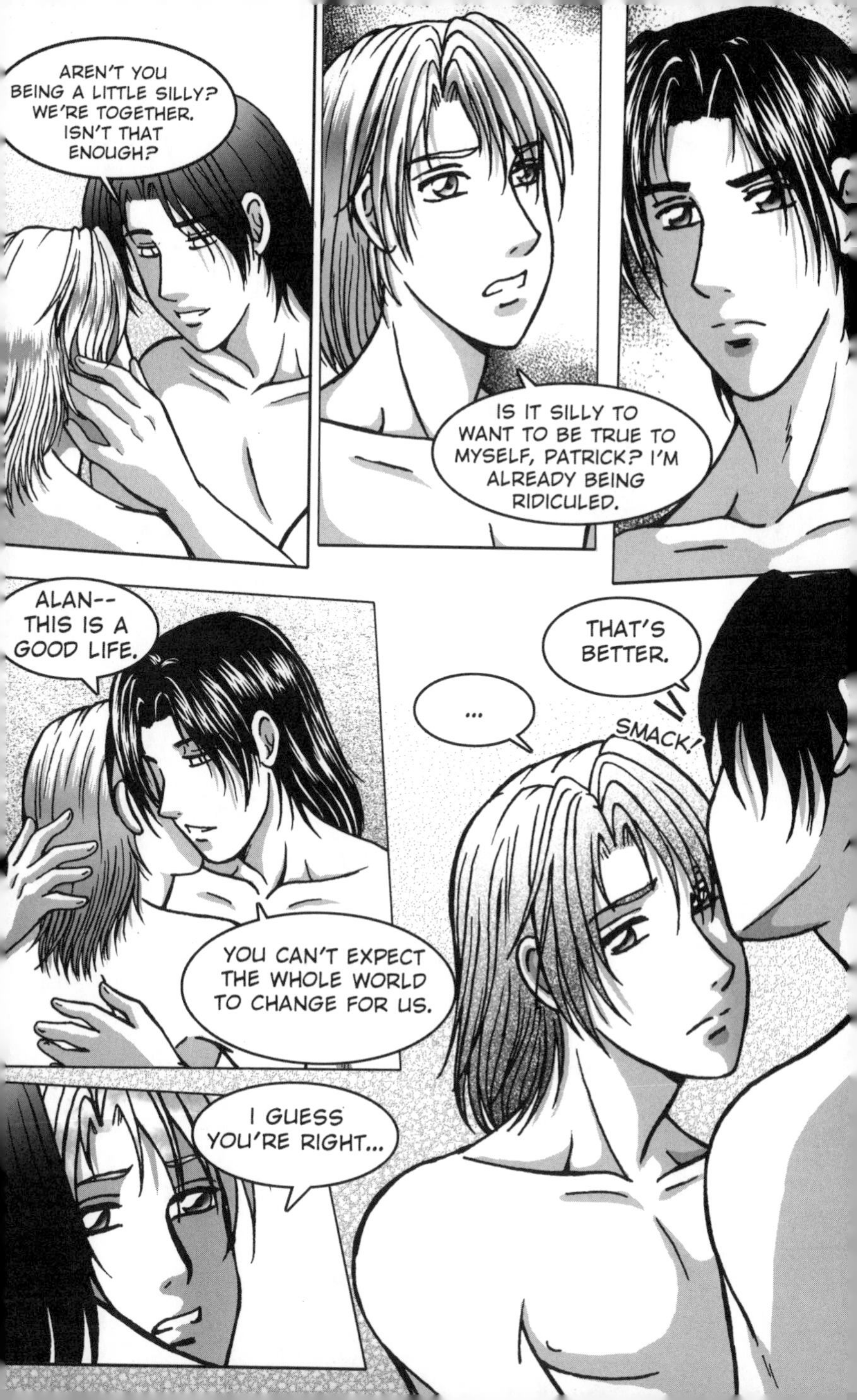
AREN'T YOU BEING A LITTLE SILLY? WE'RE TOGETHER. ISN'T THAT ENOUGH?
IS IT SILLY TO WANT TO BE TRUE TO MYSELF, PATRICK? I'M ALREADY BEING RIDICULED.
ALAN-- THIS IS A GOOD LIFE.
YOU CAN'T EXPECT THE WHOLE WORLD TO CHANGE FOR US.
I GUESS YOU'RE RIGHT...
...
THAT'S BETTER.
SMACK!

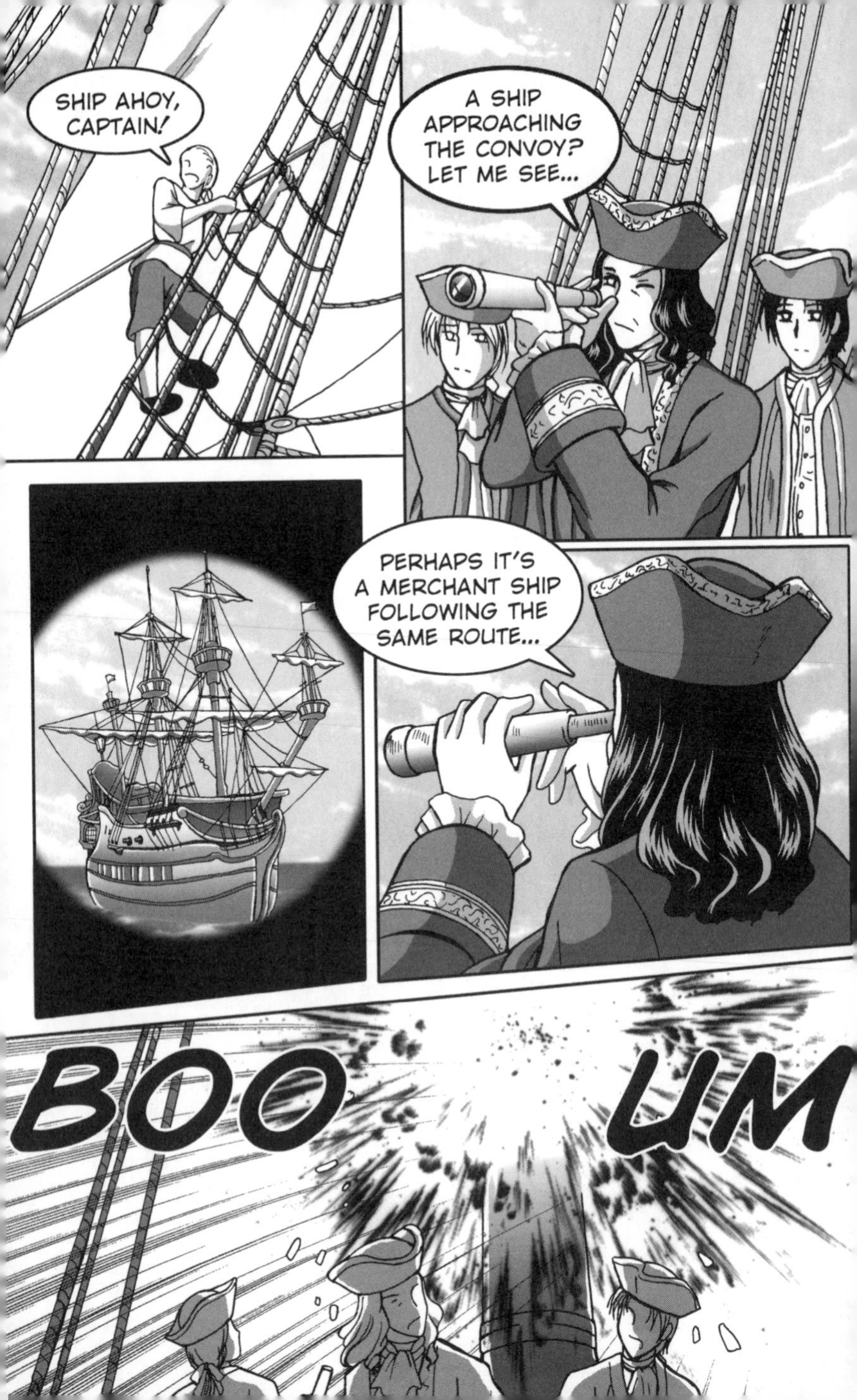
SHIP AHOY, CAPTAIN!
A SHIP APPROACHING THE CONVOY? LET ME SEE...
PERHAPS IT'S A MERCHANT SHIP FOLLOWING THE SAME ROUTE...
BOO UM

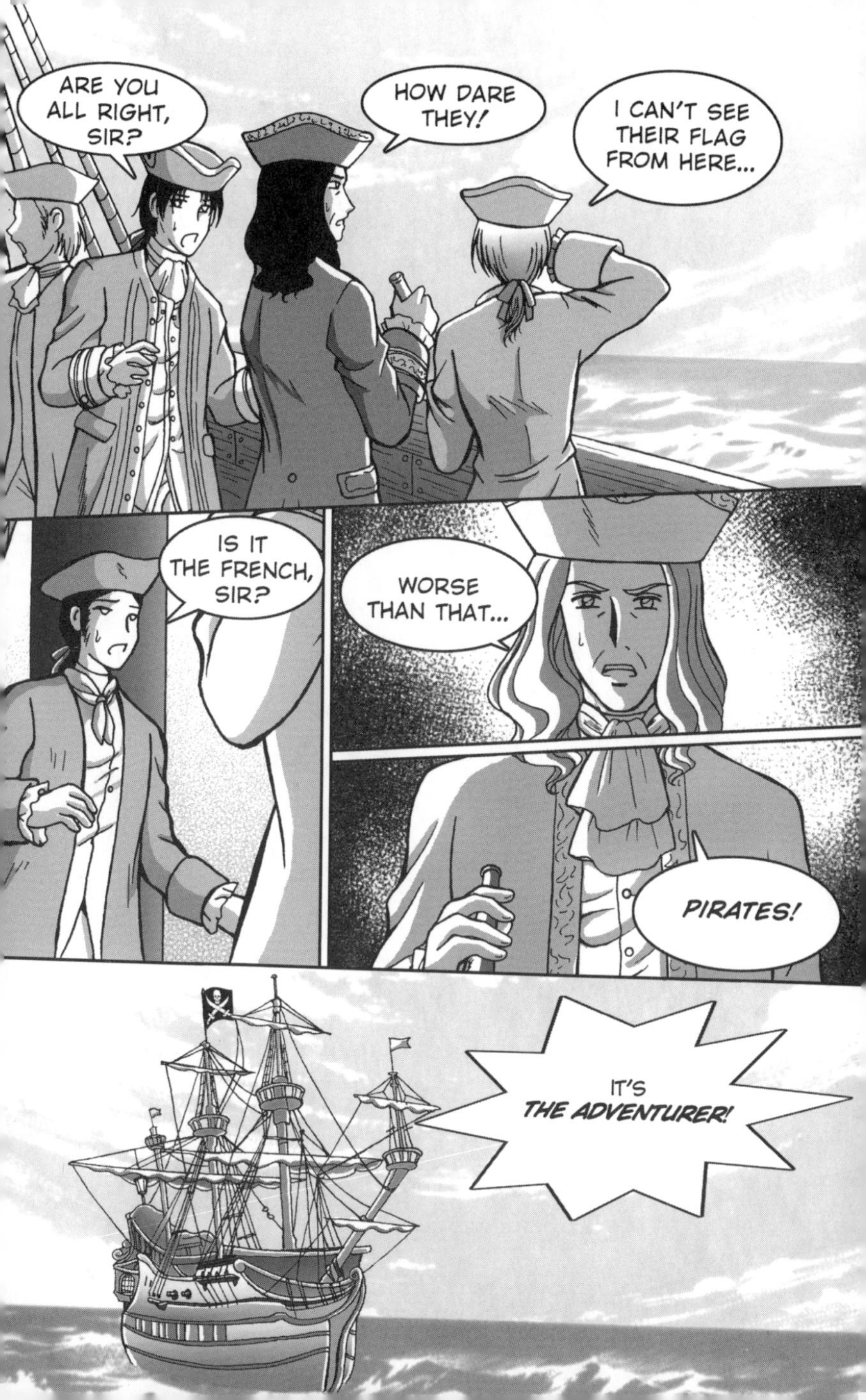
ARE YOU ALL RIGHT, SIR?
HOW DARE THEY!
I CAN'T SEE THEIR FLAG FROM HERE...
IS IT THE FRENCH, SIR?
WORSE THAN THAT...
PIRATES!
IT'S THE ADVENTURER!

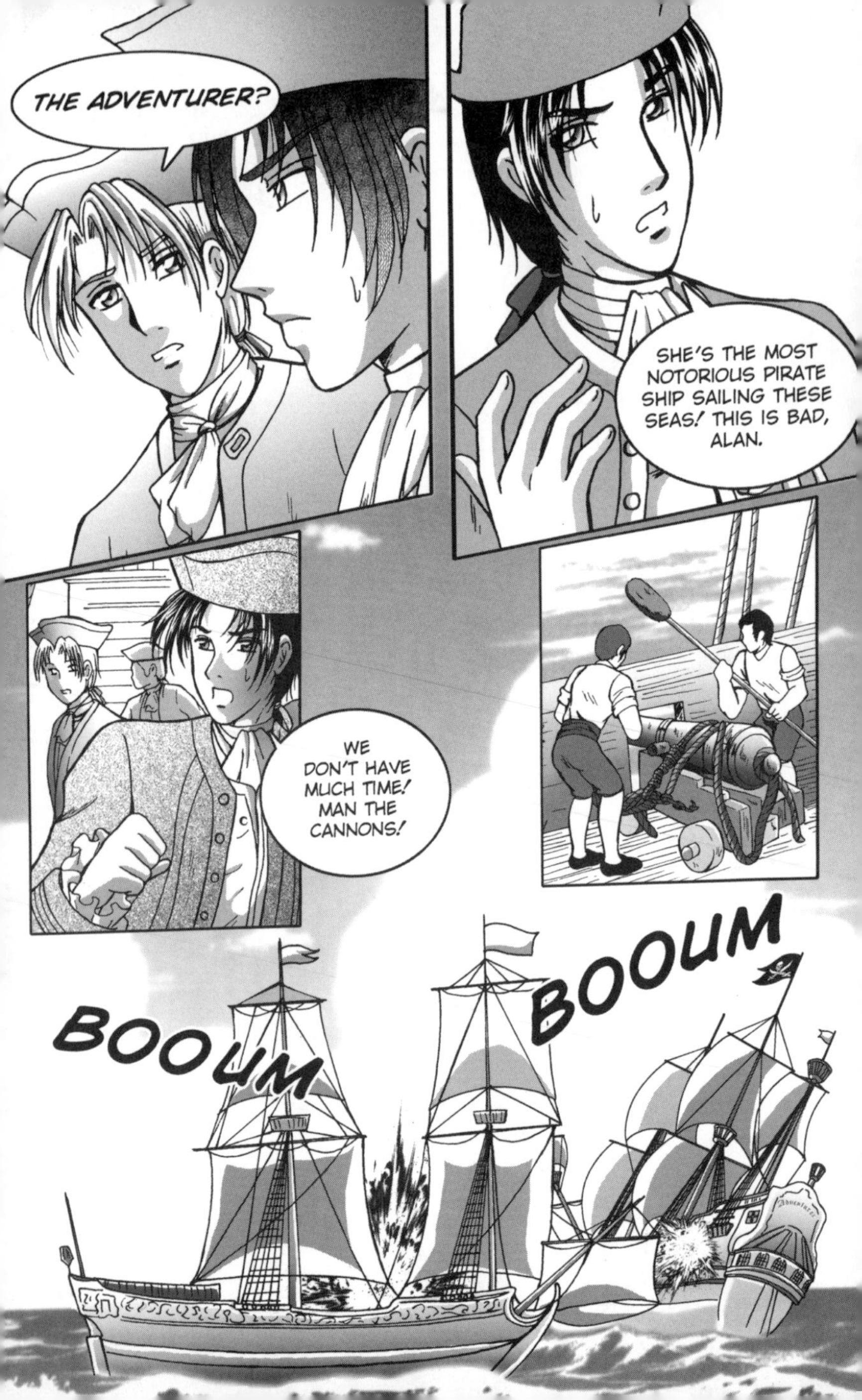
THE ADVENTURER?
SHE'S THE MOST NOTORIOUS PIRATE SHIP SAILING THESE SEAS! THIS IS BAD, ALAN.
WE DON'T HAVE MUCH TIME! MAN THE CANNONS!
BOOUM
BOOUM

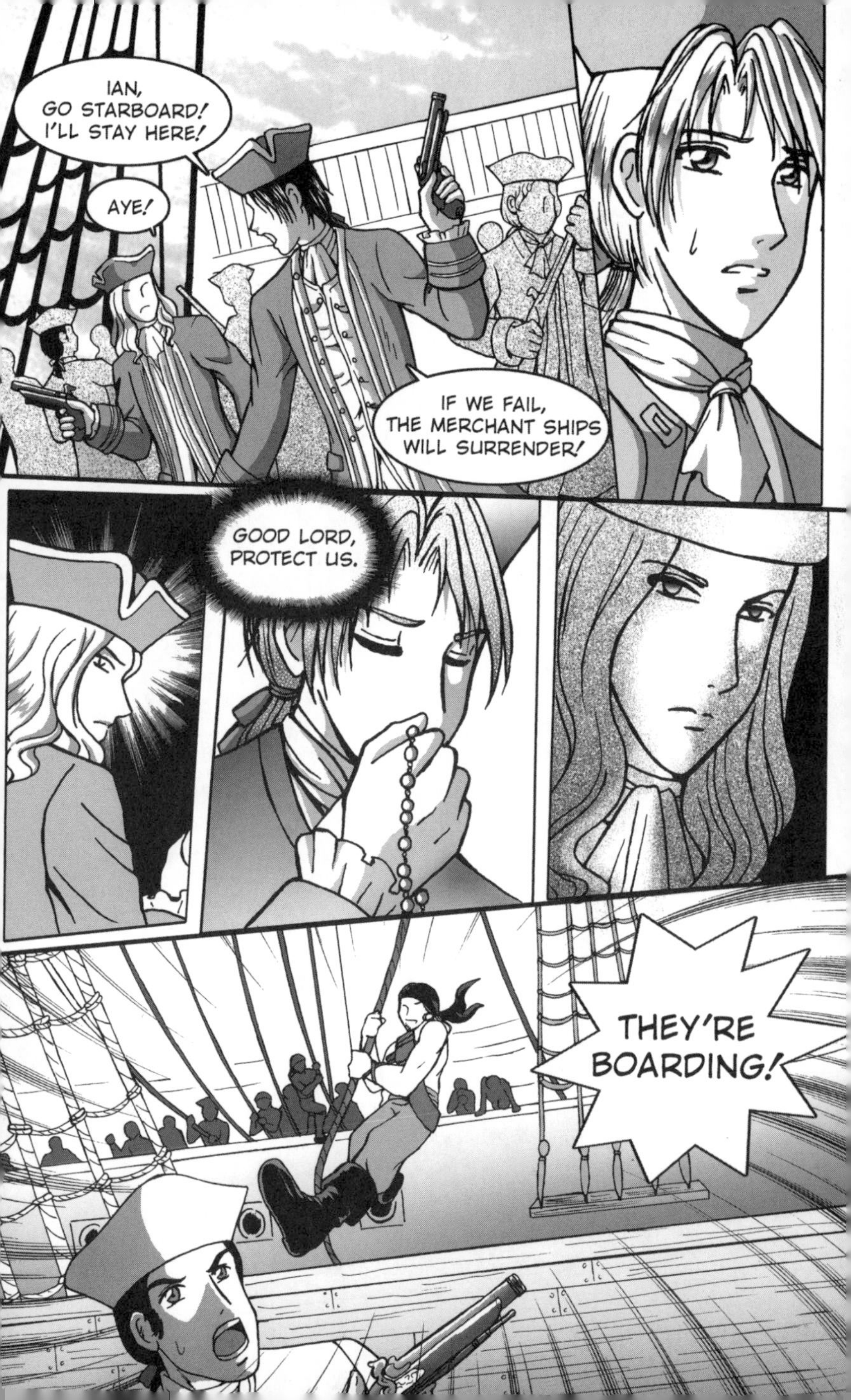
IAN, GO STARBOARD! I'LL STAY HERE!
AYE!
IF WE FAIL, THE MERCHANT SHIPS WILL SURRENDER!
GOOD LORD, PROTECT US.
THEY'RE BOARDING!

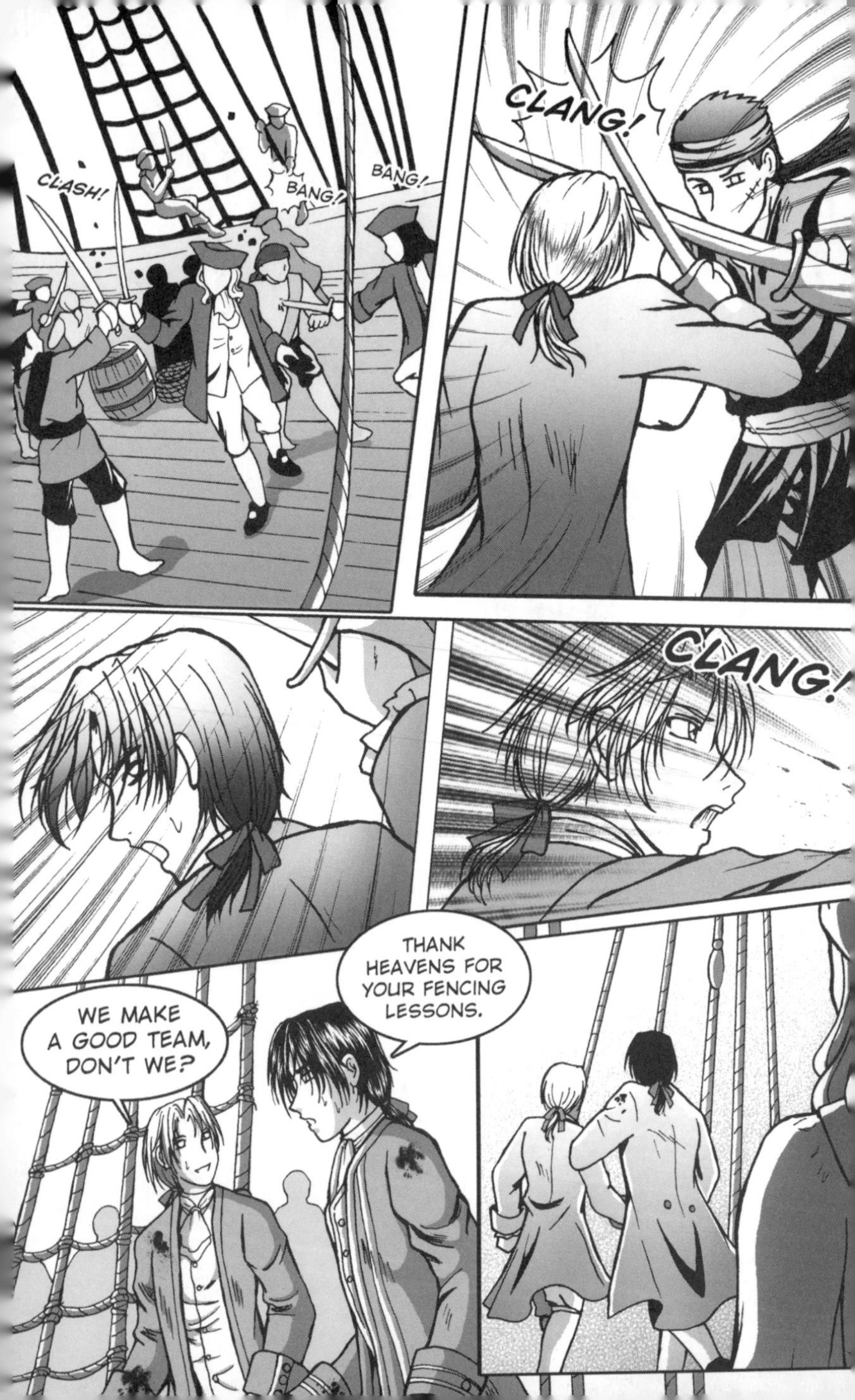
CLASH!
BANG!
BANG!
CLANG!
CLANG!
WE MAKE A GOOD TEAM, DON'T WE?
THANK HEAVENS FOR YOUR FENCING LESSONS.

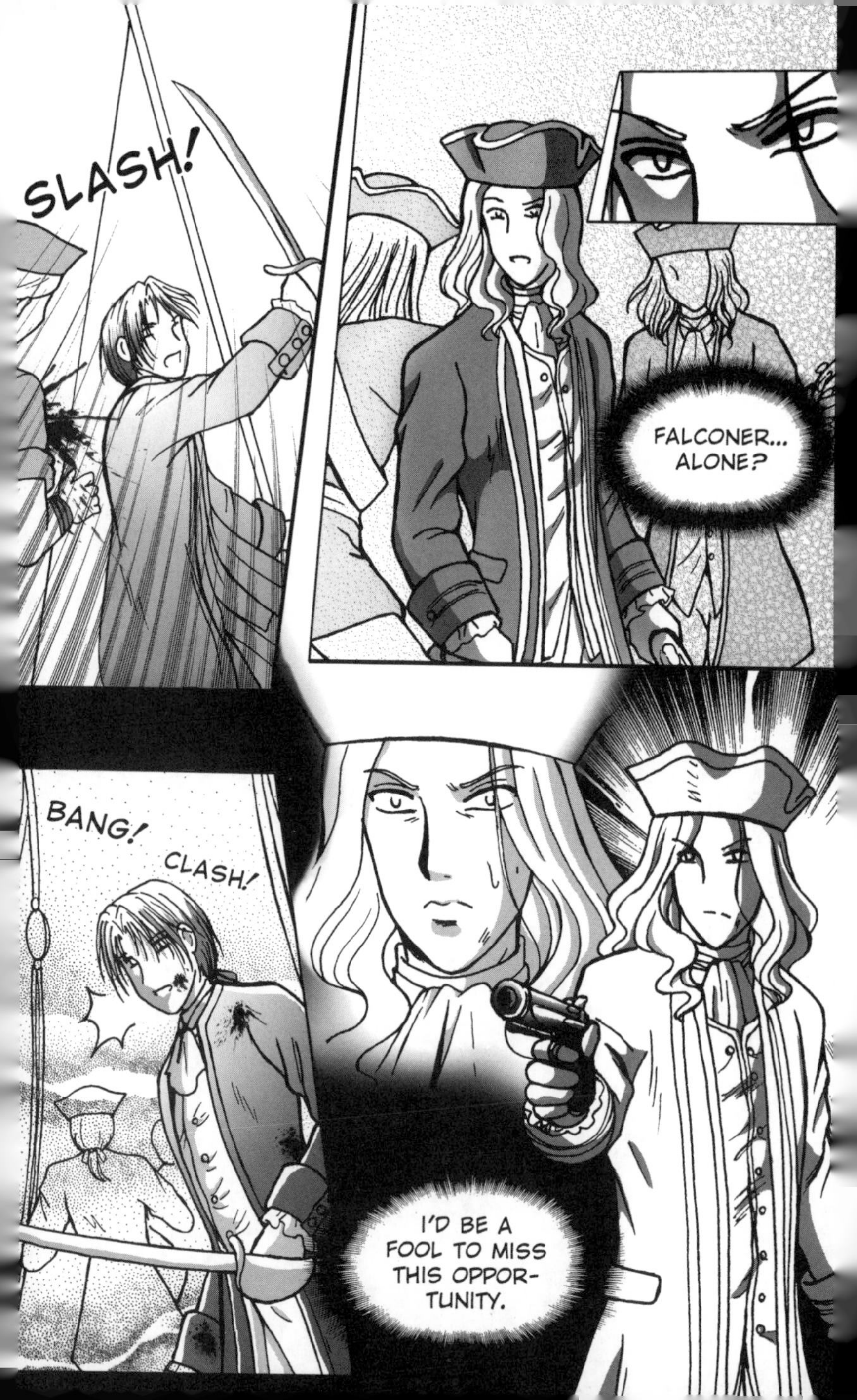
SLASH!
FALCONER... ALONE?
BANG!
CLASH!
I'D BE A FOOL TO MISS THIS OPPOR-TUNITY.

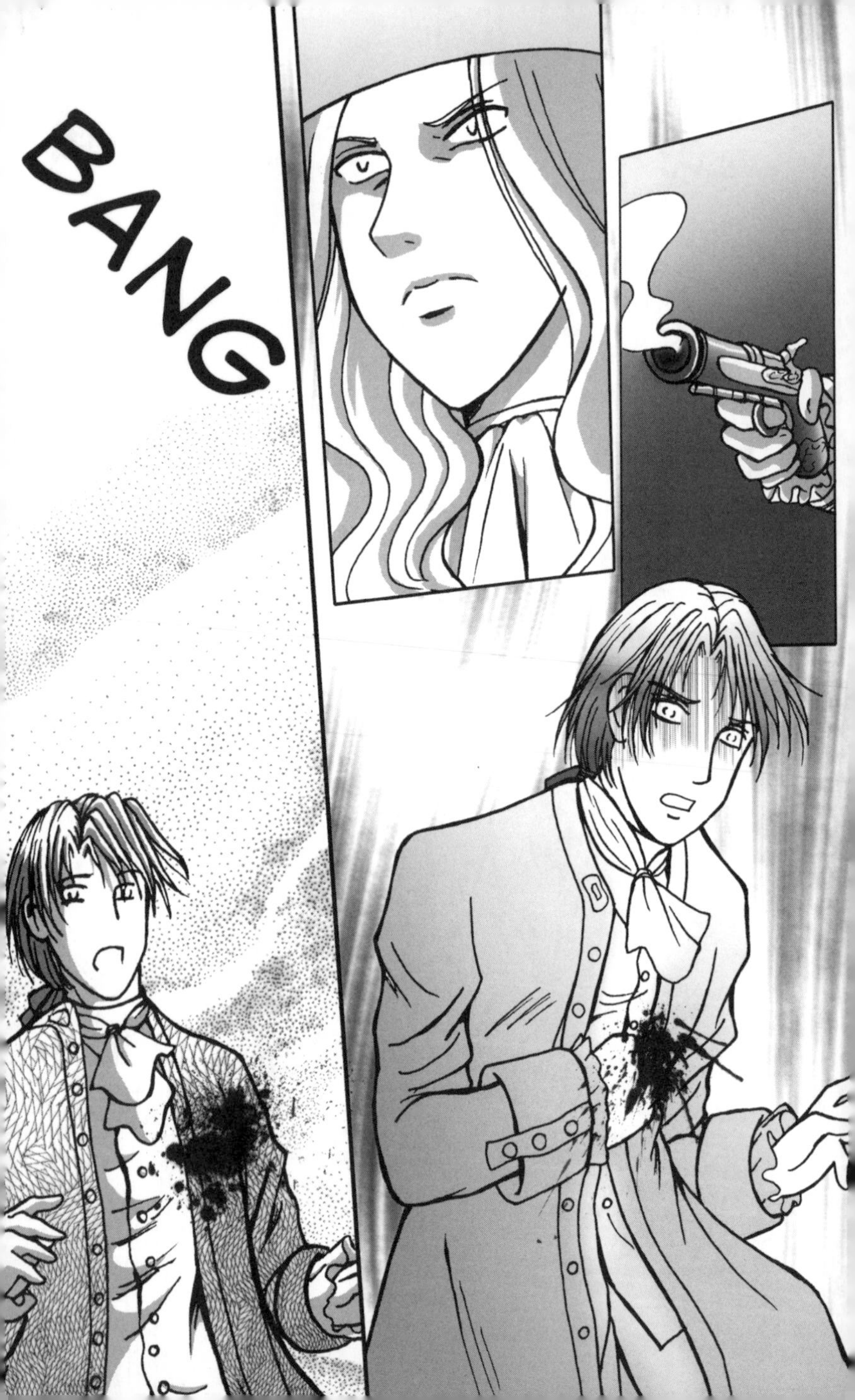
BANG

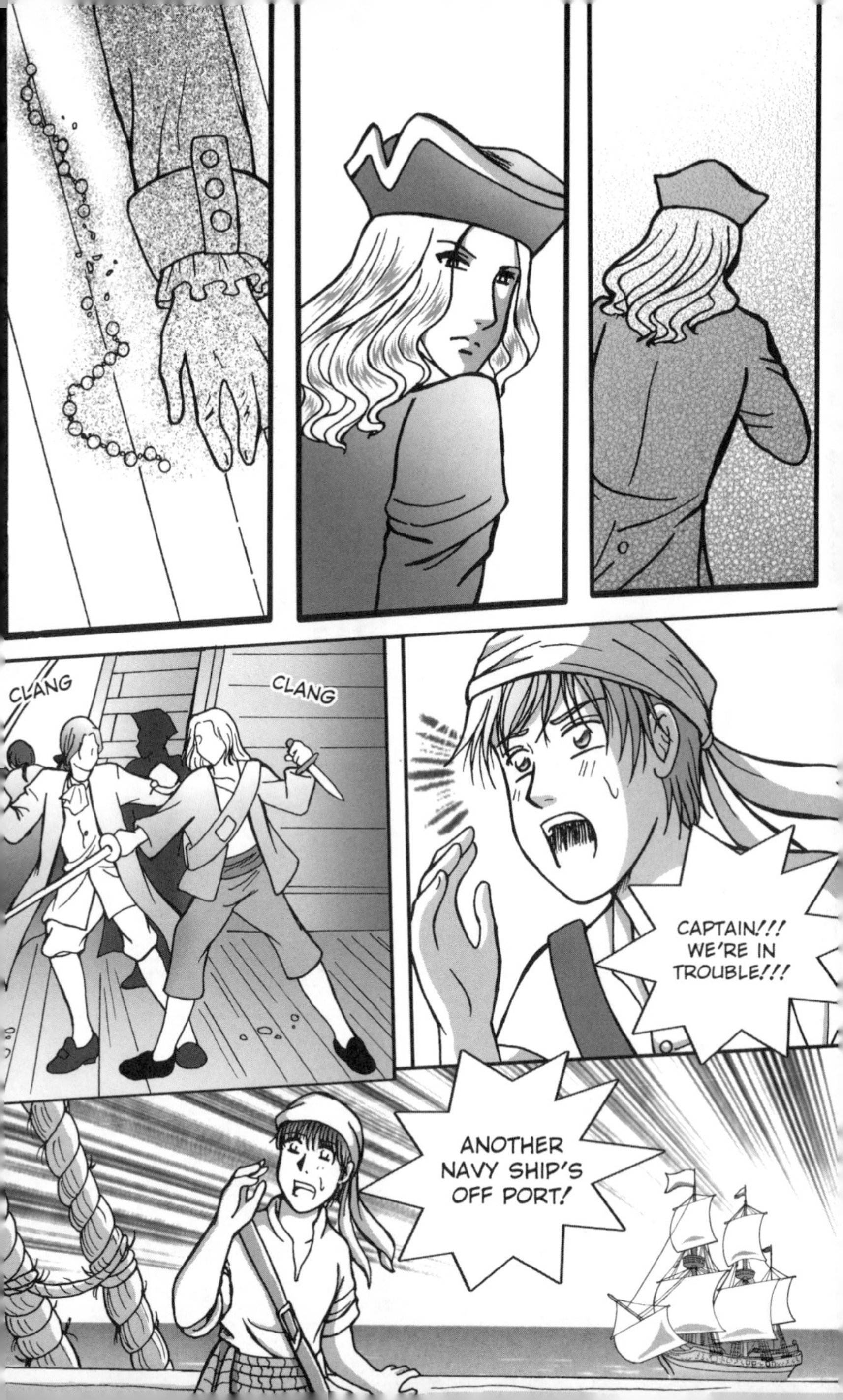
CLANG
CLANG
CAPTAIN!!! WE'RE IN TROUBLE!!!
ANOTHER NAVY SHIP'S OFF PORT!

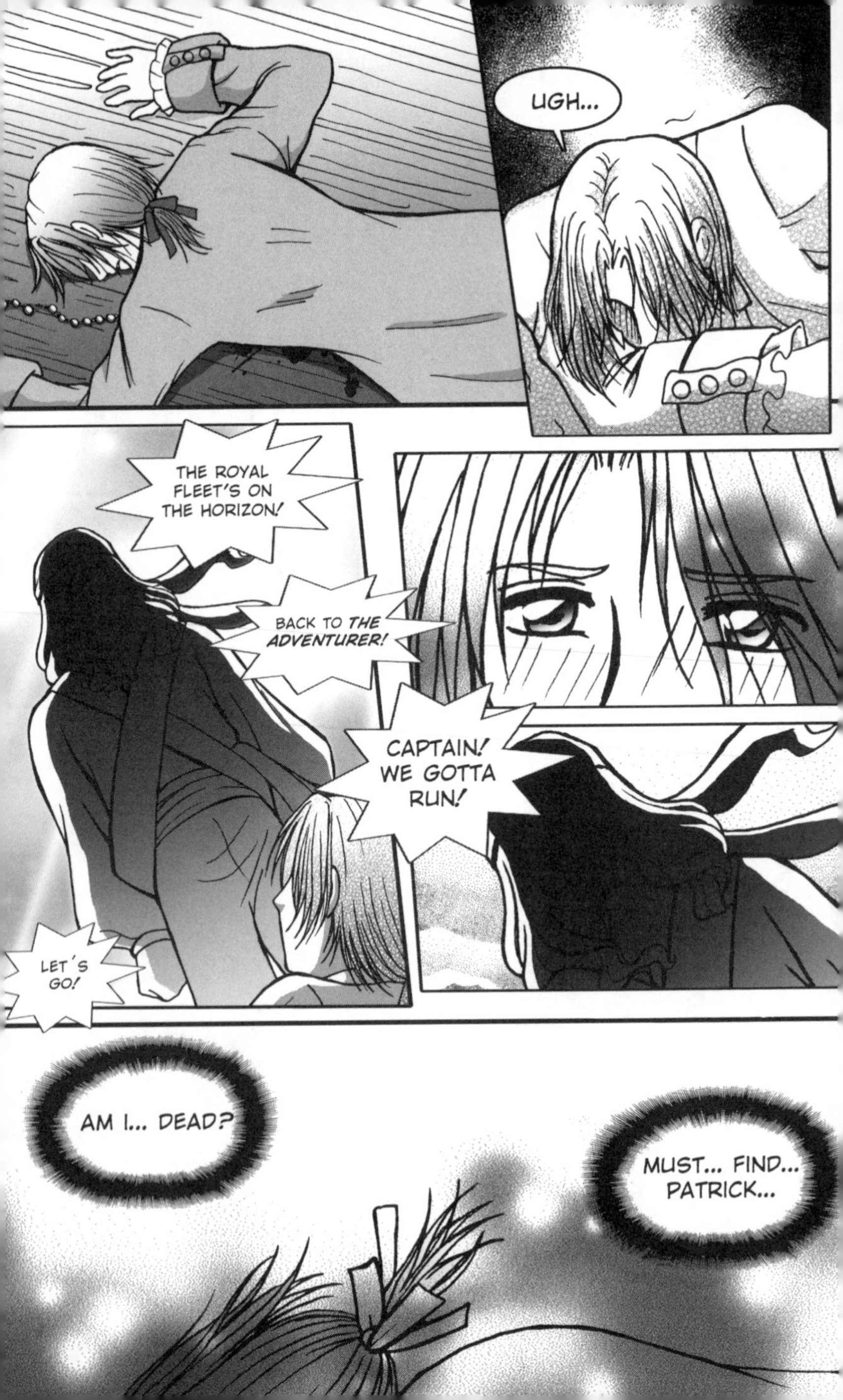
UGH...
THE ROYAL FLEET'S ON THE HORIZON!
BACK TO THE ADVENTURER!
CAPTAIN! WE GOTTA RUN!
LET'S GO!
AM I... DEAD?
MUST... FIND... PATRICK...

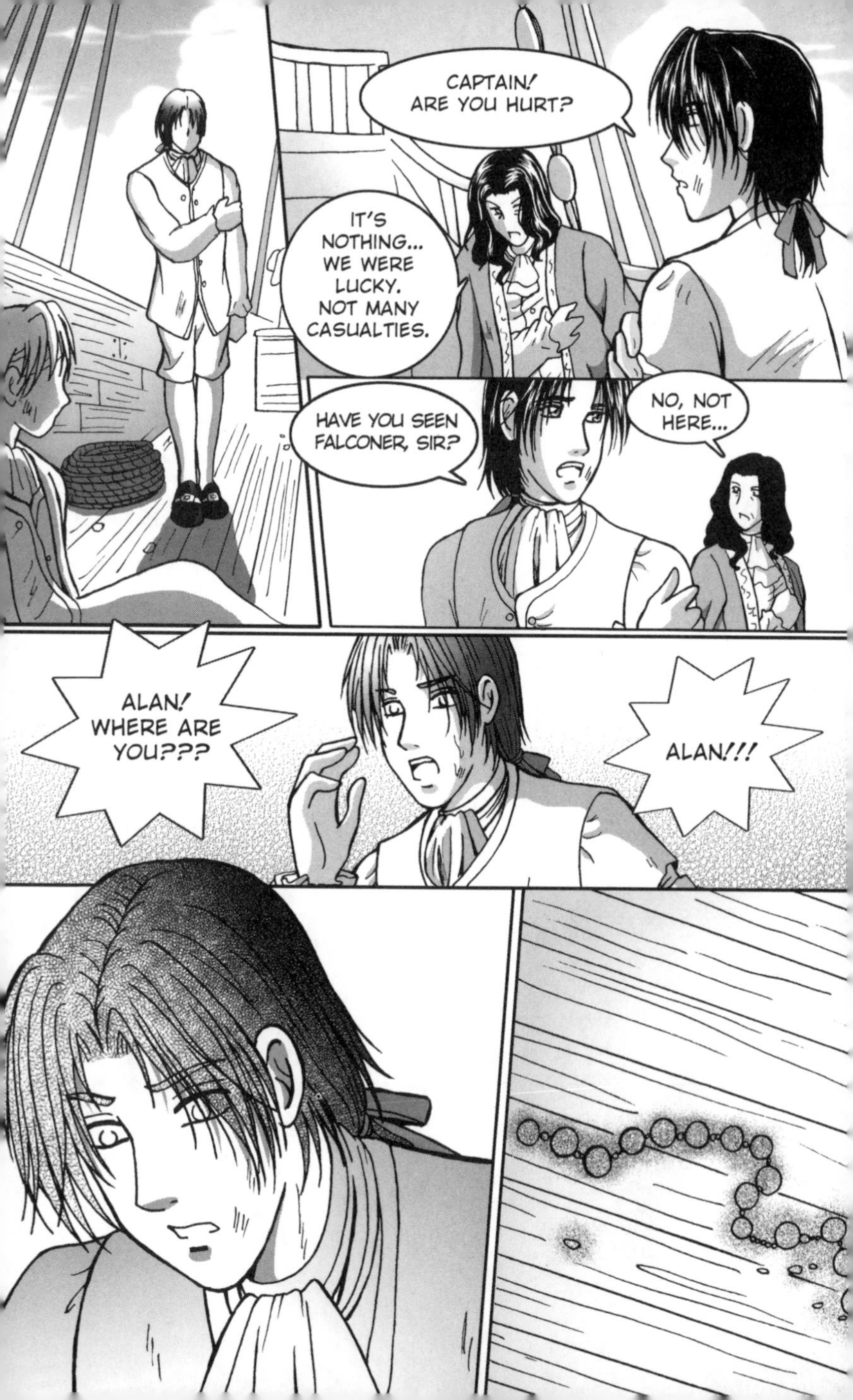
CAPTAIN! ARE YOU HURT?
IT'S NOTHING... WE WERE LUCKY. NOT MANY CASUALTIES.
HAVE YOU SEEN FALCONER, SIR?
NO, NOT HERE...
ALAN! WHERE ARE YOU???
ALAN!!!

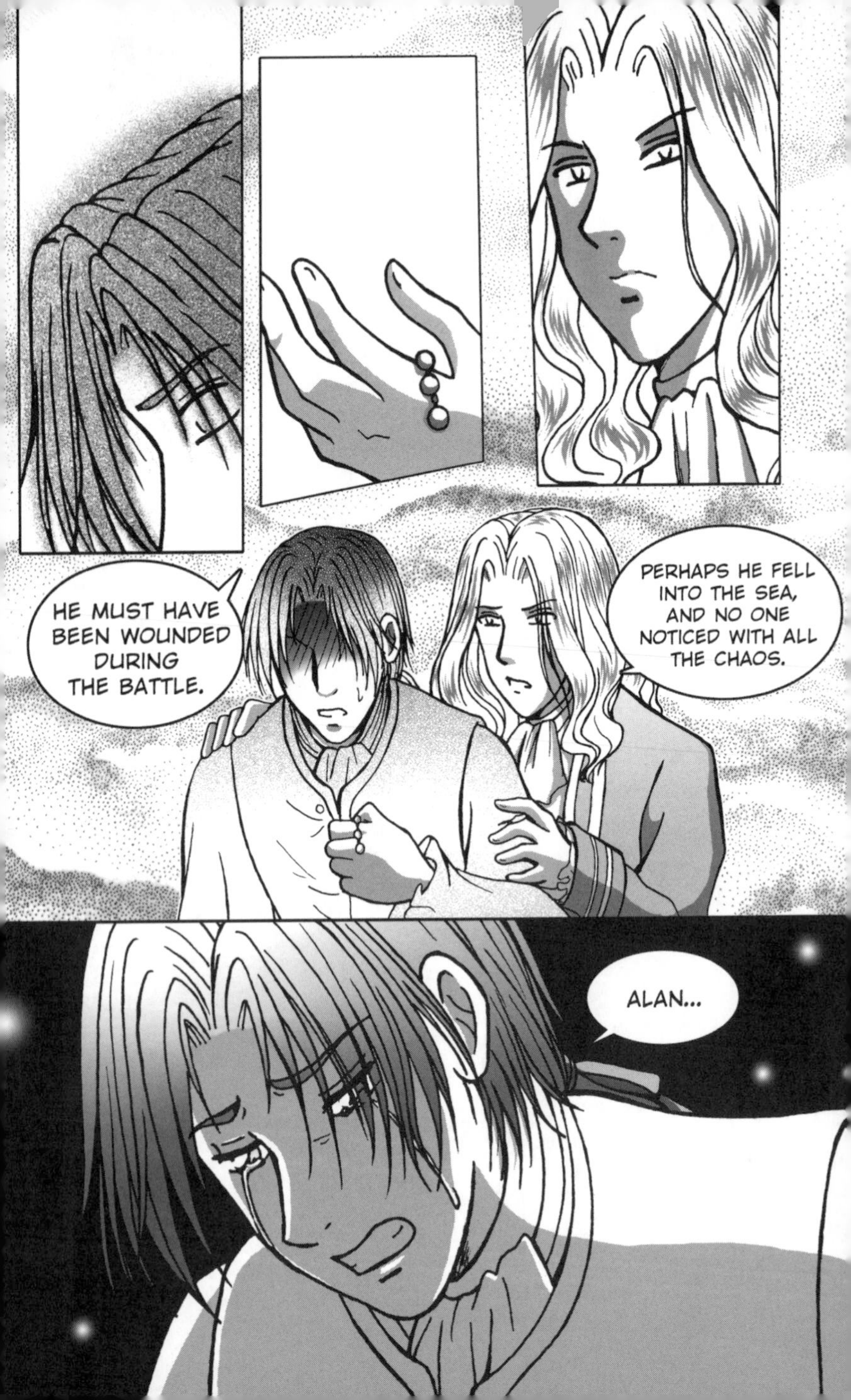
HE MUST HAVE BEEN WOUNDED DURING THE BATTLE.
PERHAPS HE FELL INTO THE SEA, AND NO ONE NOTICED WITH ALL THE CHAOS.
ALAN...

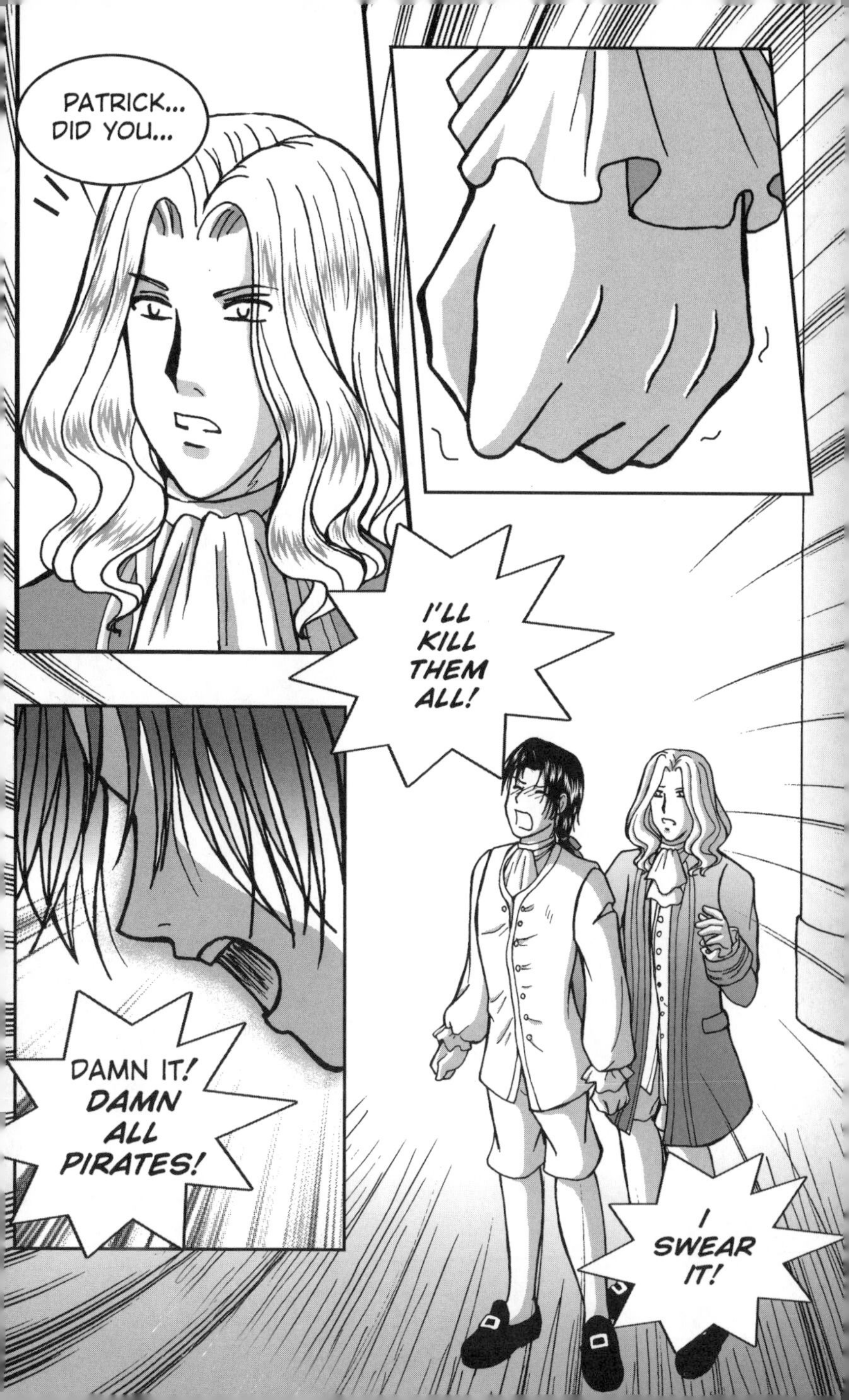
PATRICK... DID YOU...
I'LL KILL THEM ALL!
DAMN IT! DAMN ALL PIRATES!
I SWEAR IT!

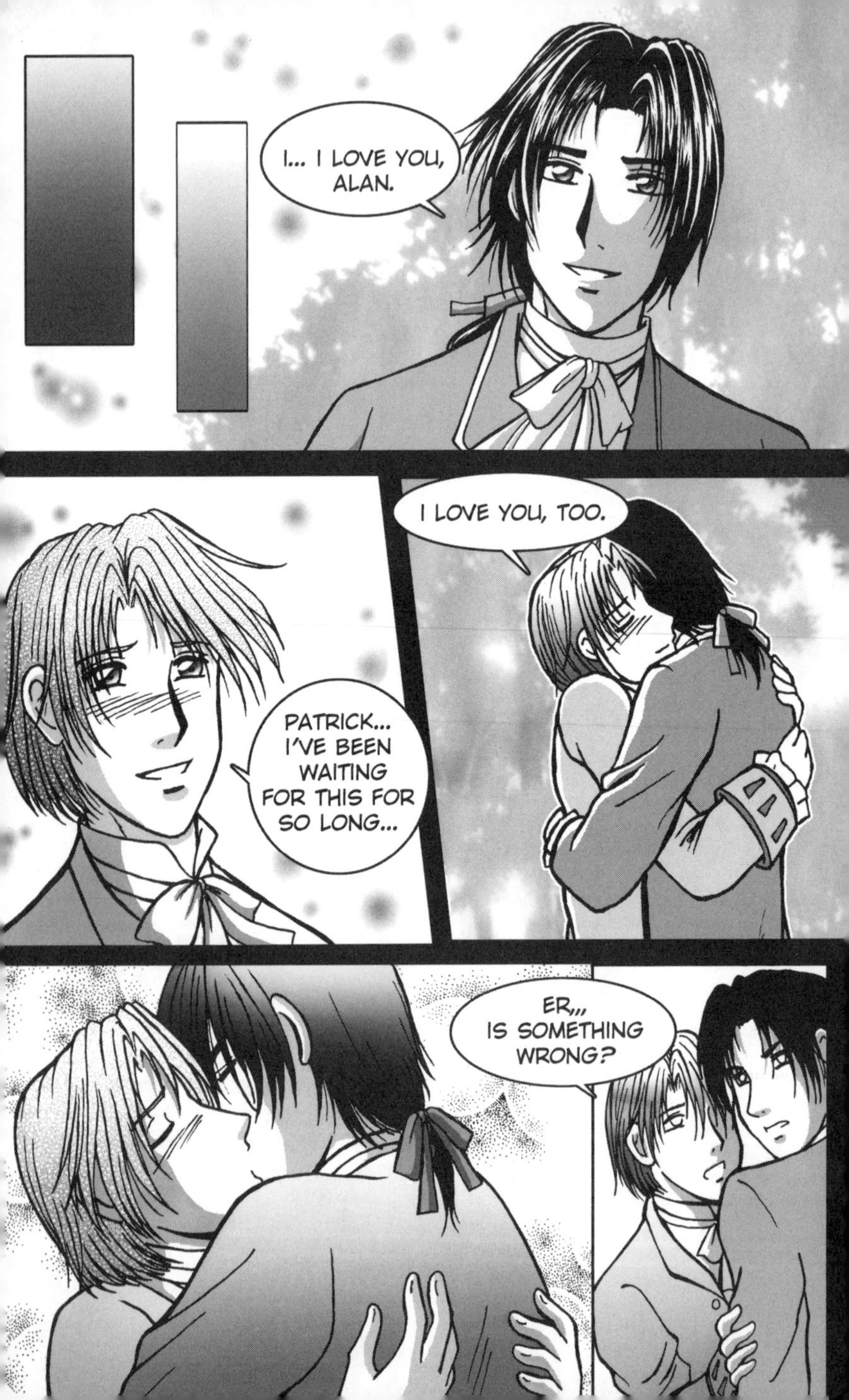
I... I LOVE YOU, ALAN.
PATRICK... I'VE BEEN WAITING FOR THIS FOR SO LONG...
I LOVE YOU, TOO.
ER,,, IS SOMETHING WRONG?

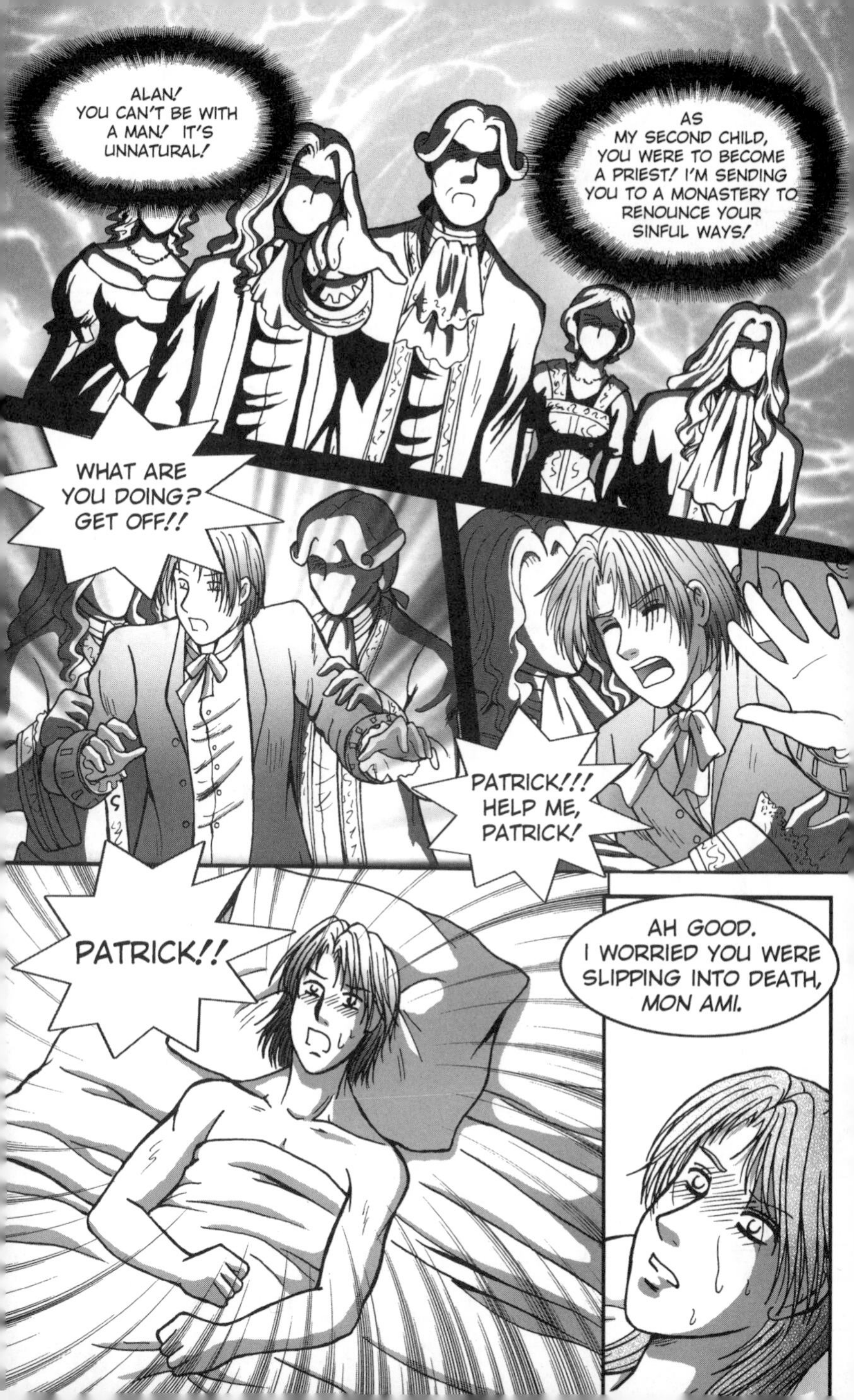
ALAN! YOU CAN'T BE WITH A MAN! IT'S UNNATURAL!
AS MY SECOND CHILD, YOU WERE TO BECOME A PRIEST! I'M SENDING YOU TO A MONASTERY TO RENOUNCE YOUR SINFUL WAYS!
WHAT ARE YOU DOING? GET OFF!!
PATRICK!!! HELP ME, PATRICK!
PATRICK!!
AH GOOD. I WORRIED YOU WERE SLIPPING INTO DEATH, MON AMI.

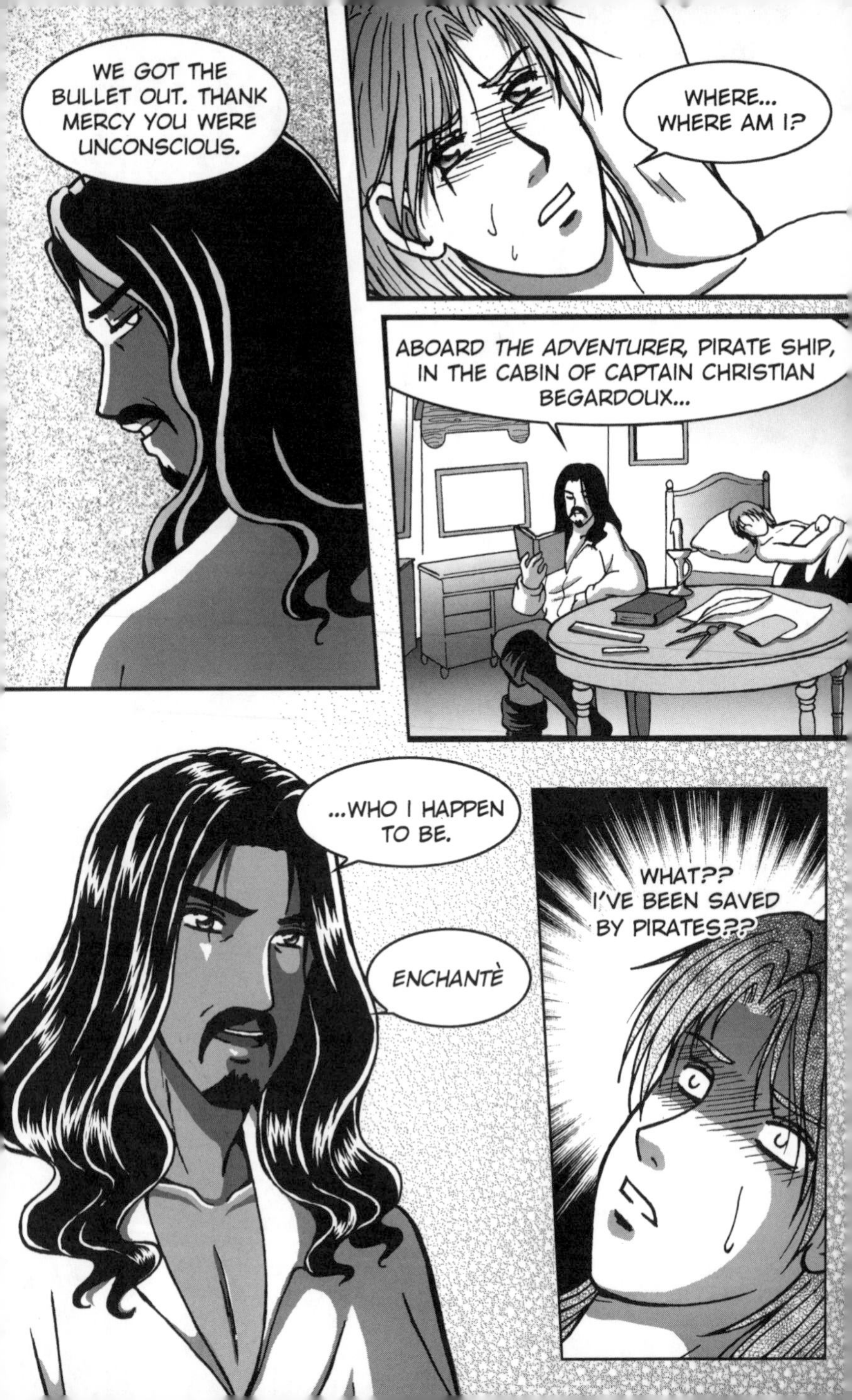
WE GOT THE BULLET OUT. THANK MERCY YOU WERE UNCONSCIOUS.
WHERE... WHERE AM I?
ABOARD THE *ADVENTURER*, PIRATE SHIP, IN THE CABIN OF CAPTAIN CHRISTIAN BEGARDOUX...
...WHO I HAPPEN TO BE.
ENCHANTÈ
WHAT?? I'VE BEEN SAVED BY PIRATES??

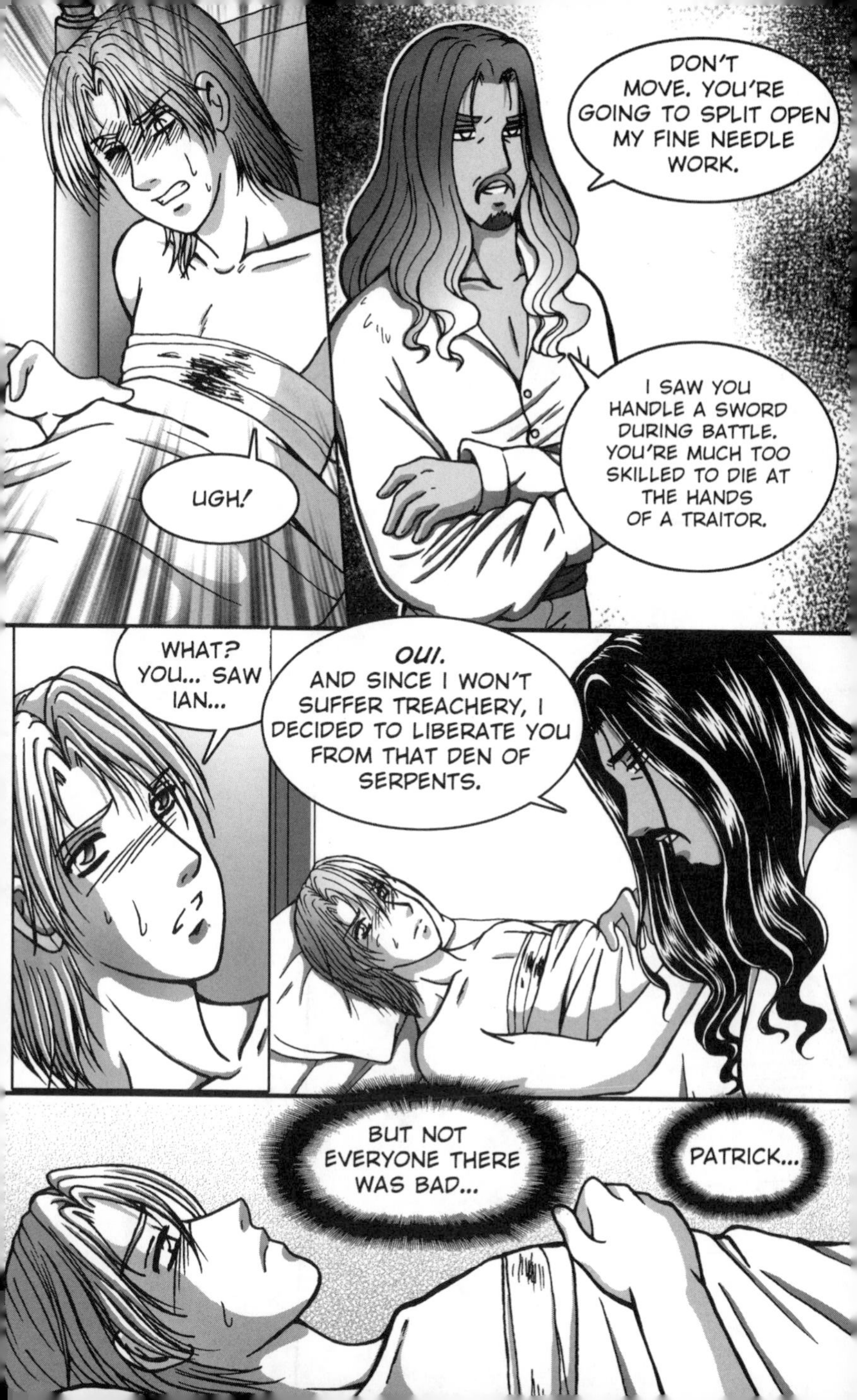
DON'T MOVE. YOU'RE GOING TO SPLIT OPEN MY FINE NEEDLE WORK.
UGH!
I SAW YOU HANDLE A SWORD DURING BATTLE. YOU'RE MUCH TOO SKILLED TO DIE AT THE HANDS OF A TRAITOR.
WHAT? YOU... SAW IAN...
OUI. AND SINCE I WON'T SUFFER TREACHERY, I DECIDED TO LIBERATE YOU FROM THAT DEN OF SERPENTS.
BUT NOT EVERYONE THERE WAS BAD...
PATRICK...

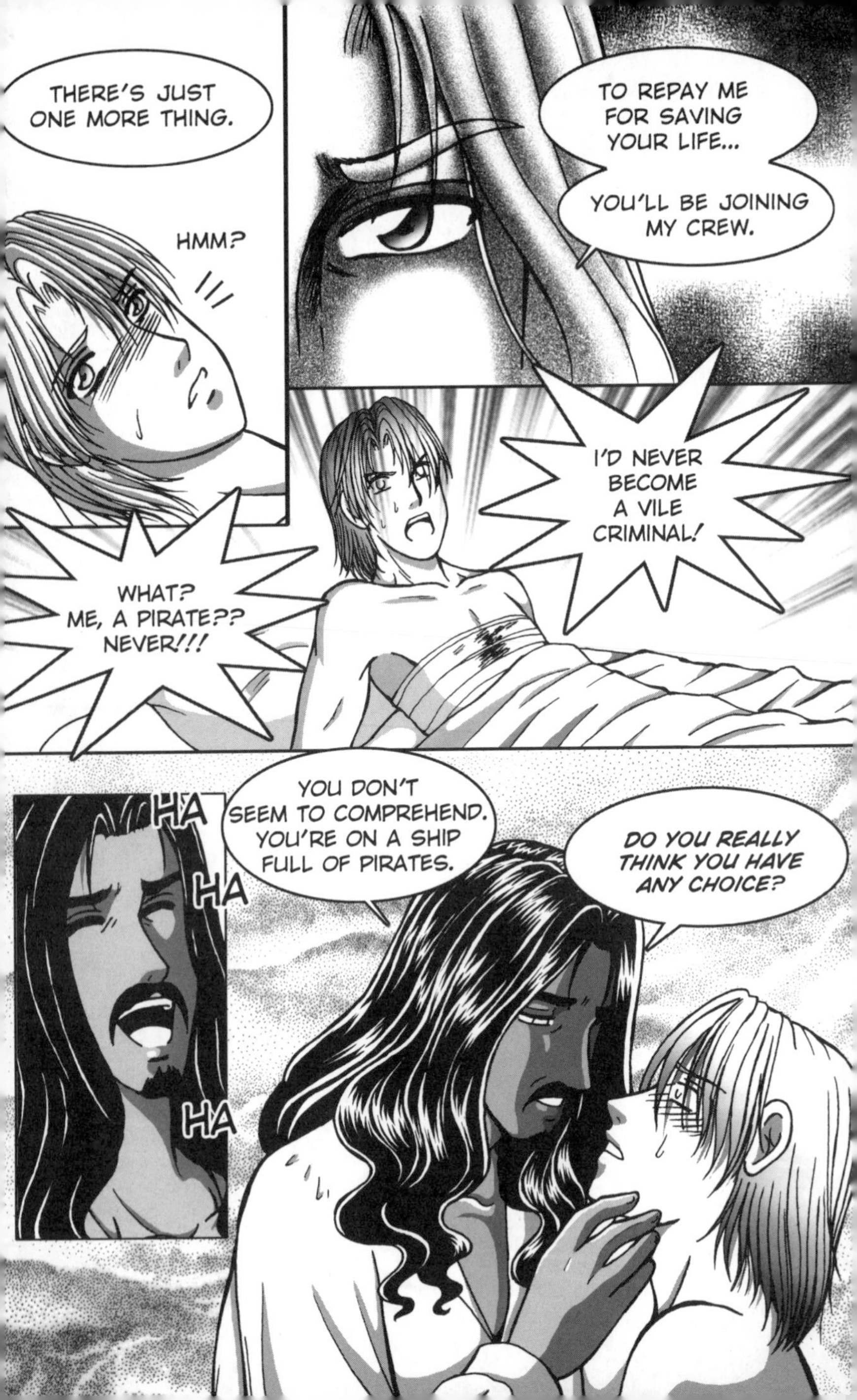
THERE'S JUST ONE MORE THING.
HMM?
TO REPAY ME FOR SAVING YOUR LIFE...
YOU'LL BE JOINING MY CREW.
WHAT? ME, A PIRATE?? NEVER!!!
I'D NEVER BECOME A VILE CRIMINAL!
HA HA HA
YOU DON'T SEEM TO COMPREHEND. YOU'RE ON A SHIP FULL OF PIRATES.
DO YOU REALLY THINK YOU HAVE ANY CHOICE?

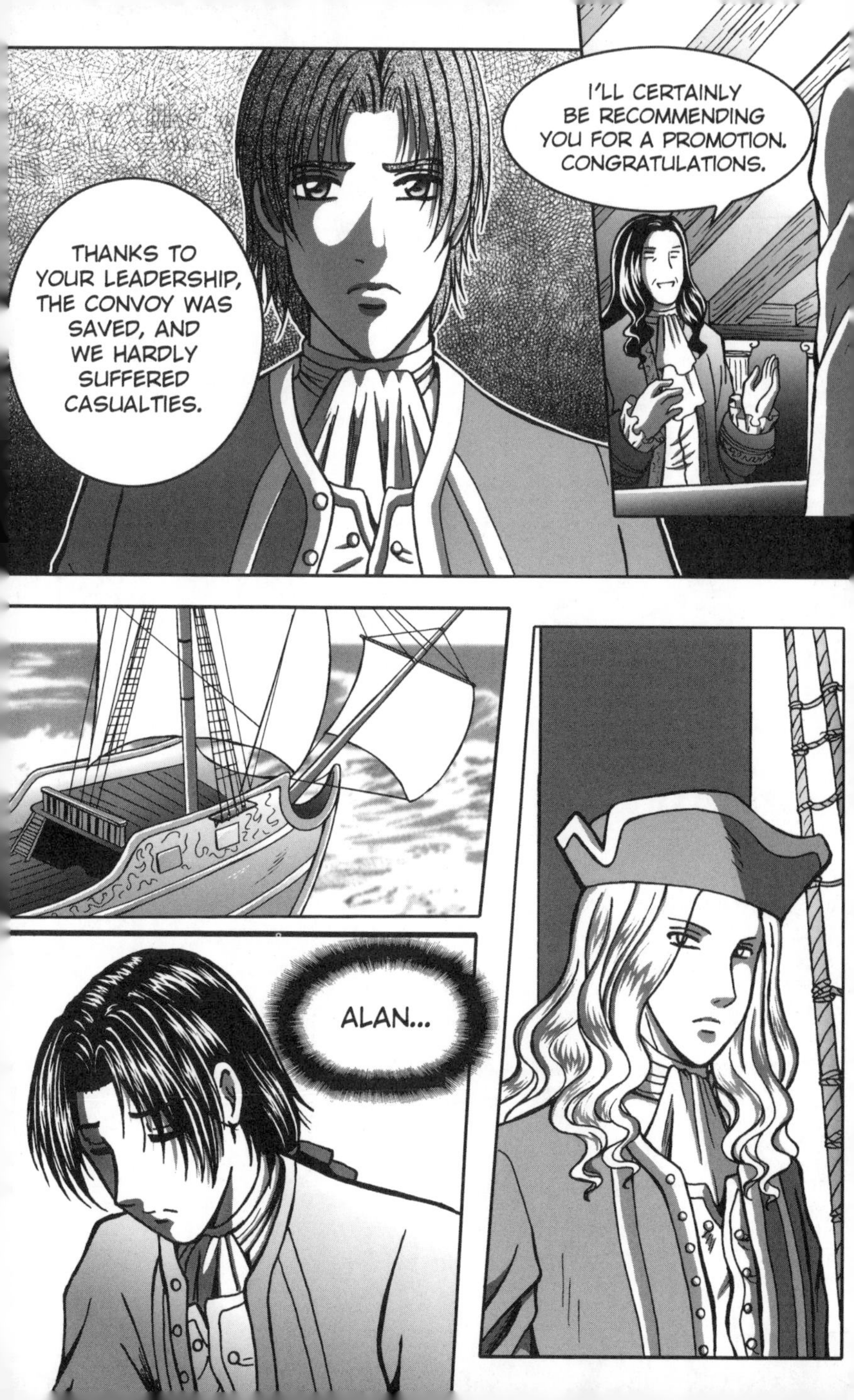
I'LL CERTAINLY BE RECOMMENDING YOU FOR A PROMOTION. CONGRATULATIONS.
THANKS TO YOUR LEADERSHIP, THE CONVOY WAS SAVED, AND WE HARDLY SUFFERED CASUALTIES.
ALAN...

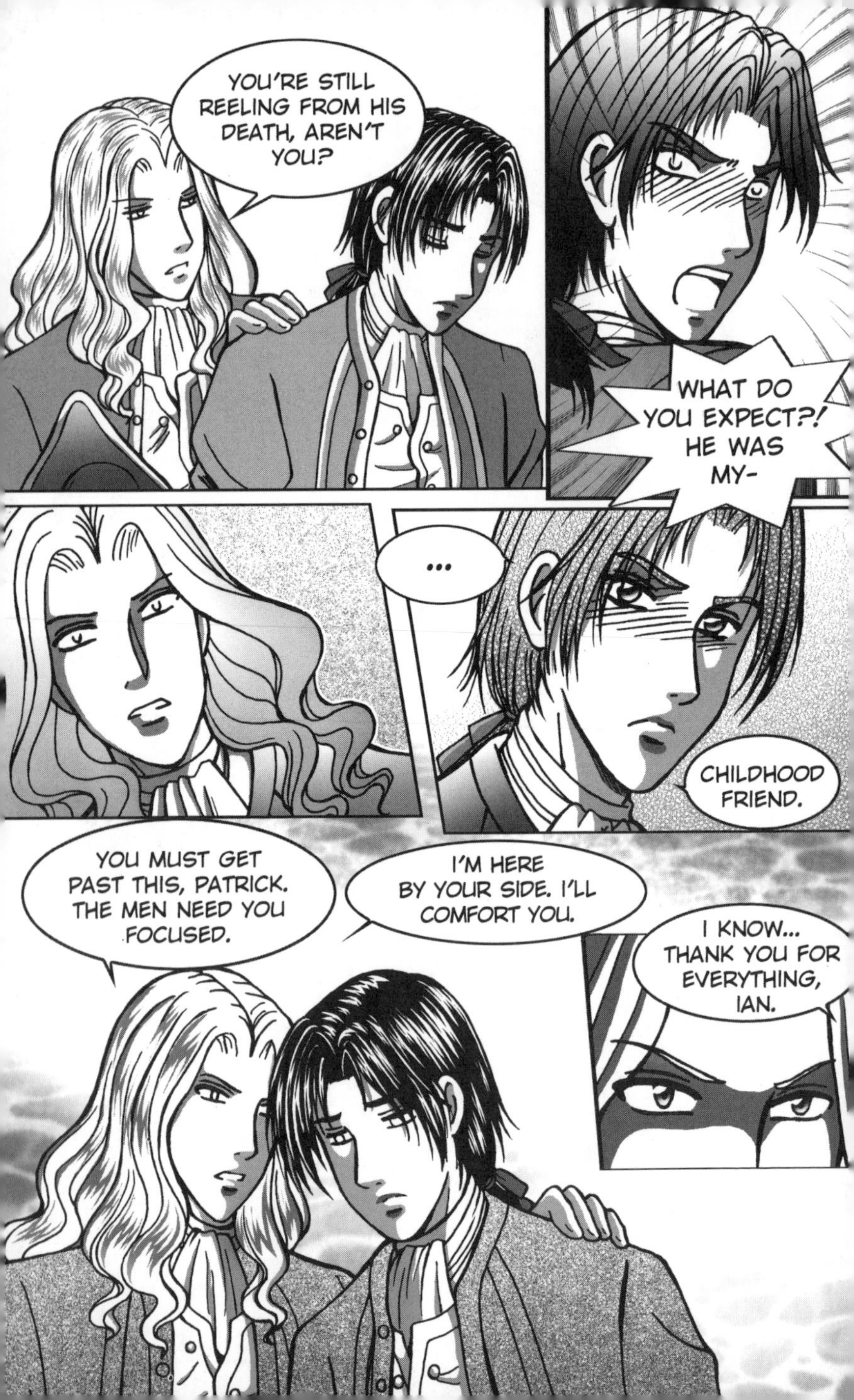
YOU'RE STILL REELING FROM HIS DEATH, AREN'T YOU?
WHAT DO YOU EXPECT?! HE WAS MY-
...
CHILDHOOD FRIEND.
YOU MUST GET PAST THIS, PATRICK. THE MEN NEED YOU FOCUSED.
I'M HERE BY YOUR SIDE. I'LL COMFORT YOU.
I KNOW... THANK YOU FOR EVERYTHING, IAN.

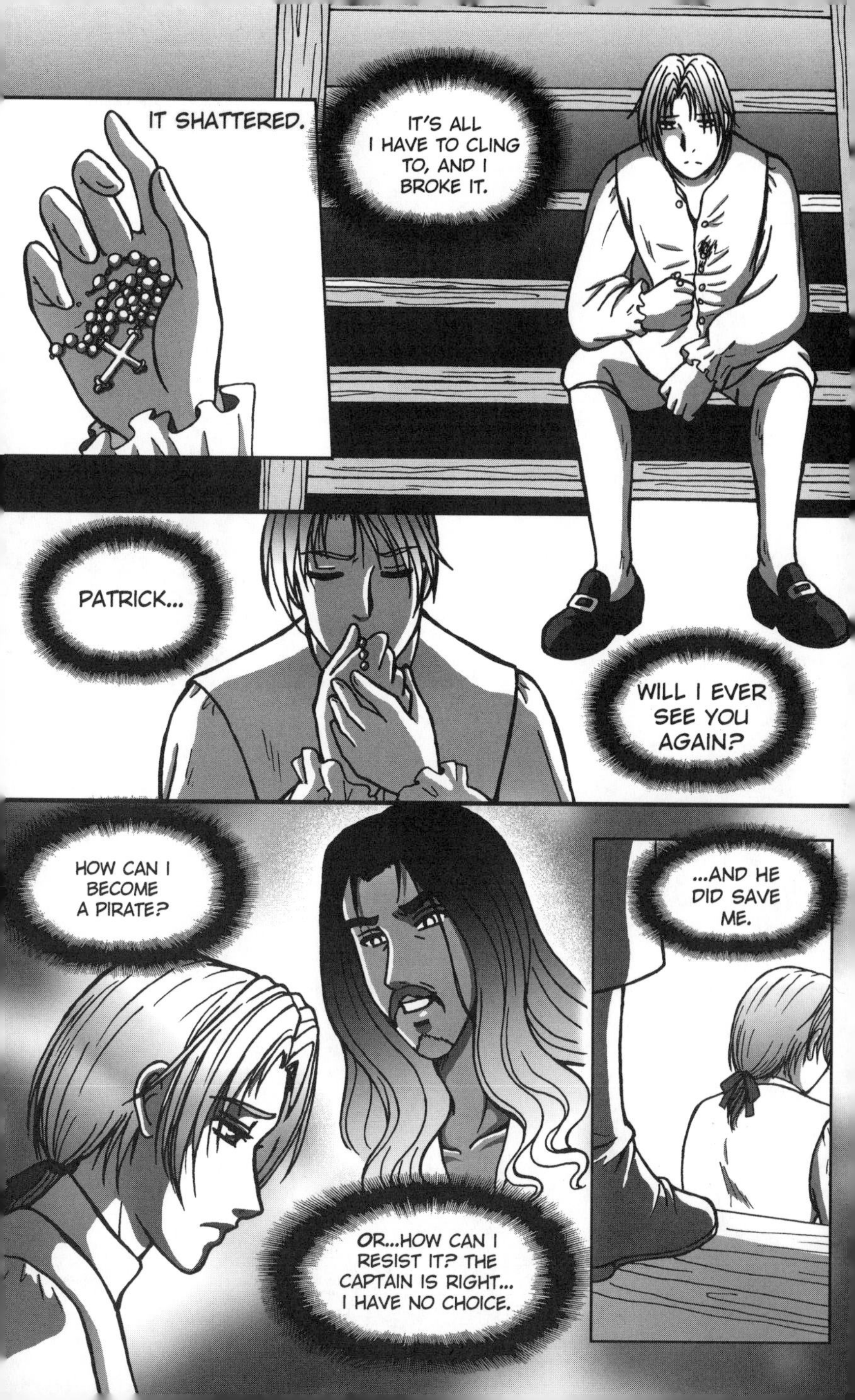
IT SHATTERED.
IT'S ALL I HAVE TO CLING TO, AND I BROKE IT.
PATRICK...
WILL I EVER SEE YOU AGAIN?
HOW CAN I BECOME A PIRATE?
OR...HOW CAN I RESIST IT? THE CAPTAIN IS RIGHT... I HAVE NO CHOICE.
...AND HE DID SAVE ME.

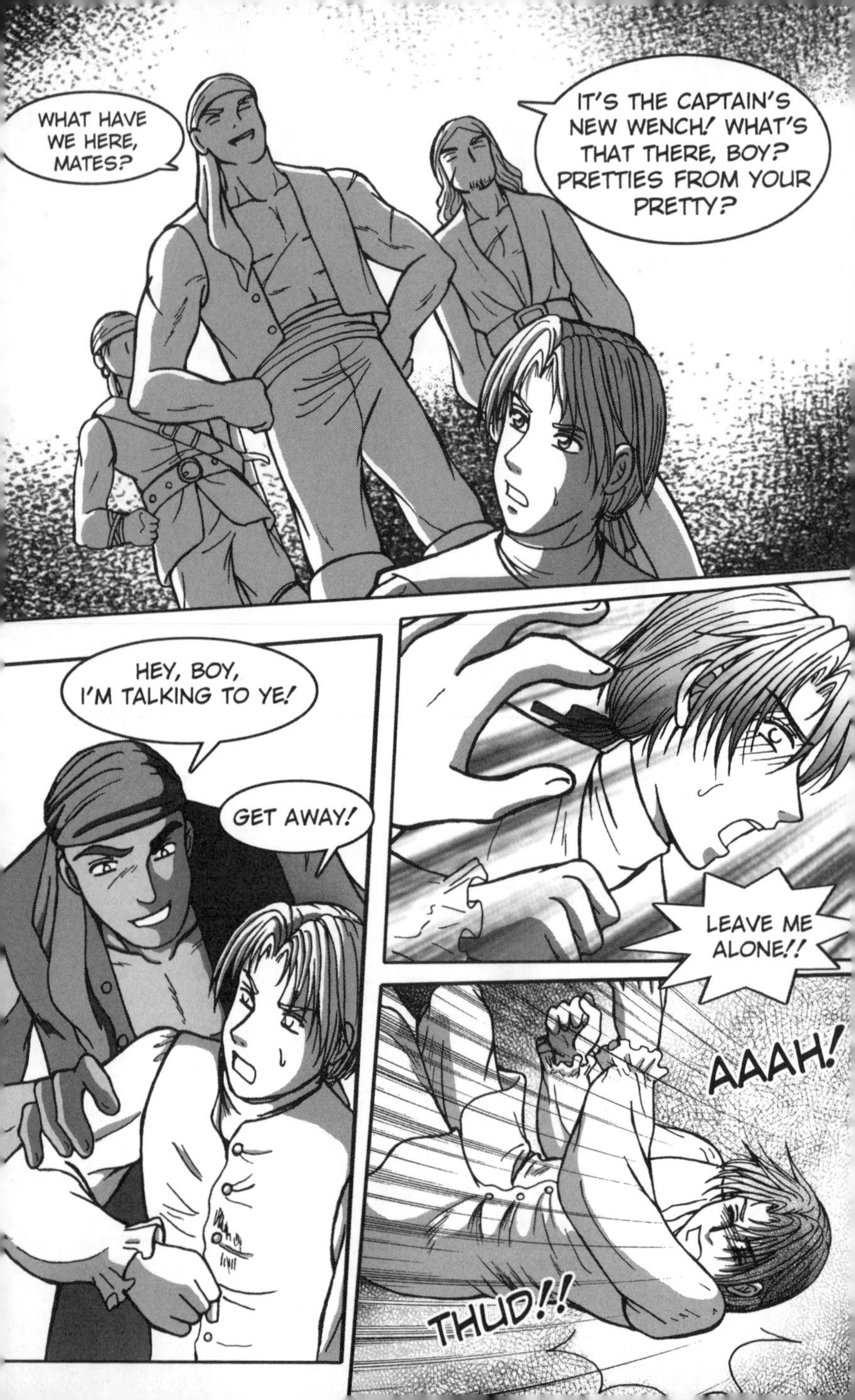
WHAT HAVE WE HERE, MATES?
IT'S THE CAPTAIN'S NEW WENCH! WHAT'S THAT THERE, BOY? PRETTIES FROM YOUR PRETTY?
HEY, BOY, I'M TALKING TO YE!
GET AWAY!
LEAVE ME ALONE!!
AAAH!
THUD!!

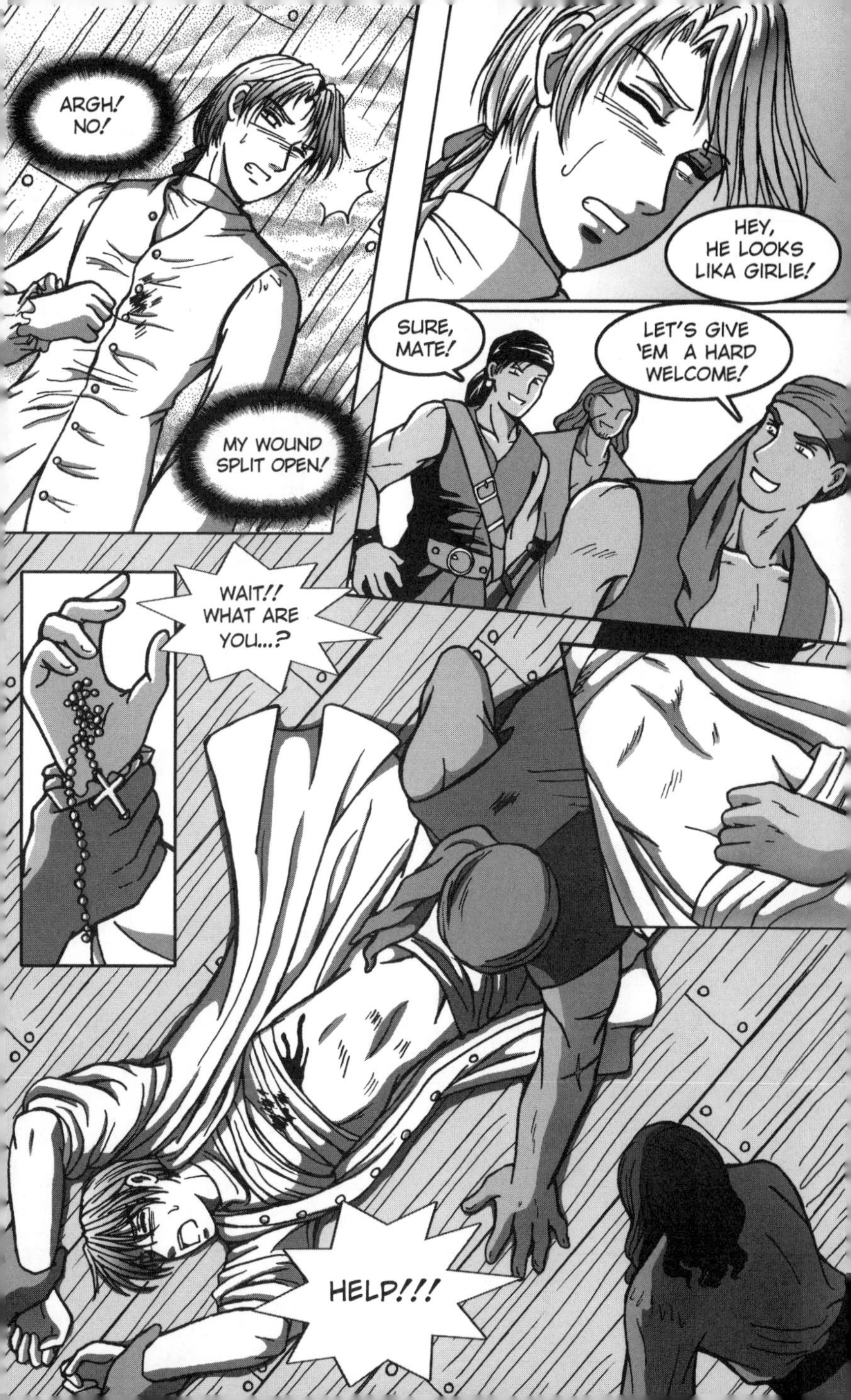
ARGH! NO!
MY WOUND SPLIT OPEN!
HEY, HE LOOKS LIKA GIRLIE!
SURE, MATE!
LET'S GIVE 'EM A HARD WELCOME!
WAIT!! WHAT ARE YOU...?
HELP!!!

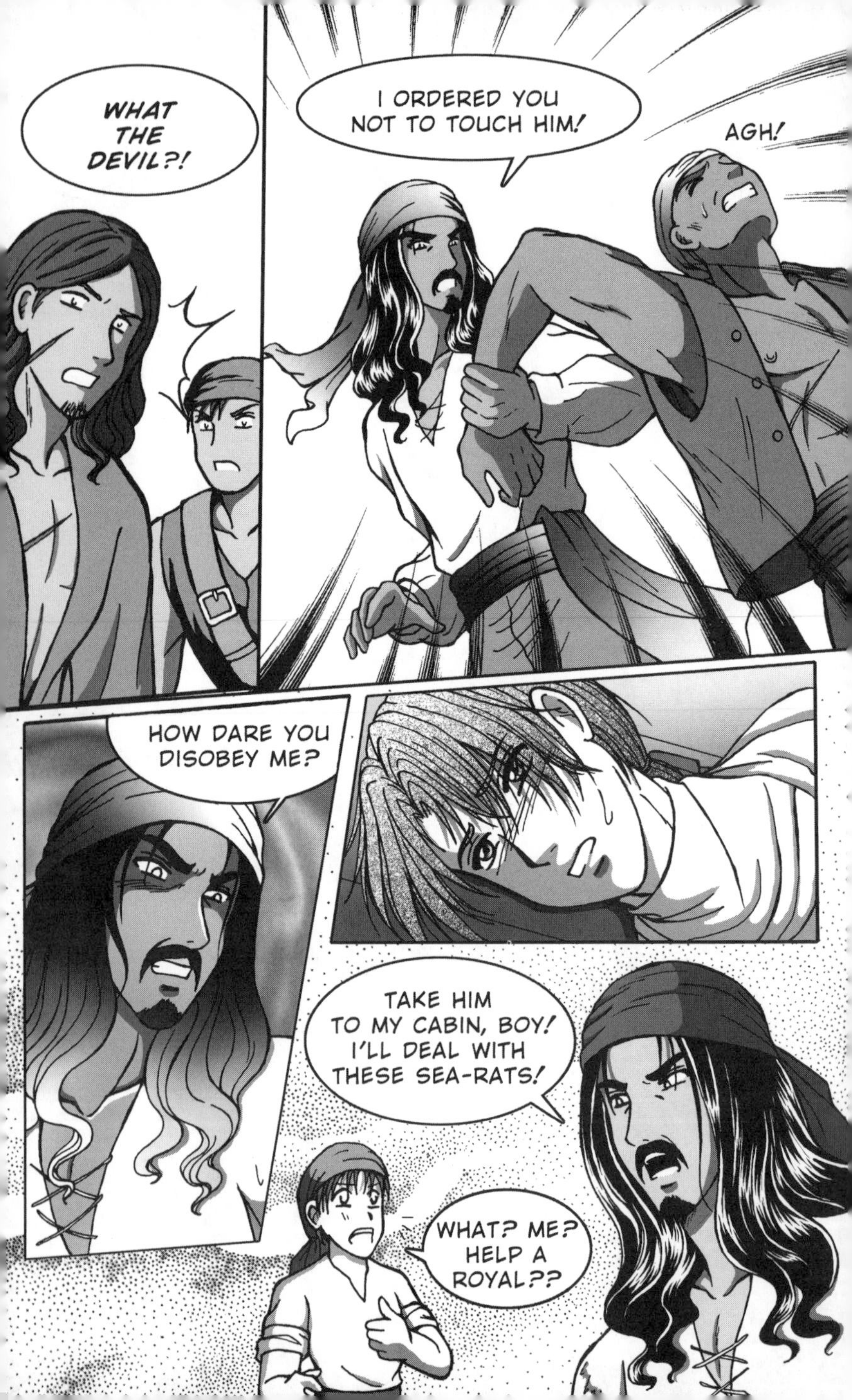
WHAT THE DEVIL?!
I ORDERED YOU NOT TO TOUCH HIM!
AGH!
HOW DARE YOU DISOBEY ME?
TAKE HIM TO MY CABIN, BOY! I'LL DEAL WITH THESE SEA-RATS!
WHAT? ME? HELP A ROYAL??

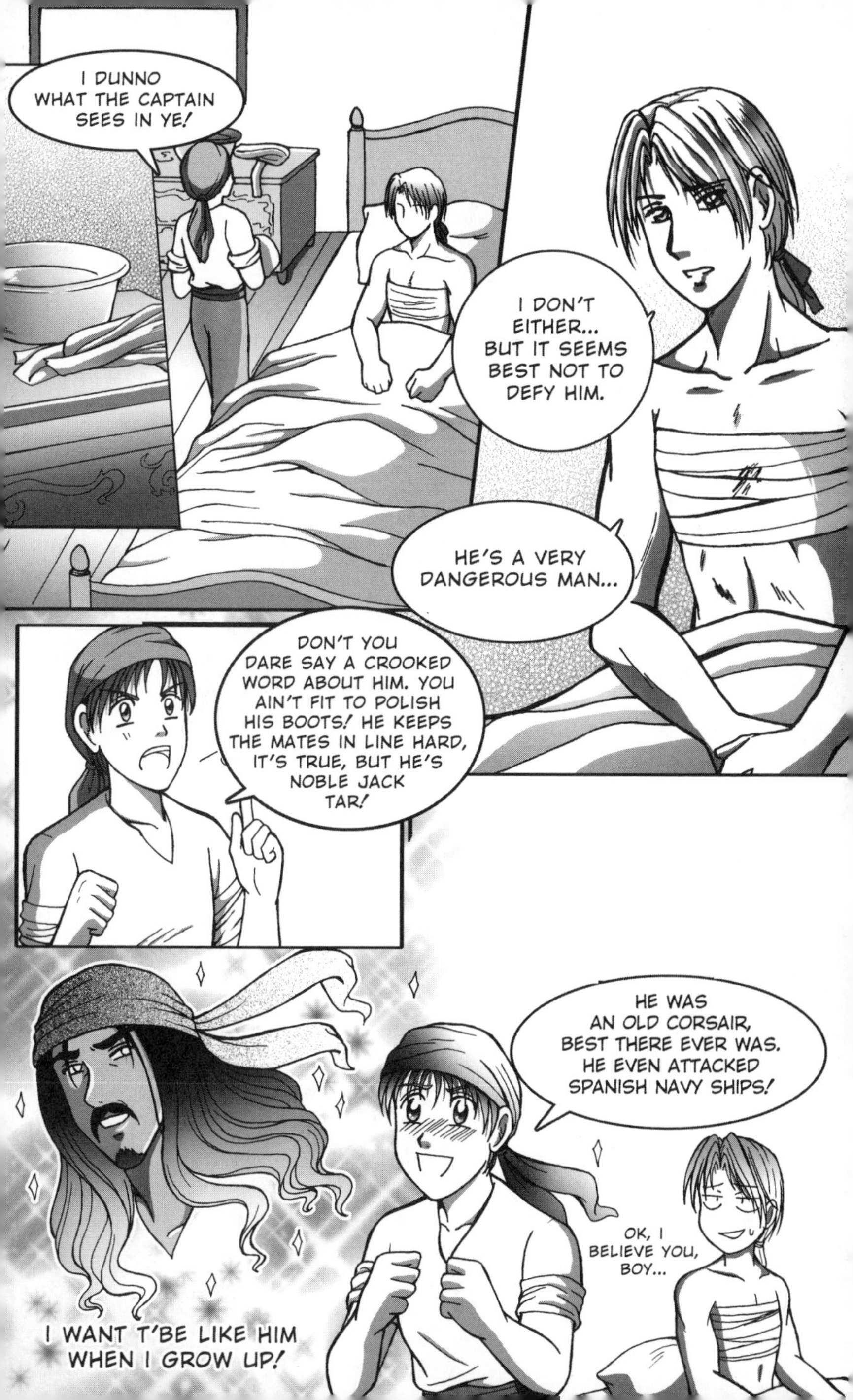
I DUNNO WHAT THE CAPTAIN SEES IN YE!
I DON'T EITHER... BUT IT SEEMS BEST NOT TO DEFY HIM.
HE'S A VERY DANGEROUS MAN...
DON'T YOU DARE SAY A CROOKED WORD ABOUT HIM. YOU AIN'T FIT TO POLISH HIS BOOTS! HE KEEPS THE MATES IN LINE HARD, IT'S TRUE, BUT HE'S NOBLE JACK TAR!
HE WAS AN OLD CORSAIR, BEST THERE EVER WAS. HE EVEN ATTACKED SPANISH NAVY SHIPS!
I WANT T'BE LIKE HIM WHEN I GROW UP!
OK, I BELIEVE YOU, BOY...

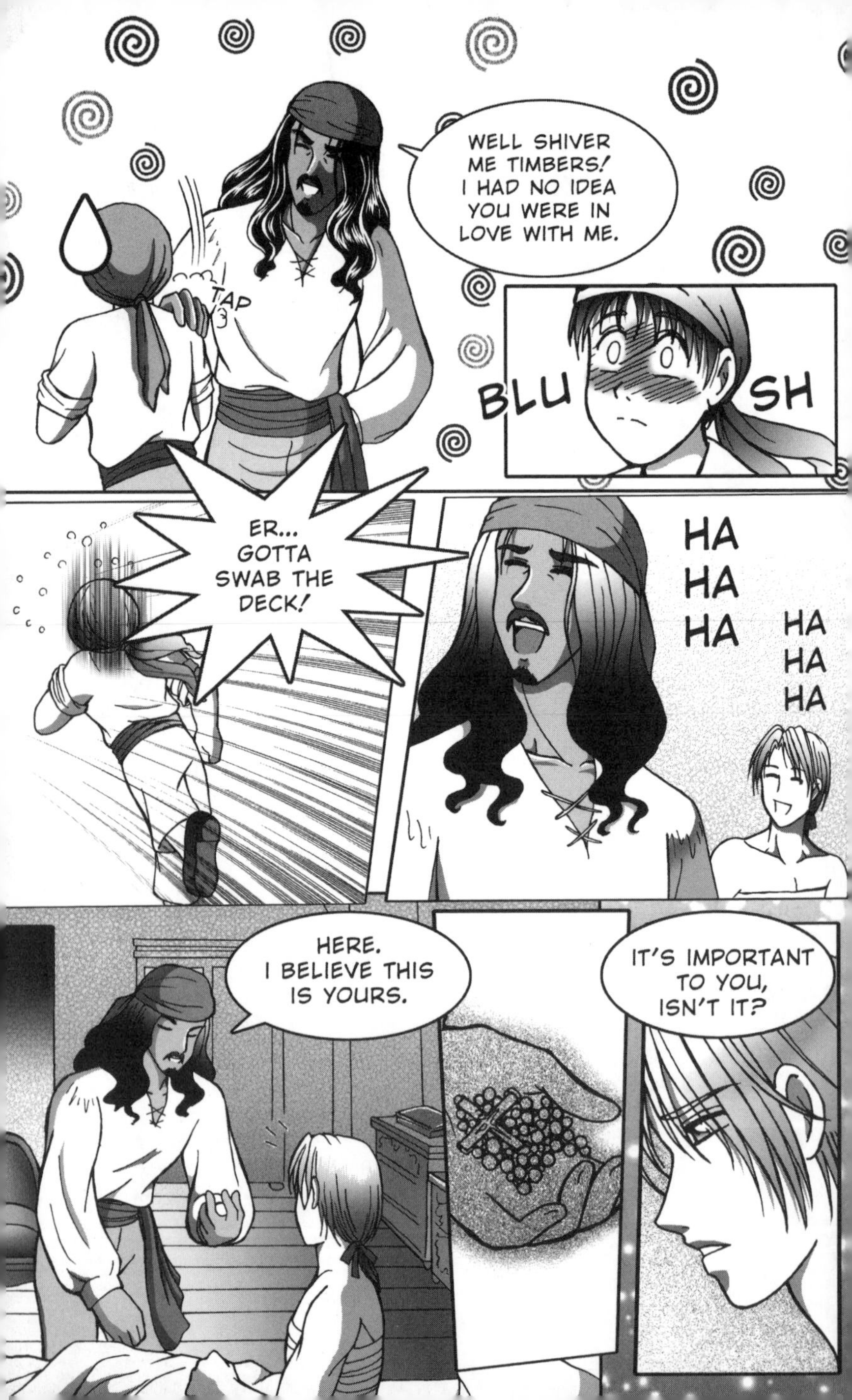

WELL SHIVER ME TIMBERS! I HAD NO IDEA YOU WERE IN LOVE WITH ME.
TAP
BLU SH
ER... GOTTA SWAB THE DECK!
HA HA HA
HA HA HA
HERE. I BELIEVE THIS IS YOURS.
IT'S IMPORTANT TO YOU, ISN'T IT?

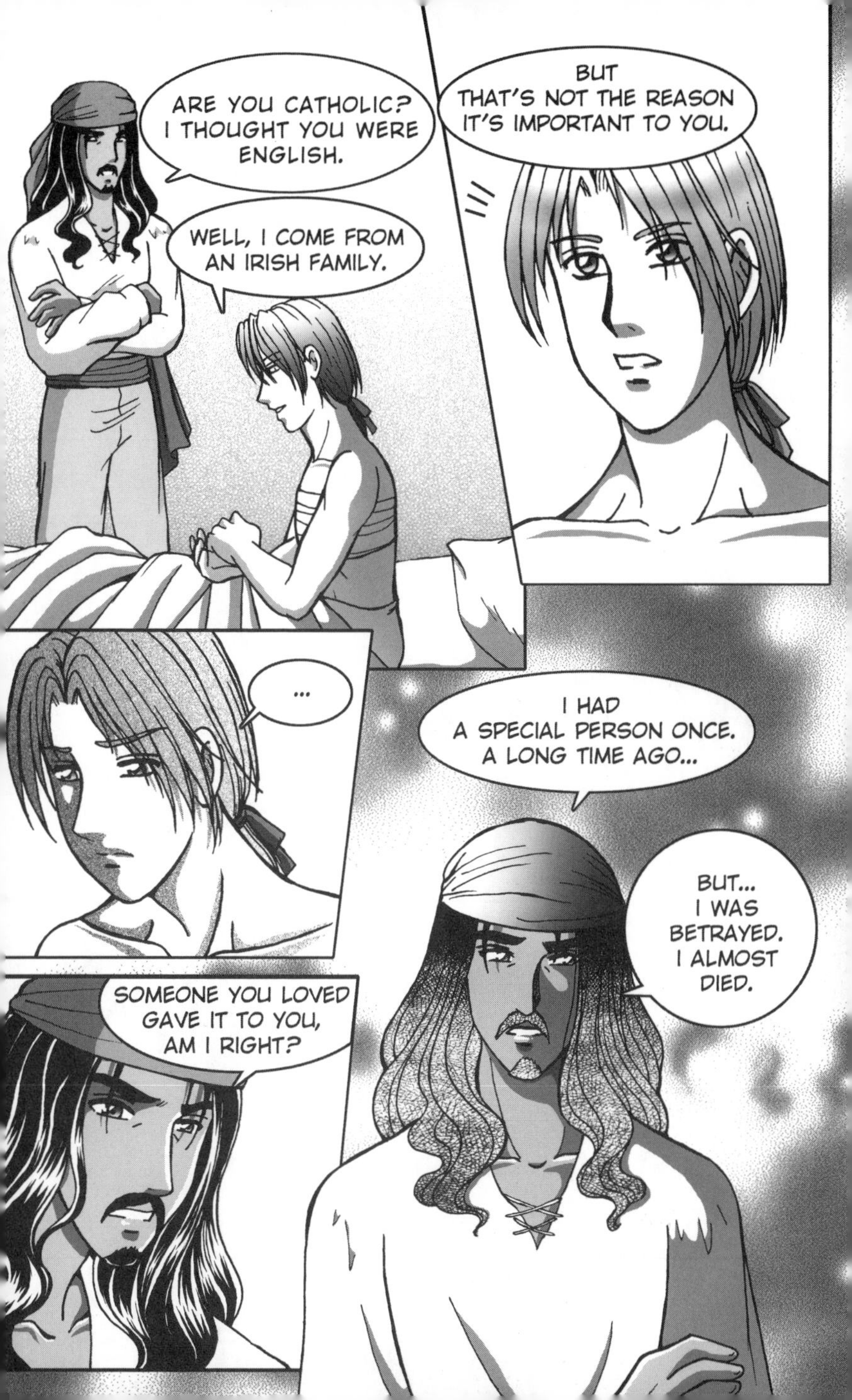
ARE YOU CATHOLIC? I THOUGHT YOU WERE ENGLISH.
WELL, I COME FROM AN IRISH FAMILY.
BUT THAT'S NOT THE REASON IT'S IMPORTANT TO YOU.
...
I HAD A SPECIAL PERSON ONCE. A LONG TIME AGO...
BUT... I WAS BETRAYED. I ALMOST DIED.
SOMEONE YOU LOVED GAVE IT TO YOU, AM I RIGHT?

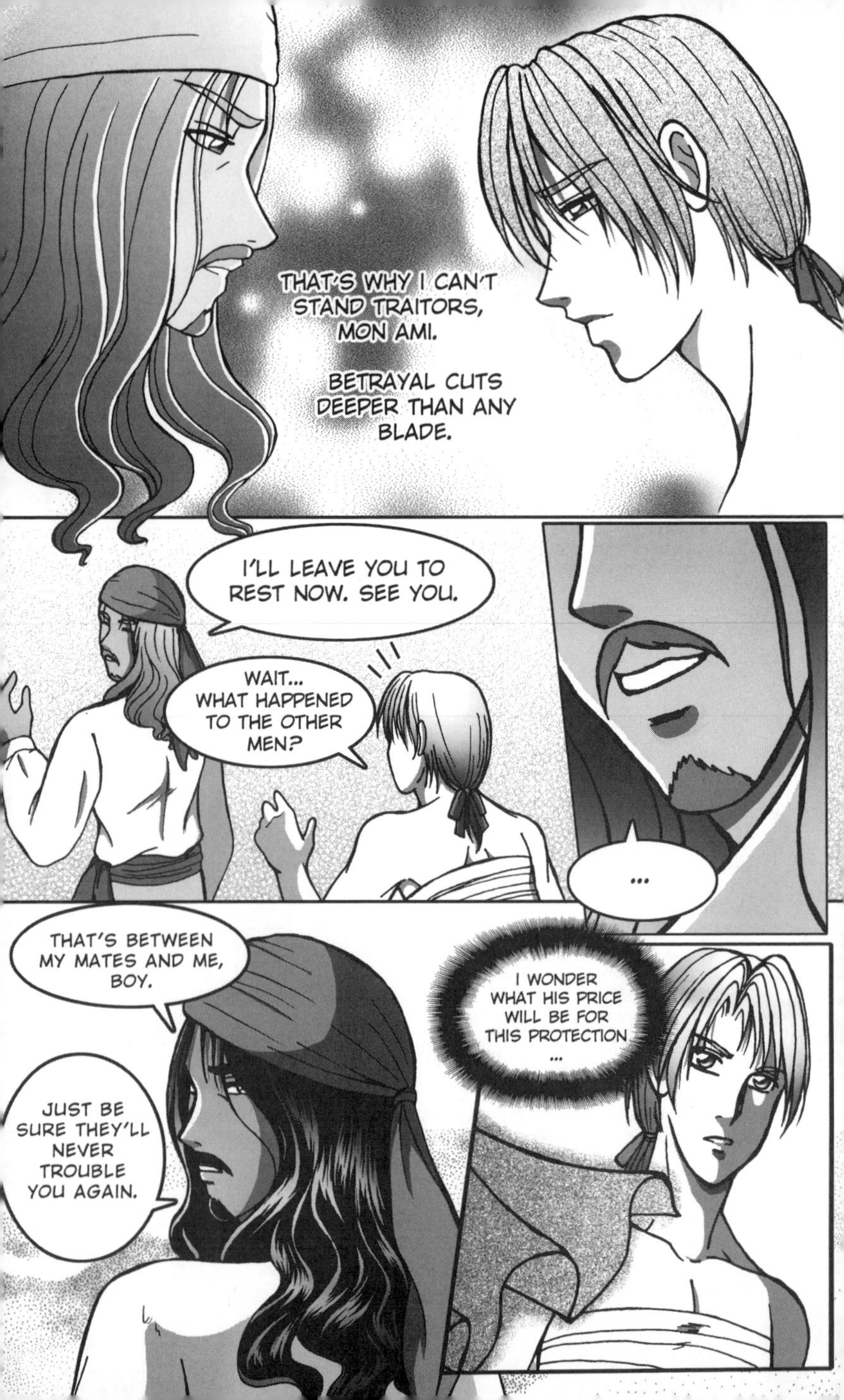
THAT'S WHY I CAN'T STAND TRAITORS, MON AMI.
BETRAYAL CUTS DEEPER THAN ANY BLADE.
I'LL LEAVE YOU TO REST NOW. SEE YOU.
WAIT... WHAT HAPPENED TO THE OTHER MEN?
...
THAT'S BETWEEN MY MATES AND ME, BOY.
JUST BE SURE THEY'LL NEVER TROUBLE YOU AGAIN.
I WONDER WHAT HIS PRICE WILL BE FOR THIS PROTECTION ...

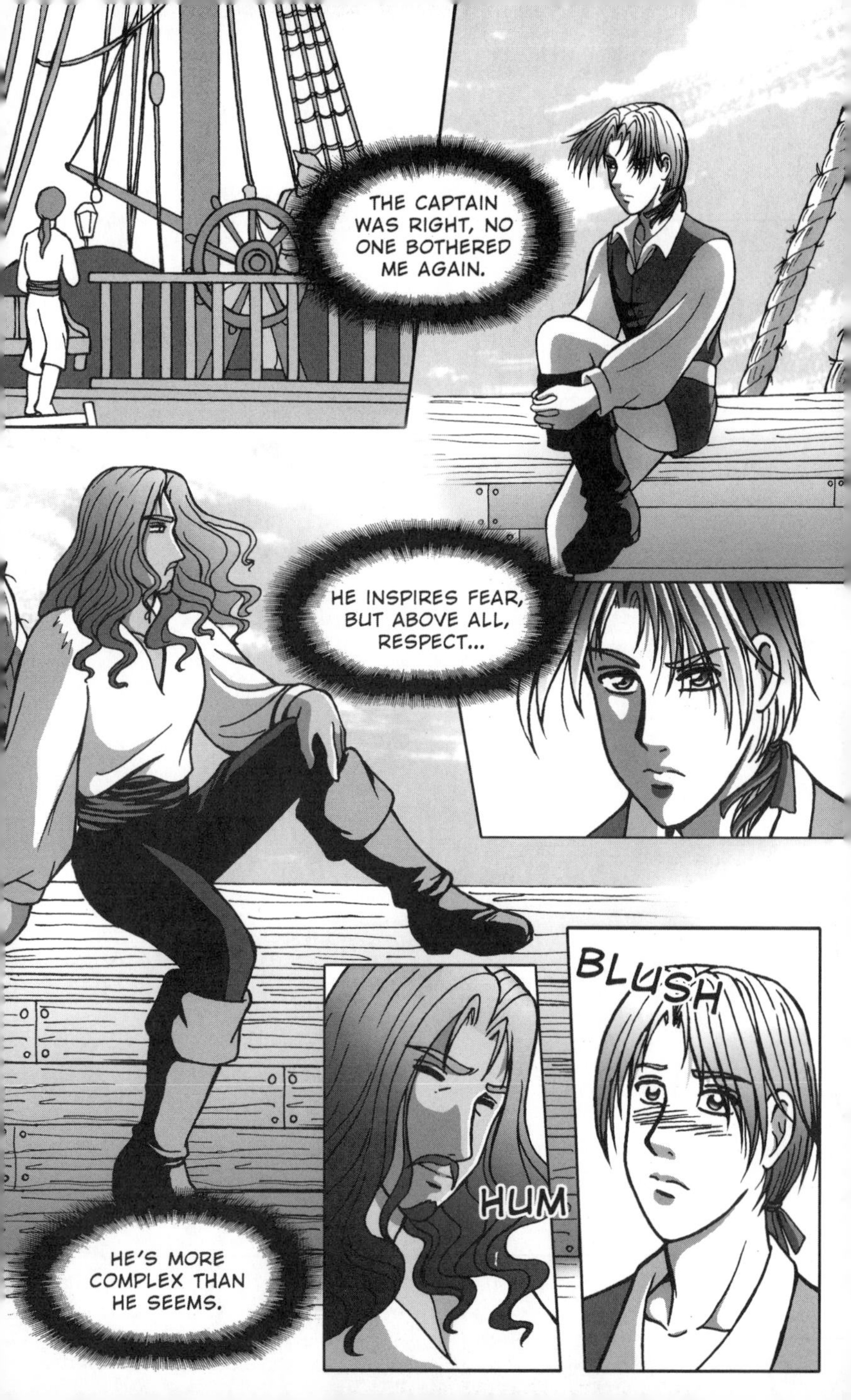
THE CAPTAIN WAS RIGHT, NO ONE BOTHERED ME AGAIN.
HE INSPIRES FEAR, BUT ABOVE ALL, RESPECT...
HE'S MORE COMPLEX THAN HE SEEMS.
BLUSH
HUM

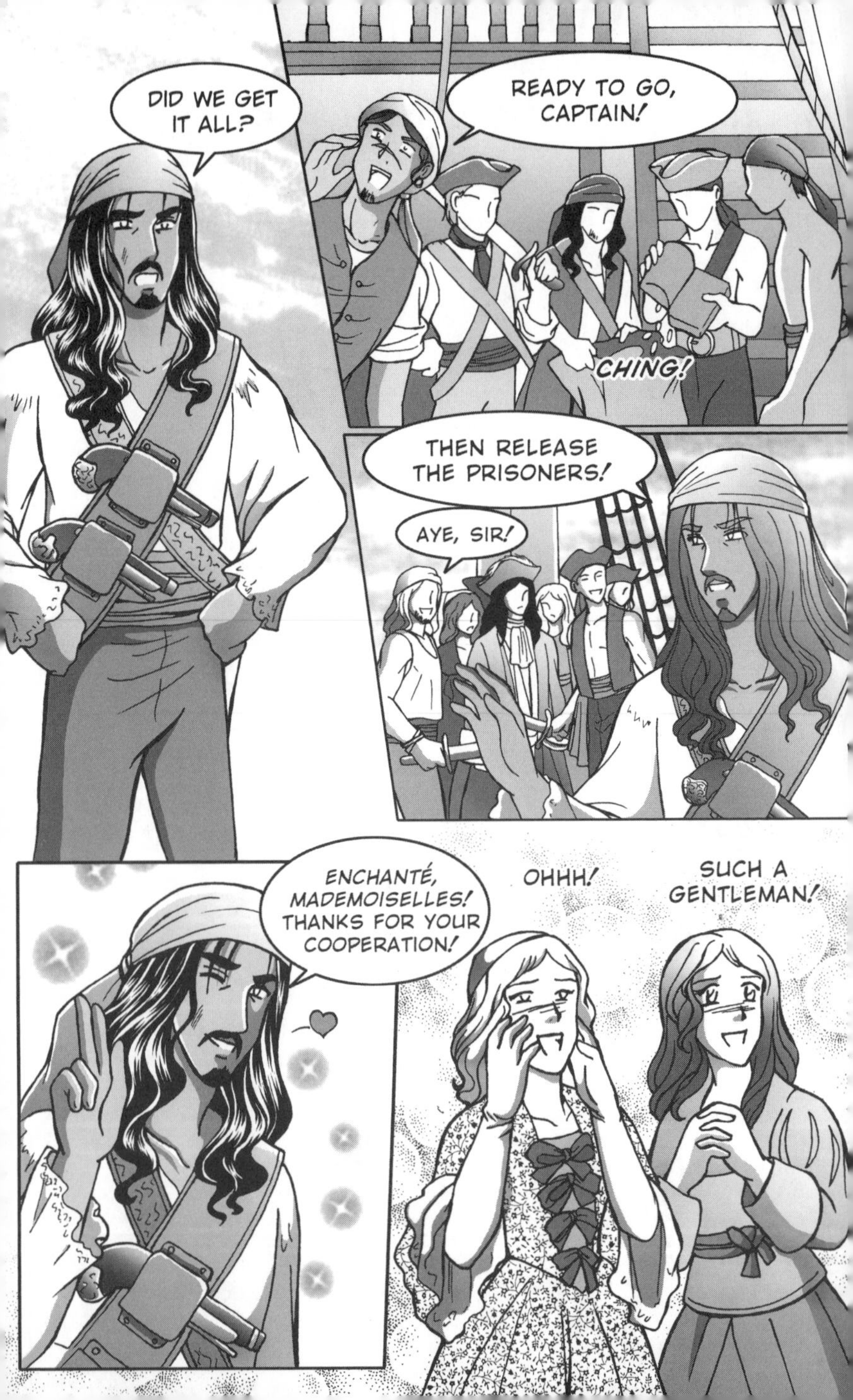
DID WE GET IT ALL?
READY TO GO, CAPTAIN!
CHING!
THEN RELEASE THE PRISONERS!
AYE, SIR!
ENCHANTÉ, MADEMOISELLES! THANKS FOR YOUR COOPERATION!
OHHH!
SUCH A GENTLEMAN!

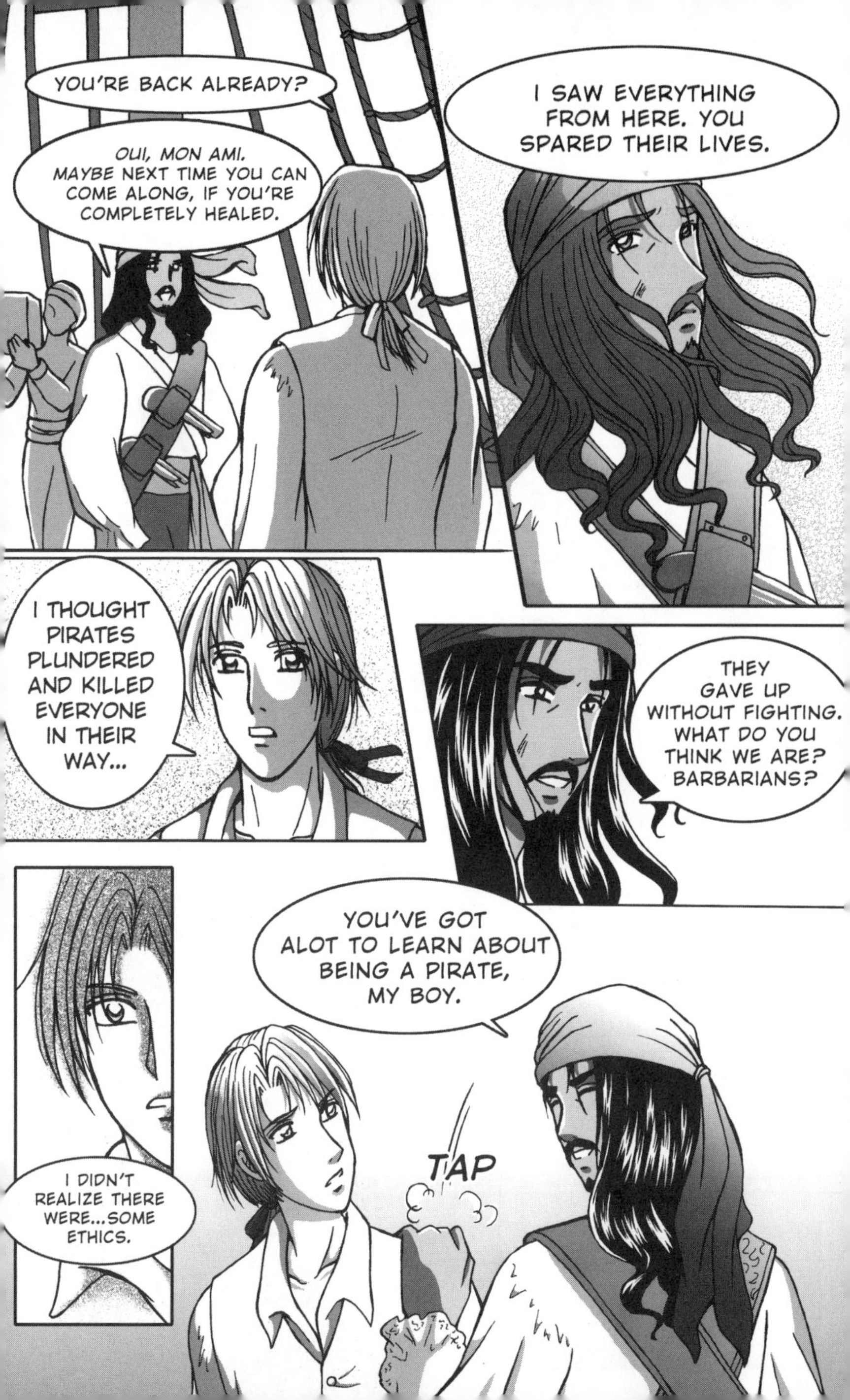
YOU'RE BACK ALREADY?
OUI, MON AMI. MAYBE NEXT TIME YOU CAN COME ALONG, IF YOU'RE COMPLETELY HEALED.
I SAW EVERYTHING FROM HERE. YOU SPARED THEIR LIVES.
I THOUGHT PIRATES PLUNDERED AND KILLED EVERYONE IN THEIR WAY...
THEY GAVE UP WITHOUT FIGHTING. WHAT DO YOU THINK WE ARE? BARBARIANS?
I DIDN'T REALIZE THERE WERE...SOME ETHICS.
YOU'VE GOT ALOT TO LEARN ABOUT BEING A PIRATE, MY BOY.
TAP

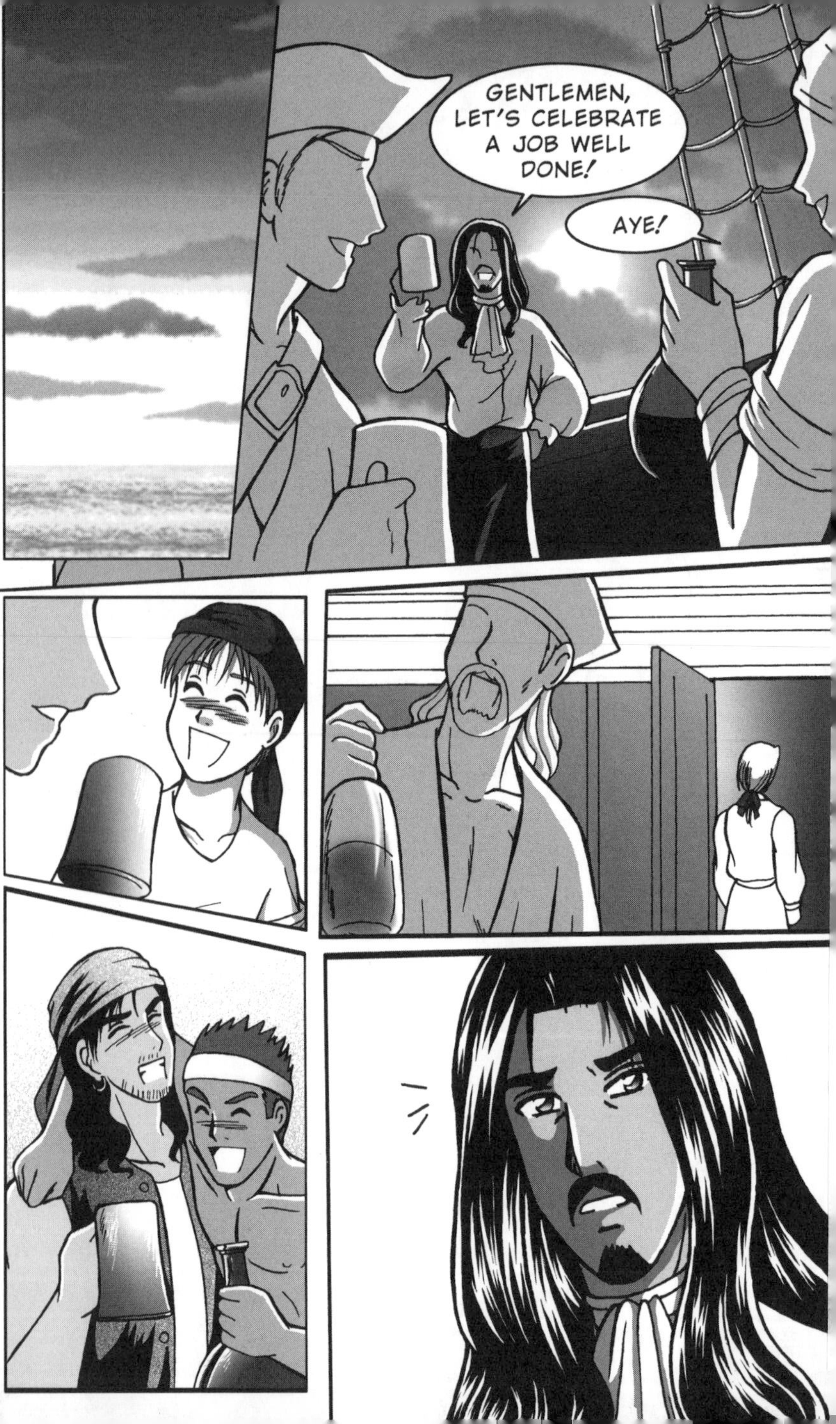
GENTLEMEN, LET'S CELEBRATE A JOB WELL DONE!
AYE!

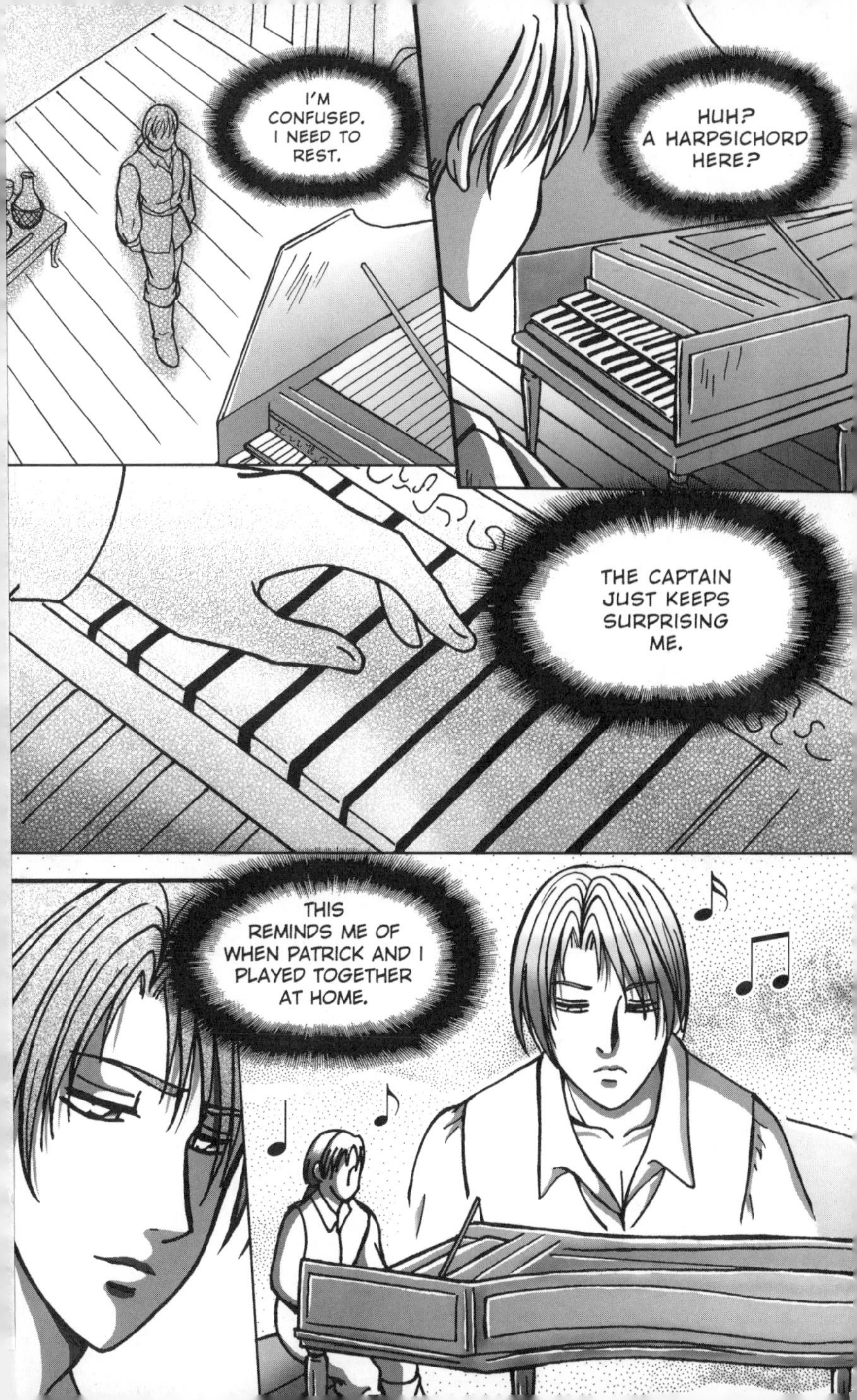
I'M CONFUSED. I NEED TO REST.
HUH? A HARPSICHORD HERE?
THE CAPTAIN JUST KEEPS SURPRISING ME.
THIS REMINDS ME OF WHEN PATRICK AND I PLAYED TOGETHER AT HOME.

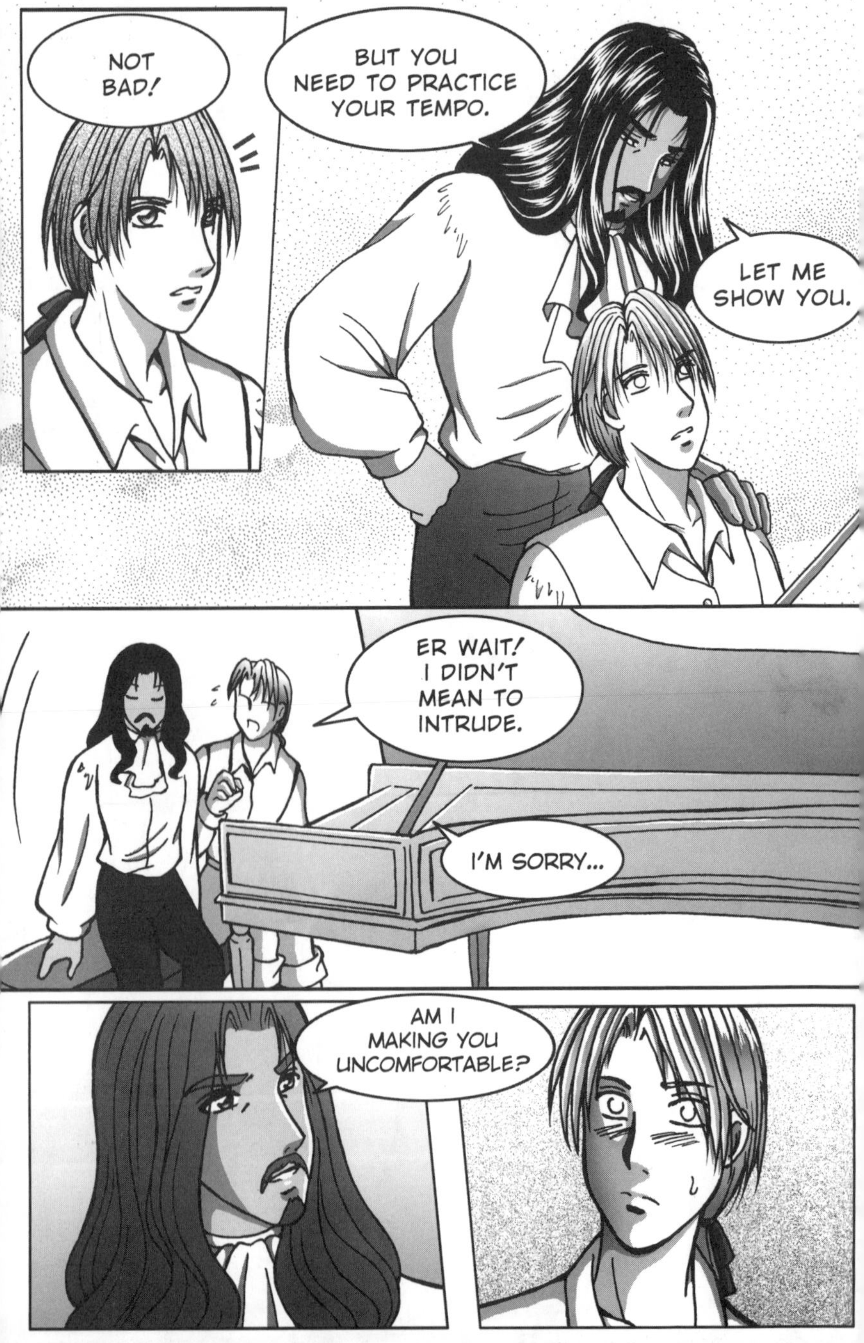
NOT BAD!
BUT YOU NEED TO PRACTICE YOUR TEMPO.
LET ME SHOW YOU.
ER WAIT! I DIDN'T MEAN TO INTRUDE.
I'M SORRY...
AM I MAKING YOU UNCOMFORTABLE?

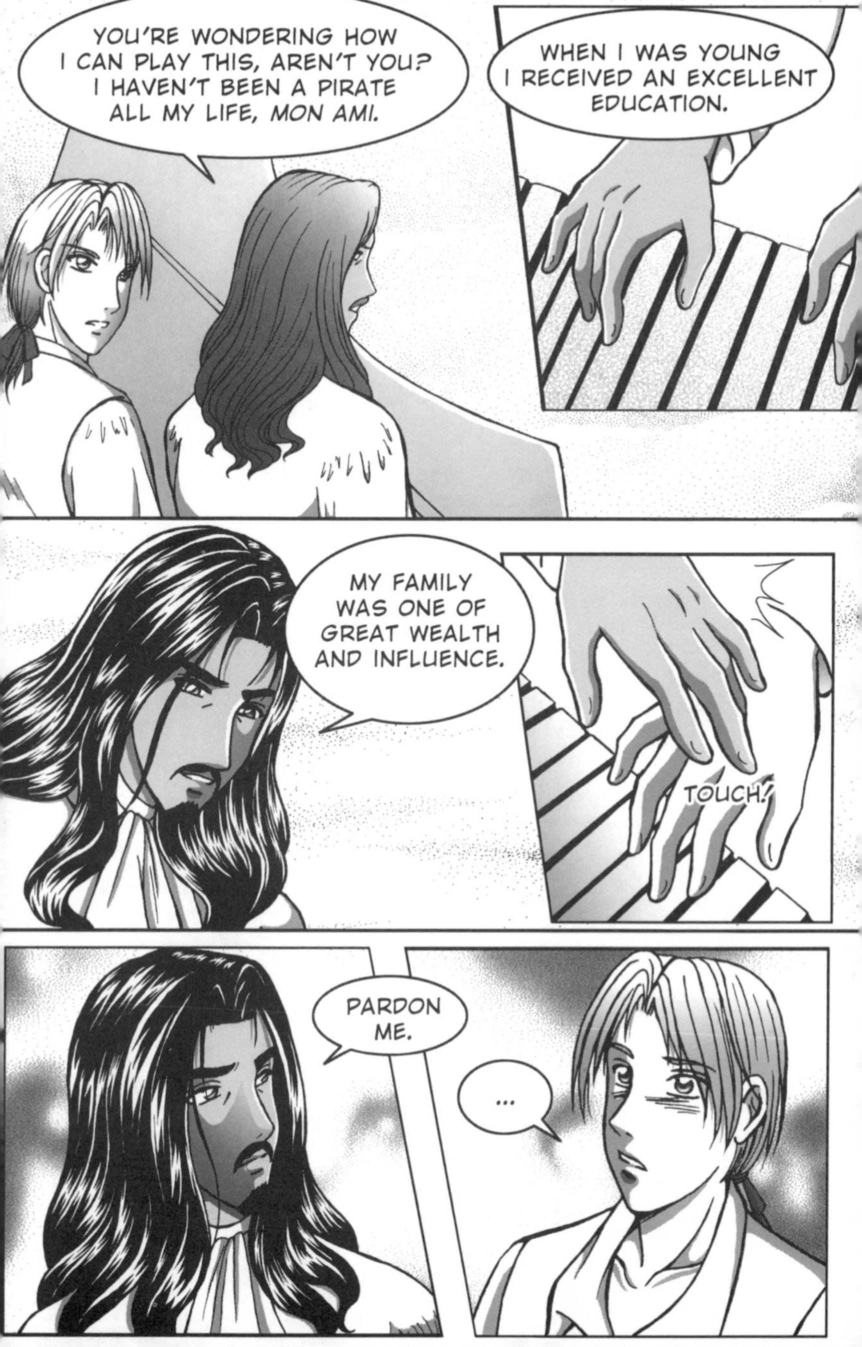
YOU'RE WONDERING HOW I CAN PLAY THIS, AREN'T YOU? I HAVEN'T BEEN A PIRATE ALL MY LIFE, *MON AMI.*
WHEN I WAS YOUNG I RECEIVED AN EXCELLENT EDUCATION.
MY FAMILY WAS ONE OF GREAT WEALTH AND INFLUENCE.
TOUCH!
PARDON ME.
...

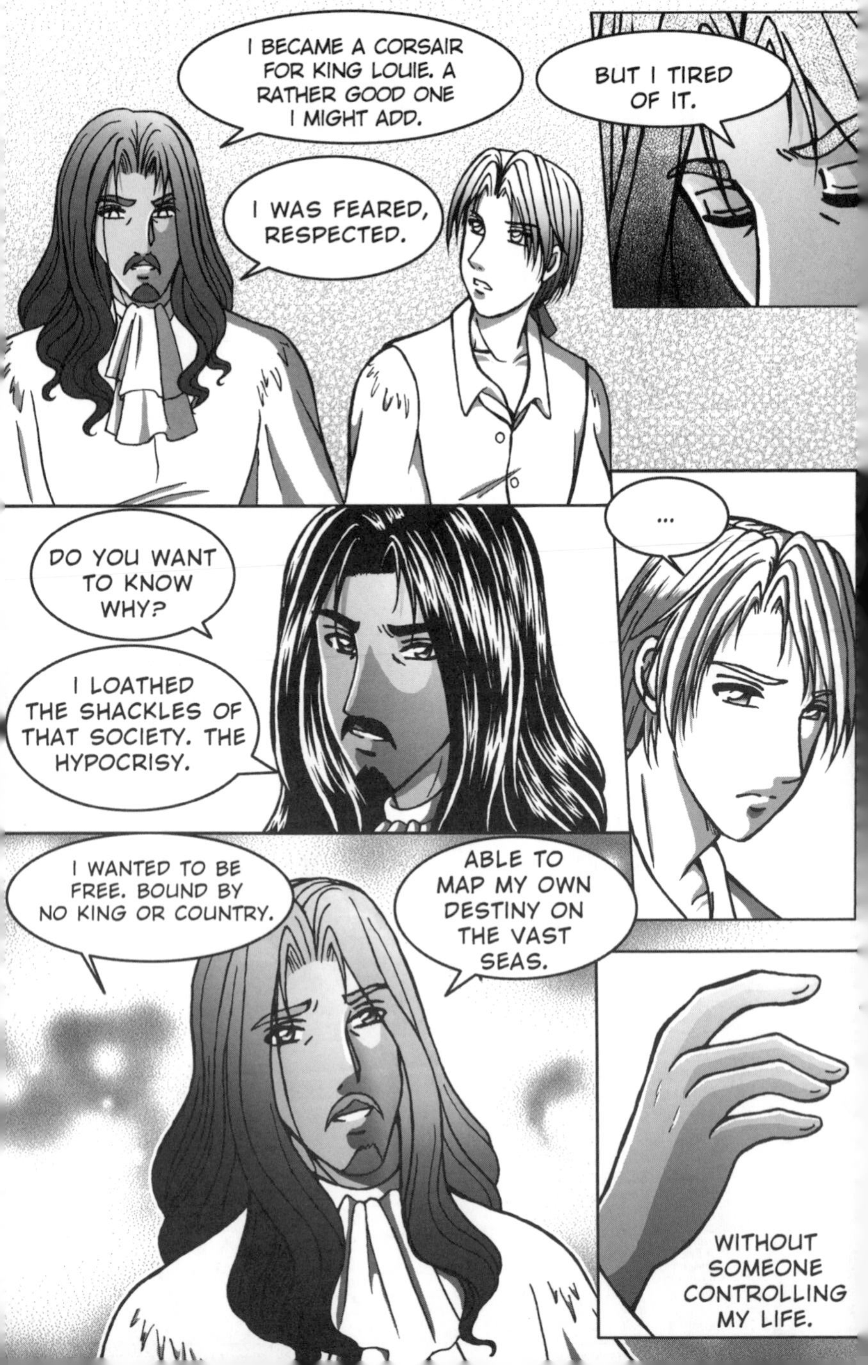
I BECAME A CORSAIR FOR KING LOUIE. A RATHER GOOD ONE I MIGHT ADD.
I WAS FEARED, RESPECTED.
BUT I TIRED OF IT.
DO YOU WANT TO KNOW WHY?
I LOATHED THE SHACKLES OF THAT SOCIETY. THE HYPOCRISY.
...
I WANTED TO BE FREE. BOUND BY NO KING OR COUNTRY.
ABLE TO MAP MY OWN DESTINY ON THE VAST SEAS.
WITHOUT SOMEONE CONTROLLING MY LIFE.

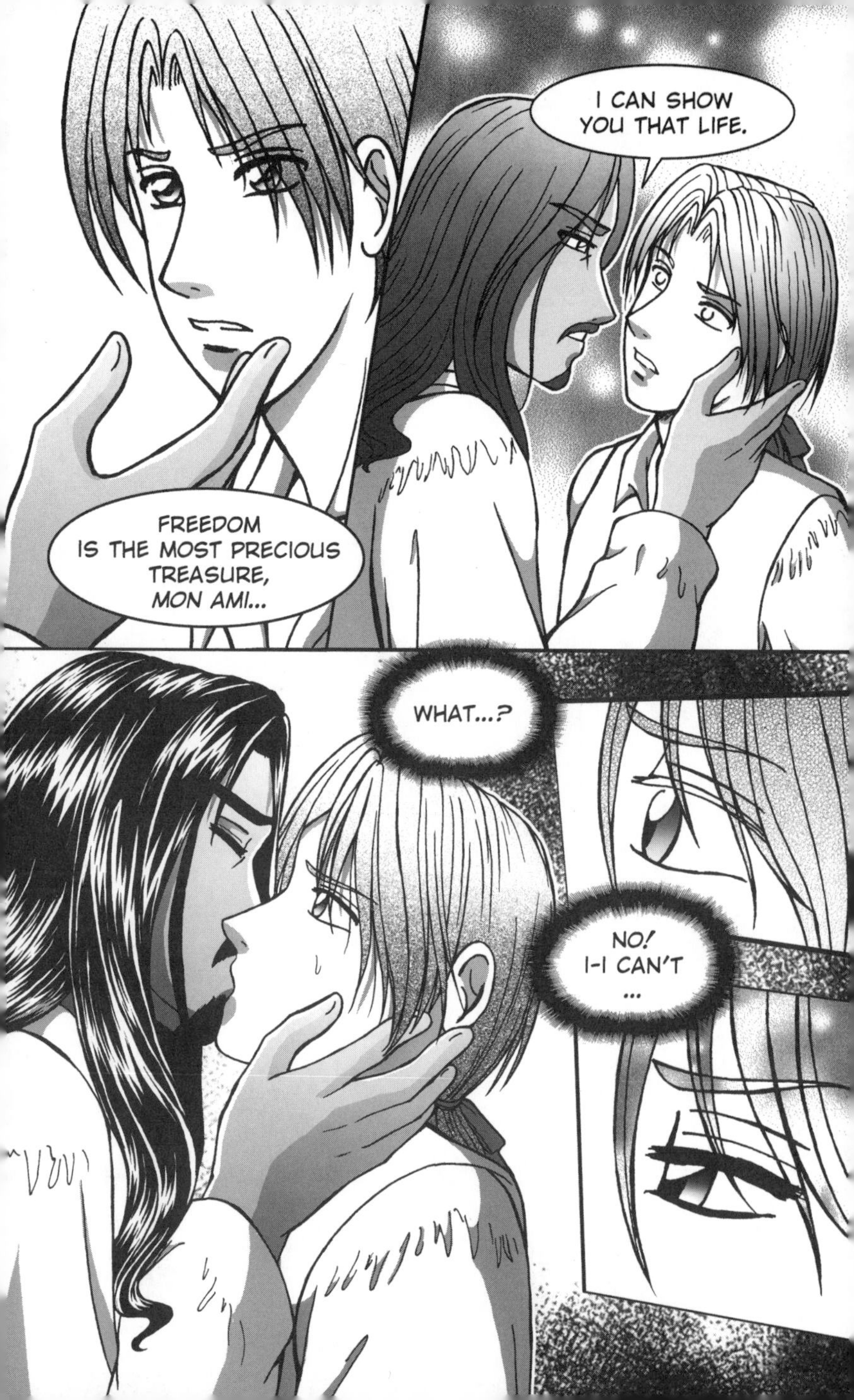
I CAN SHOW YOU THAT LIFE.
FREEDOM IS THE MOST PRECIOUS TREASURE, MON AMI...
WHAT...?
NO! I-I CAN'T ...

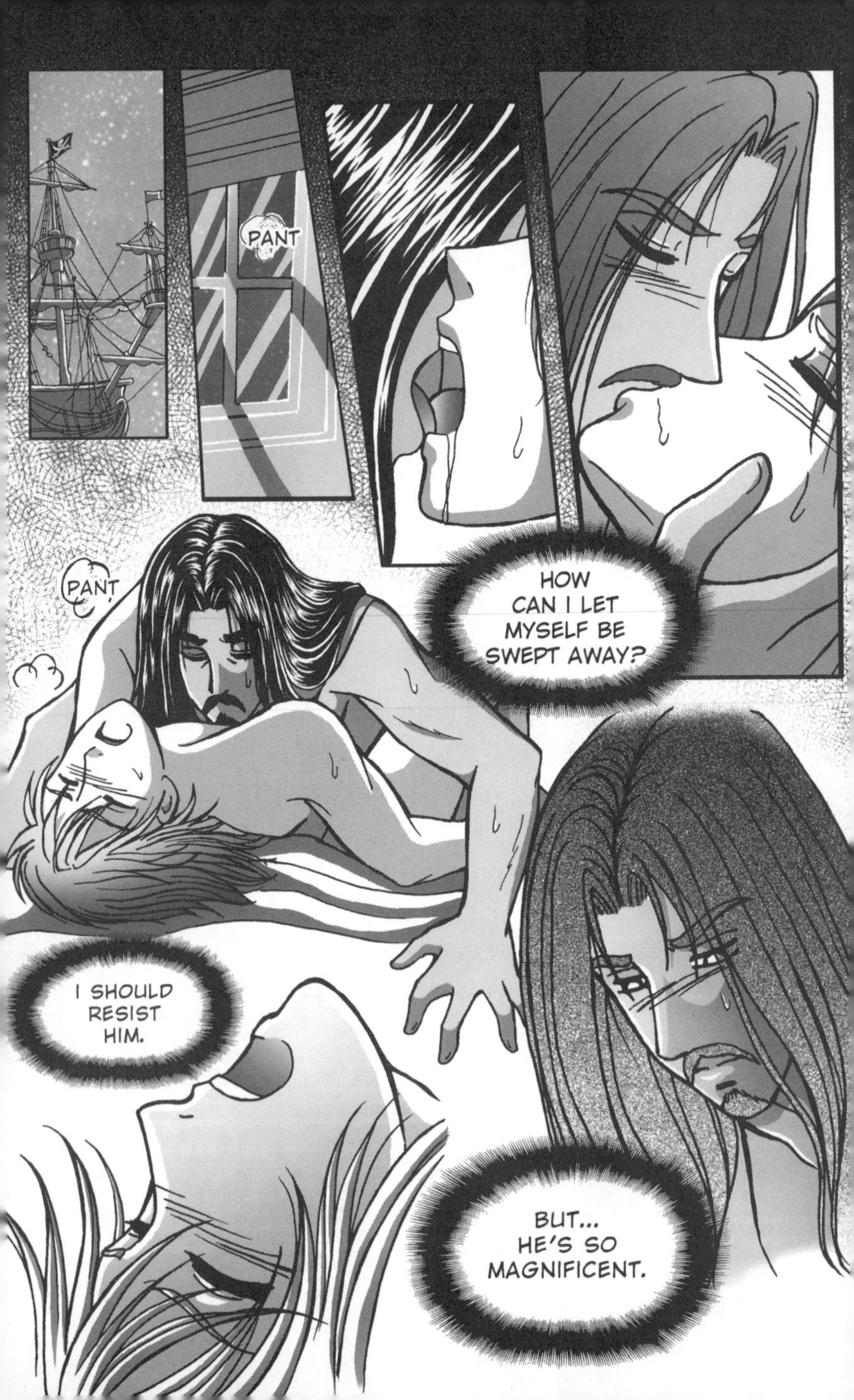
PANT
PANT
HOW CAN I LET MYSELF BE SWEPT AWAY?
I SHOULD RESIST HIM.
BUT... HE'S SO MAGNIFICENT.

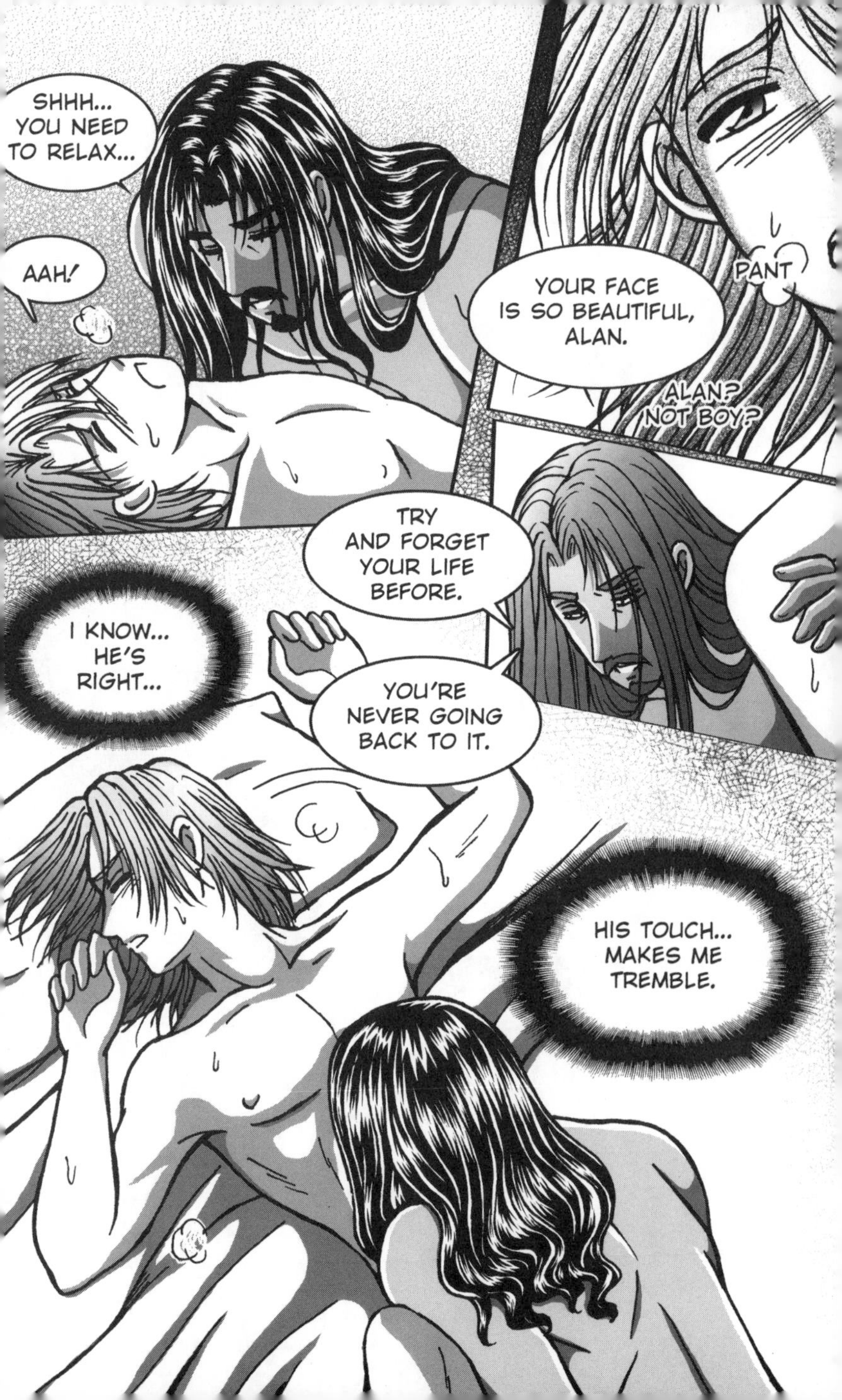
SHHH... YOU NEED TO RELAX...
AAH!
YOUR FACE IS SO BEAUTIFUL, ALAN.
PANT
ALAN? NOT BOY?
TRY AND FORGET YOUR LIFE BEFORE.
YOU'RE NEVER GOING BACK TO IT.
I KNOW... HE'S RIGHT...
HIS TOUCH... MAKES ME TREMBLE.

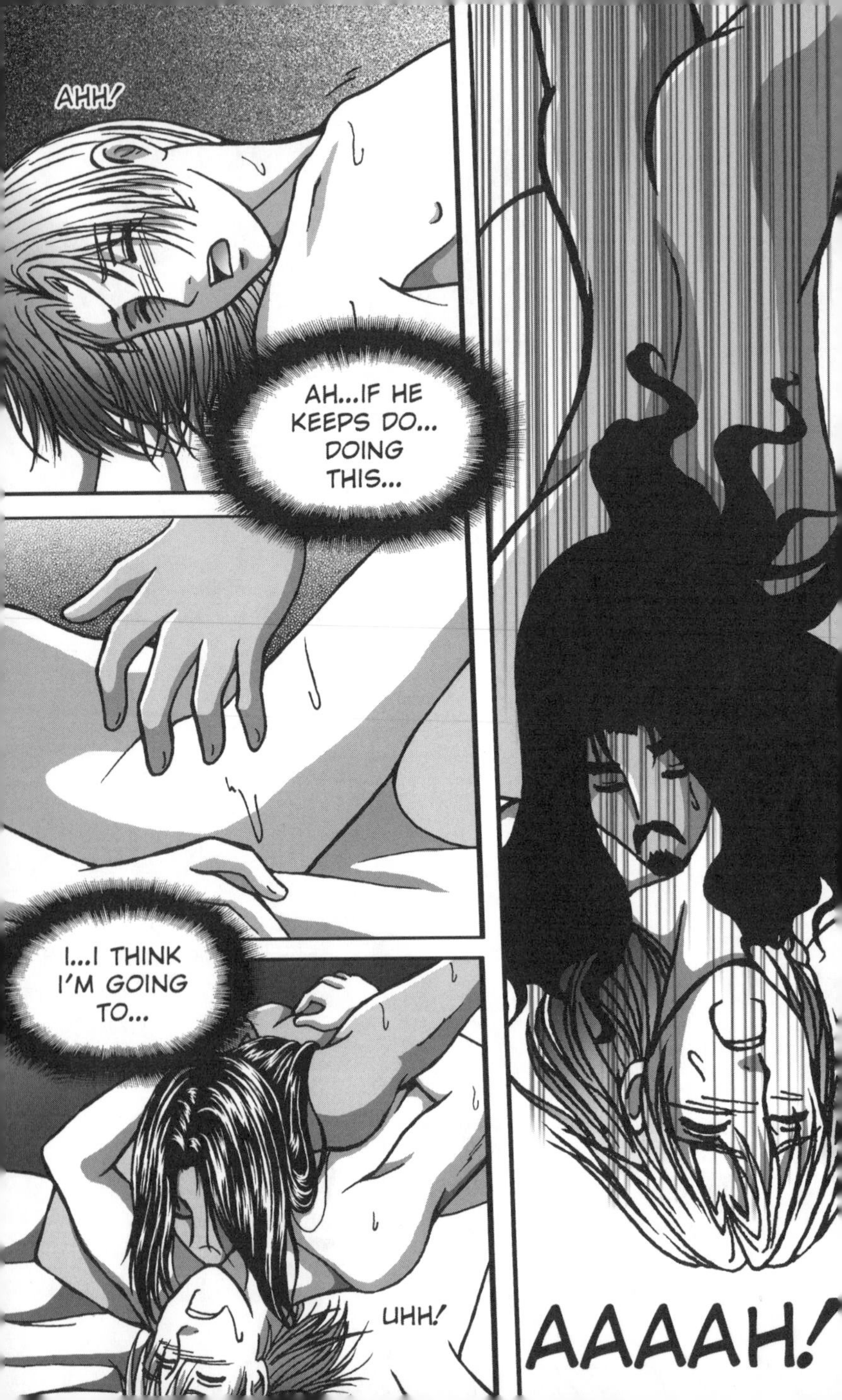
AHH!
AH...IF HE KEEPS DO... DOING THIS...
I...I THINK I'M GOING TO...
UHH!
AAAAH!

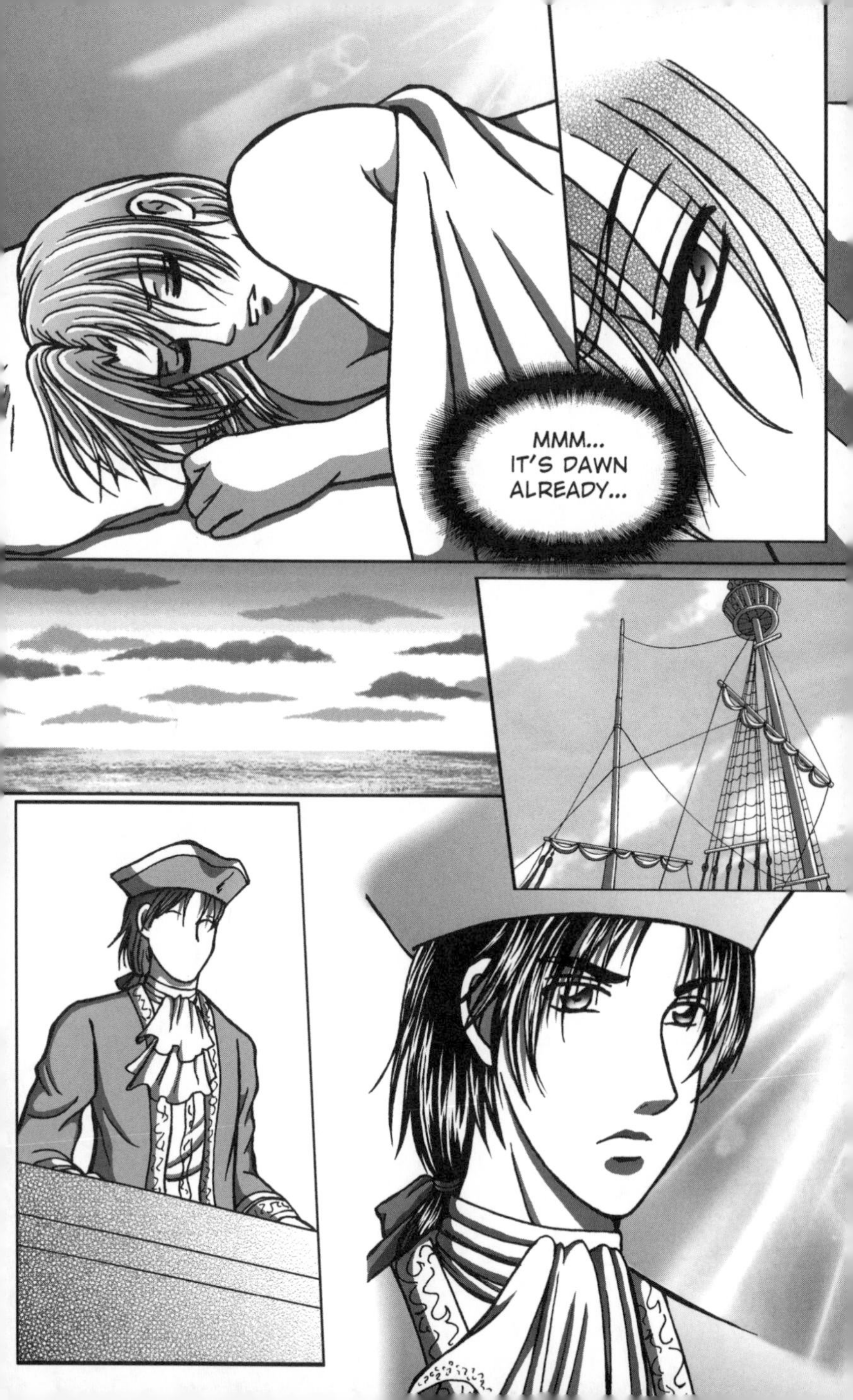
MMM... IT'S DAWN ALREADY...

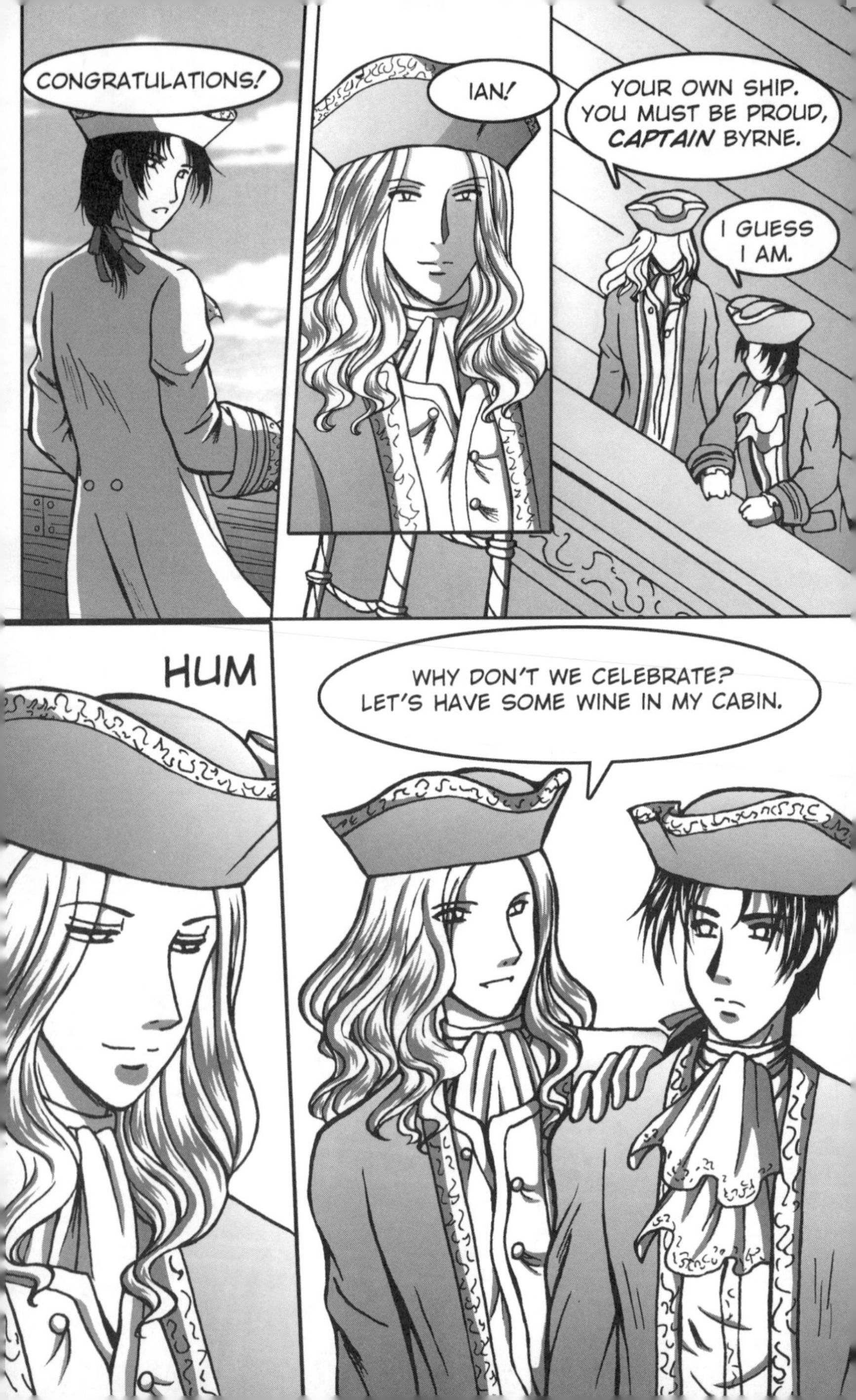
CONGRATULATIONS!
IAN!
YOUR OWN SHIP. YOU MUST BE PROUD, CAPTAIN BYRNE.
I GUESS I AM.
HUM
WHY DON'T WE CELEBRATE? LET'S HAVE SOME WINE IN MY CABIN.

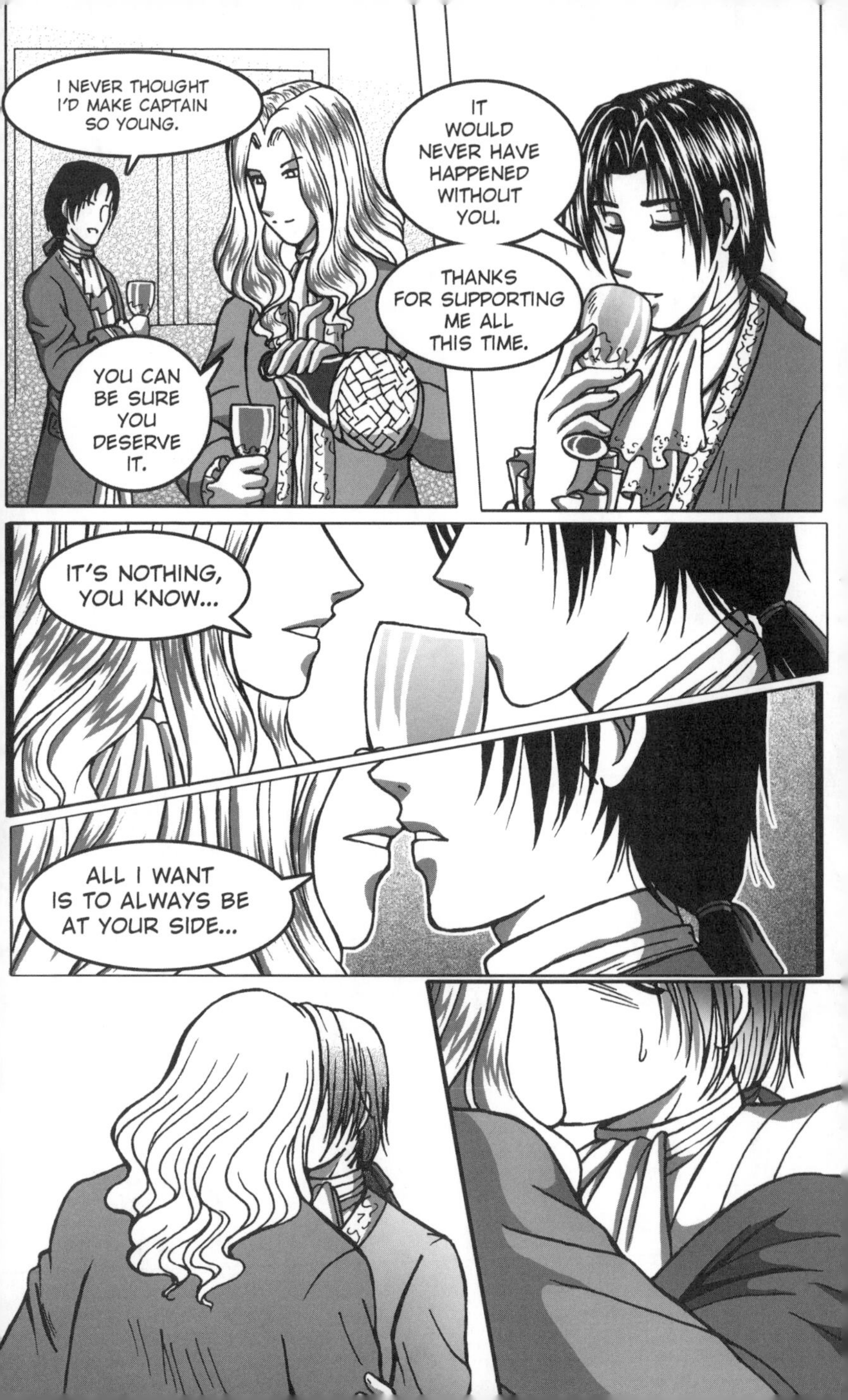
I NEVER THOUGHT I'D MAKE CAPTAIN SO YOUNG.
YOU CAN BE SURE YOU DESERVE IT.
IT WOULD NEVER HAVE HAPPENED WITHOUT YOU.
THANKS FOR SUPPORTING ME ALL THIS TIME.
IT'S NOTHING, YOU KNOW...
ALL I WANT IS TO ALWAYS BE AT YOUR SIDE...

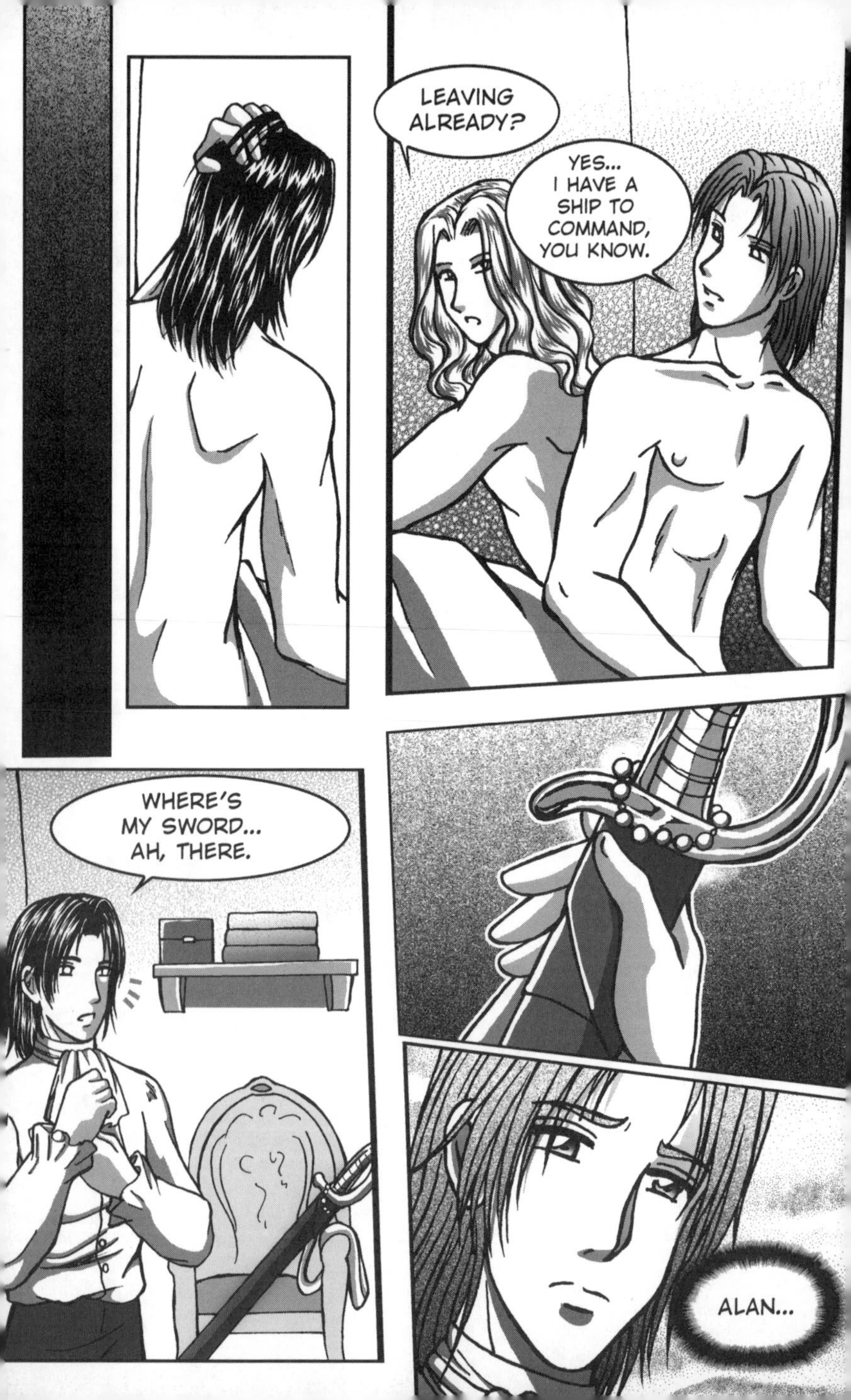
LEAVING ALREADY?
YES... I HAVE A SHIP TO COMMAND, YOU KNOW.
WHERE'S MY SWORD... AH, THERE.
ALAN...

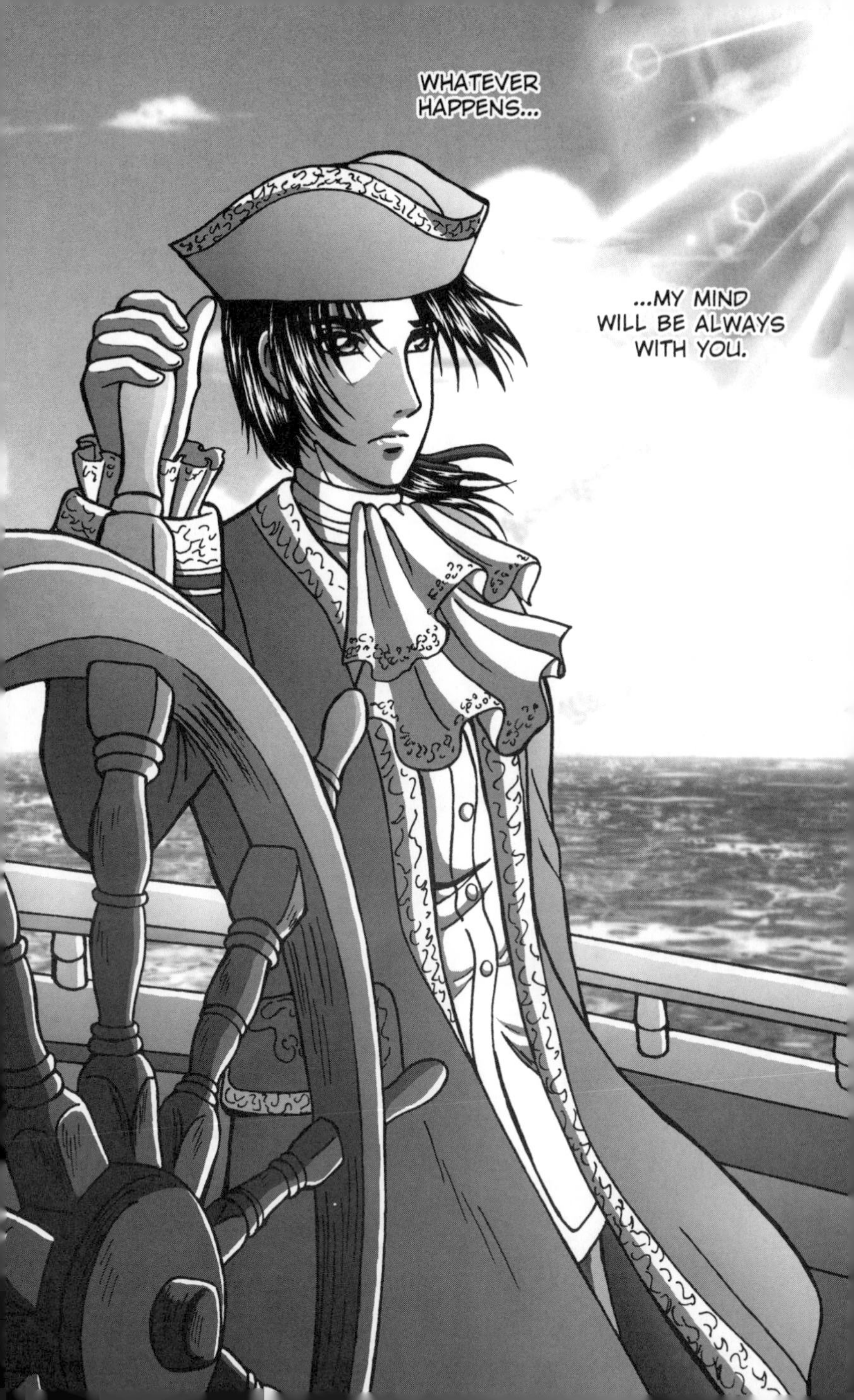
WHATEVER HAPPENS...
...MY MIND WILL BE ALWAYS WITH YOU.

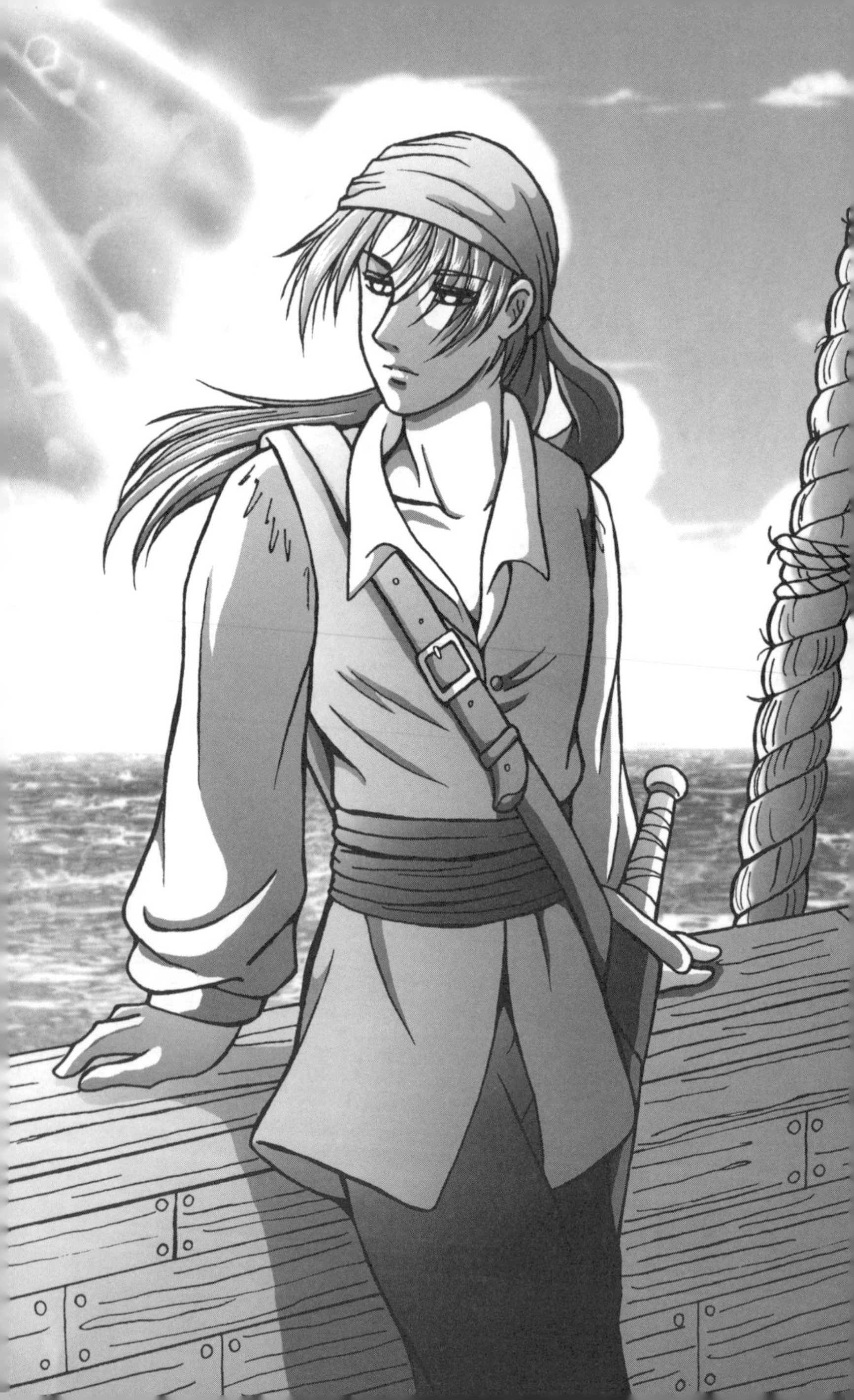

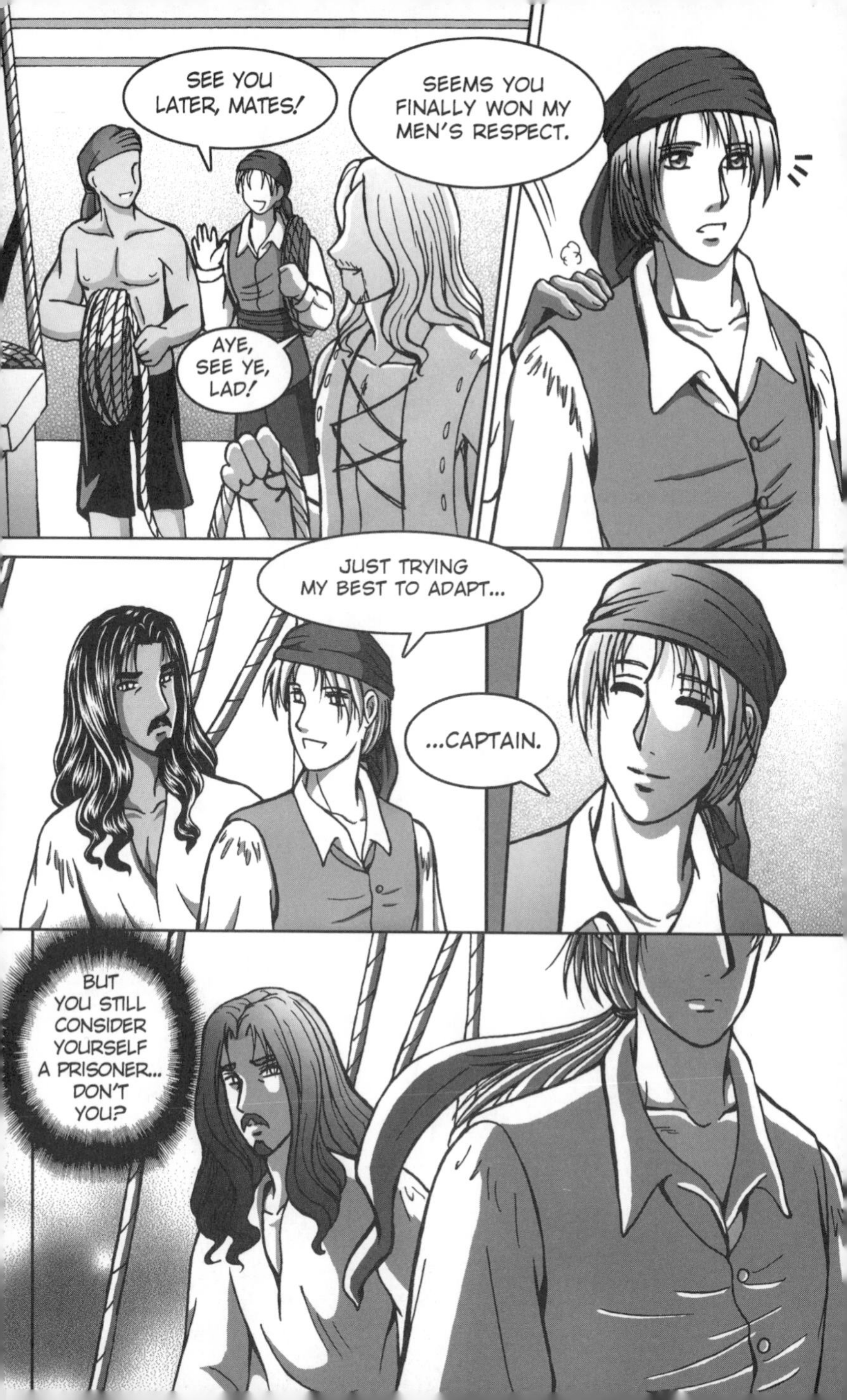
SEE YOU
LATER, MATES!
AYE,
SEE YE,
LAD!
SEEMS YOU
FINALLY WON MY
MEN'S RESPECT.
JUST TRYING
MY BEST TO ADAPT...
...CAPTAIN.
BUT
YOU STILL
CONSIDER
YOURSELF
A PRISONER...
DON'T
YOU?

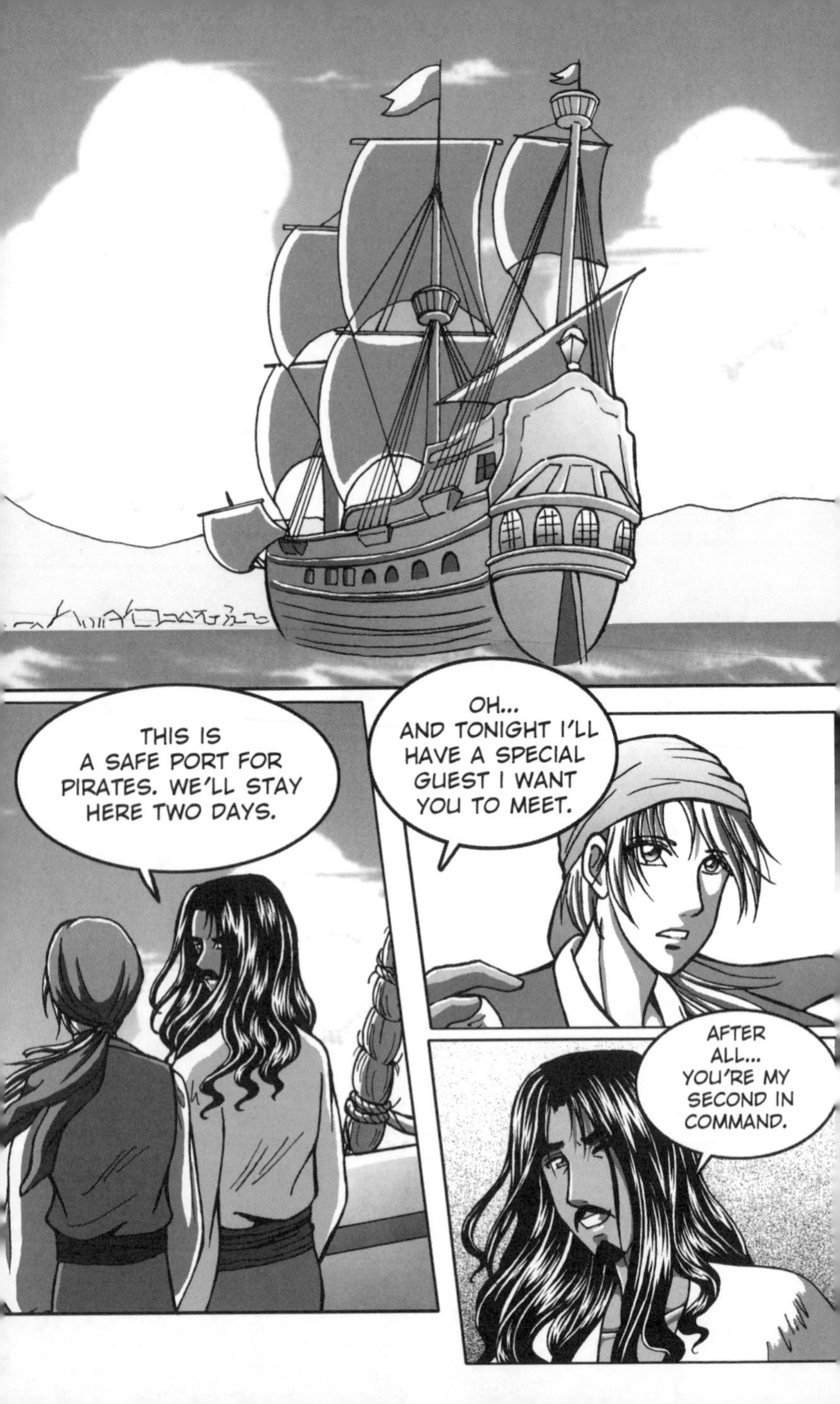
THIS IS A SAFE PORT FOR PIRATES. WE'LL STAY HERE TWO DAYS.
OH... AND TONIGHT I'LL HAVE A SPECIAL GUEST I WANT YOU TO MEET.
AFTER ALL... YOU'RE MY SECOND IN COMMAND.

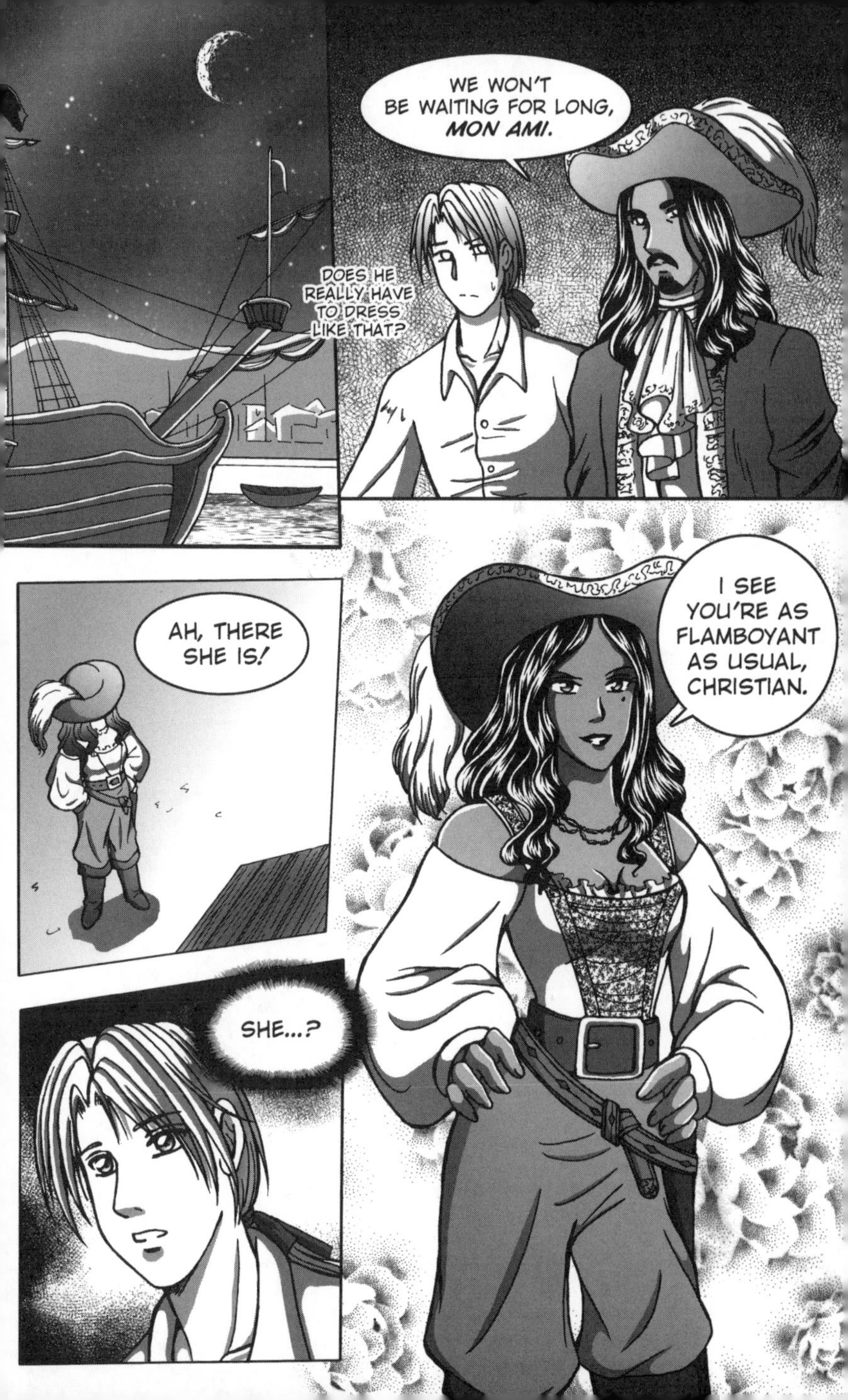
WE WON'T BE WAITING FOR LONG, *MON AMI*.
DOES HE REALLY HAVE TO DRESS LIKE THAT?
AH, THERE SHE IS!
SHE...?
I SEE YOU'RE AS FLAMBOYANT AS USUAL, CHRISTIAN.

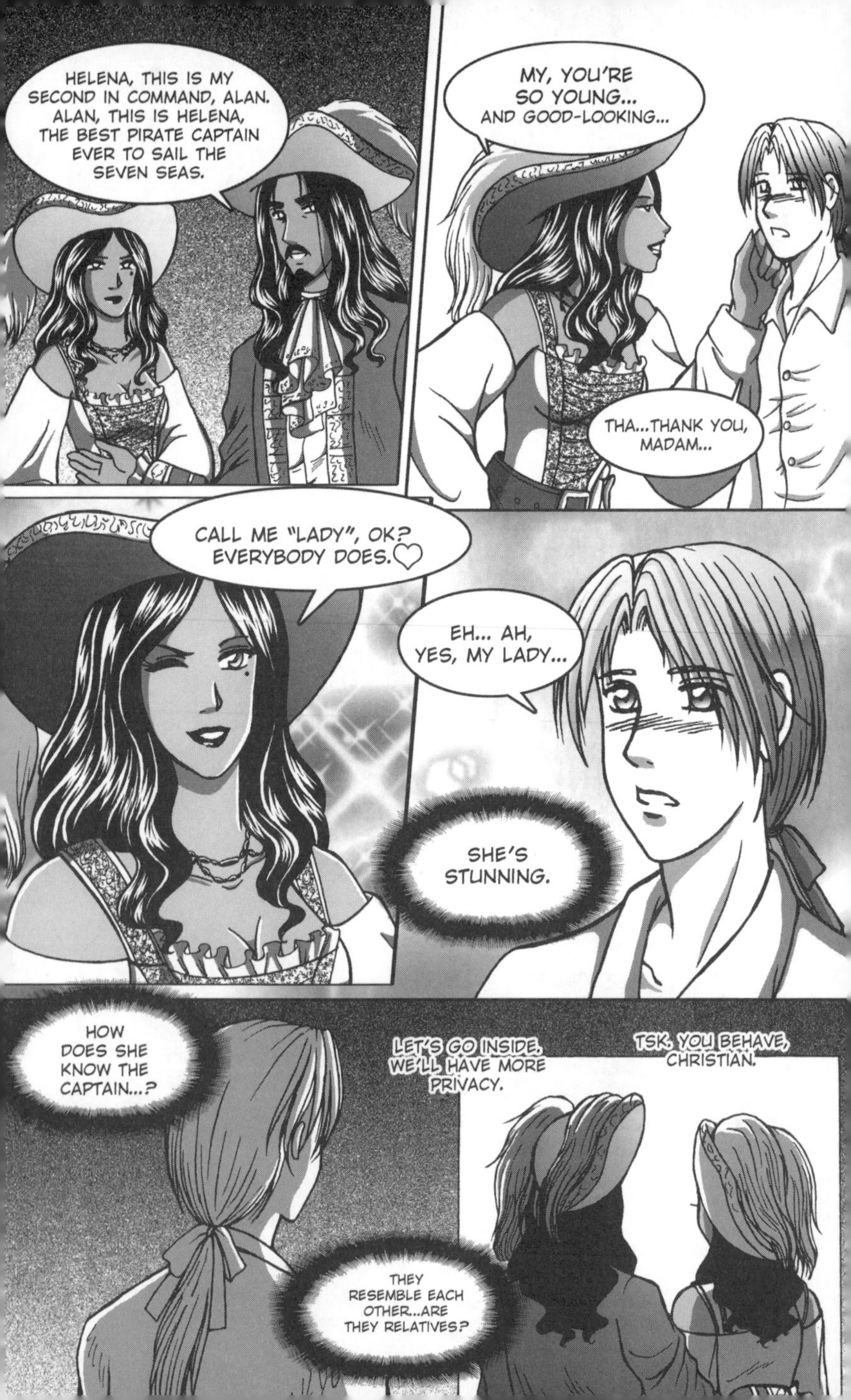
HELENA, THIS IS MY SECOND IN COMMAND, ALAN. ALAN, THIS IS HELENA, THE BEST PIRATE CAPTAIN EVER TO SAIL THE SEVEN SEAS.
MY, YOU'RE SO YOUNG... AND GOOD-LOOKING...
THA...THANK YOU, MADAM...
CALL ME "LADY", OK? EVERYBODY DOES.♡
EH... AH, YES, MY LADY...
SHE'S STUNNING.
HOW DOES SHE KNOW THE CAPTAIN...?
LET'S GO INSIDE. WE'LL HAVE MORE PRIVACY.
TSK, YOU BEHAVE, CHRISTIAN.
THEY RESEMBLE EACH OTHER...ARE THEY RELATIVES?

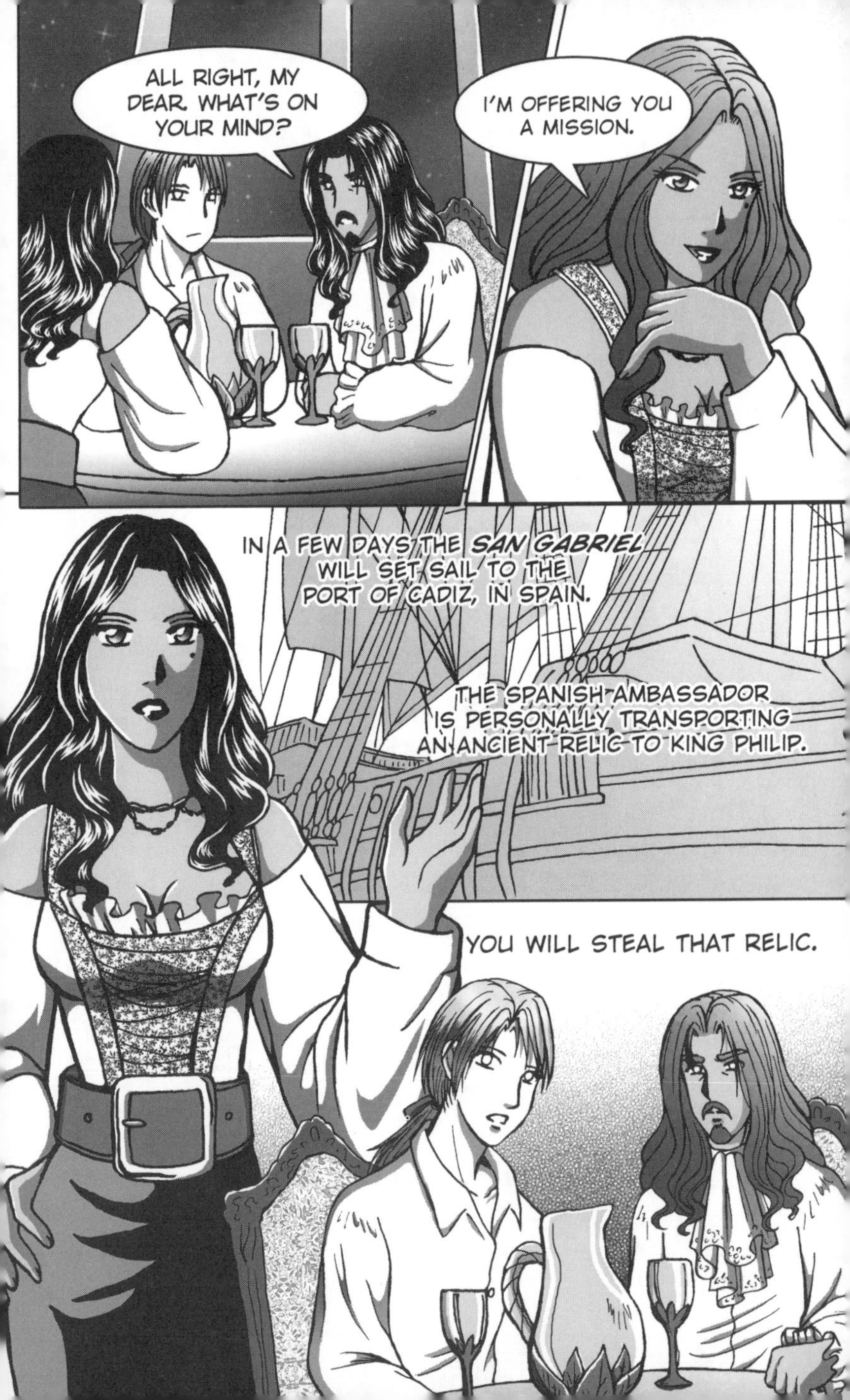
ALL RIGHT, MY DEAR. WHAT'S ON YOUR MIND?
I'M OFFERING YOU A MISSION.
IN A FEW DAYS THE *SAN GABRIEL* WILL SET SAIL TO THE PORT OF CADIZ, IN SPAIN.
THE SPANISH AMBASSADOR IS PERSONALLY TRANSPORTING AN ANCIENT RELIC TO KING PHILIP.
YOU WILL STEAL THAT RELIC.

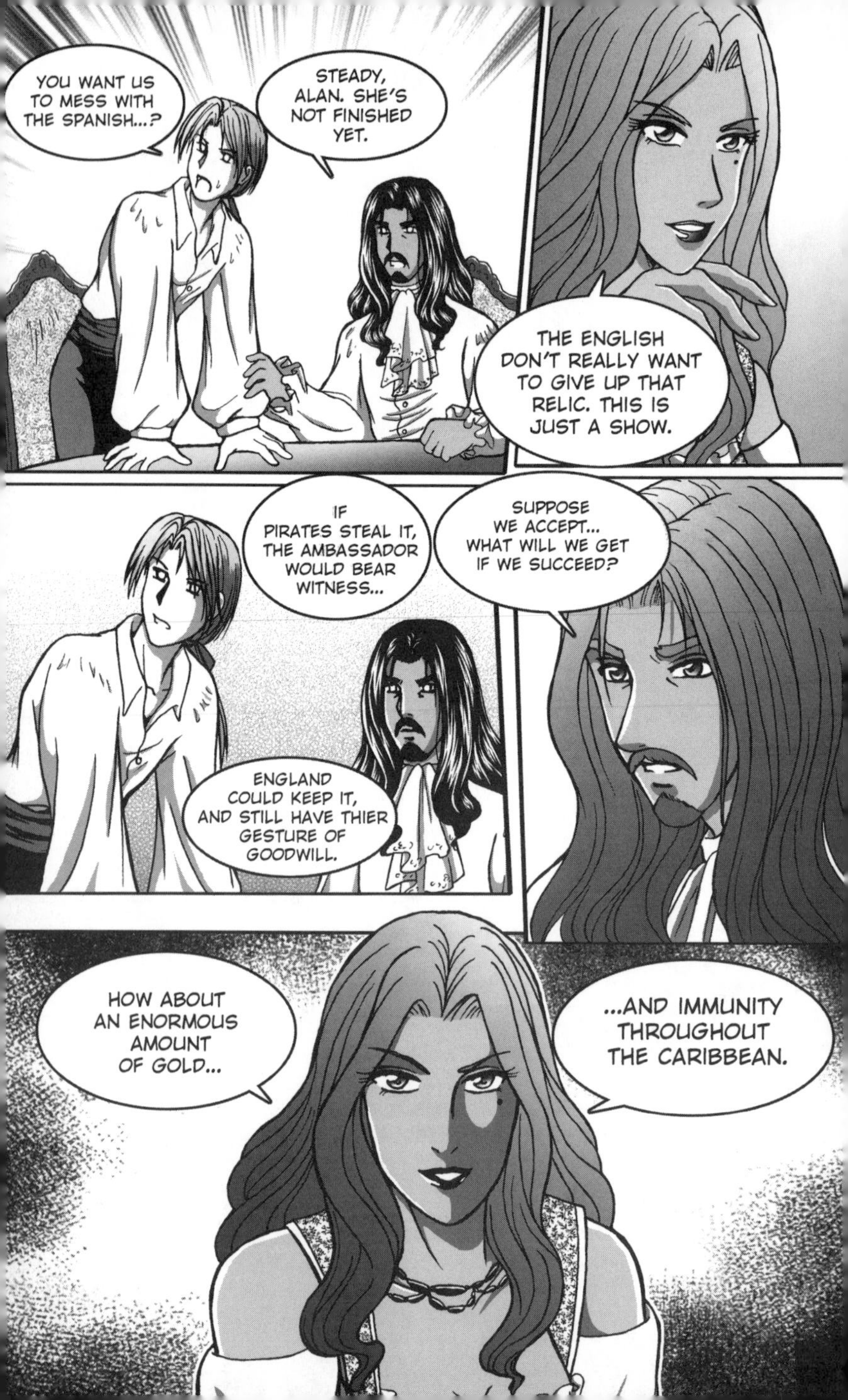
YOU WANT US TO MESS WITH THE SPANISH...?
STEADY, ALAN. SHE'S NOT FINISHED YET.
THE ENGLISH DON'T REALLY WANT TO GIVE UP THAT RELIC. THIS IS JUST A SHOW.
IF PIRATES STEAL IT, THE AMBASSADOR WOULD BEAR WITNESS...
ENGLAND COULD KEEP IT, AND STILL HAVE THIER GESTURE OF GOODWILL.
SUPPOSE WE ACCEPT... WHAT WILL WE GET IF WE SUCCEED?
HOW ABOUT AN ENORMOUS AMOUNT OF GOLD...
...AND IMMUNITY THROUGHOUT THE CARIBBEAN.

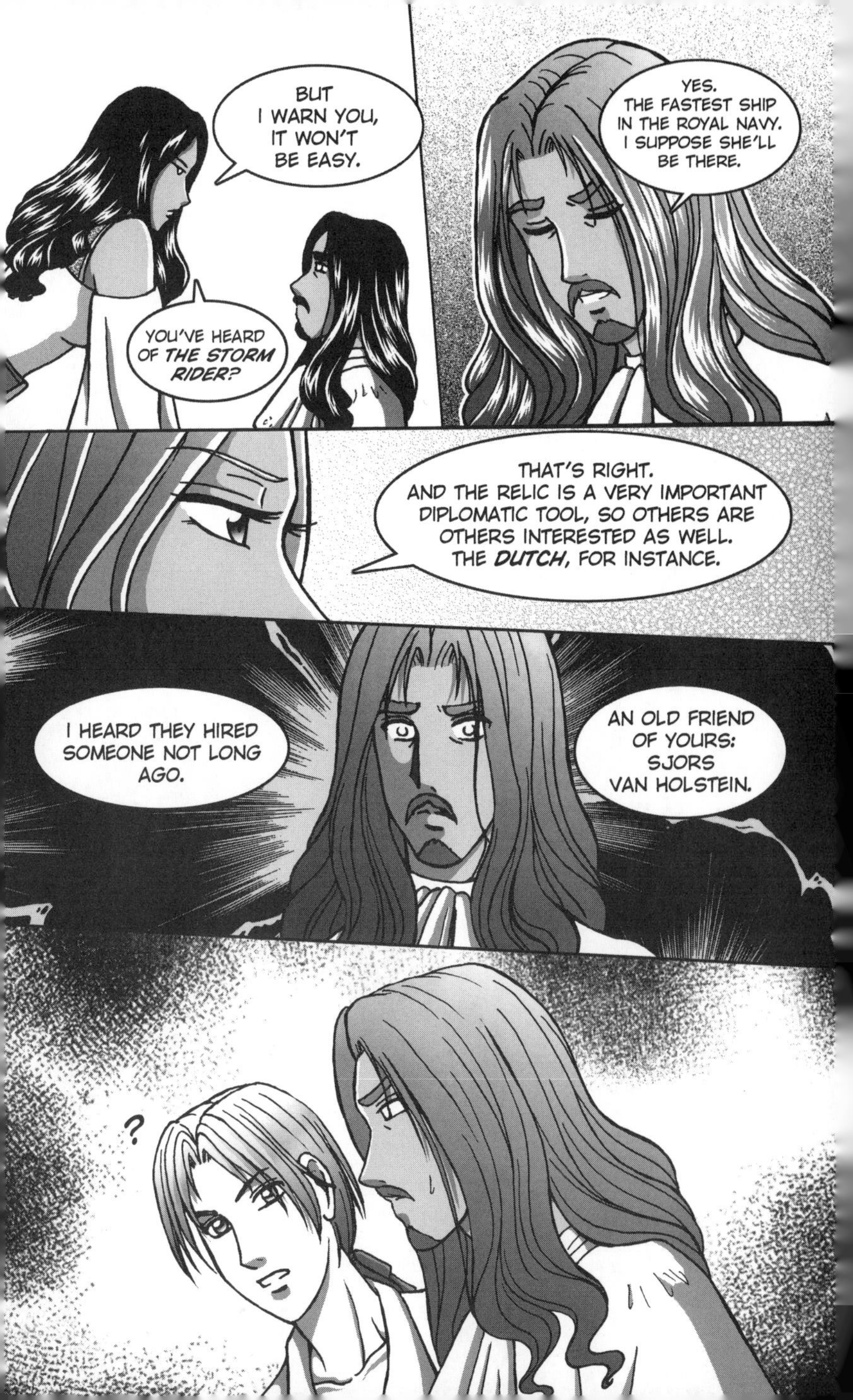
BUT I WARN YOU, IT WON'T BE EASY.
YOU'VE HEARD OF *THE STORM RIDER?*
YES. THE FASTEST SHIP IN THE ROYAL NAVY. I SUPPOSE SHE'LL BE THERE.
THAT'S RIGHT. AND THE RELIC IS A VERY IMPORTANT DIPLOMATIC TOOL, SO OTHERS ARE OTHERS INTERESTED AS WELL. THE *DUTCH*, FOR INSTANCE.
I HEARD THEY HIRED SOMEONE NOT LONG AGO.
AN OLD FRIEND OF YOURS: SJORS VAN HOLSTEIN.
?

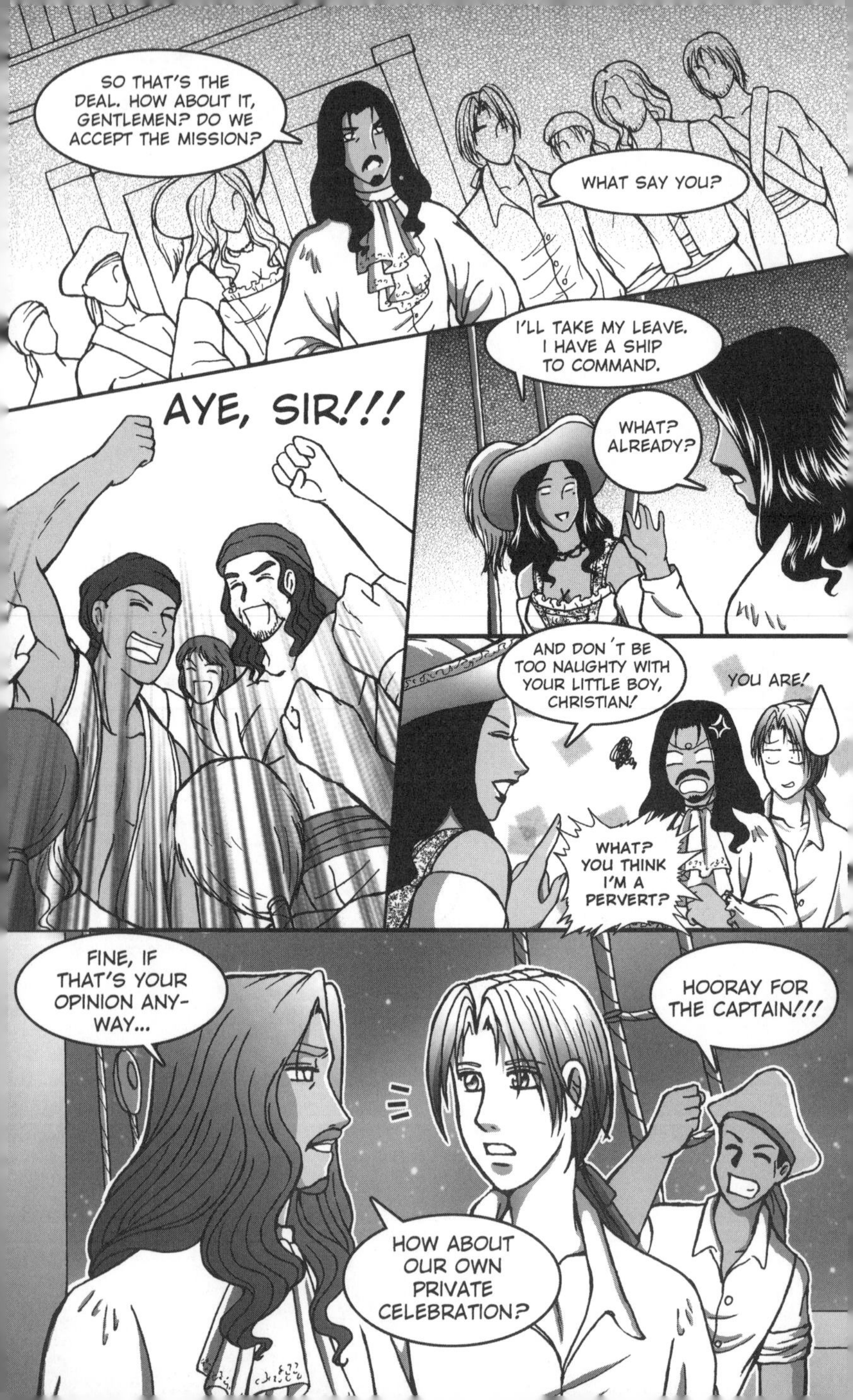
SO THAT'S THE DEAL. HOW ABOUT IT, GENTLEMEN? DO WE ACCEPT THE MISSION?
WHAT SAY YOU?
AYE, SIR!!!
I'LL TAKE MY LEAVE. I HAVE A SHIP TO COMMAND.
WHAT? ALREADY?
AND DON´T BE TOO NAUGHTY WITH YOUR LITTLE BOY, CHRISTIAN!
WHAT? YOU THINK I'M A PERVERT?
YOU ARE!
FINE, IF THAT'S YOUR OPINION ANY-WAY...
HOORAY FOR THE CAPTAIN!!!
HOW ABOUT OUR OWN PRIVATE CELEBRATION?

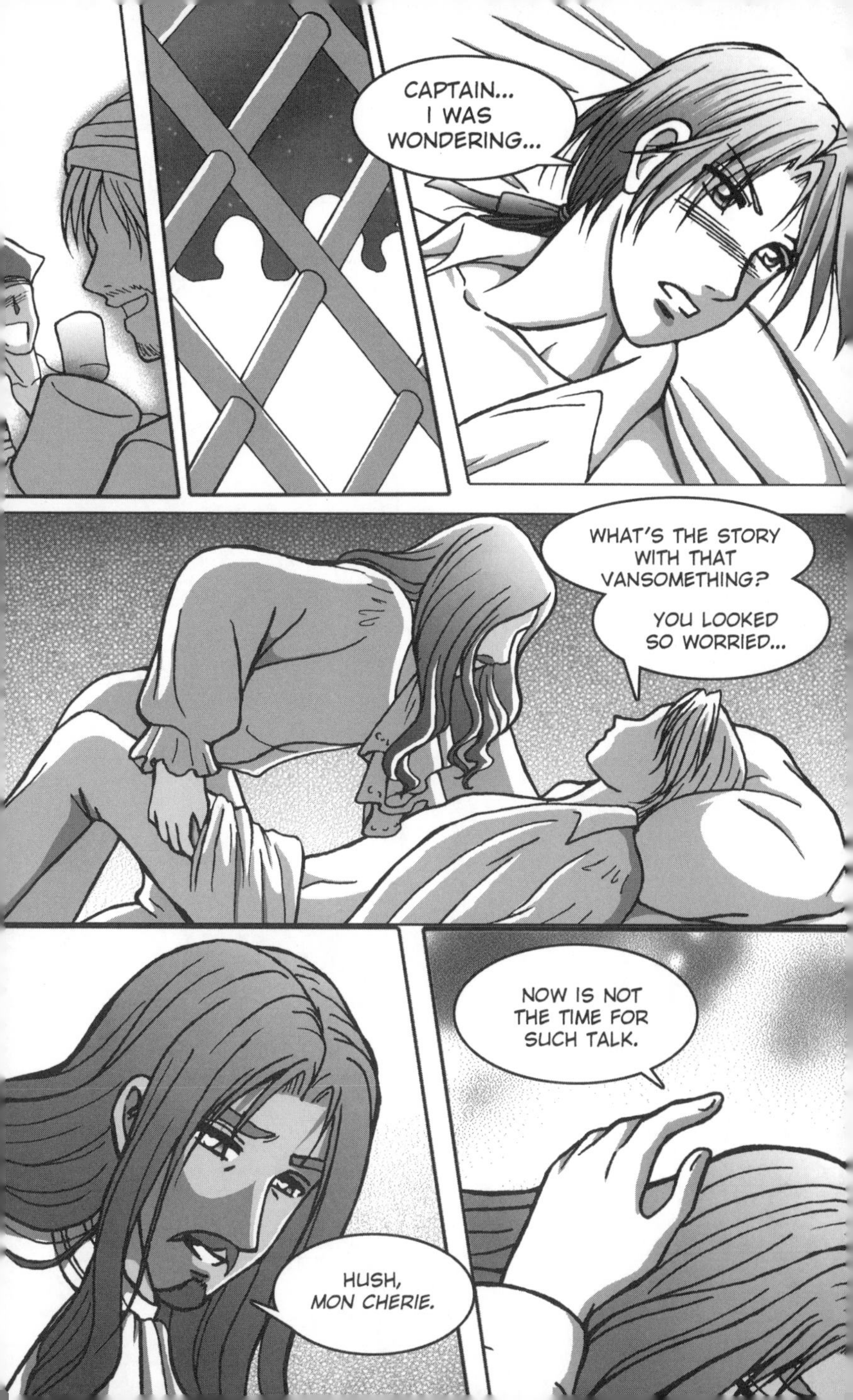
CAPTAIN... I WAS WONDERING...
WHAT'S THE STORY WITH THAT VANSOMETHING?
YOU LOOKED SO WORRIED...
NOW IS NOT THE TIME FOR SUCH TALK.
HUSH, MON CHERIE.

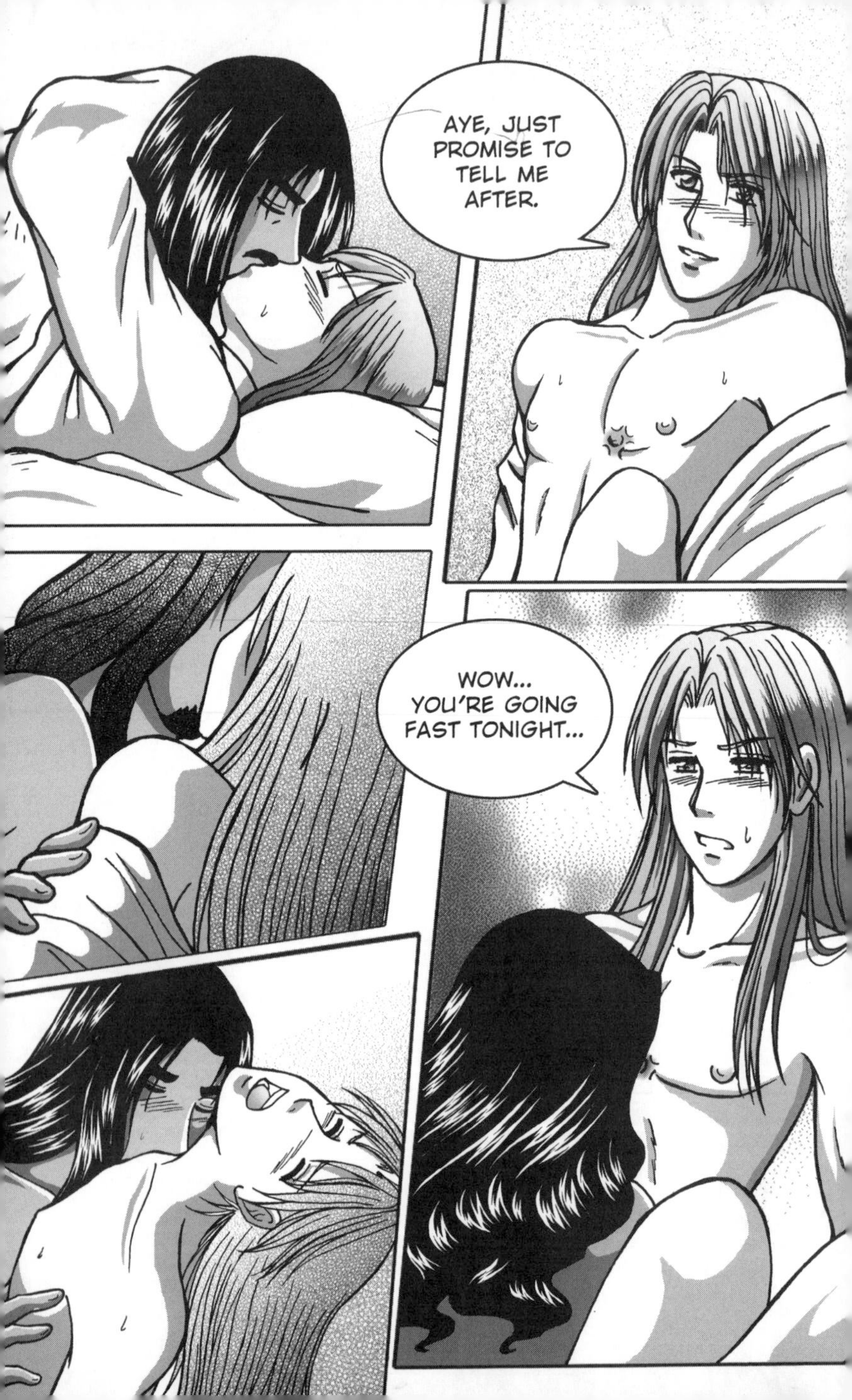
AYE, JUST PROMISE TO TELL ME AFTER.
WOW... YOU'RE GOING FAST TONIGHT...

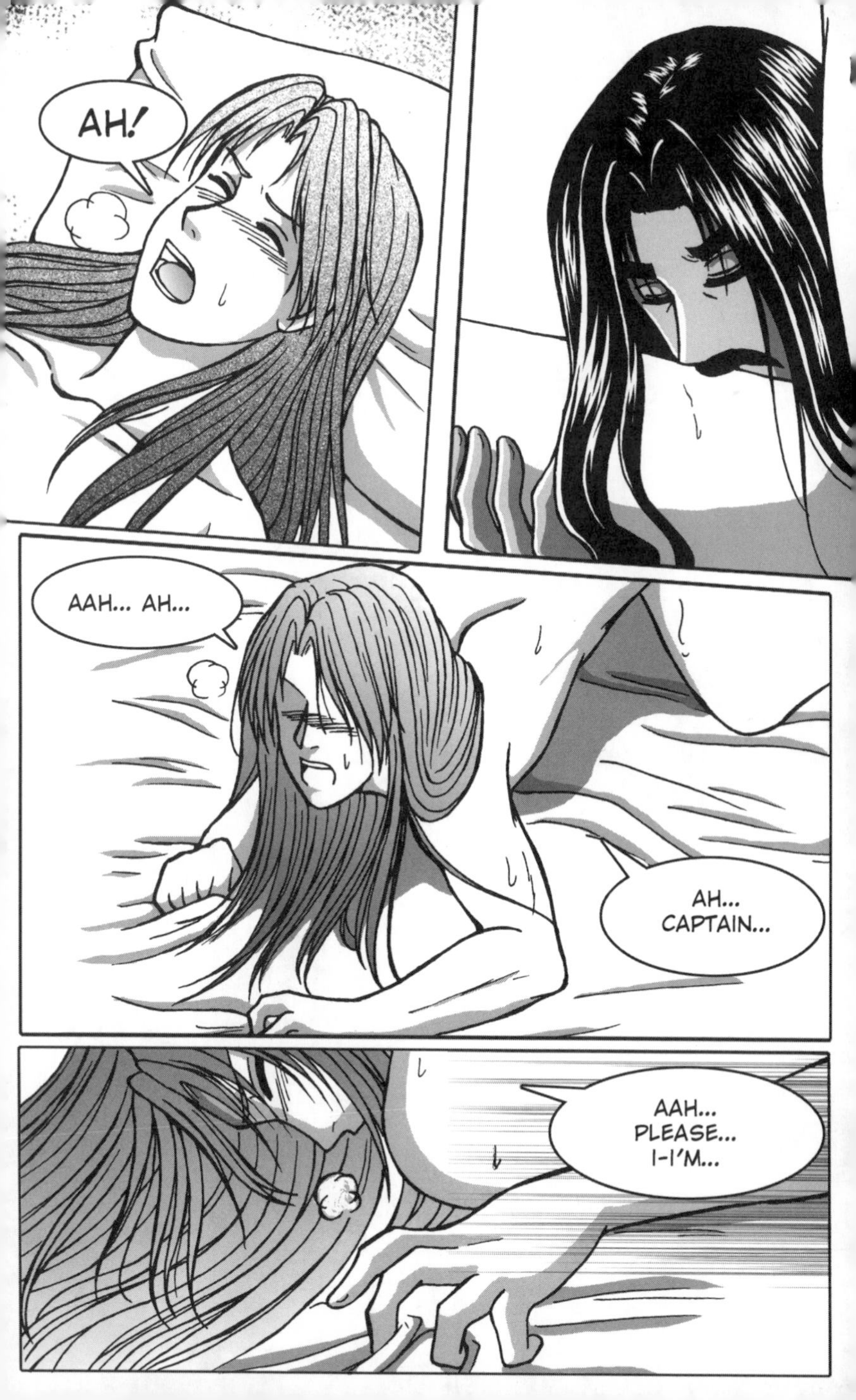
AH!
AAH... AH...
AH... CAPTAIN...
AAH... PLEASE... I-I'M...

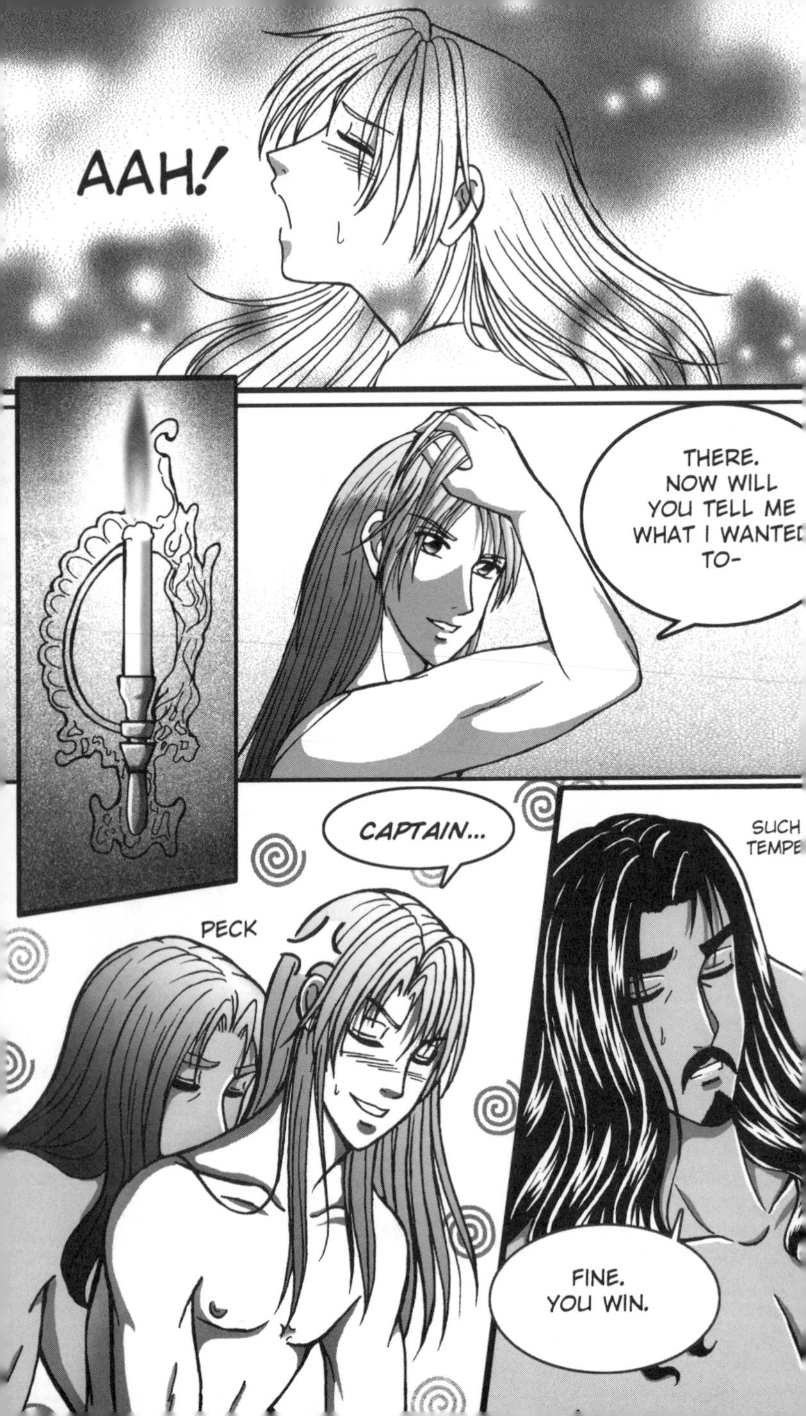
AAH!
THERE. NOW WILL YOU TELL ME WHAT I WANTED TO-
CAPTAIN...
PECK
SUCH TEMPE
FINE. YOU WIN.

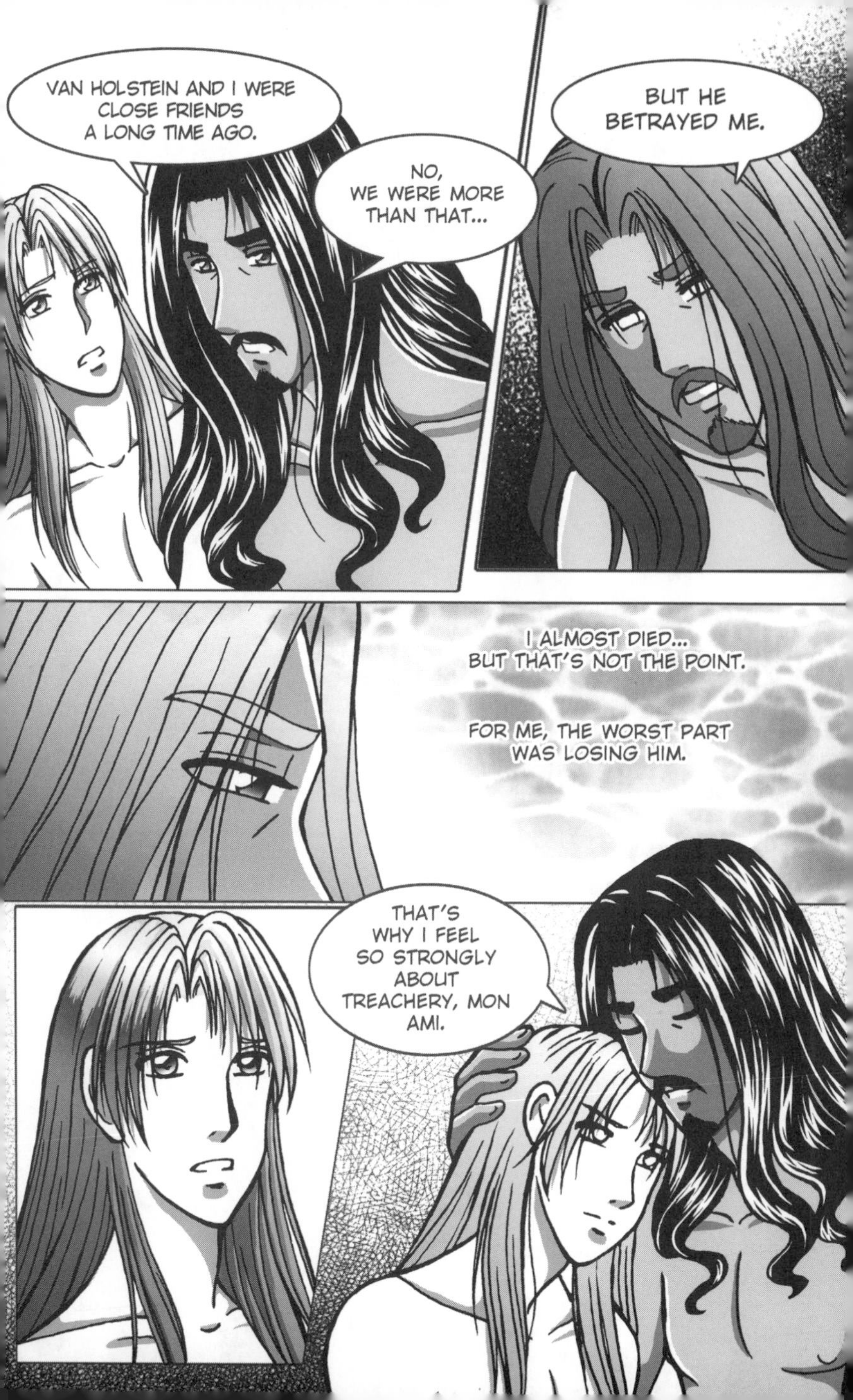
VAN HOLSTEIN AND I WERE CLOSE FRIENDS A LONG TIME AGO.
NO, WE WERE MORE THAN THAT...
BUT HE BETRAYED ME.
I ALMOST DIED... BUT THAT'S NOT THE POINT.
FOR ME, THE WORST PART WAS LOSING HIM.
THAT'S WHY I FEEL SO STRONGLY ABOUT TREACHERY, MON AMI.

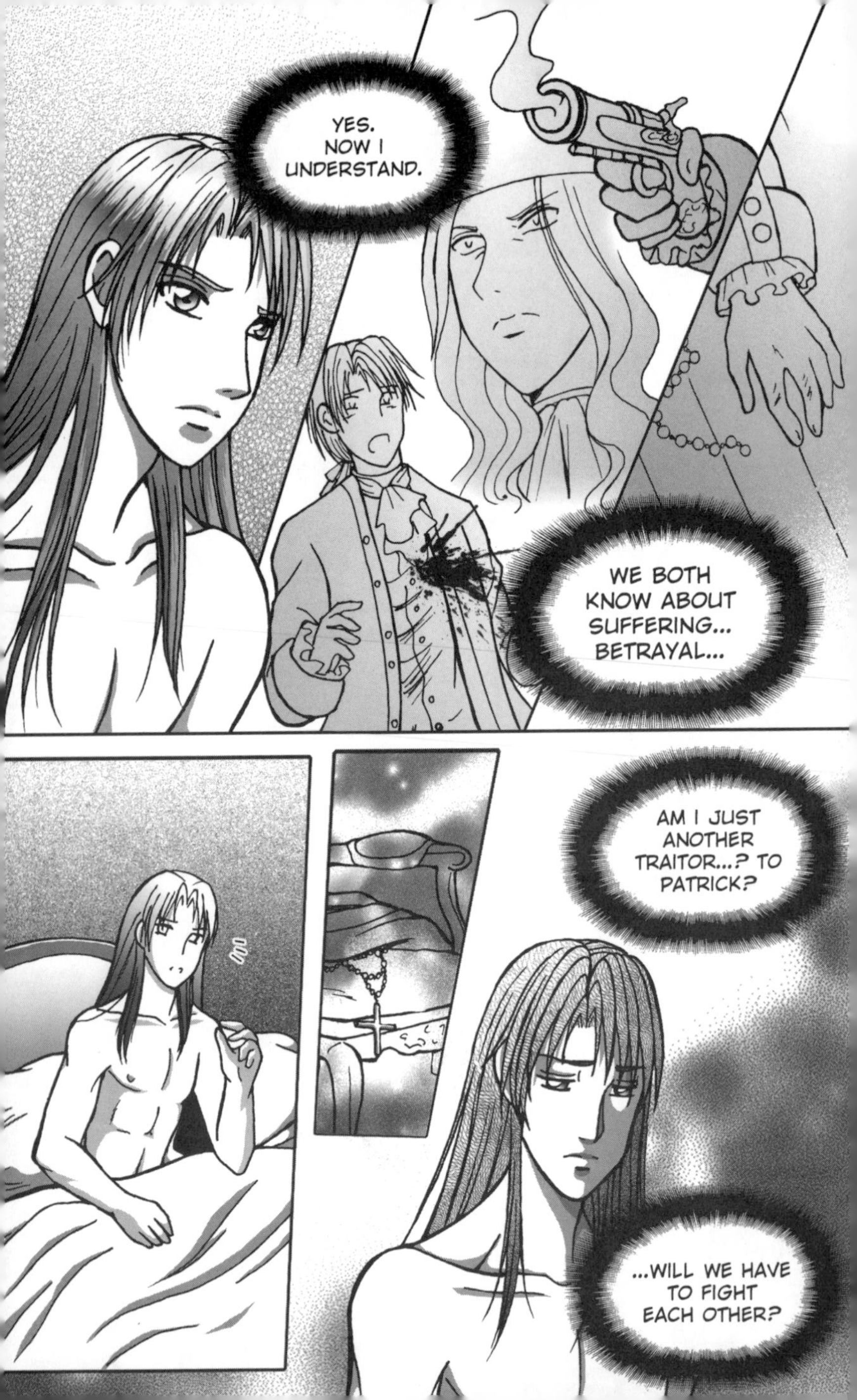
YES. NOW I UNDERSTAND.
WE BOTH KNOW ABOUT SUFFERING... BETRAYAL...
AM I JUST ANOTHER TRAITOR...? TO PATRICK?
...WILL WE HAVE TO FIGHT EACH OTHER?

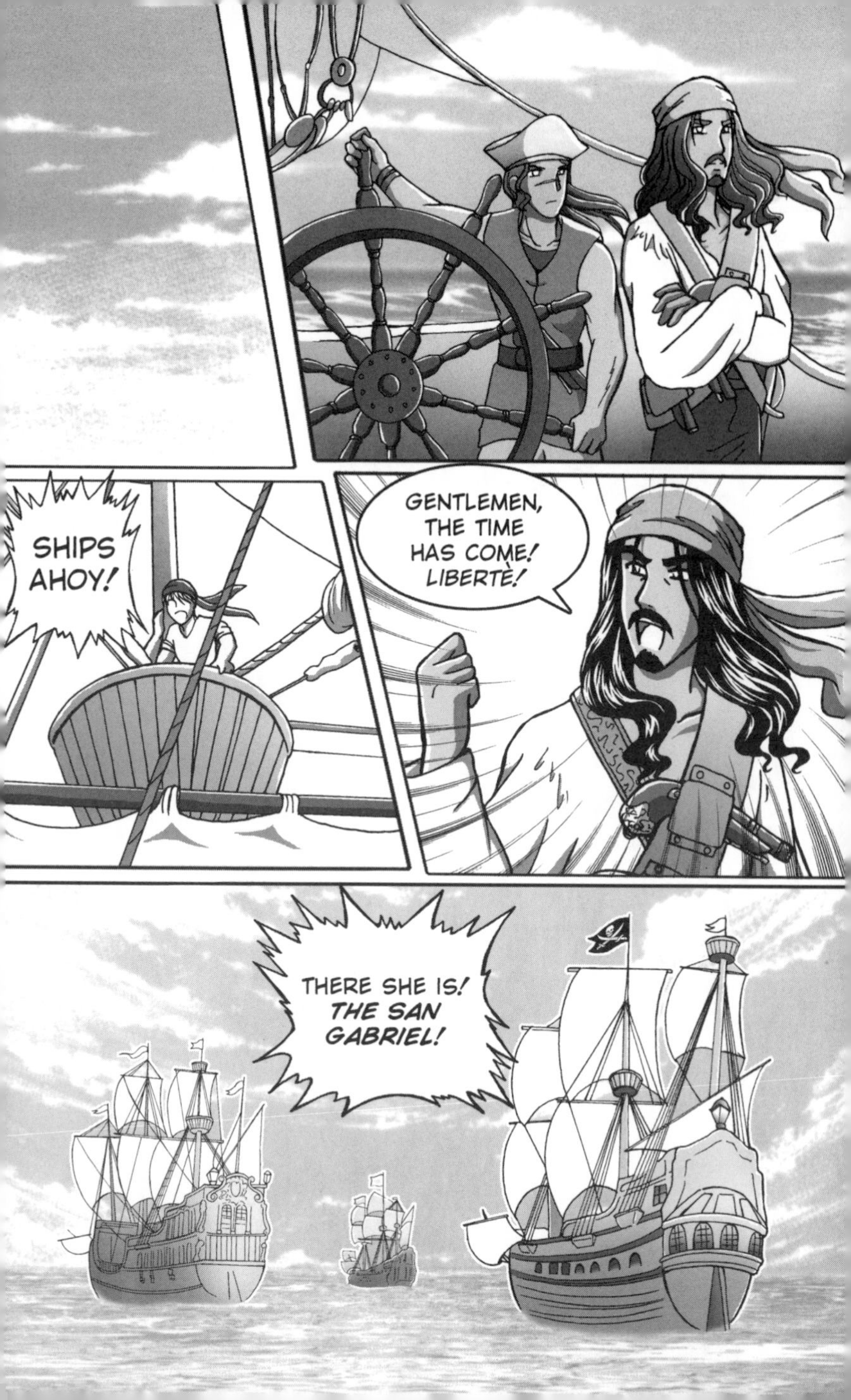
SHIPS AHOY!
GENTLEMEN, THE TIME HAS COME! LIBERTÈ!
THERE SHE IS! THE SAN GABRIEL!

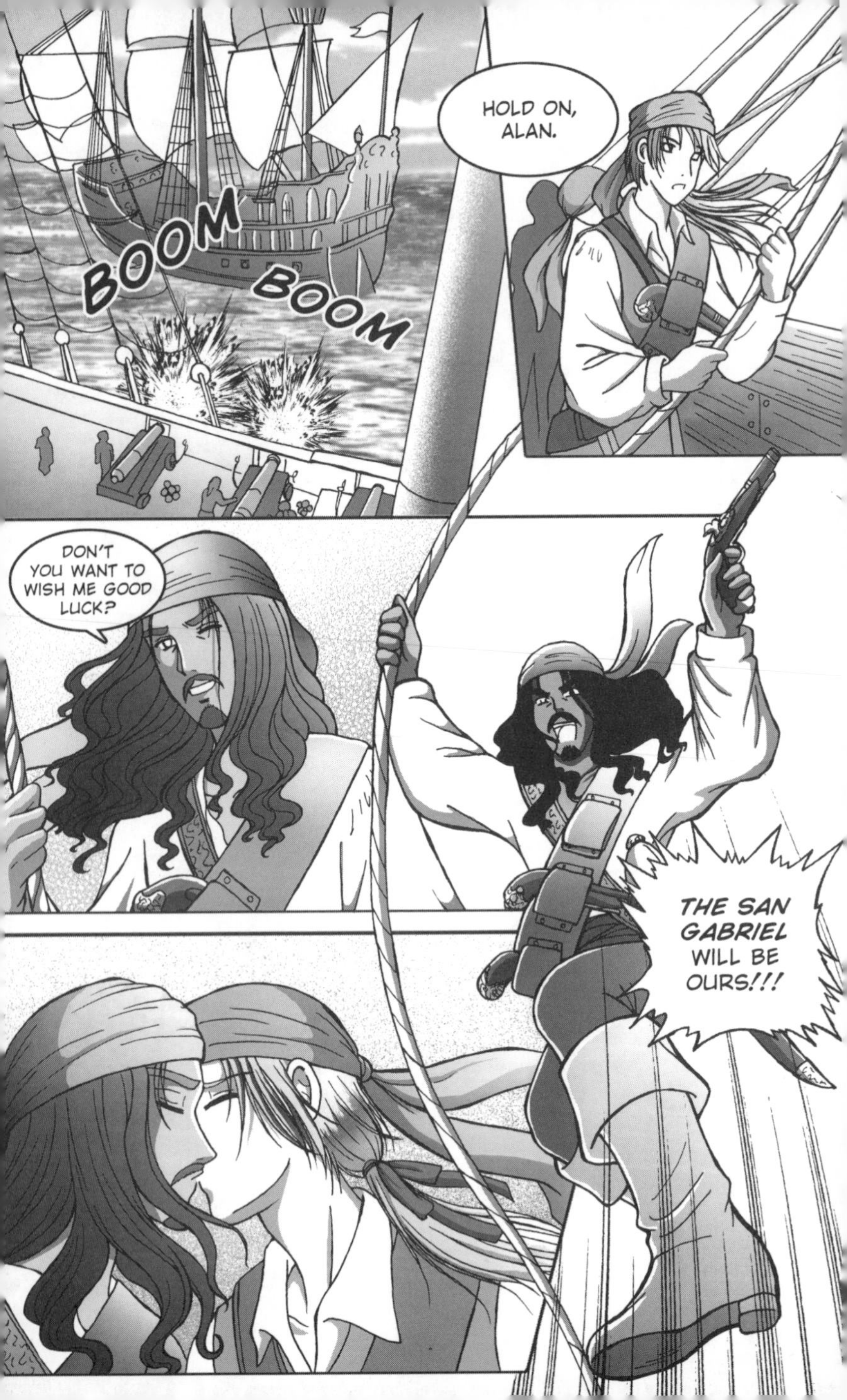
BOOM
BOOM
HOLD ON, ALAN.
DON'T YOU WANT TO WISH ME GOOD LUCK?
THE SAN GABRIEL WILL BE OURS!!!

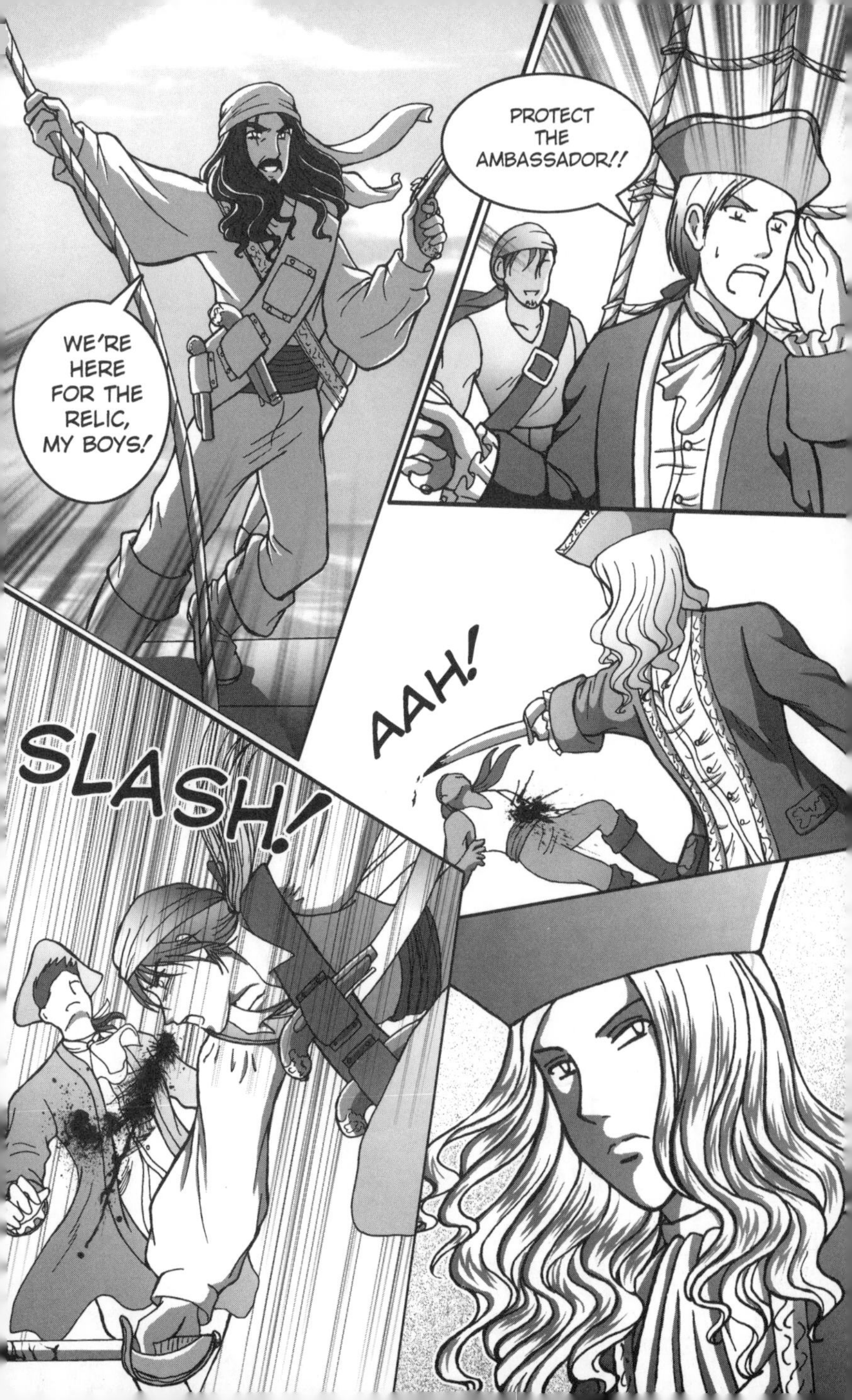
WE'RE HERE FOR THE RELIC, MY BOYS!
PROTECT THE AMBASSADOR!!
AAH!
SLASH!

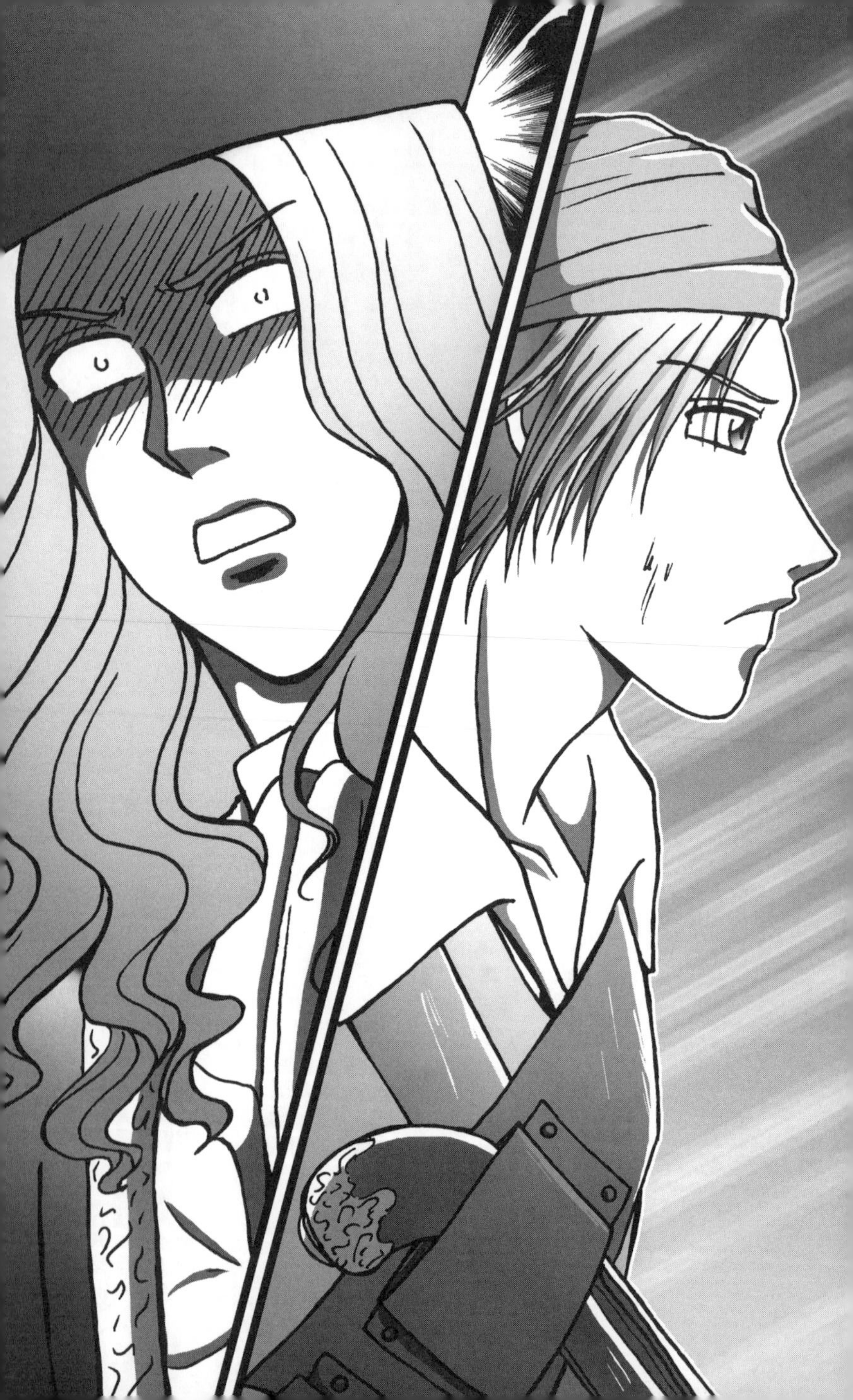

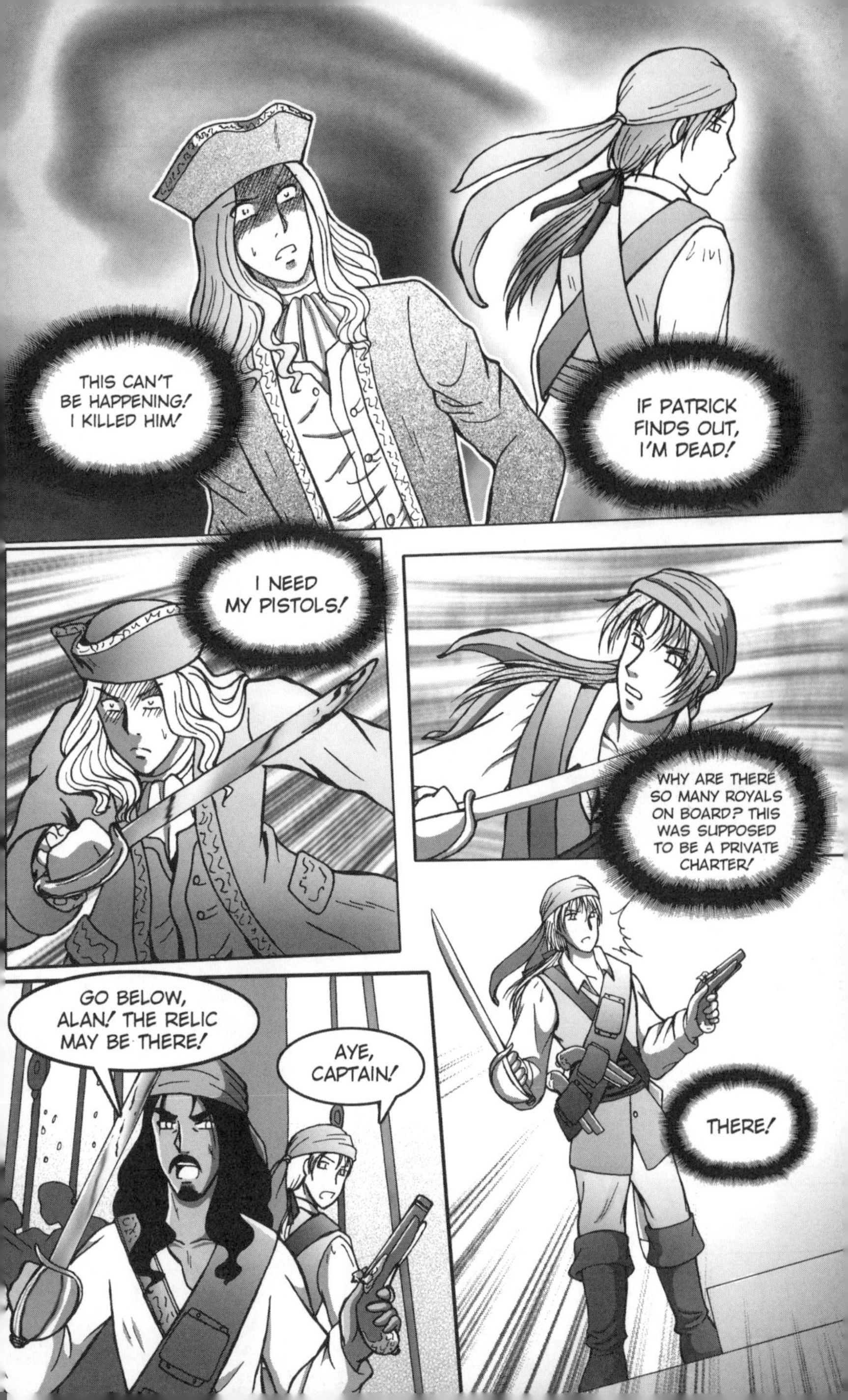
THIS CAN'T BE HAPPENING! I KILLED HIM!
IF PATRICK FINDS OUT, I'M DEAD!
I NEED MY PISTOLS!
WHY ARE THERE SO MANY ROYALS ON BOARD? THIS WAS SUPPOSED TO BE A PRIVATE CHARTER!
GO BELOW, ALAN! THE RELIC MAY BE THERE!
AYE, CAPTAIN!
THERE!

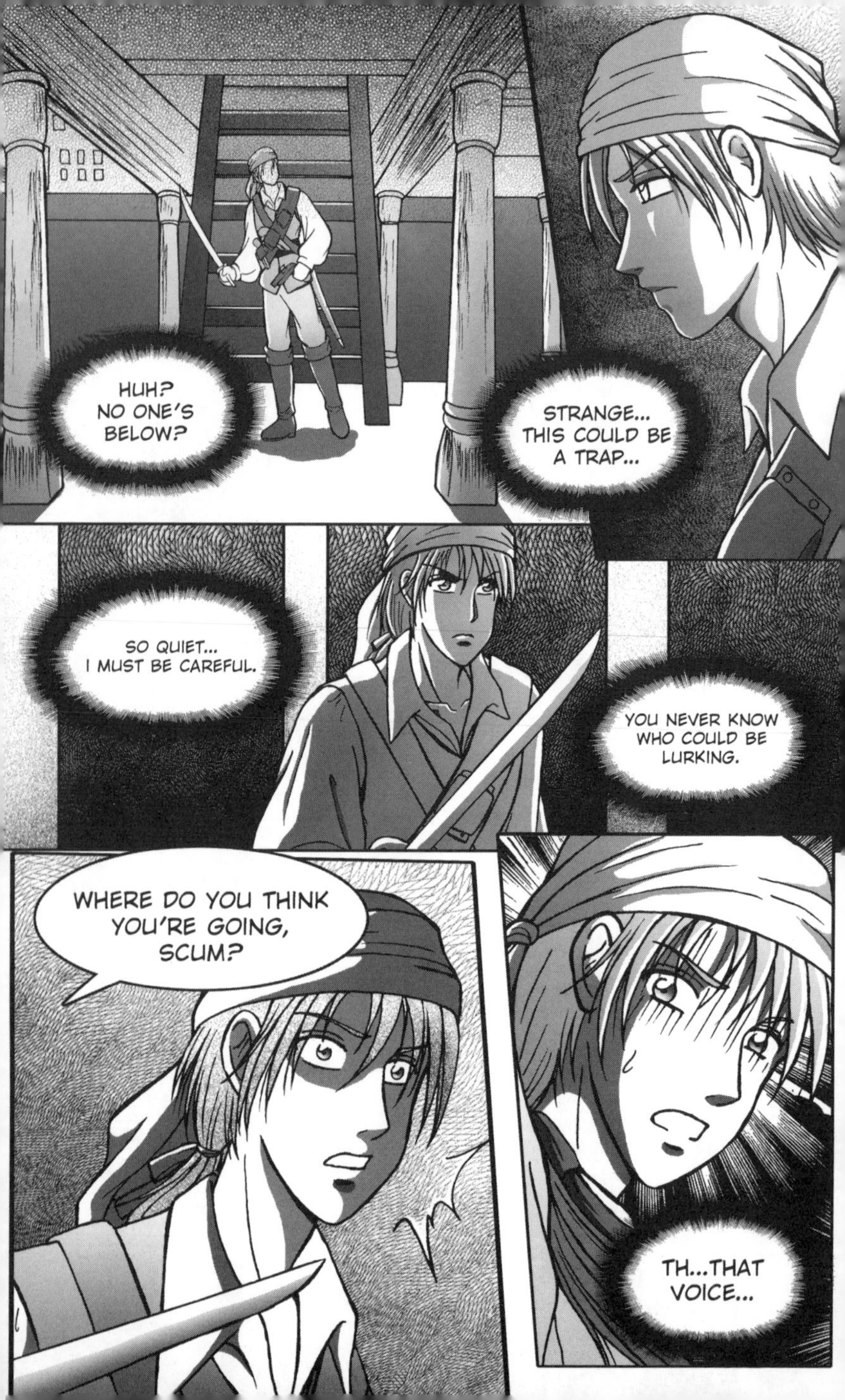
HUH? NO ONE'S BELOW?
STRANGE... THIS COULD BE A TRAP...
SO QUIET... I MUST BE CAREFUL.
YOU NEVER KNOW WHO COULD BE LURKING.
WHERE DO YOU THINK YOU'RE GOING, SCUM?
TH...THAT VOICE...

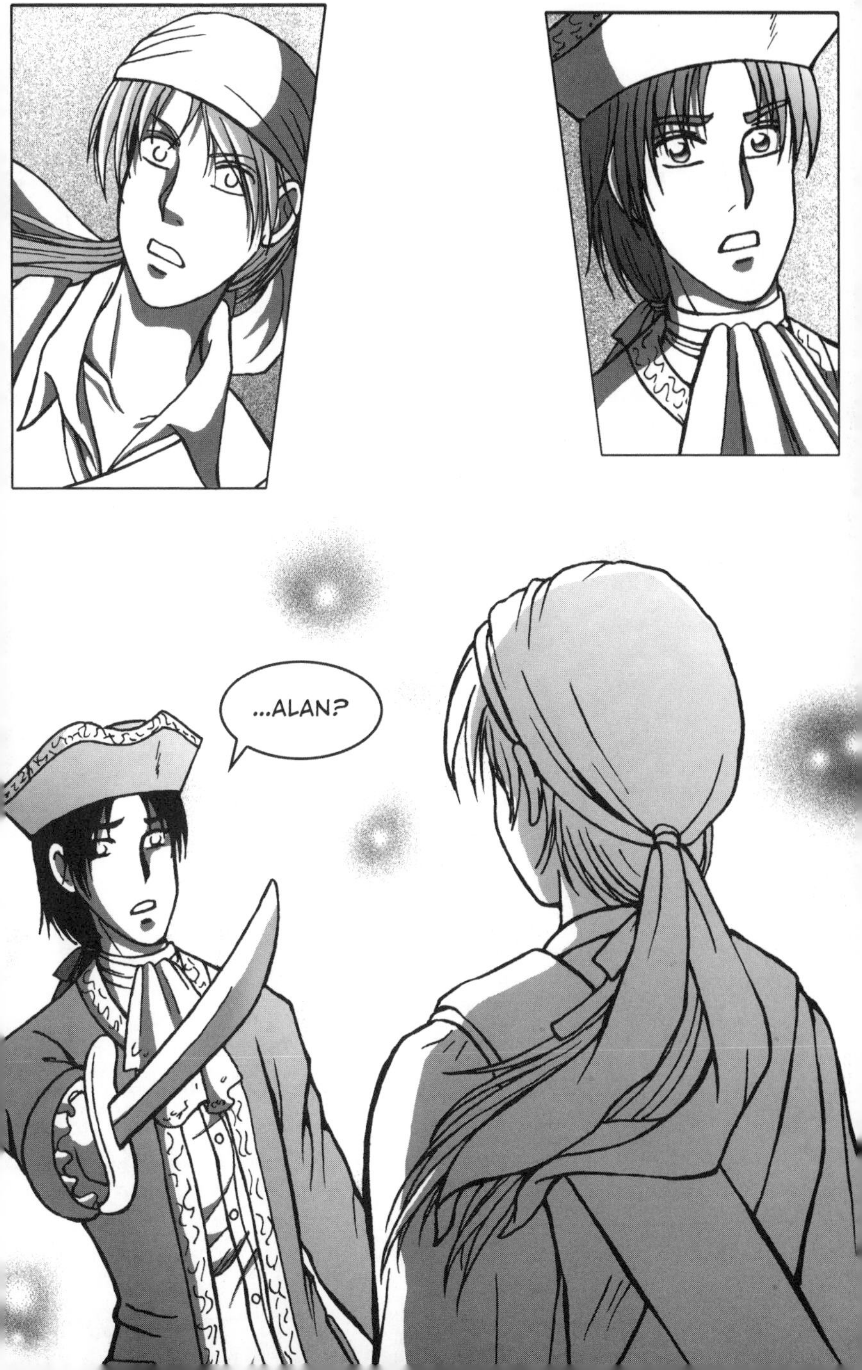
...ALAN?

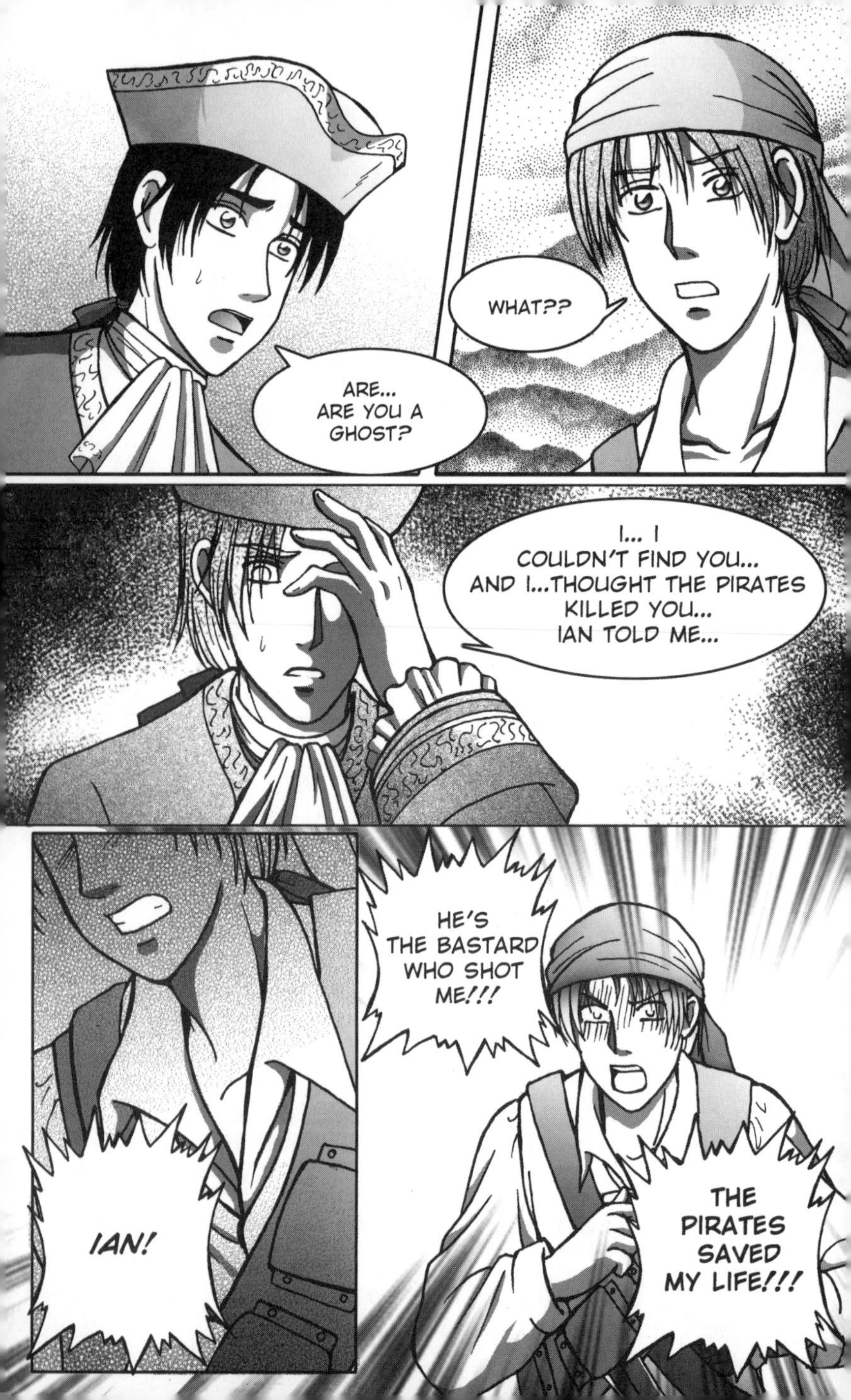
WHAT??
ARE... ARE YOU A GHOST?
I... I COULDN'T FIND YOU... AND I...THOUGHT THE PIRATES KILLED YOU... IAN TOLD ME...
HE'S THE BASTARD WHO SHOT ME!!!
IAN!
THE PIRATES SAVED MY LIFE!!!

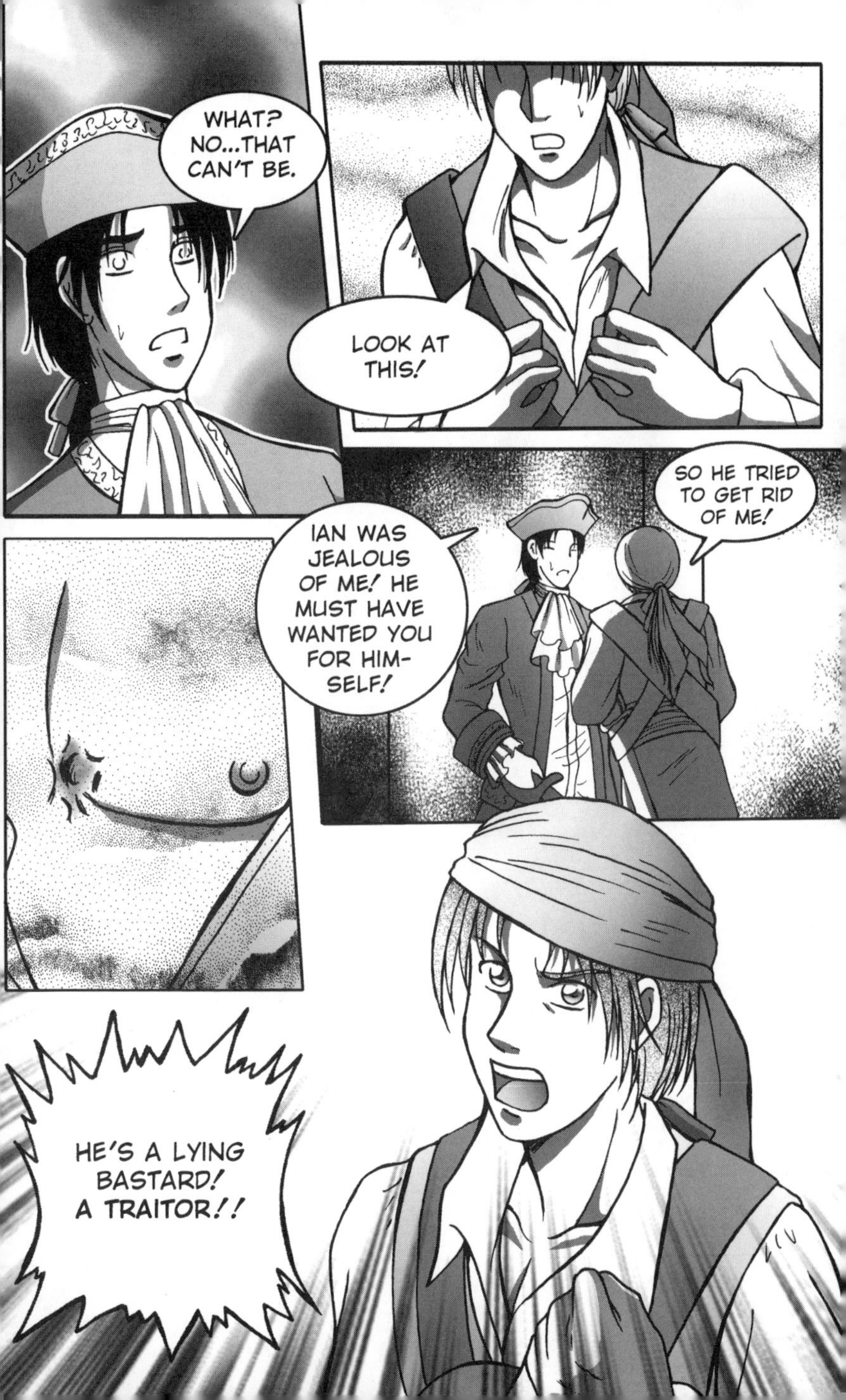
WHAT? NO...THAT CAN'T BE.
LOOK AT THIS!
IAN WAS JEALOUS OF ME! HE MUST HAVE WANTED YOU FOR HIM-SELF!
SO HE TRIED TO GET RID OF ME!
HE'S A LYING BASTARD! A TRAITOR!!

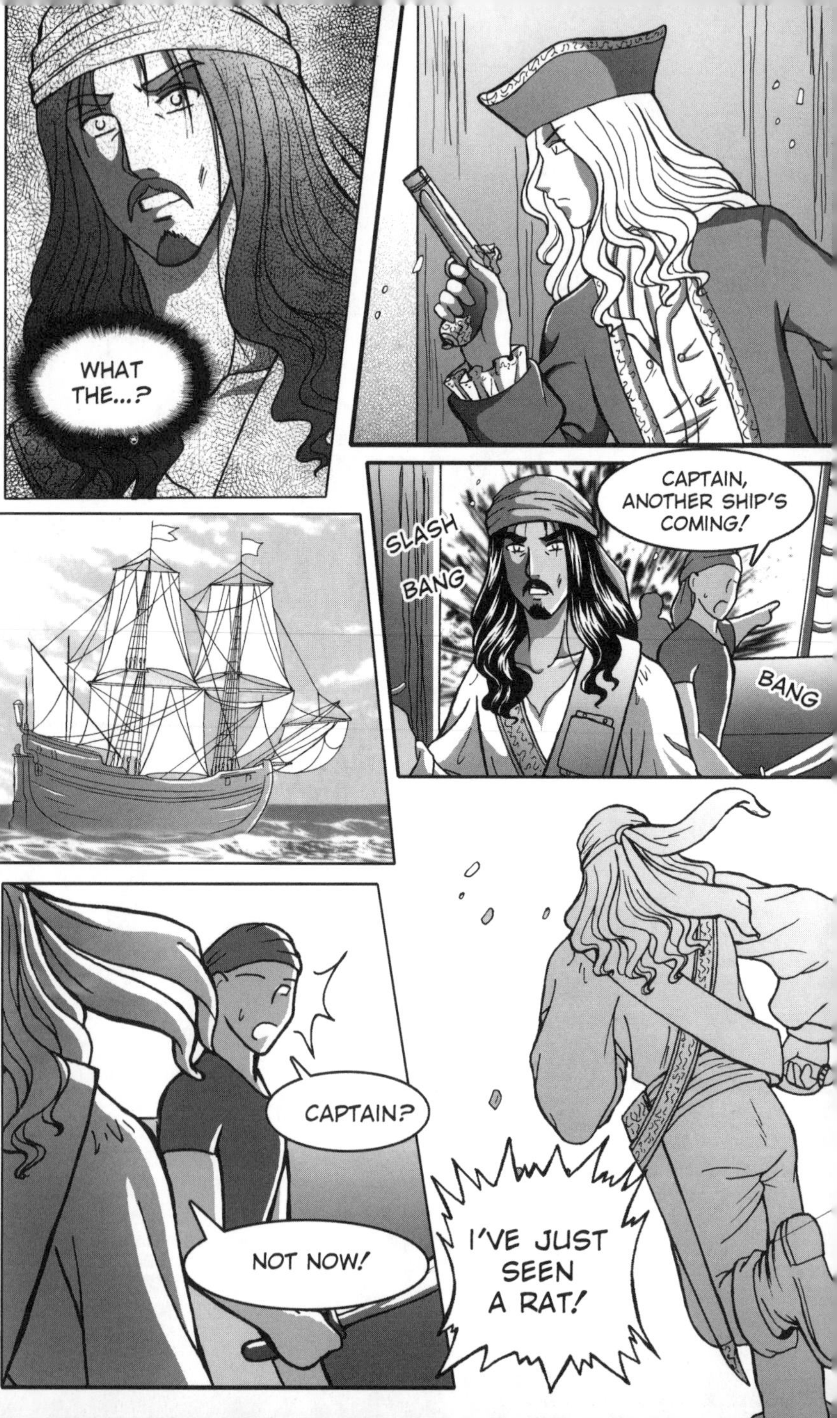
WHAT THE...?
CAPTAIN, ANOTHER SHIP'S COMING!
SLASH
BANG
BANG
CAPTAIN?
NOT NOW!
I'VE JUST SEEN A RAT!

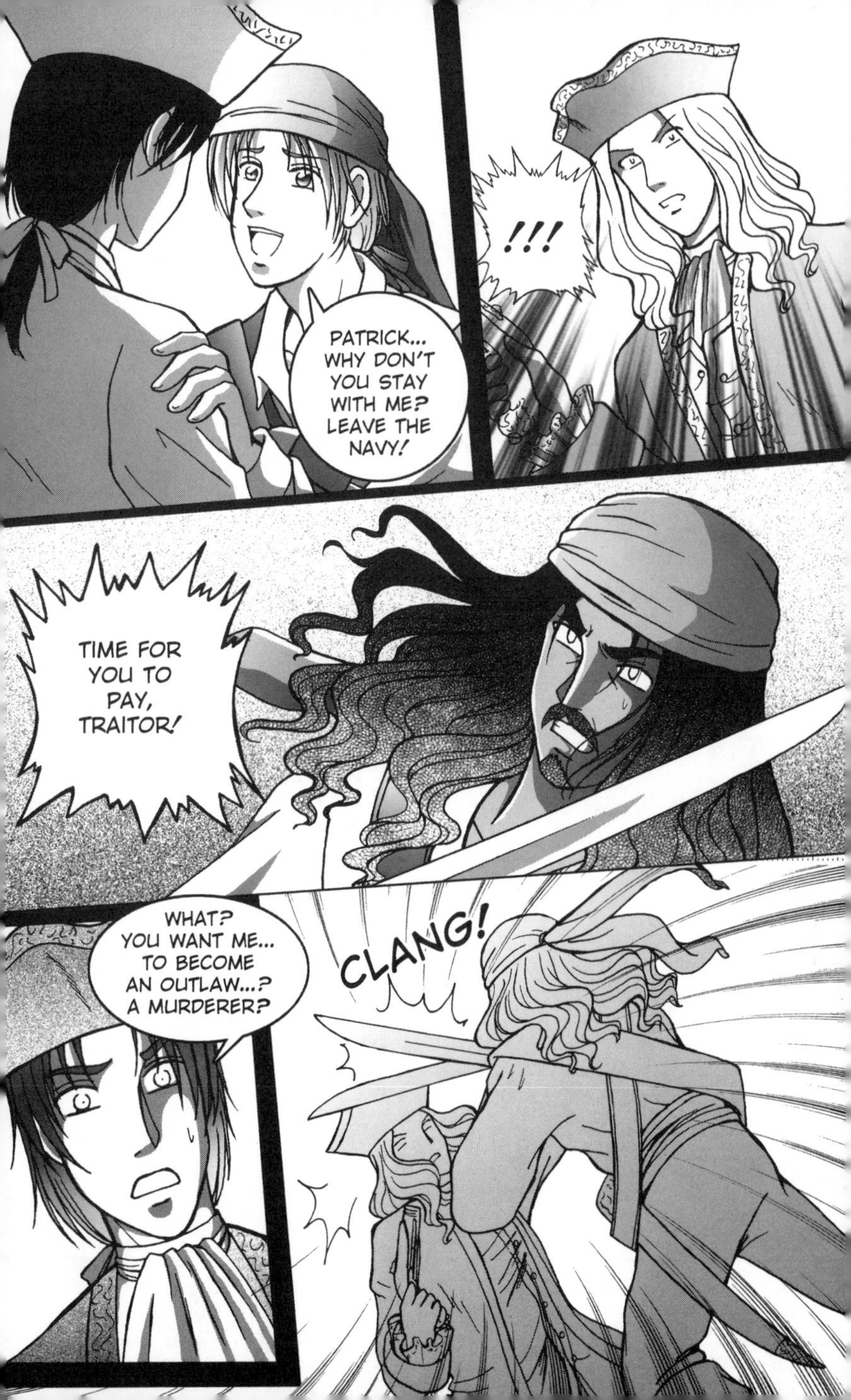
PATRICK... WHY DON'T YOU STAY WITH ME? LEAVE THE NAVY!
!!!
TIME FOR YOU TO PAY, TRAITOR!
WHAT? YOU WANT ME... TO BECOME AN OUTLAW...? A MURDERER?
CLANG!

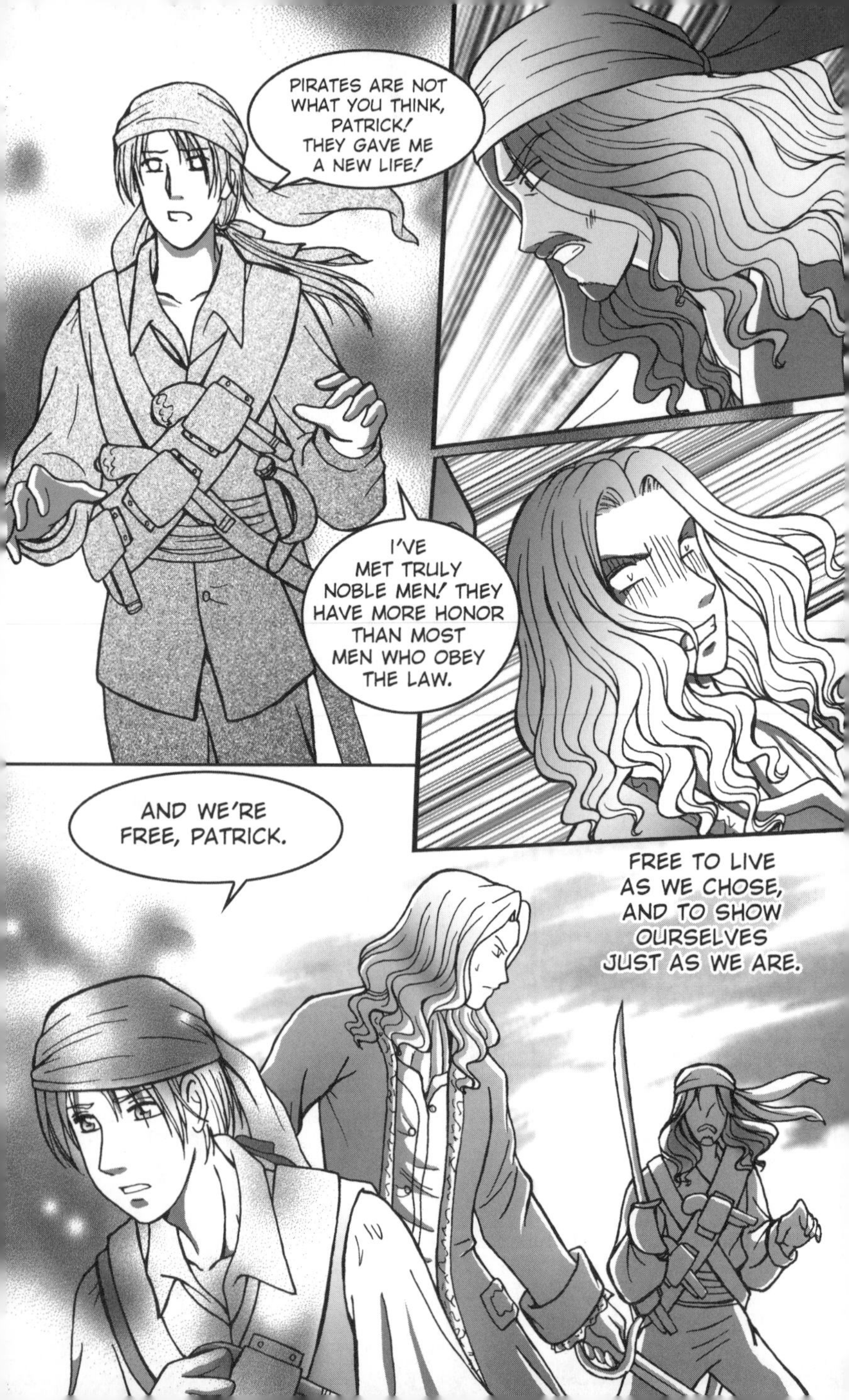
PIRATES ARE NOT WHAT YOU THINK, PATRICK! THEY GAVE ME A NEW LIFE!
I'VE MET TRULY NOBLE MEN! THEY HAVE MORE HONOR THAN MOST MEN WHO OBEY THE LAW.
AND WE'RE FREE, PATRICK.
FREE TO LIVE AS WE CHOSE, AND TO SHOW OURSELVES JUST AS WE ARE.

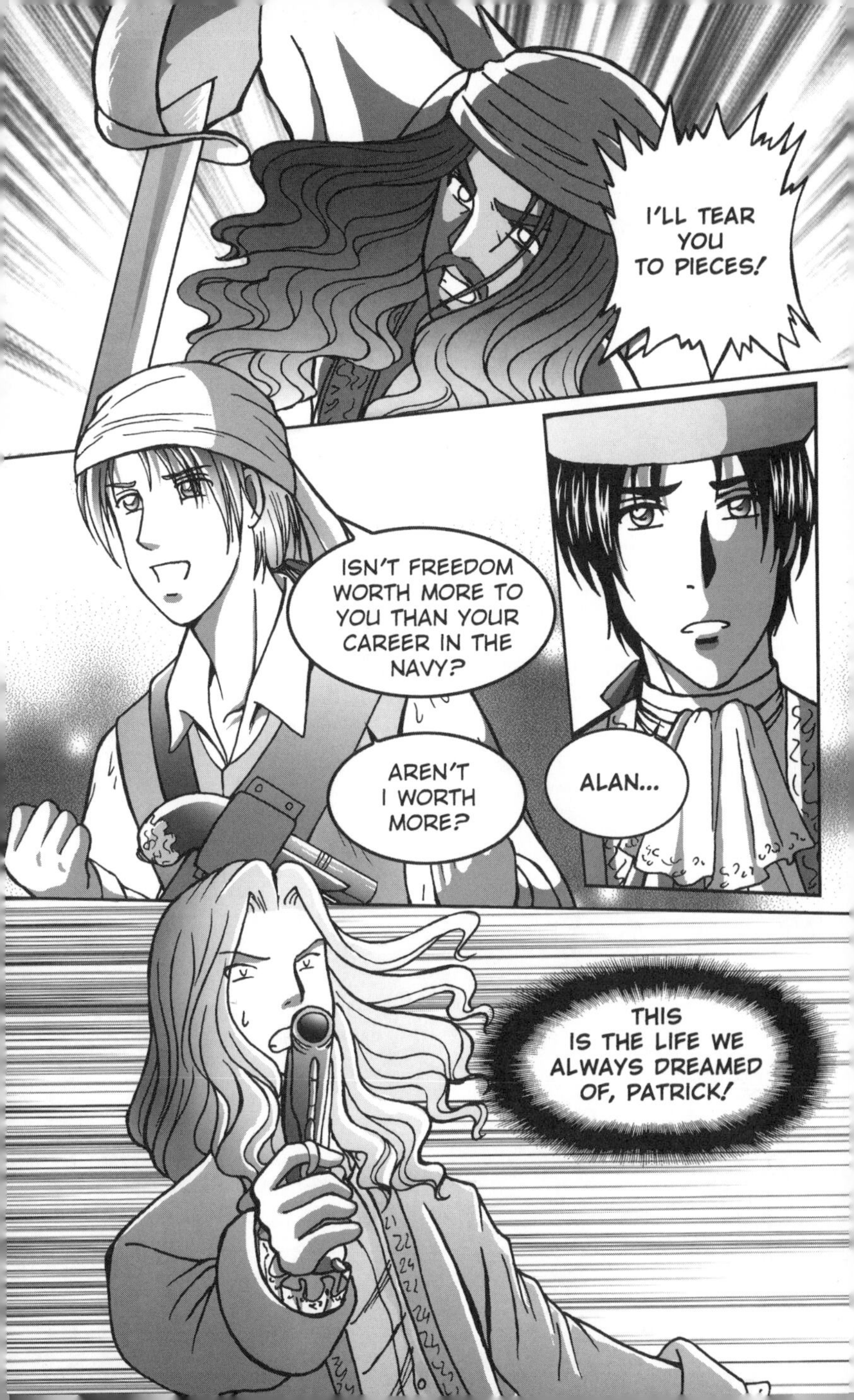
I'LL TEAR YOU TO PIECES!
ISN'T FREEDOM WORTH MORE TO YOU THAN YOUR CAREER IN THE NAVY?
ALAN...
AREN'T I WORTH MORE?
THIS IS THE LIFE WE ALWAYS DREAMED OF, PATRICK!

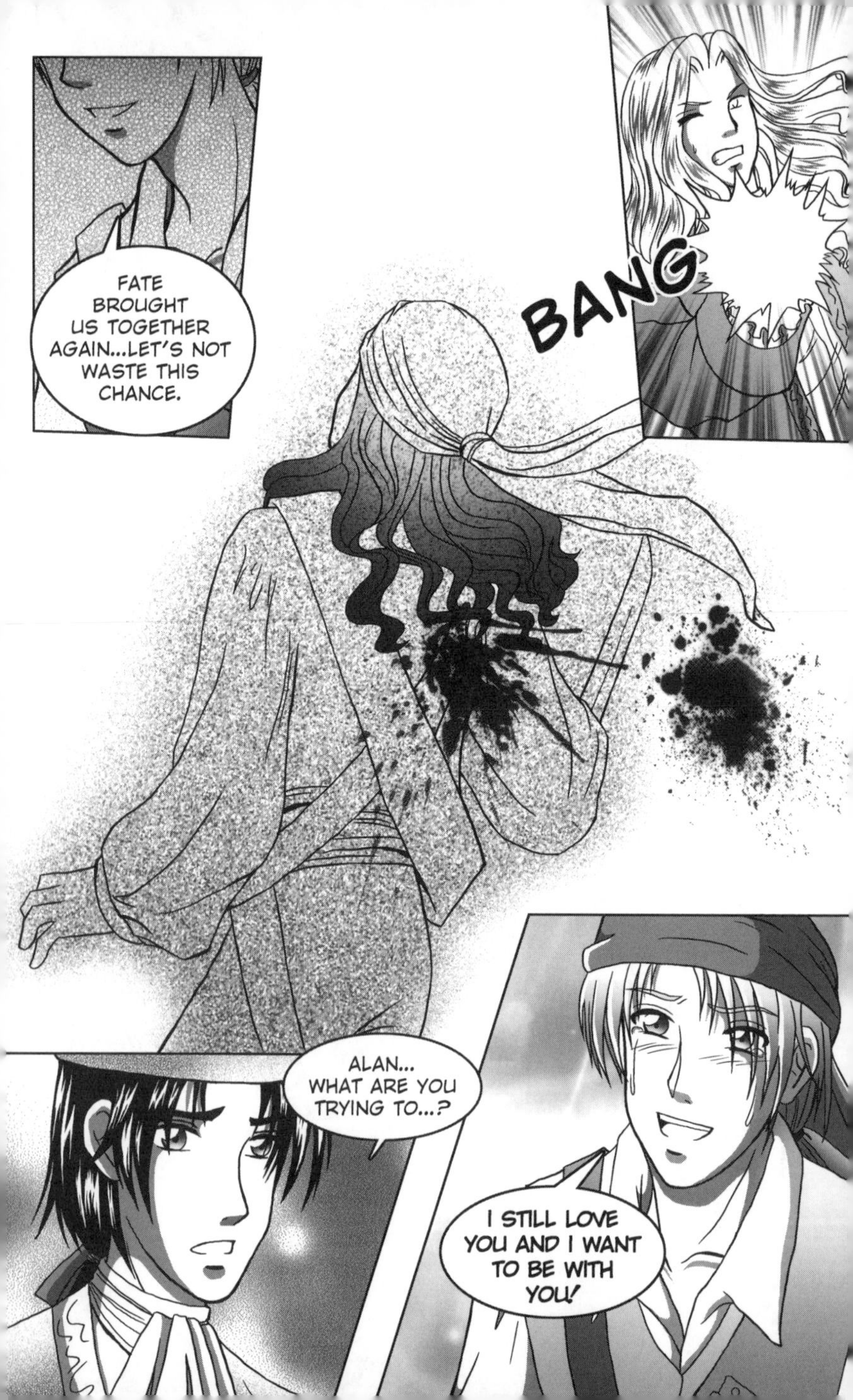
FATE BROUGHT US TOGETHER AGAIN...LET'S NOT WASTE THIS CHANCE.
BANG
ALAN... WHAT ARE YOU TRYING TO...?
I STILL LOVE YOU AND I WANT TO BE WITH YOU!

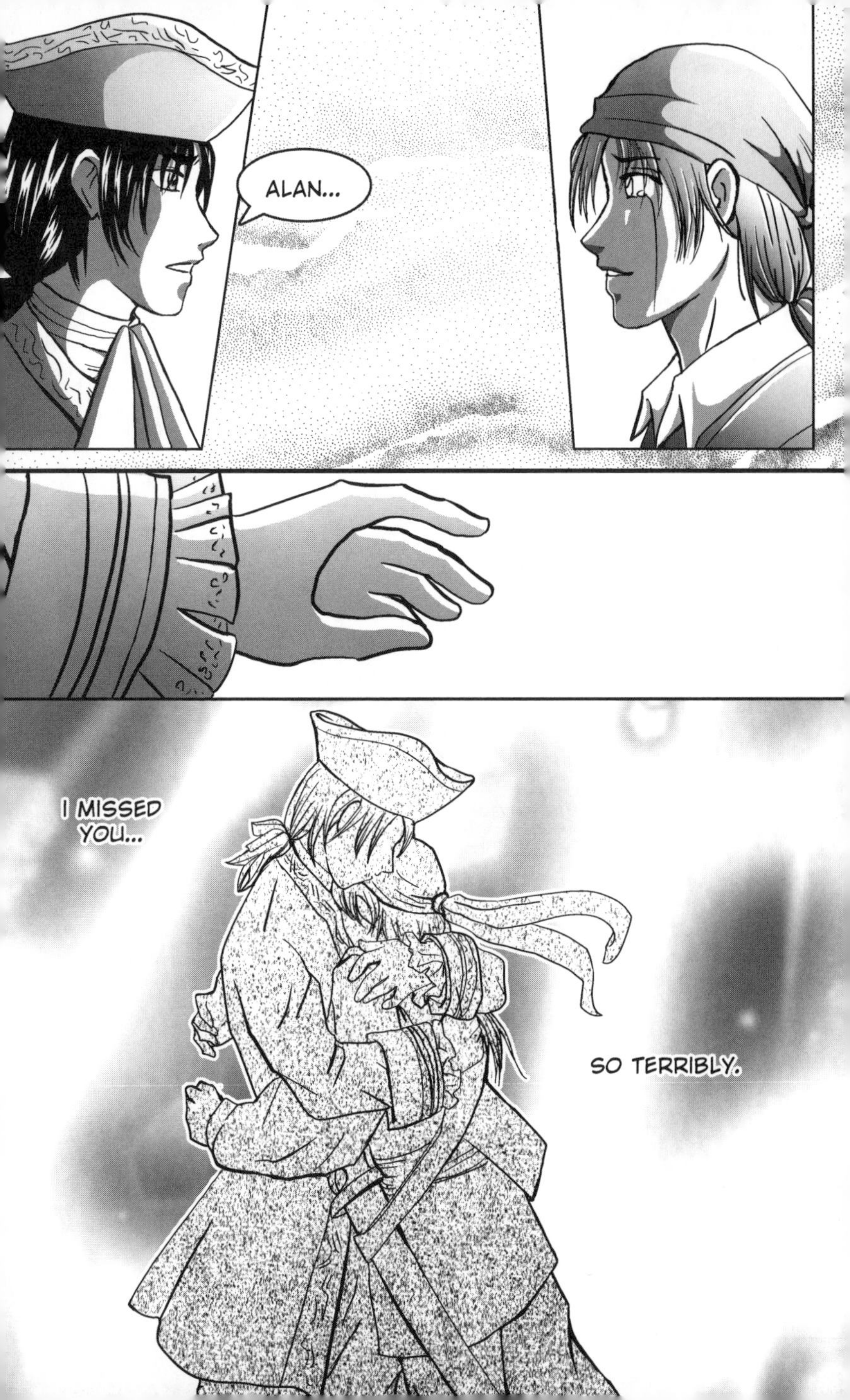
ALAN...
I MISSED YOU...
SO TERRIBLY.

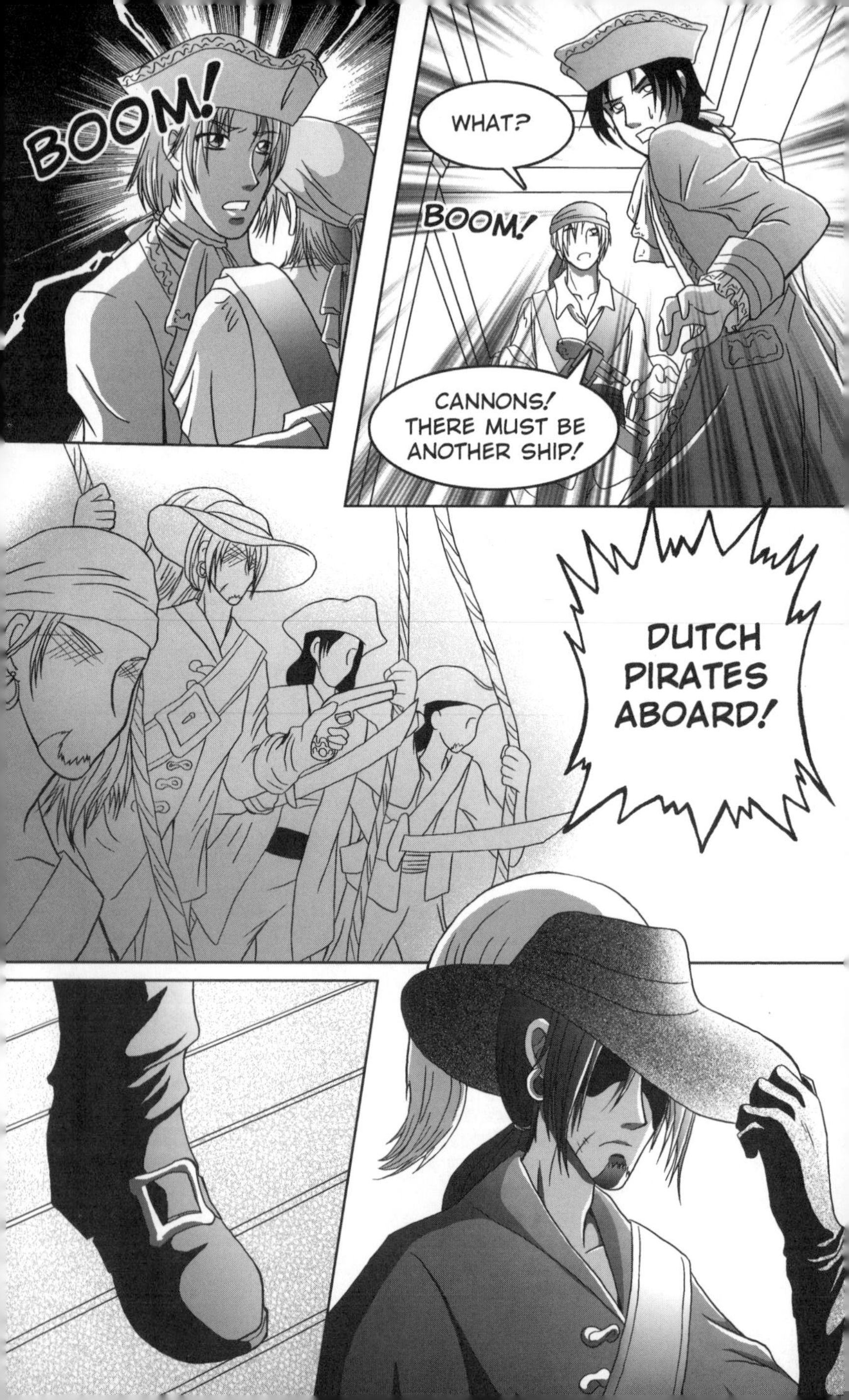
BOOM!
WHAT?
BOOM!
CANNONS! THERE MUST BE ANOTHER SHIP!
DUTCH PIRATES ABOARD!

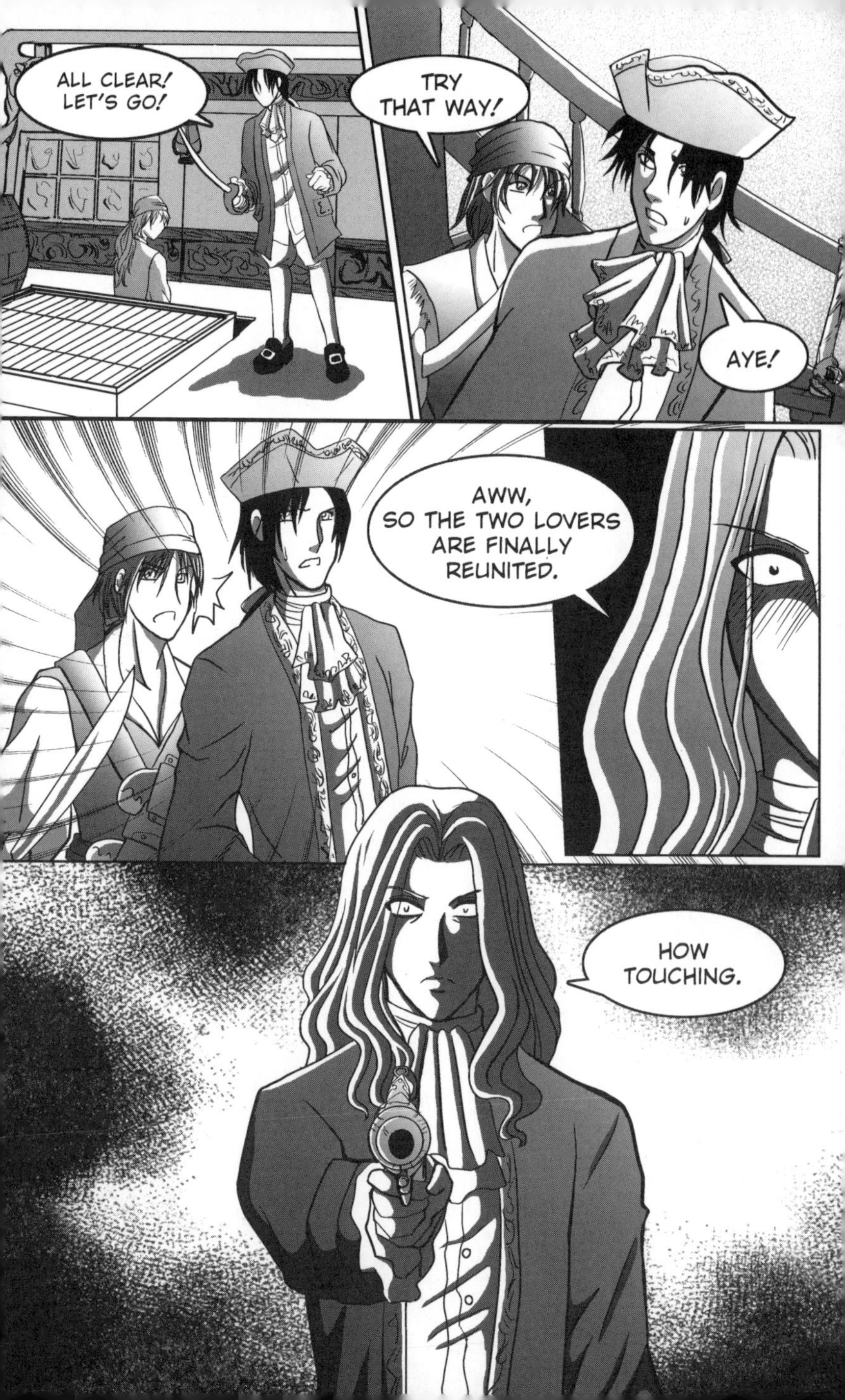
ALL CLEAR! LET'S GO!
TRY THAT WAY!
AYE!
AWW, SO THE TWO LOVERS ARE FINALLY REUNITED.
HOW TOUCHING.

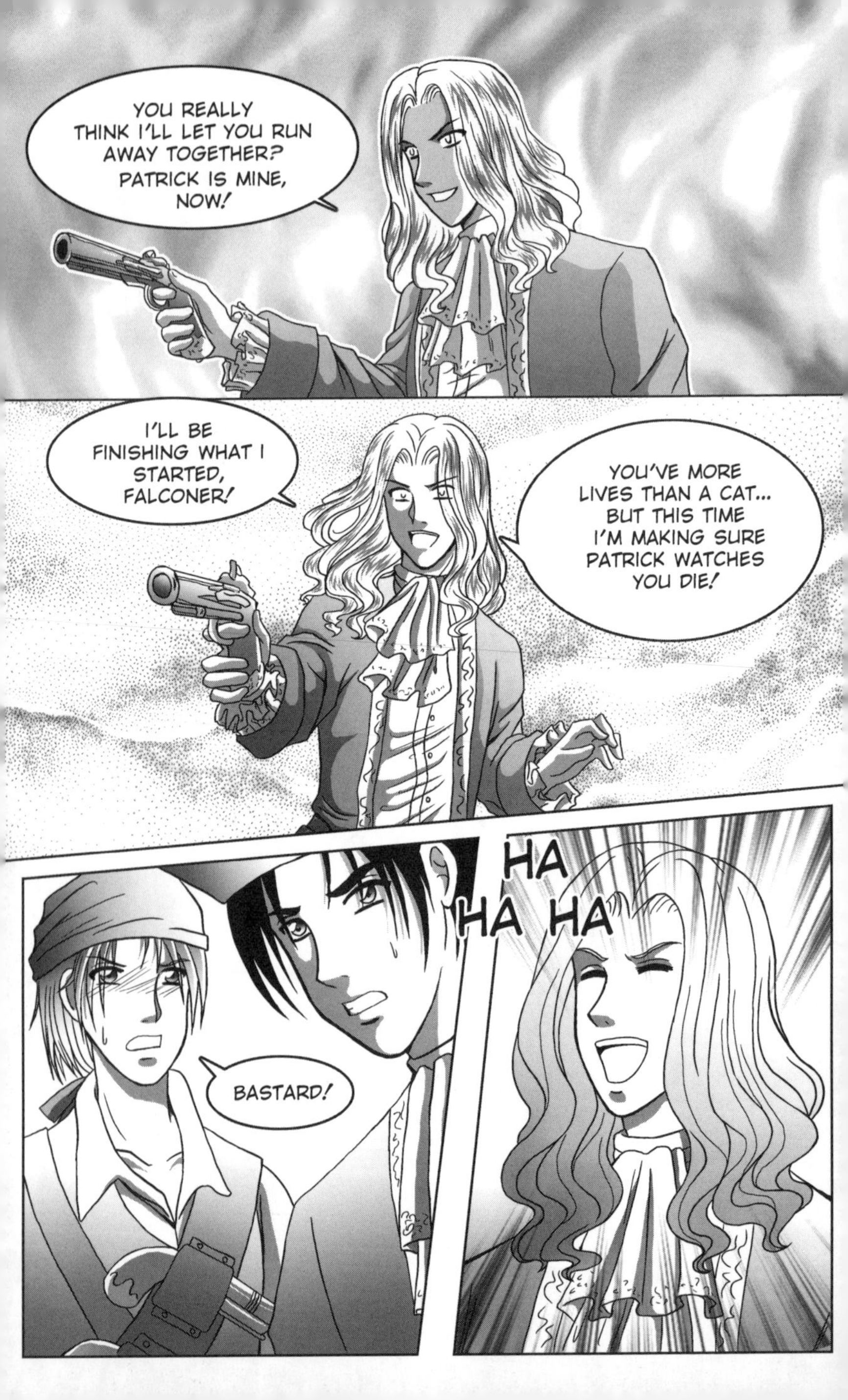
YOU REALLY THINK I'LL LET YOU RUN AWAY TOGETHER? PATRICK IS MINE, NOW!
I'LL BE FINISHING WHAT I STARTED, FALCONER!
YOU'VE MORE LIVES THAN A CAT... BUT THIS TIME I'M MAKING SURE PATRICK WATCHES YOU DIE!
HA HA HA
BASTARD!

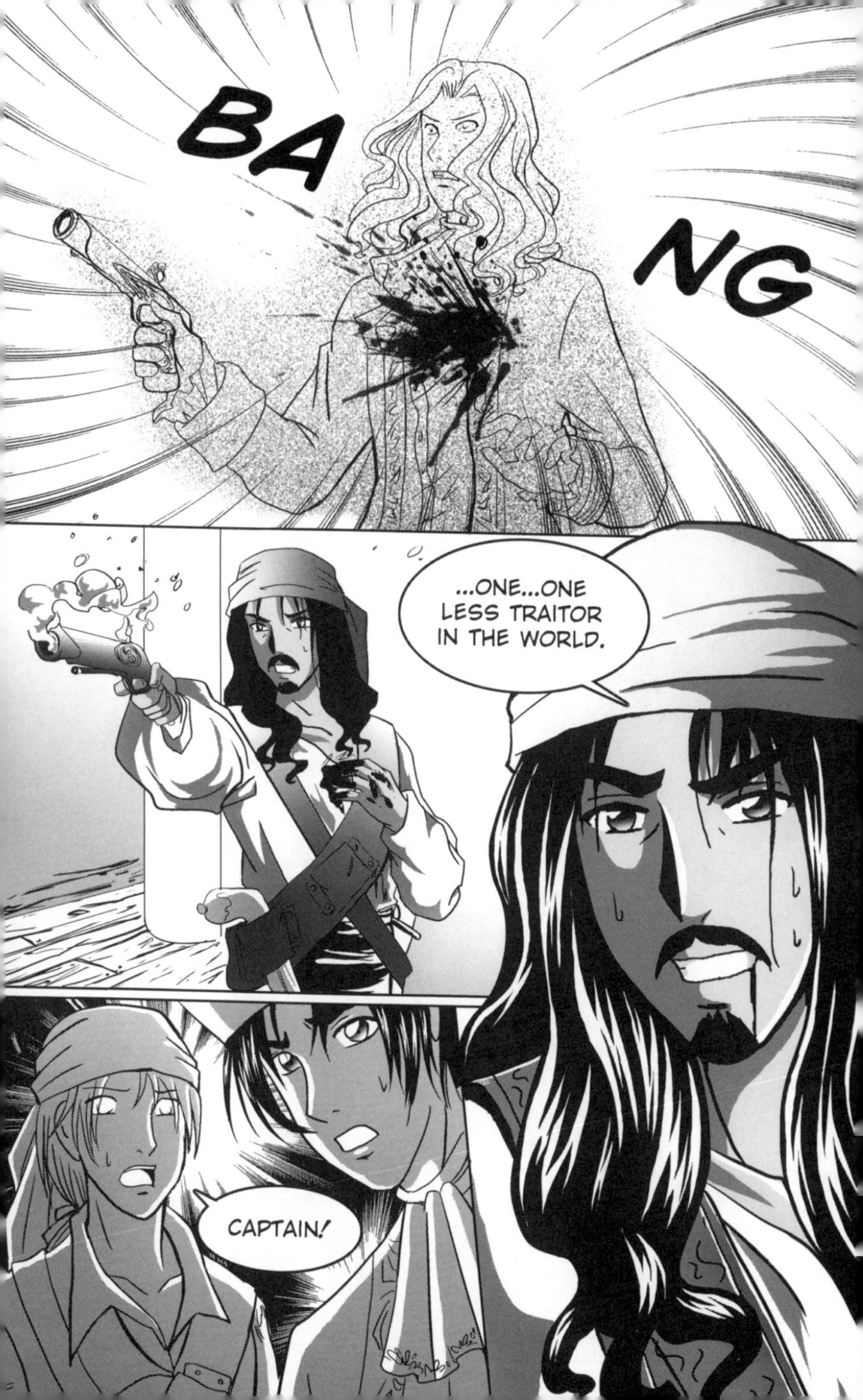
BA
NG
...ONE...ONE LESS TRAITOR IN THE WORLD.
CAPTAIN!

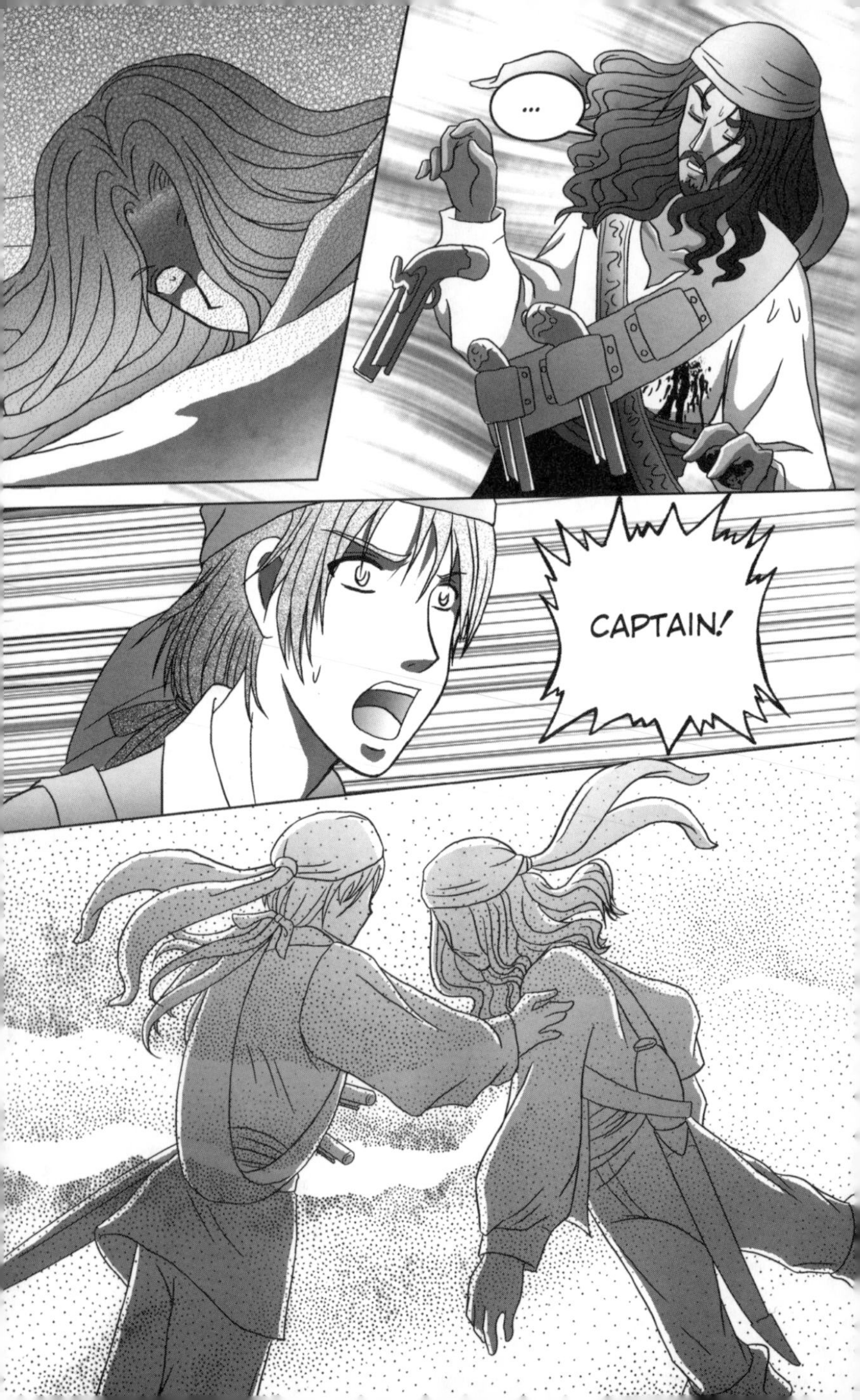
...
CAPTAIN!

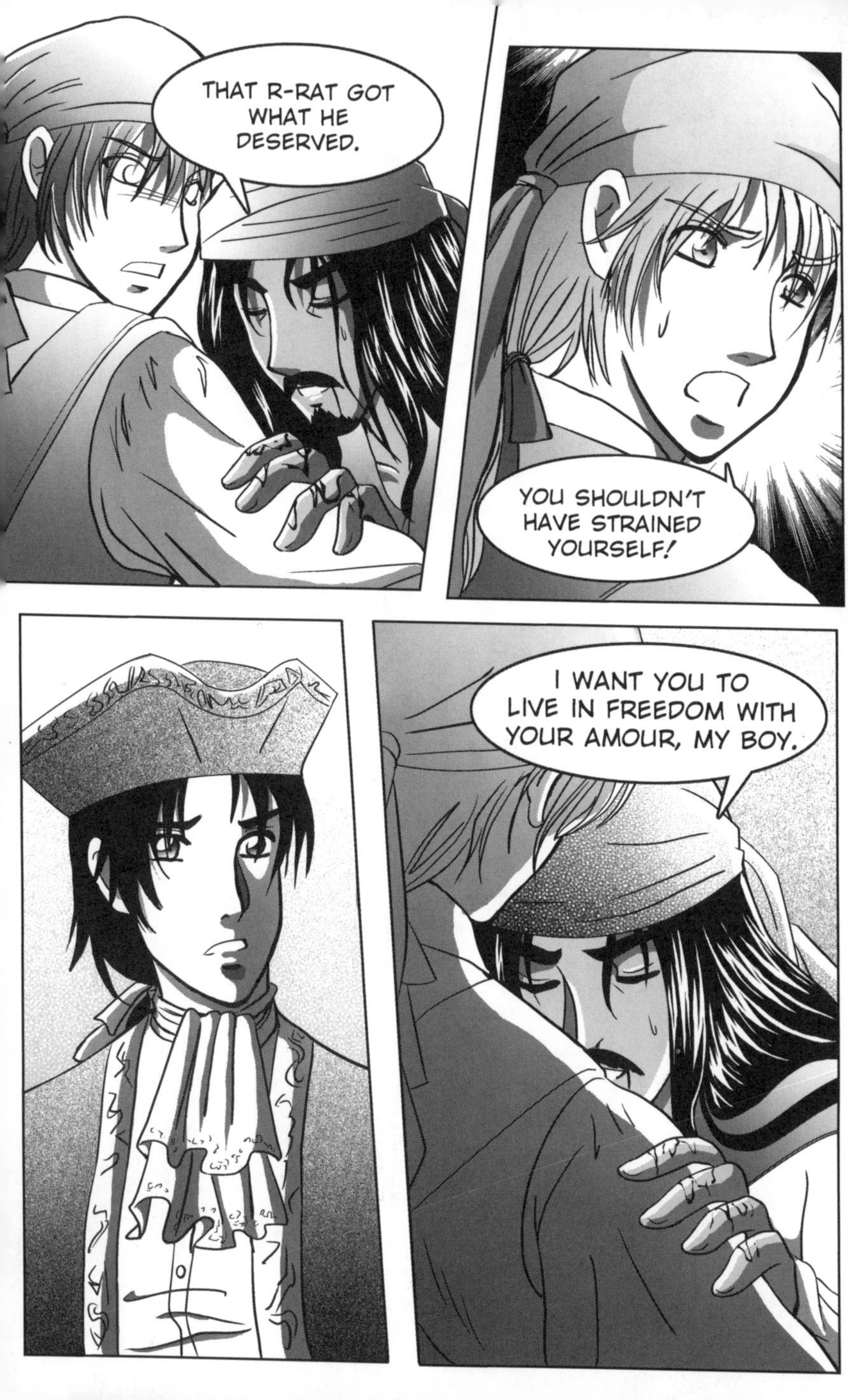
THAT R-RAT GOT WHAT HE DESERVED.
YOU SHOULDN'T HAVE STRAINED YOURSELF!
I WANT YOU TO LIVE IN FREEDOM WITH YOUR AMOUR, MY BOY.

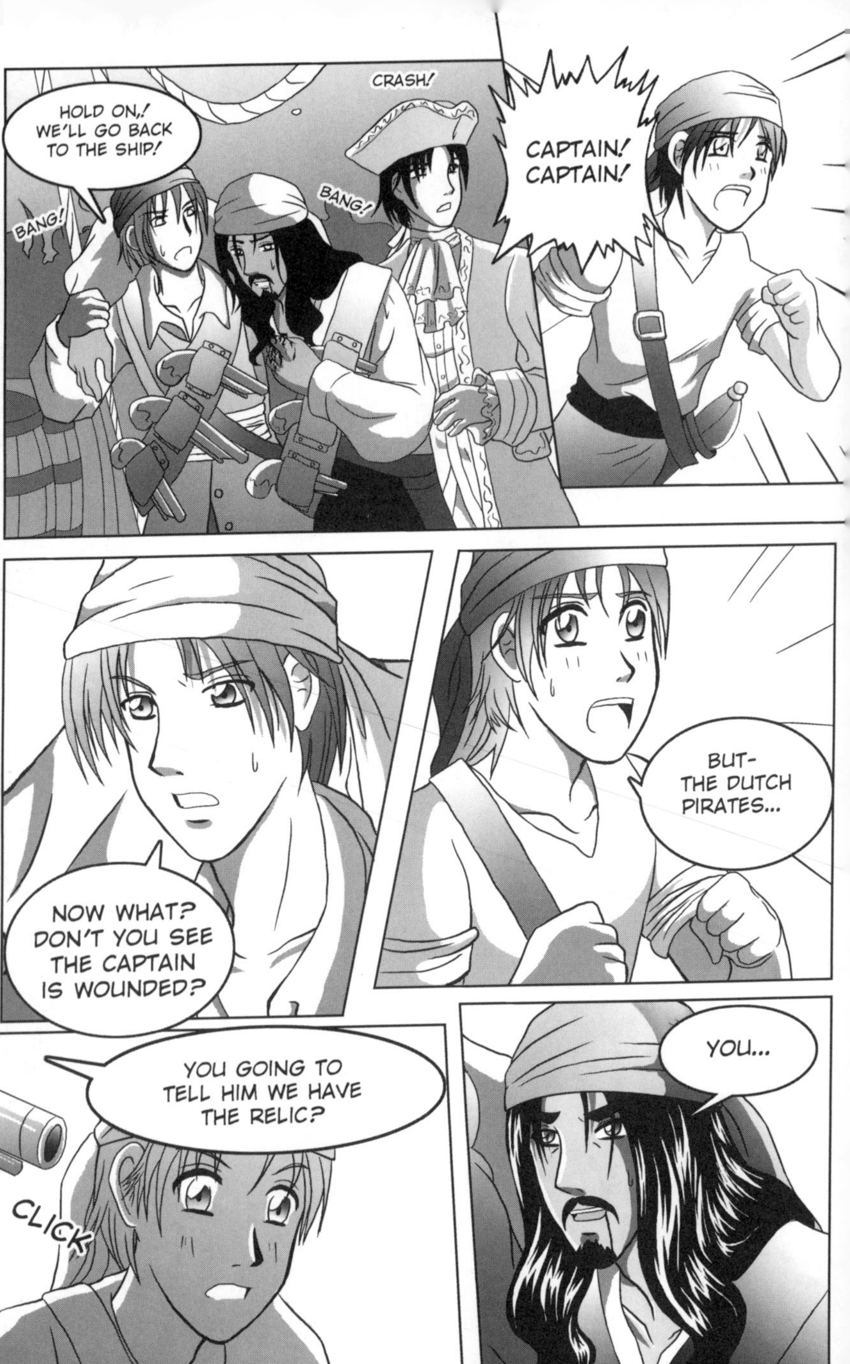
HOLD ON,! WE'LL GO BACK TO THE SHIP!
CRASH!
BANG!
BANG!
CAPTAIN! CAPTAIN!
BUT- THE DUTCH PIRATES...
NOW WHAT? DON'T YOU SEE THE CAPTAIN IS WOUNDED?
YOU GOING TO TELL HIM WE HAVE THE RELIC?
CLICK
YOU...

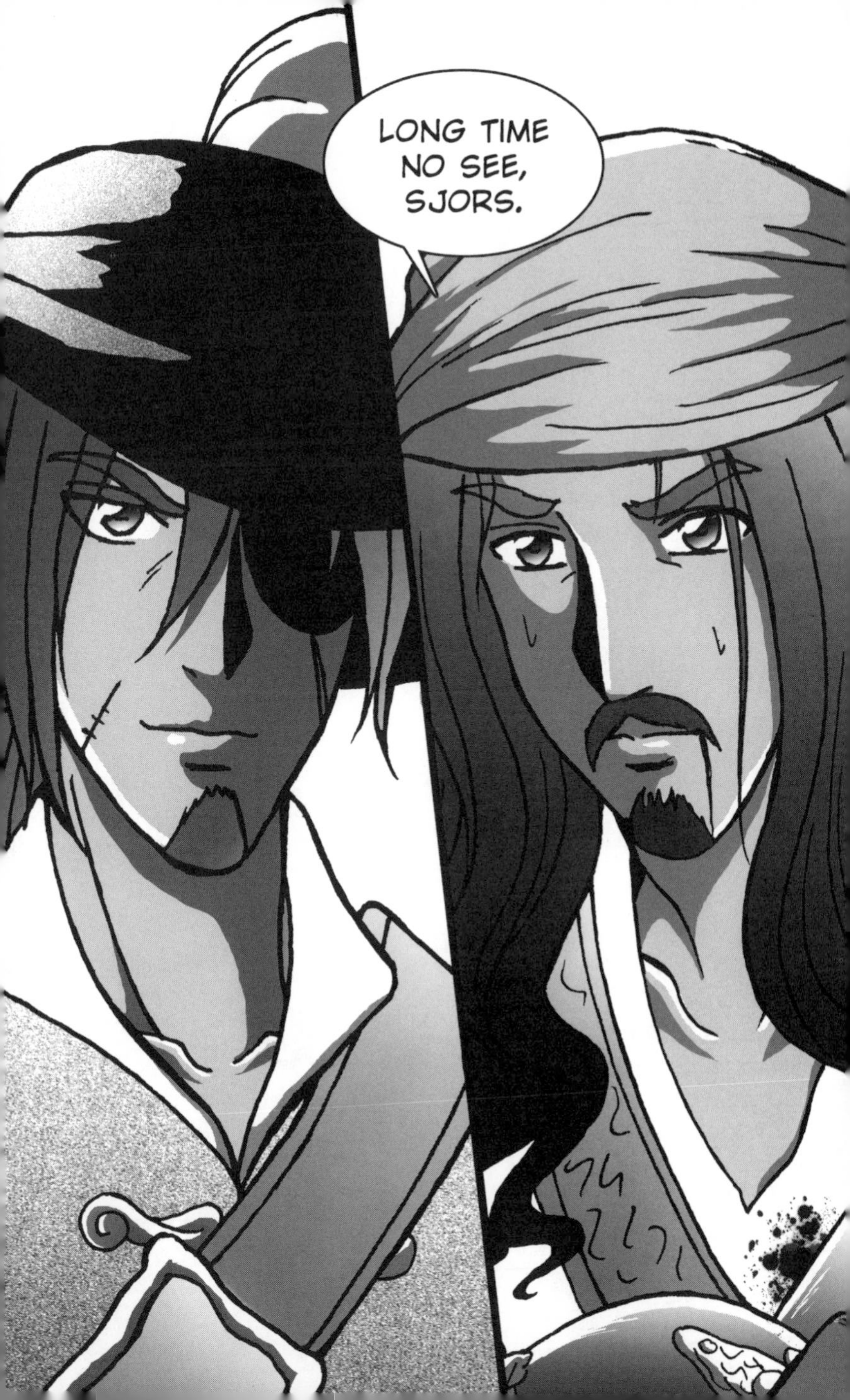
LONG TIME NO SEE, SJORS.

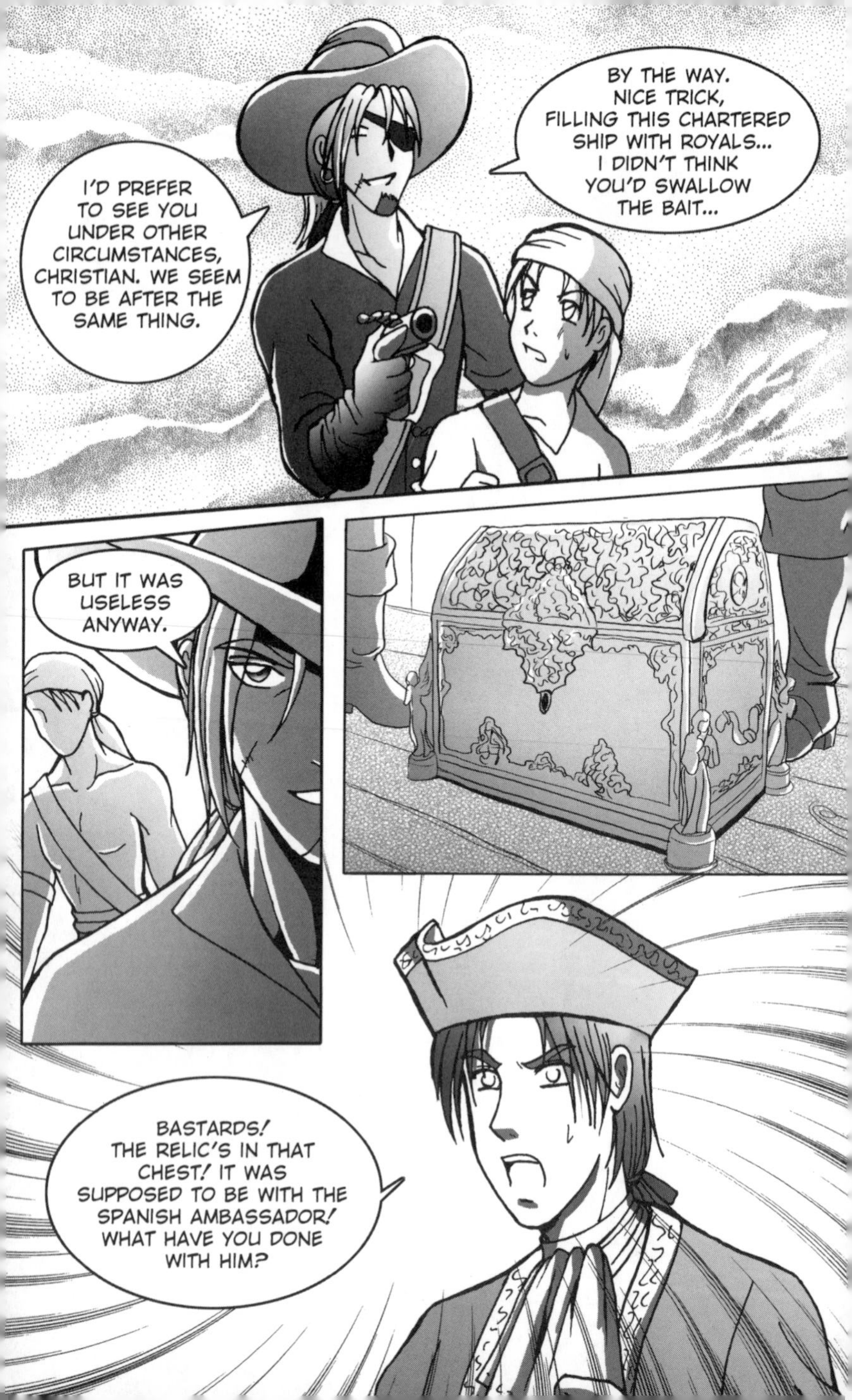

I'D PREFER TO SEE YOU UNDER OTHER CIRCUMSTANCES, CHRISTIAN. WE SEEM TO BE AFTER THE SAME THING.
BY THE WAY. NICE TRICK, FILLING THIS CHARTERED SHIP WITH ROYALS... I DIDN'T THINK YOU'D SWALLOW THE BAIT...
BUT IT WAS USELESS ANYWAY.
BASTARDS! THE RELIC'S IN THAT CHEST! IT WAS SUPPOSED TO BE WITH THE SPANISH AMBASSADOR! WHAT HAVE YOU DONE WITH HIM?

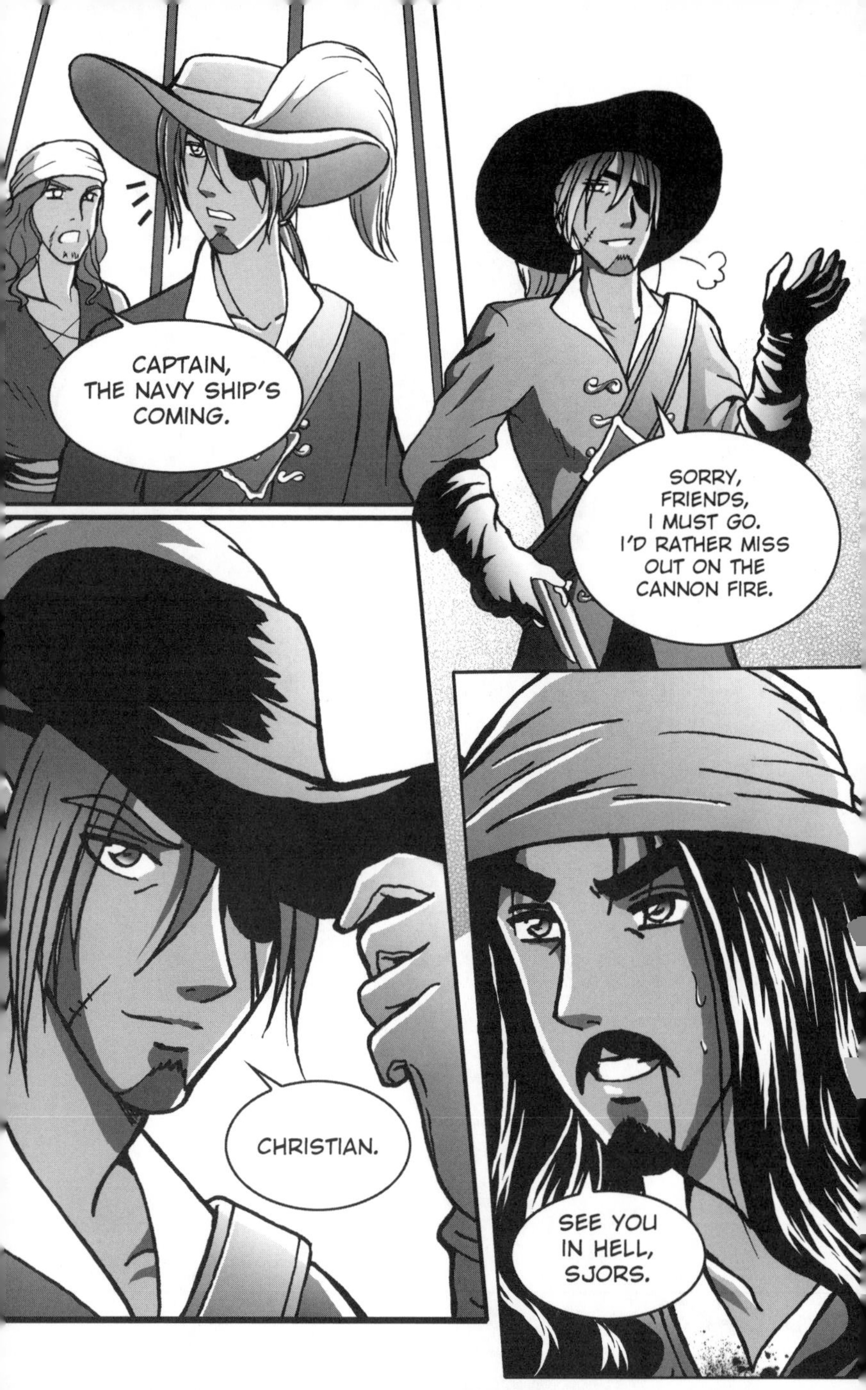
CAPTAIN, THE NAVY SHIP'S COMING.
SORRY, FRIENDS, I MUST GO. I'D RATHER MISS OUT ON THE CANNON FIRE.
CHRISTIAN.
SEE YOU IN HELL, SJORS.

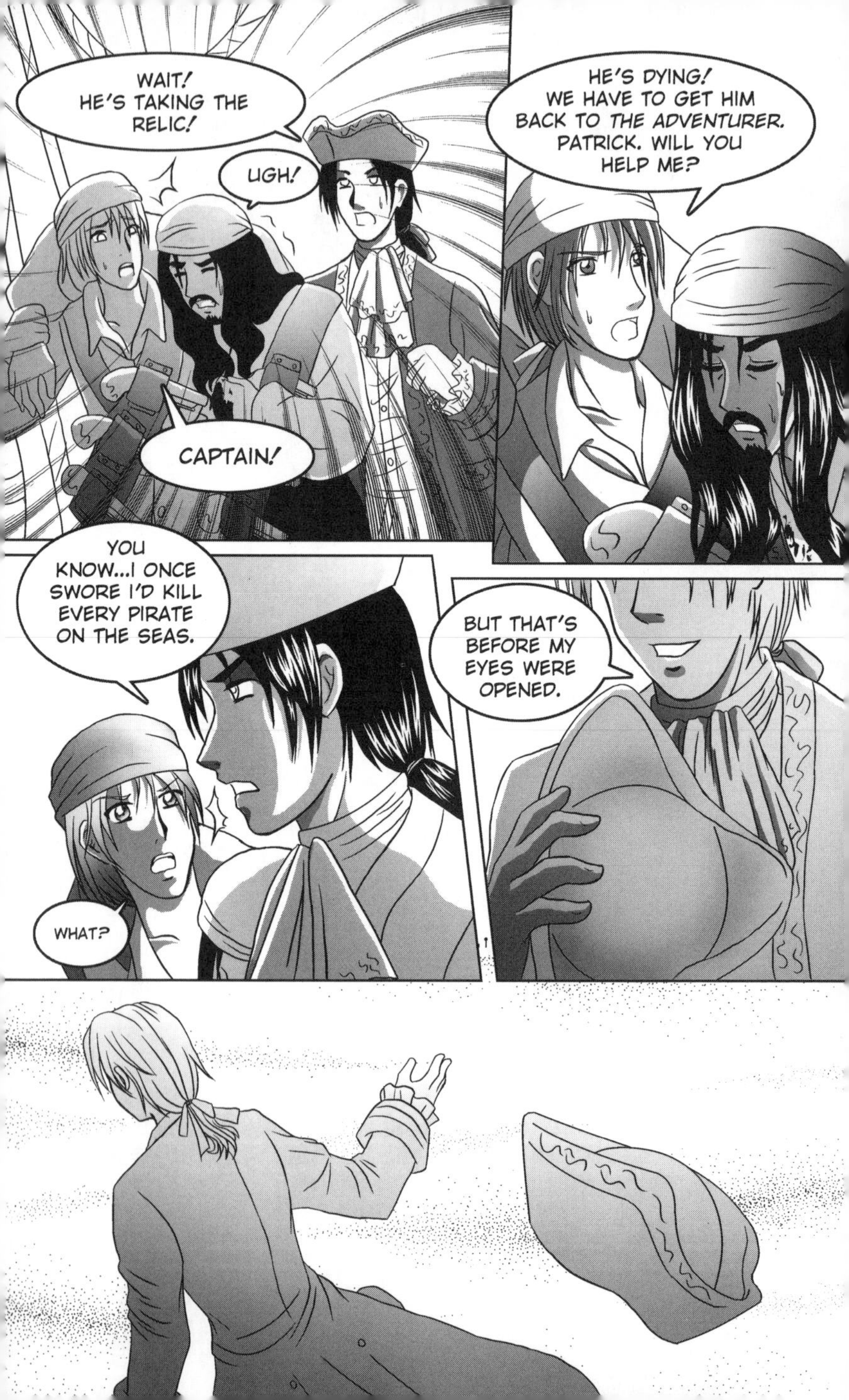
WAIT! HE'S TAKING THE RELIC!
UGH!
CAPTAIN!
HE'S DYING! WE HAVE TO GET HIM BACK TO THE ADVENTURER. PATRICK. WILL YOU HELP ME?
YOU KNOW...I ONCE SWORE I'D KILL EVERY PIRATE ON THE SEAS.
WHAT?
BUT THAT'S BEFORE MY EYES WERE OPENED.

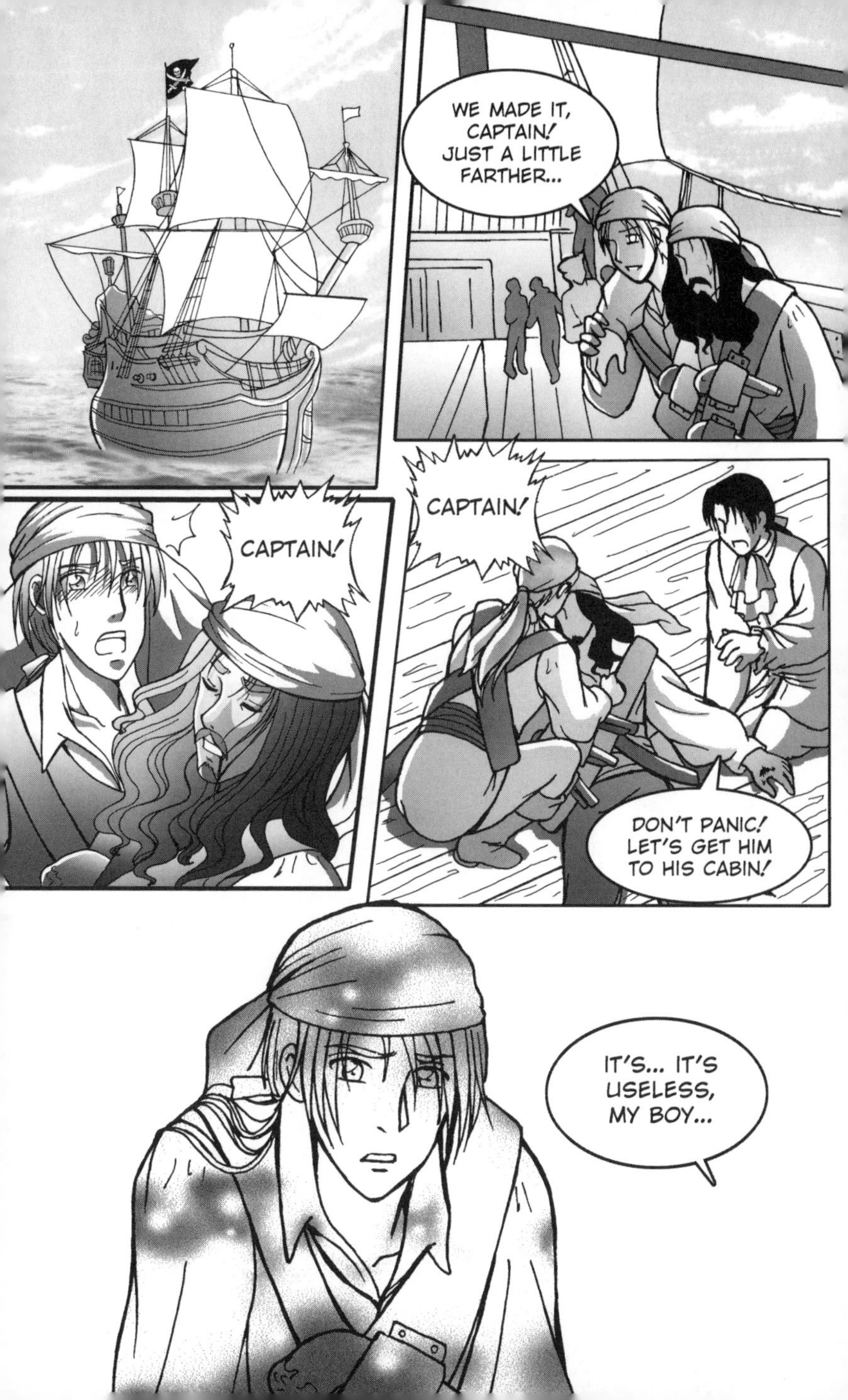
WE MADE IT, CAPTAIN! JUST A LITTLE FARTHER...
CAPTAIN!
CAPTAIN!
DON'T PANIC! LET'S GET HIM TO HIS CABIN!
IT'S... IT'S USELESS, MY BOY...

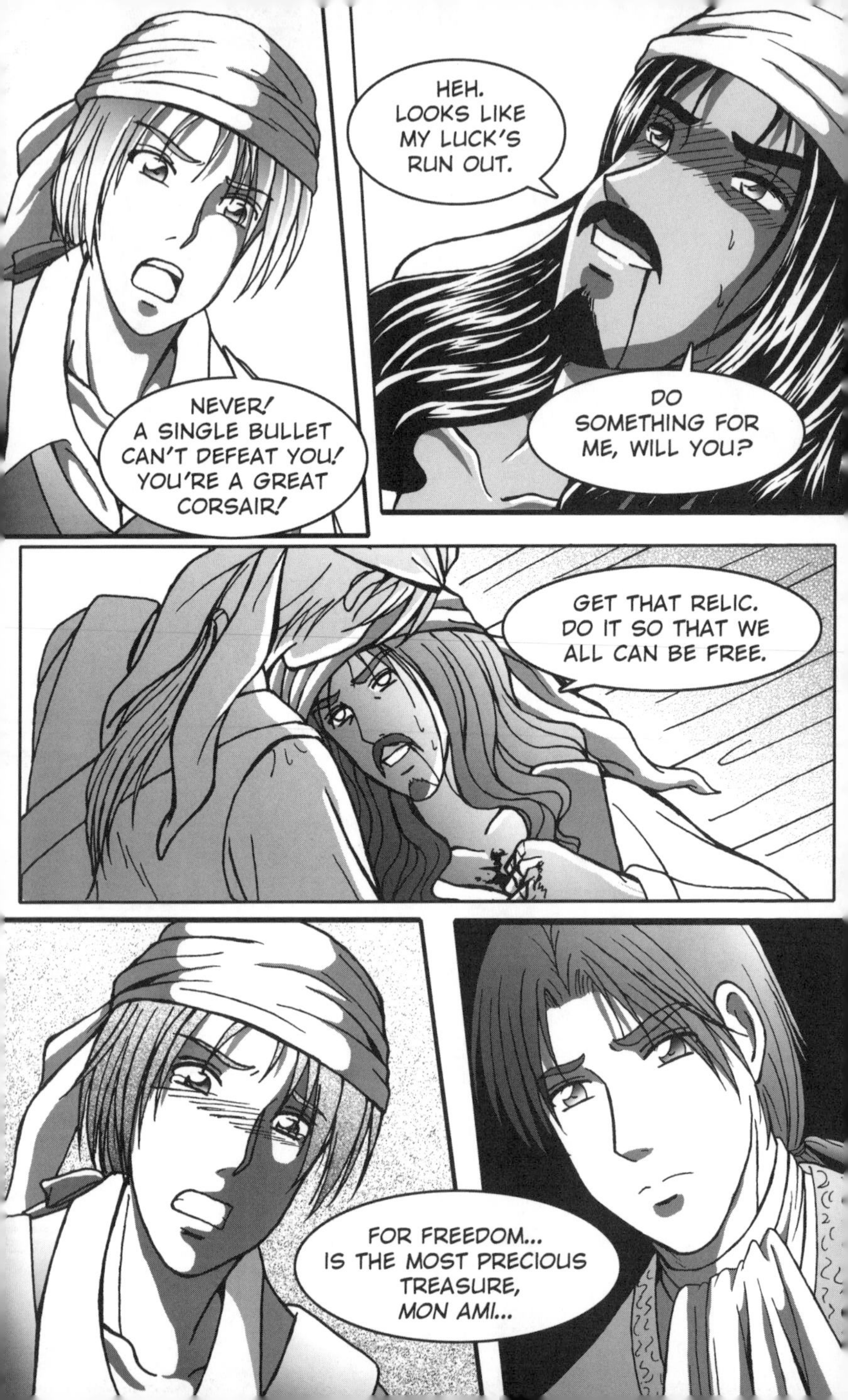
NEVER! A SINGLE BULLET CAN'T DEFEAT YOU! YOU'RE A GREAT CORSAIR!
HEH. LOOKS LIKE MY LUCK'S RUN OUT.
DO SOMETHING FOR ME, WILL YOU?
GET THAT RELIC. DO IT SO THAT WE ALL CAN BE FREE.
FOR FREEDOM... IS THE MOST PRECIOUS TREASURE, MON AMI...

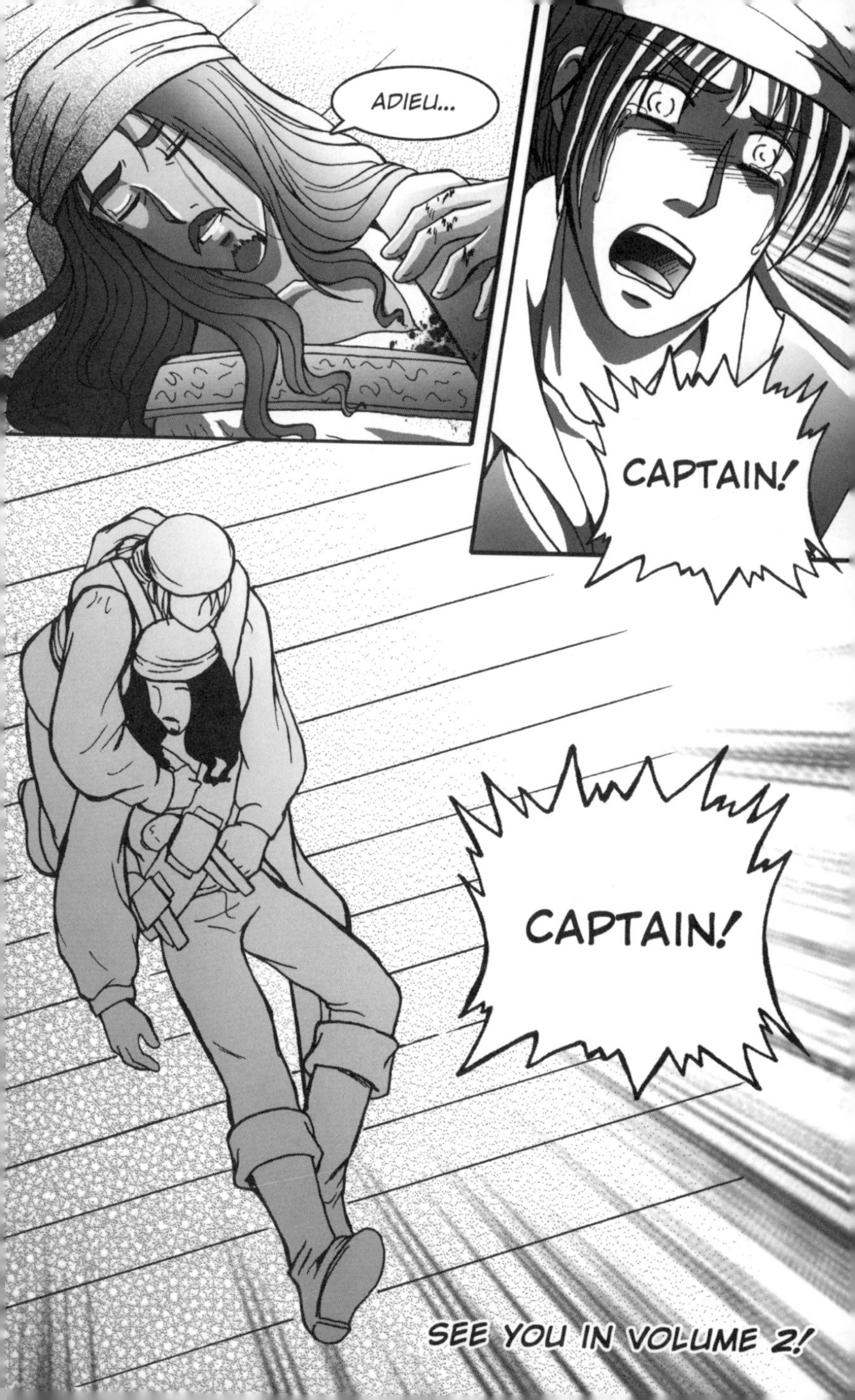
ADIEU...
CAPTAIN!
CAPTAIN!
SEE YOU IN VOLUME 2!

"THE BREEZE FAIR AFT, ALL SAILS ON HIGH,
TEN GUNS ON EACH SIDE MOUNTED SEEN,
SHE DOES NOT CUT THE SEA, BUT FLY,
A SWIFTLY SAILING BRIGANTINE;
A PIRATE BARK, THE "DREADED" NAMED,
FOR HER SURPASSING BOLDNESS FAMED,
ON EVERY SEA WELL-KNOWN AND SHORE,
FROM SIDE TO SIDE THEIR BOUNDARIES O'ER,
THE MOON IN STREAKS THE WAVES ILLUMES
HOARSE GROANS THE WIND THE RIGGING THROUGH;

IN GENTLE MOTION RAISED ASSUMES
THE SEA A SILVERY SHADE WITH BLUE;
WHILST SINGING GAILY ON THE POOP
THE PIRATE CAPTAIN, IN A GROUP,
SEES EUROPE HERE, THERE ASIA LIES,
AND STAMBOUL IN THE FRONT ARISE.

SAIL ON, MY SWIFT ONE! NOTHING FEAR;
NOR CALM, NOR STORM, NOR FOEMAN'S FORCE,
SHALL MAKE THEE YIELD IN THY CAREER
OR TURN THEE FROM THY COURSE.
DESPITE THE ENGLISH CRUISERS FLEET
WE HAVE FULL TWENTY PRIZES MADE;
AND SEE THEIR FLAGS BENEATH MY FEET
A HUNDRED NATIONS LAID.

MY TREASURE IS MY GALLANT BARK,
MY ONLY GOD IS LIBERTY;
MY LAW IS MIGHT, THE WIND MY MARK,
MY COUNTRY IS THE SEA.

...

LOOK WHEN A SHIP OUR SIGNALS RING,
FULL SAIL TO FLY HOW QUICK SHE'S VEERED!
FOR OF THE SEA I AM THE KING,
MY FURY'S TO BE FEARED;
BUT EQUALLY WITH ALL I SHARE
WHATE'ER THE WEALTH WE TAKE SUPPLIES;
I ONLY SEEK THE MATCHLESS FAIR,
MY PORTION OF THE PRIZE.

MY TREASURE IS MY GALLANT BARK,
MY ONLY GOD IS LIBERTY;
MY LAW IS MIGHT, THE WIND MY MARK,
MY COUNTRY IS THE SEA.

"I AM CONDEMNED TO DIE ! I LAUGH;
FOR, IF MY FATES ARE KINDLY SPED,
MY DOOMER FROM HIS OWN SHIP'S STAFF
PERHAPS I'LL HANG INSTEAD.
AND IF I FALL, WHY WHAT IS LIFE?
FOR LOST I GAVE IT THEN AS DUE,
WHEN FROM SLAVERY'S YOKE IN STRIFE
A ROVER! I WITHDREW.

MY TREASURE IS MY GALLANT BARK;
MY ONLY GOD IS LIBERTY;
MY LAW IS MIGHT, THE WIND MY MARK,
MY COUNTRY IS THE SEA. "

JOSÉ DE ESPRONCEDA (1808-1842)
CANCIÓN OF THE PIRATE (FRAGMENTS)

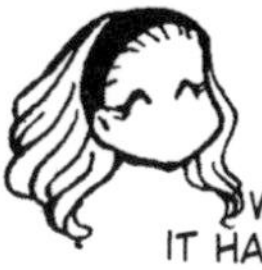

HI! THIS IS ANA AND MERCEDES, AKA STUDIO KAWAII.

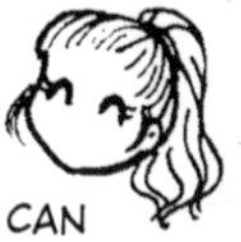

WE HOPE YOU LIKED THE STORY OF ALAN AND PATRICK. IT HAS BEEN MONTHS OF HARD WORK, BUT AT LAST ALL YOU CAN ENJOY IT!!

THIS IS OUR FIRST FULL-LENGTH NOVEL FOR *YAOI PRESS*. SO FAR OUR WORKS HAD BEEN SHORT STORIES, LIKE *THE ONE WHO GILLES DE RAIS LET LIVE* AND *SIR GAWAIN AND THE GREEN KNIGHT*. SO WHEN WE DECIDED TO WRITE *TREASURE*. WE FELT SO SCARED! (LAUGHS) WHY PIRATES? WELL, WE´VE ALWAYS LOVED SWASHBUCKLING STORIES...

WHEN WE BEGIN TO WORK ON A COMIC, FIRST THING WE THINK IS: "WHAT WOULD I WANT TO READ? SO THIS NOVEL IS THE RESULT OF THAT: ADVENTURE, BOY´S LOVE, COMEDY, TRAGEDY (AND A BIT OF SEX!), ALL SET IN THE GOLDEN AGE OF PIRACY AN IDEAL ENVIRONMENT FOR ROMANCE AND ADVENTURE, DON´T YOU THINK SO?

WE DIDN´T WANT *TREASURE* TO BE JUST A BOY´S LOVE STORY, BUT ALSO A STORY ABOUT,FREEDOM, ADVENTURE AND LOYALTY. THAT´S THE POINT OF ESPRONCEDA´S POEM. WE BELIEVE IT CONTAINS EVERYTHING WE WANTED TO DEPICT IN THIS BOOK, SO WE KEPT IT IN MIND ALL THE TIME WHILE CREATING THIS STORY.

THE CHARA DESIGNS WERE VERY CLEAR FROM THE BEGINNING. ALAN AND PATRICK ARE SUCH A SWEET COUPLE, AREN´T THEY? BUT OUR FAVOURITE IS CAPTAIN BEGARDOUX (CALL HIM, CAPTAIN B, OUR FRENCH SUCKS), THOUGH. HE WAS THE CLEAREST IMAGE WE HAD IN MIND. BRAVE, NOBLE AND LOYAL... AND OF COURSE DARK HAIR AND TANNED SKIN...(IF HE WASN´T GAY WE WOULD MARRY HIM!, HA HA!) IT WAS VERY HARD FOR US TO KILL HIM, WE ACTUALLY CRIED WHILE DRAWING THE SCENE... BUT..., IS HE REALLY DEAD? (*EVIL LAUGHS*)

THE BIG SURPRISE HAS BEEN SJORS VAN HOLSTEIN. HE WAS THE LAST CHARACTER DESIGNED, SINCE HE ONLY APPEARS AT THE END OF THIS BOOK. BUT DESPITE THIS AND DESPITE BEING "A BAD GUY", HE´S EVEN MORE POPULAR THAN BEGARDOUX! (OK, HE´S HOT, WE KNOW)

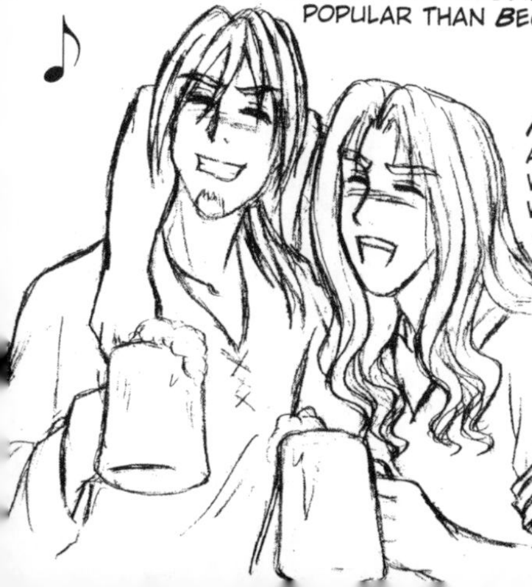

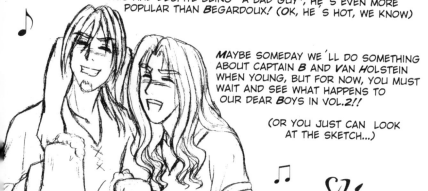

MAYBE SOMEDAY WE´LL DO SOMETHING ABOUT CAPTAIN B AND VAN HOLSTEIN WHEN YOUNG, BUT FOR NOW, YOU MUST WAIT AND SEE WHAT HAPPENS TO OUR DEAR BOYS IN VOL.2!!

(OR YOU JUST CAN LOOK AT THE SKETCH...)

♫

S Kawaii

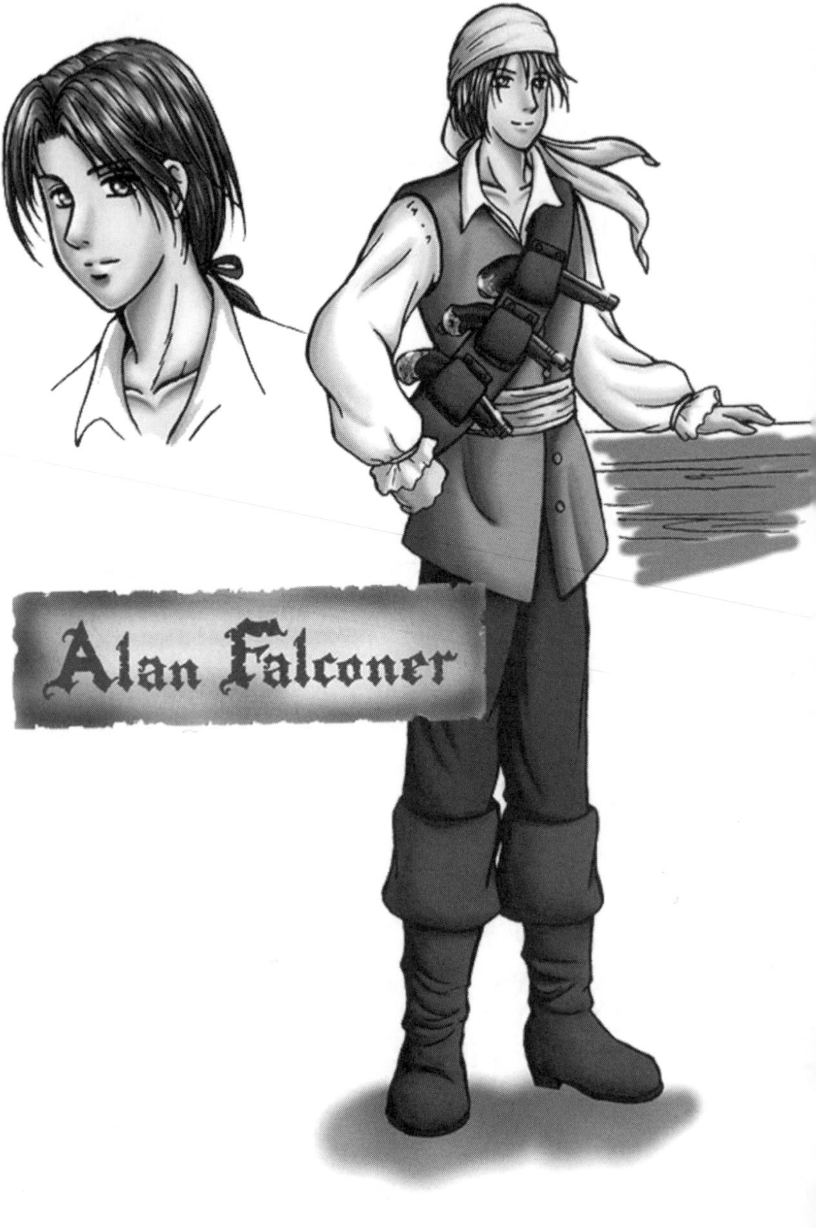
Alan Falconer

Capt. Christian Begardoux

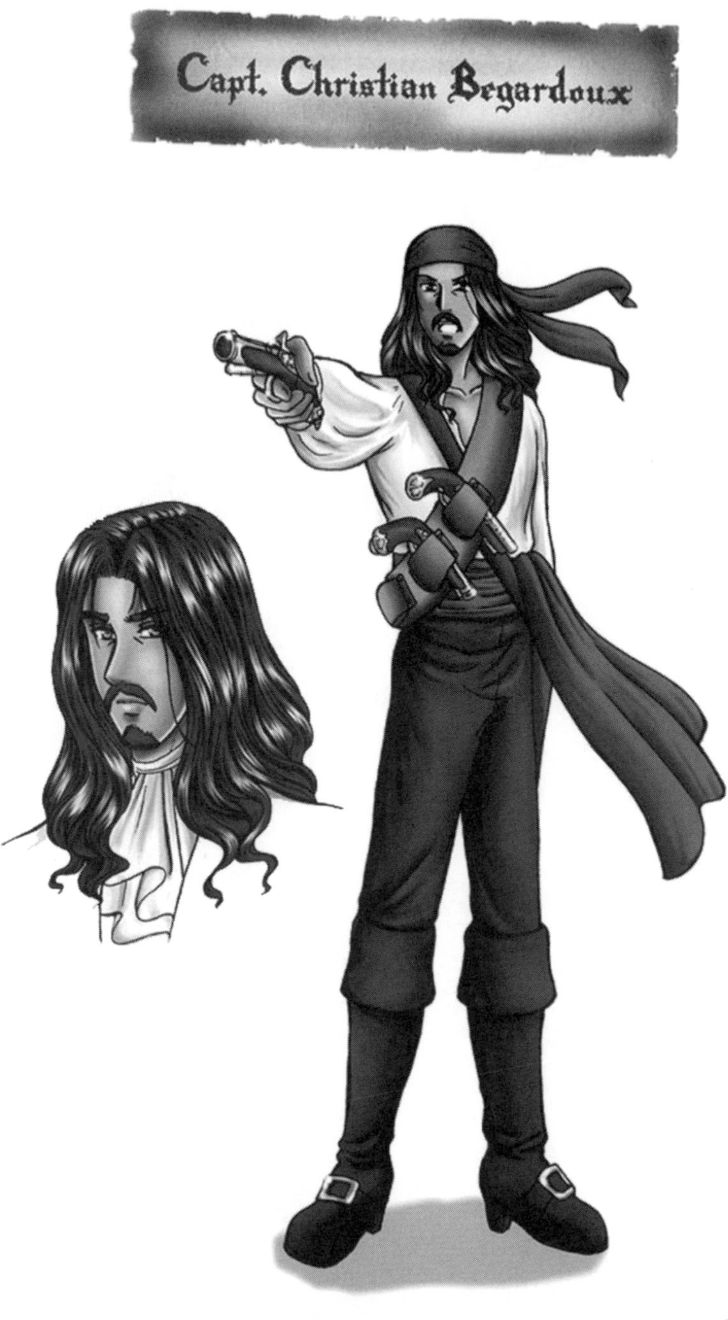

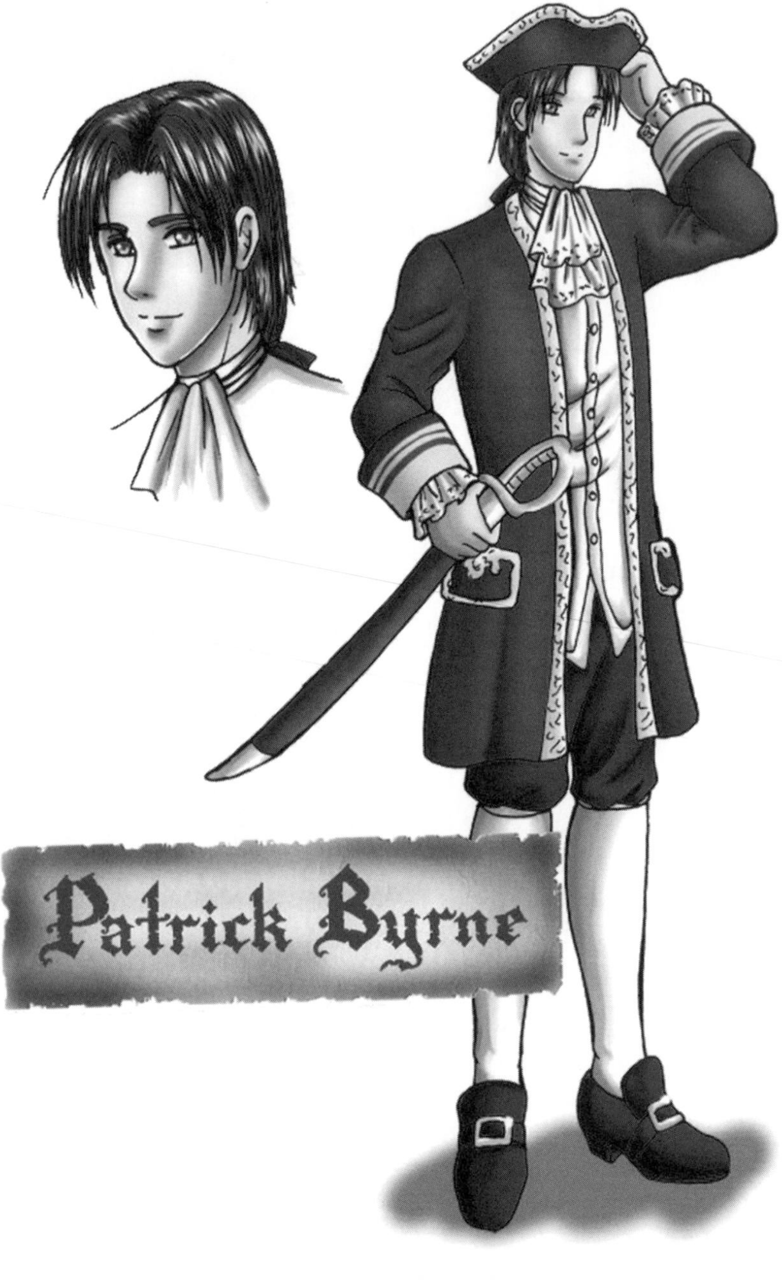
Patrick Byrne

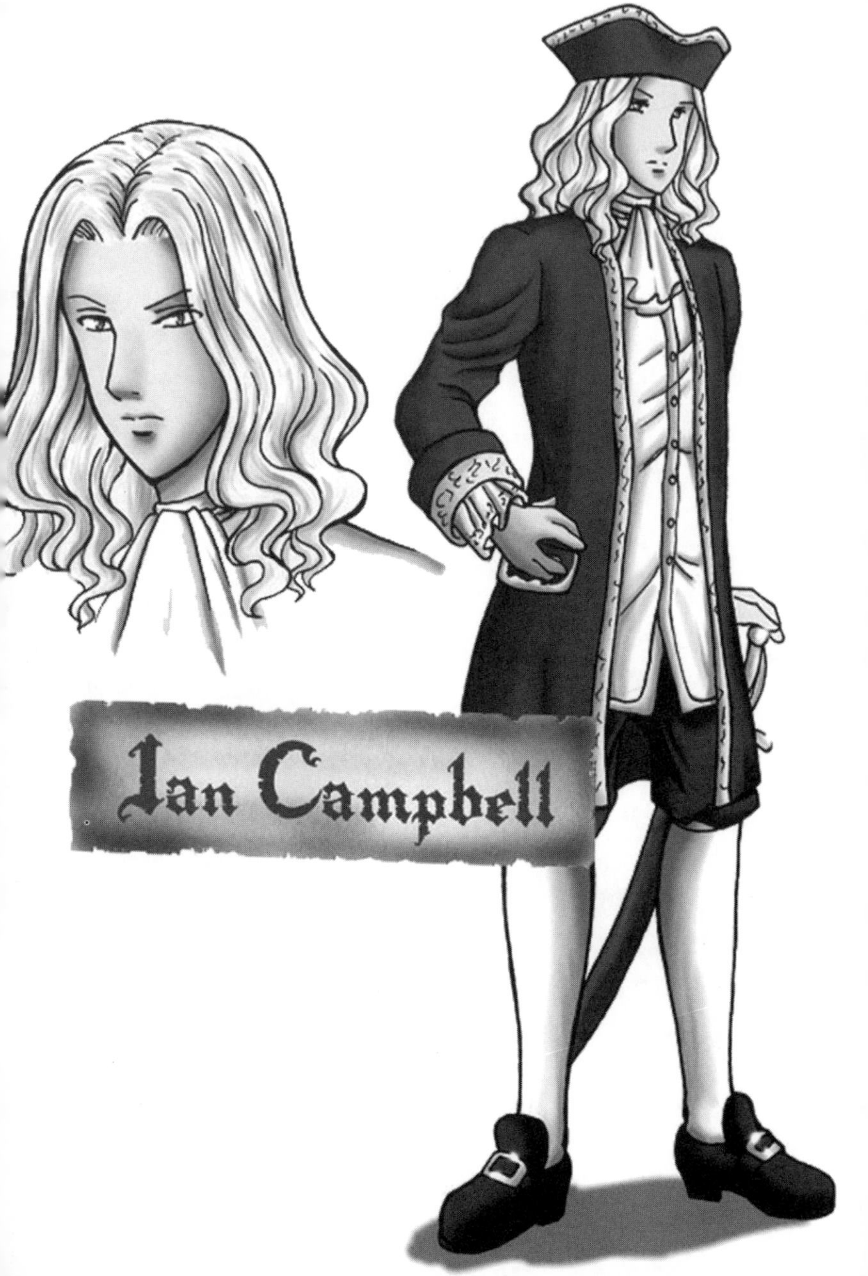
Ian Campbell

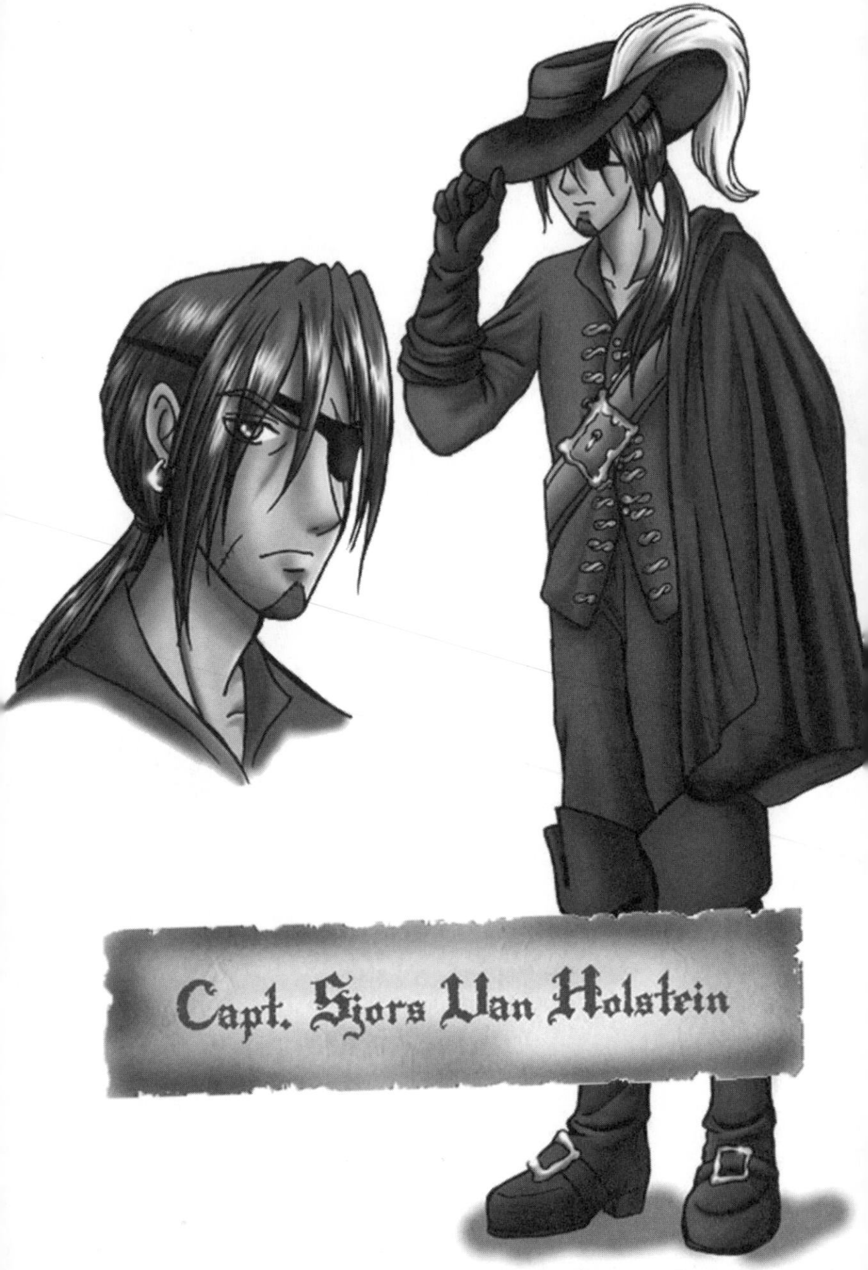
Capt. Sjors Van Holstein

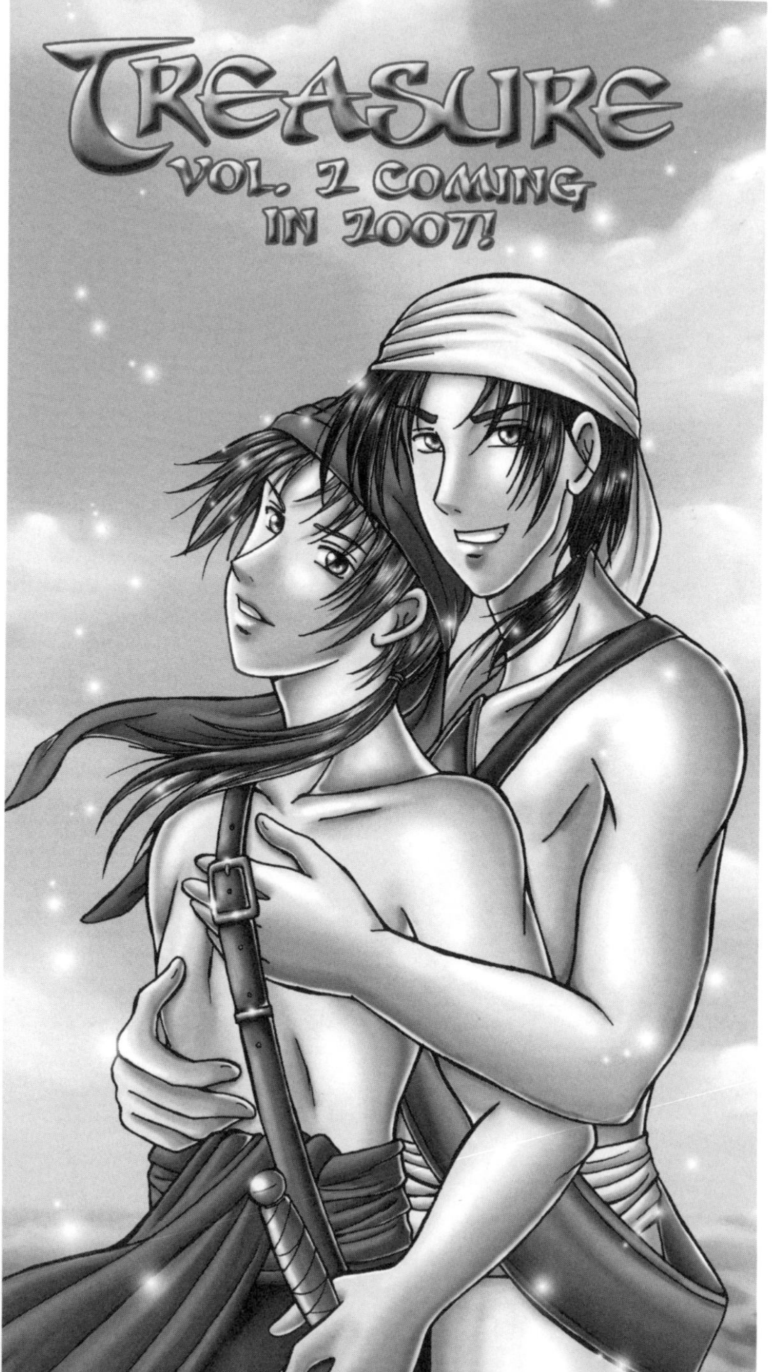
TREASURE
VOL. 2 COMING
IN 2007!

Coming Sept. 2006!

By KÔSEN
Saihôshi
THE GUARDIAN Vol.2

Saihôshi the Guardian Vol 2
by KÔSEN

The second and final volume of the smash hit series. If the guardian Sastre wants to avoid a death sentence he must rescue Prince Anel, defeat his rival Riot, and prevail against a rogue guardian. That leaves little time to protect Anel's decoy, who he's fallen in love with.

THUD
BEWARE!!
DON'T MOVE.
WHAT THE...?!

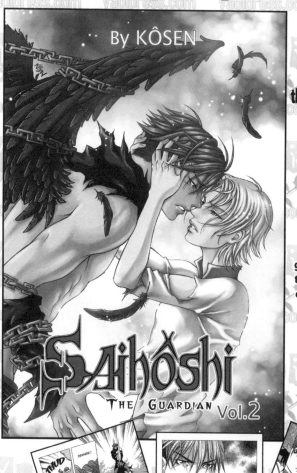

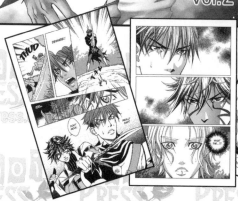

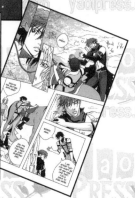

Coming Jan. 2007!

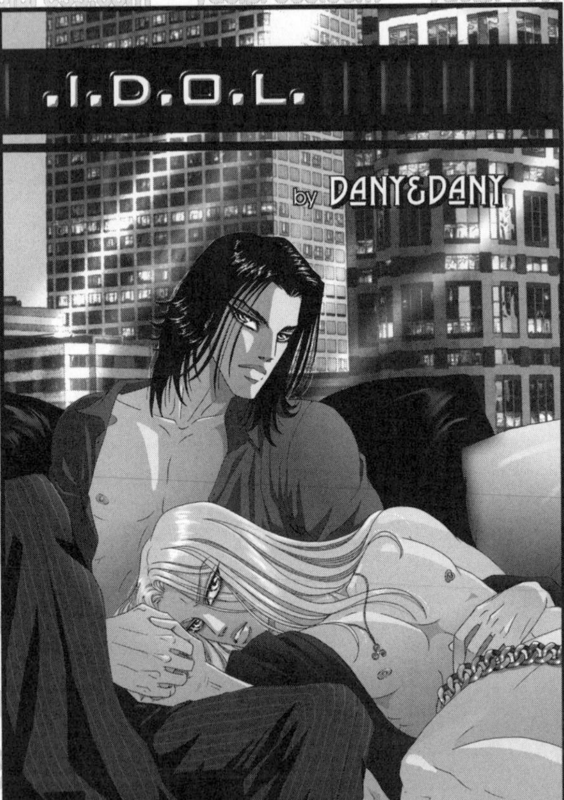
.I.D.O.L.
by DANY&DANY

Idol

by Dany&Dany

The jaded artist David hires the hustler Adam as an art model. This painting finally conveys the passion in David's heart. His model stirs passions of another kind. Acting on these feelings draws David into Adam's dark world of dangerous liaisons and jealous lovers.

THE ENGLISH LANGUAGE DEBUT OF THE RENOWNED ITALIAN YAOI STUDIO DANY&DANY!

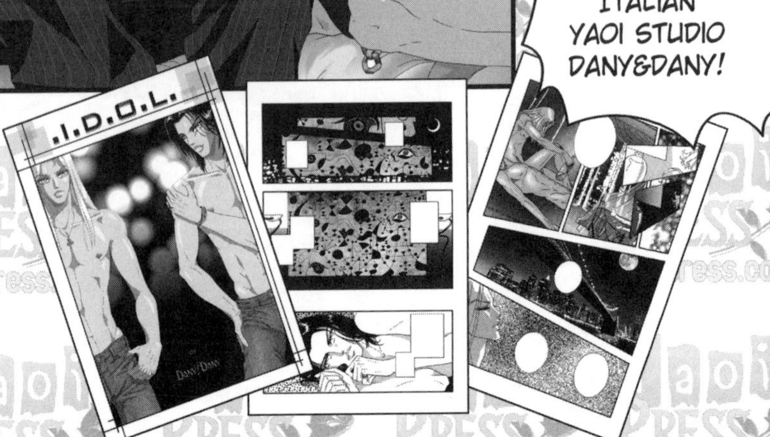
.I.D.O.L.

Coming Mar. 2007!

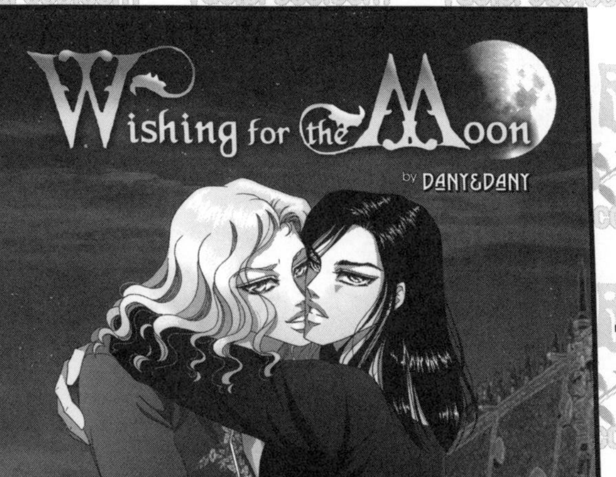
Wishing for the Moon
by DANY&DANY

Wishing for the Moon

by Dany&Dany

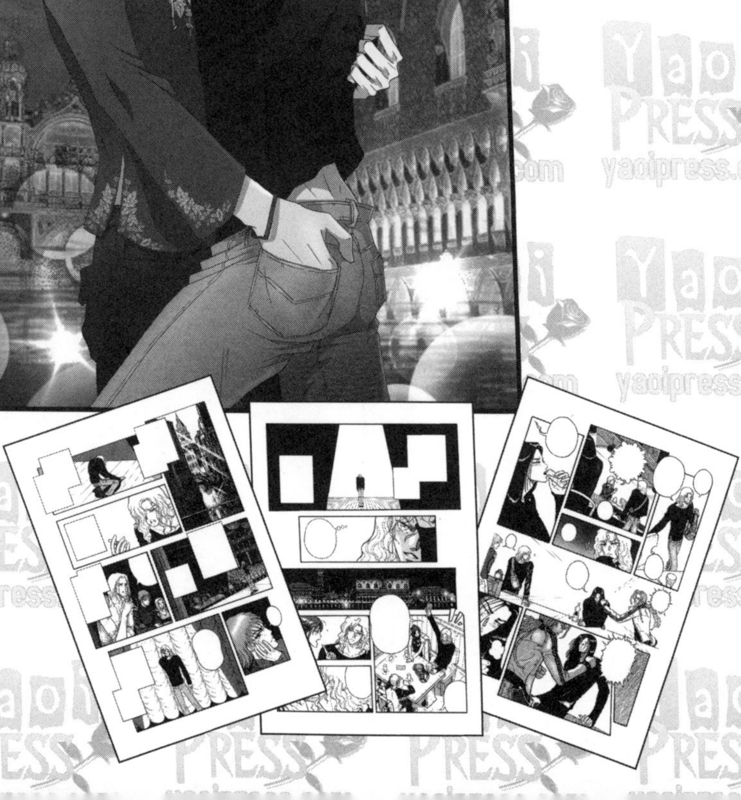

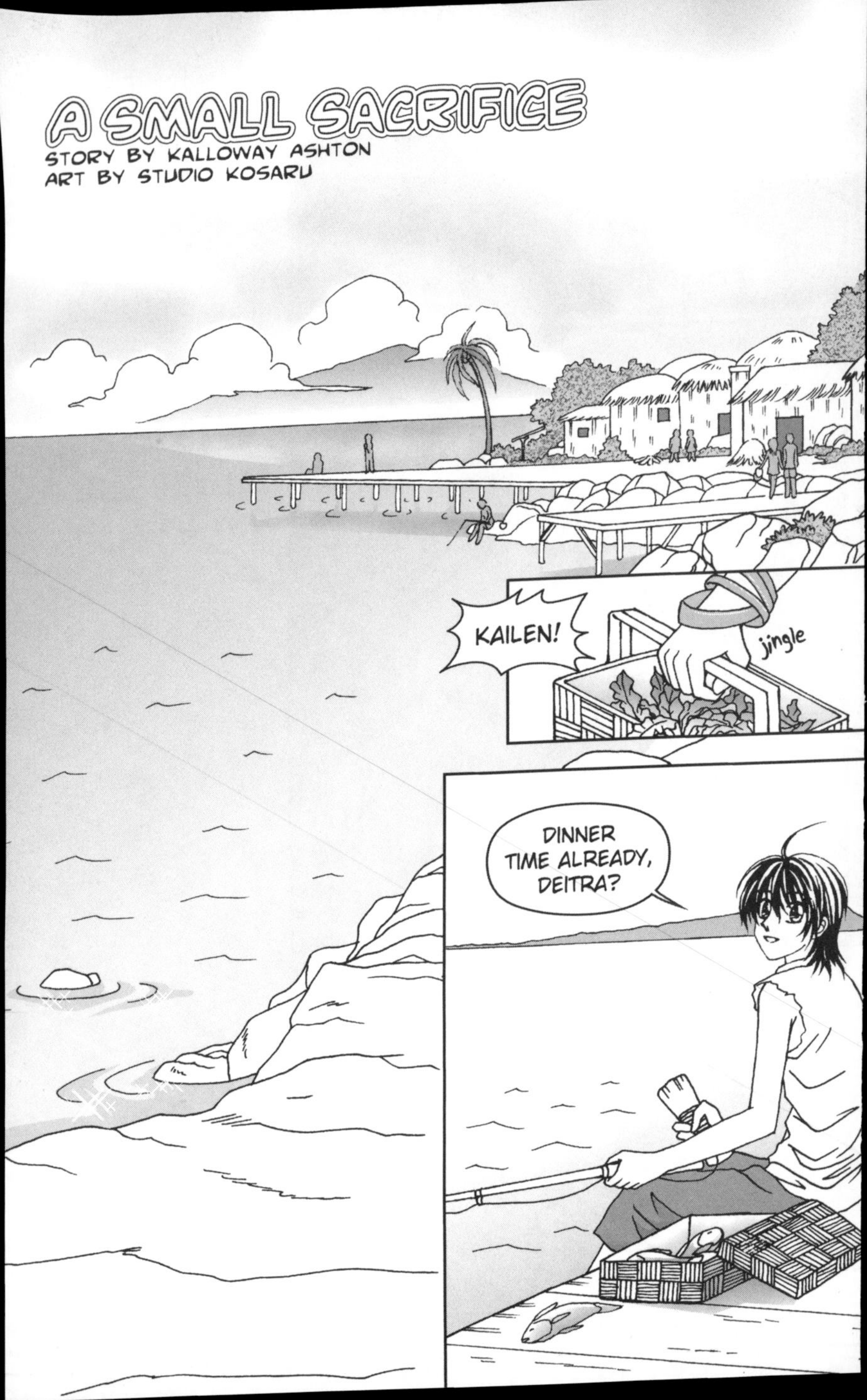
A SMALL SACRIFICE
STORY BY KALLOWAY ASHTON
ART BY STUDIO KOSARU
KAILEN!
jingle
DINNER TIME ALREADY, DEITRA?

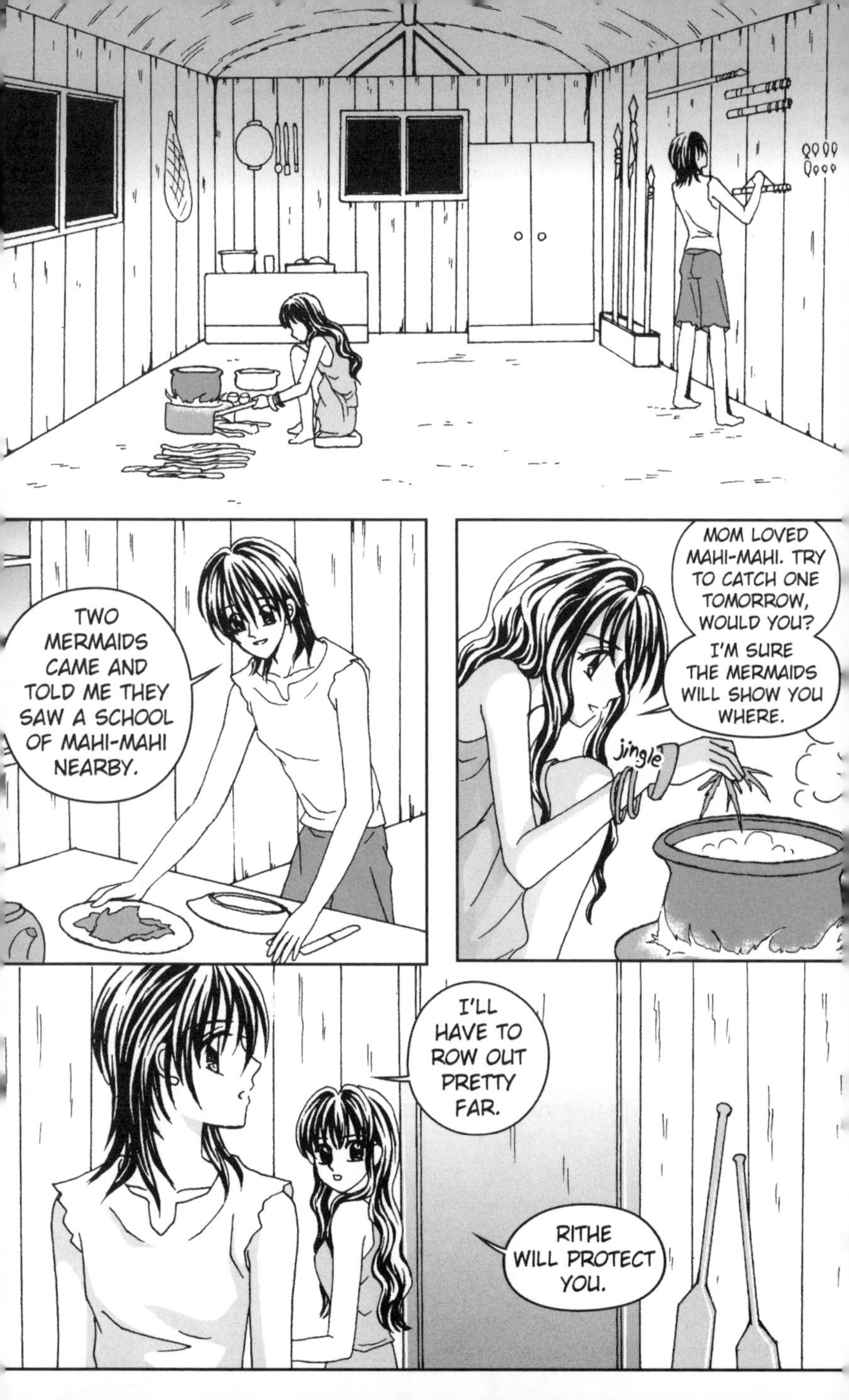

TWO MERMAIDS CAME AND TOLD ME THEY SAW A SCHOOL OF MAHI-MAHI NEARBY.
MOM LOVED MAHI-MAHI. TRY TO CATCH ONE TOMORROW, WOULD YOU?
I'M SURE THE MERMAIDS WILL SHOW YOU WHERE.
jingle
I'LL HAVE TO ROW OUT PRETTY FAR.
RITHE WILL PROTECT YOU.

"I KNOW, SIS."

"HE'S ALWAYS WATCHING OVER US."

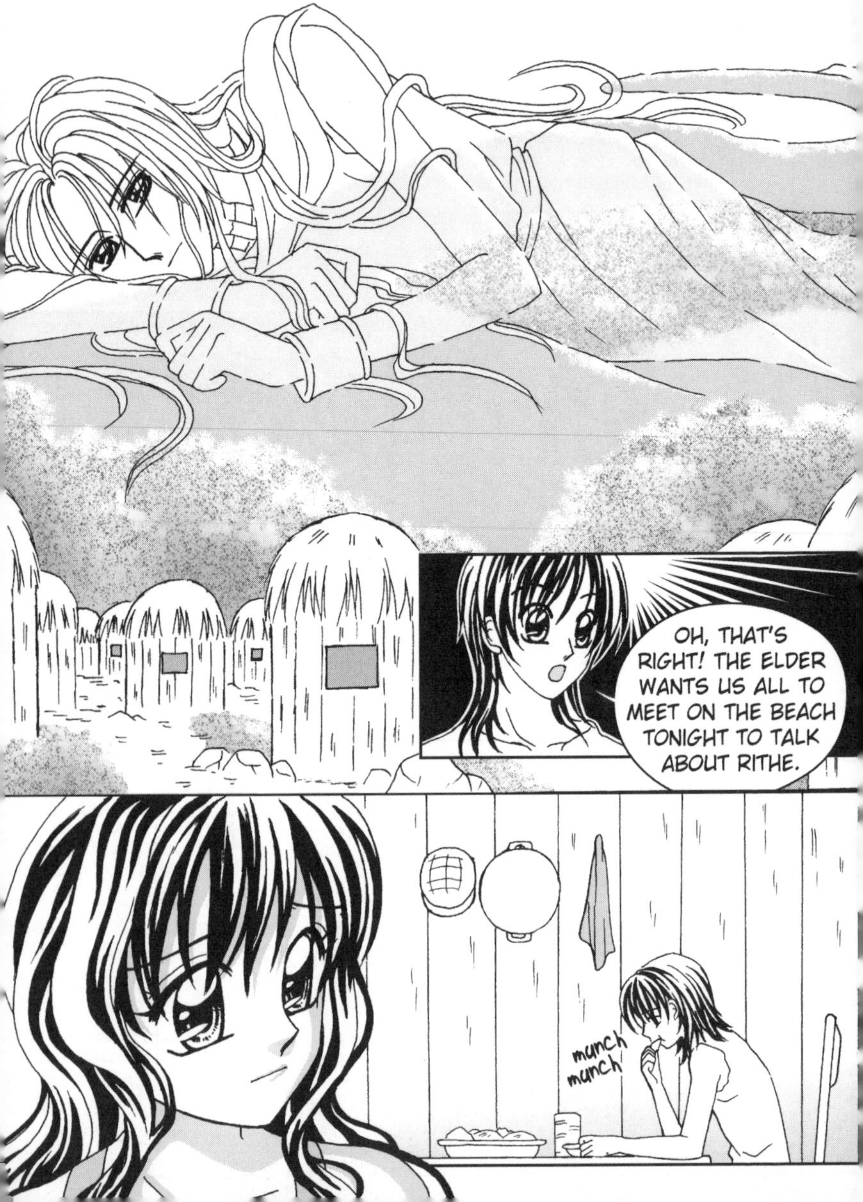
OH, THAT'S RIGHT! THE ELDER WANTS US ALL TO MEET ON THE BEACH TONIGHT TO TALK ABOUT RITHE.
munch munch

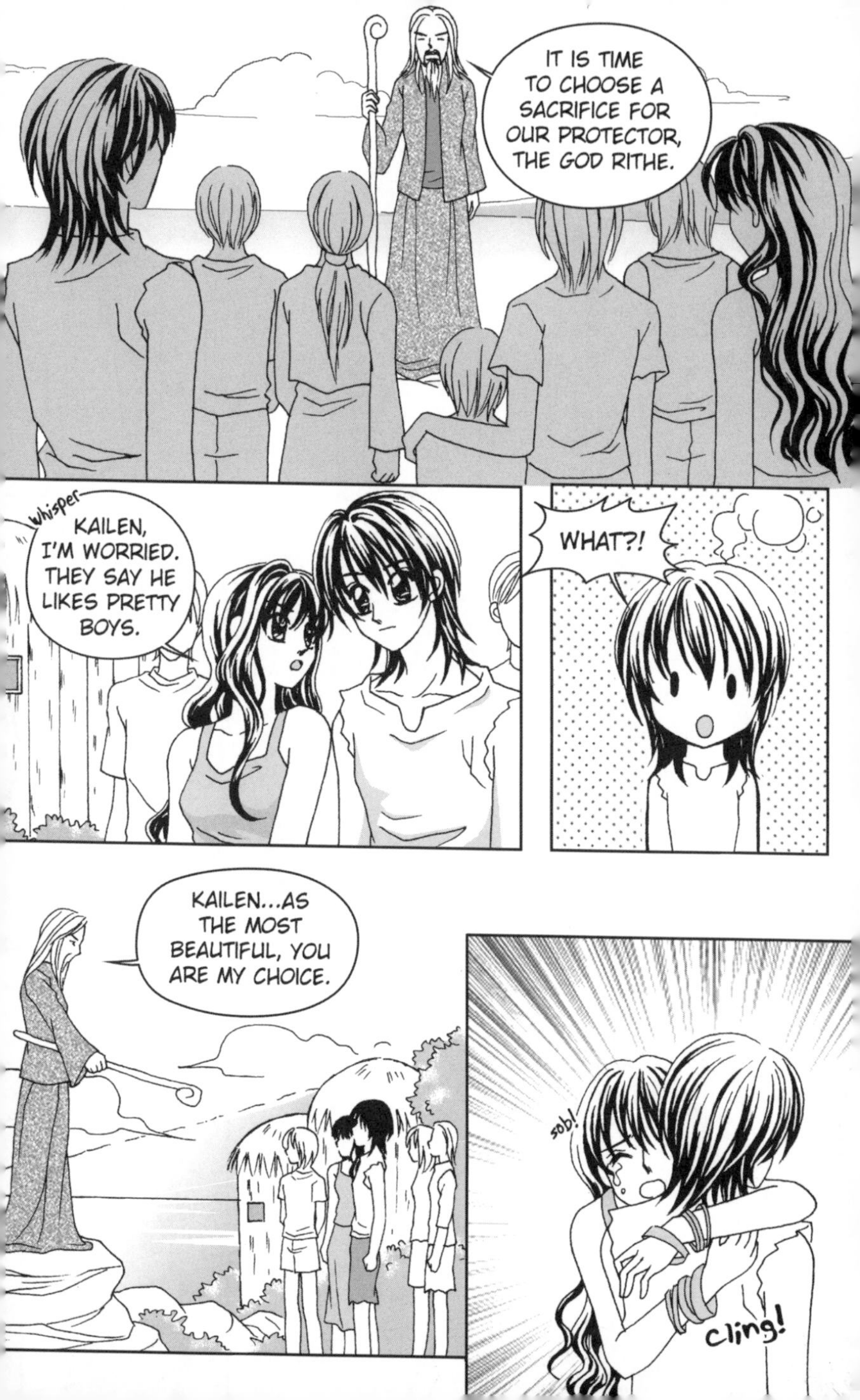
IT IS TIME TO CHOOSE A SACRIFICE FOR OUR PROTECTOR, THE GOD RITHE.
whisper
KAILEN, I'M WORRIED. THEY SAY HE LIKES PRETTY BOYS.
WHAT?!
KAILEN...AS THE MOST BEAUTIFUL, YOU ARE MY CHOICE.
sob!
cling!

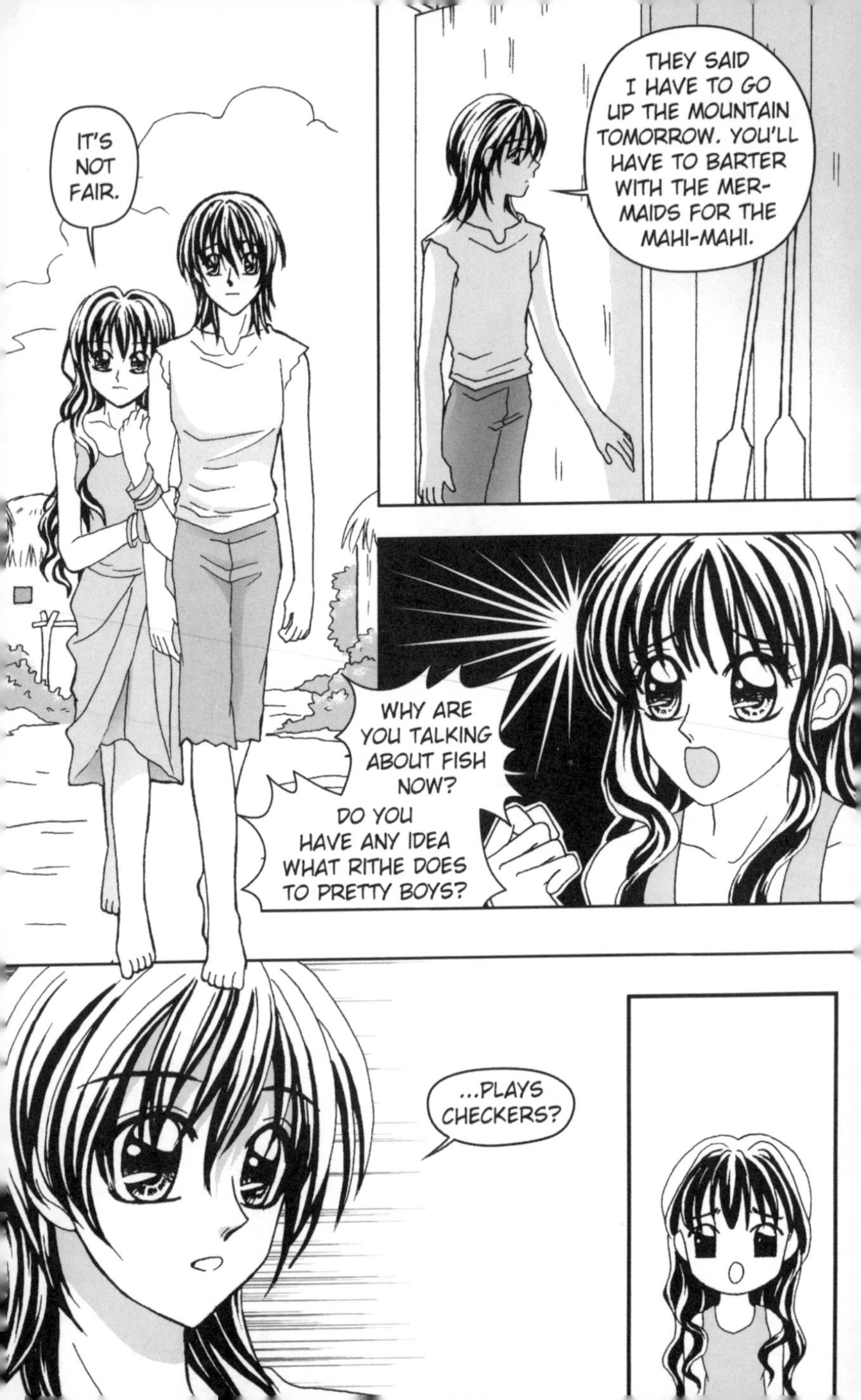
IT'S NOT FAIR.
THEY SAID I HAVE TO GO UP THE MOUNTAIN TOMORROW. YOU'LL HAVE TO BARTER WITH THE MER-MAIDS FOR THE MAHI-MAHI.
WHY ARE YOU TALKING ABOUT FISH NOW?
DO YOU HAVE ANY IDEA WHAT RITHE DOES TO PRETTY BOYS?
...PLAYS CHECKERS?

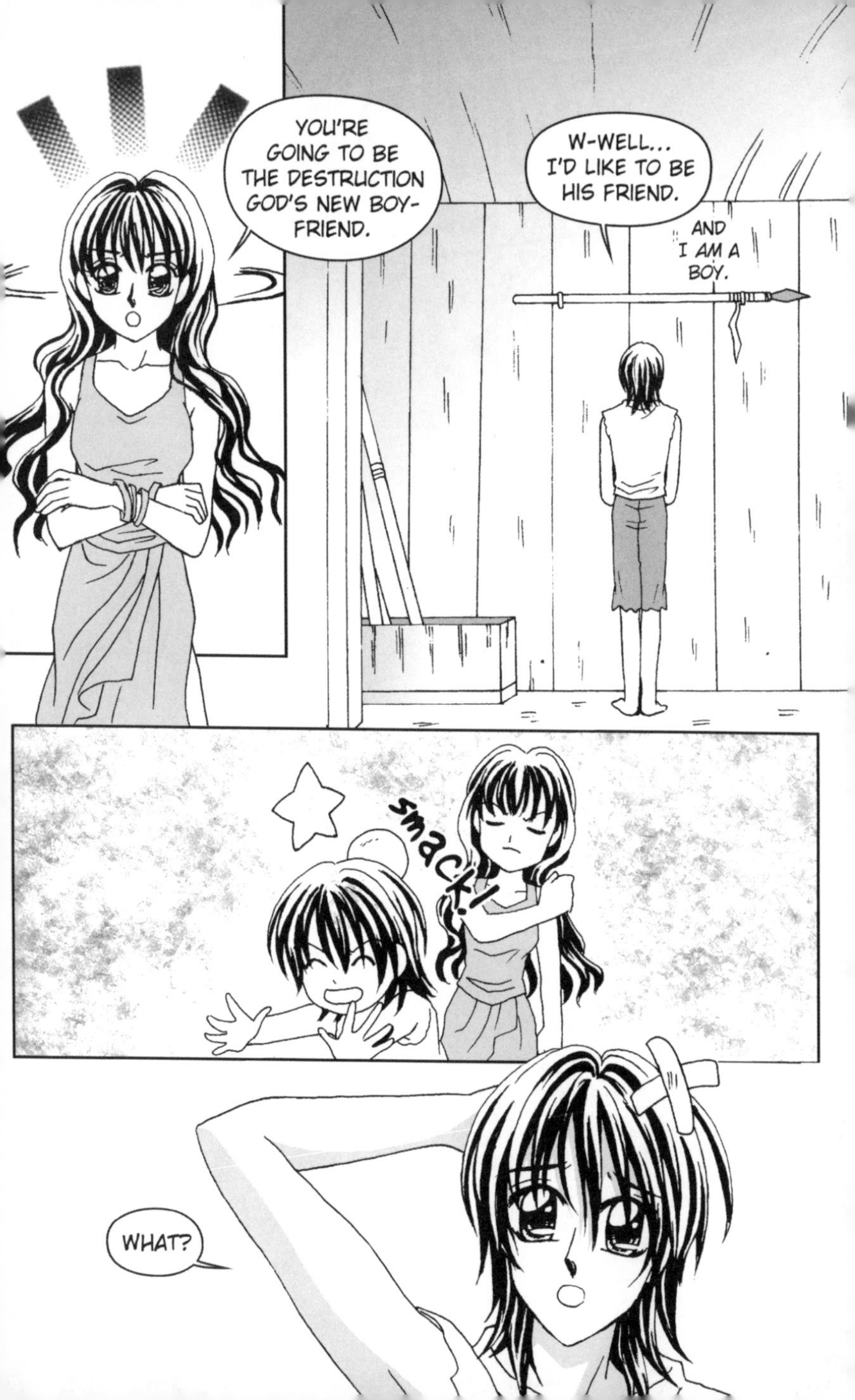
YOU'RE GOING TO BE THE DESTRUCTION GOD'S NEW BOY-FRIEND.
W-WELL... I'D LIKE TO BE HIS FRIEND.
AND I AM A BOY.
SMACK!
WHAT?

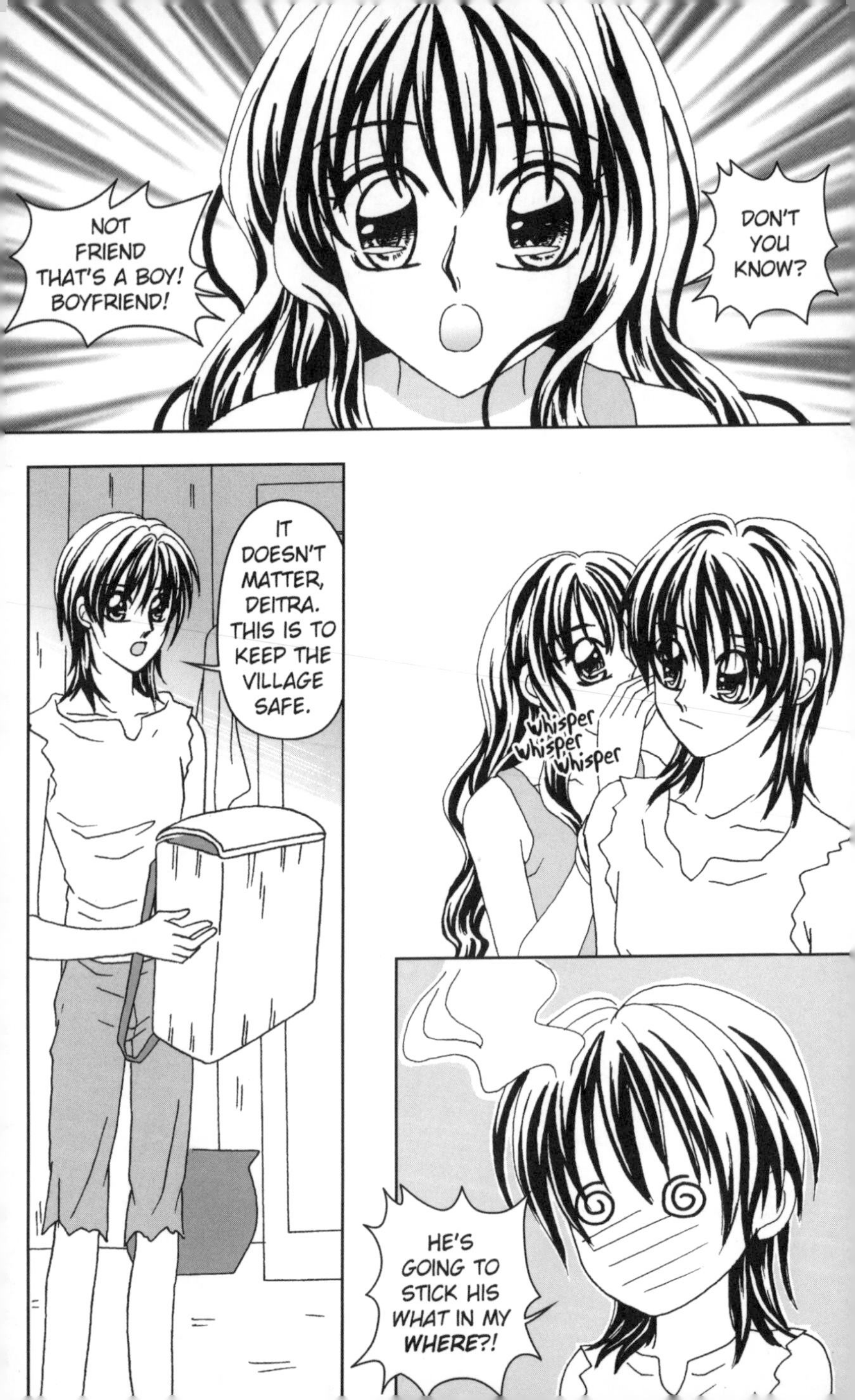
NOT FRIEND THAT'S A BOY! BOYFRIEND!
DON'T YOU KNOW?
IT DOESN'T MATTER, DEITRA. THIS IS TO KEEP THE VILLAGE SAFE.
Whisper Whisper Whisper
HE'S GOING TO STICK HIS WHAT IN MY WHERE?!

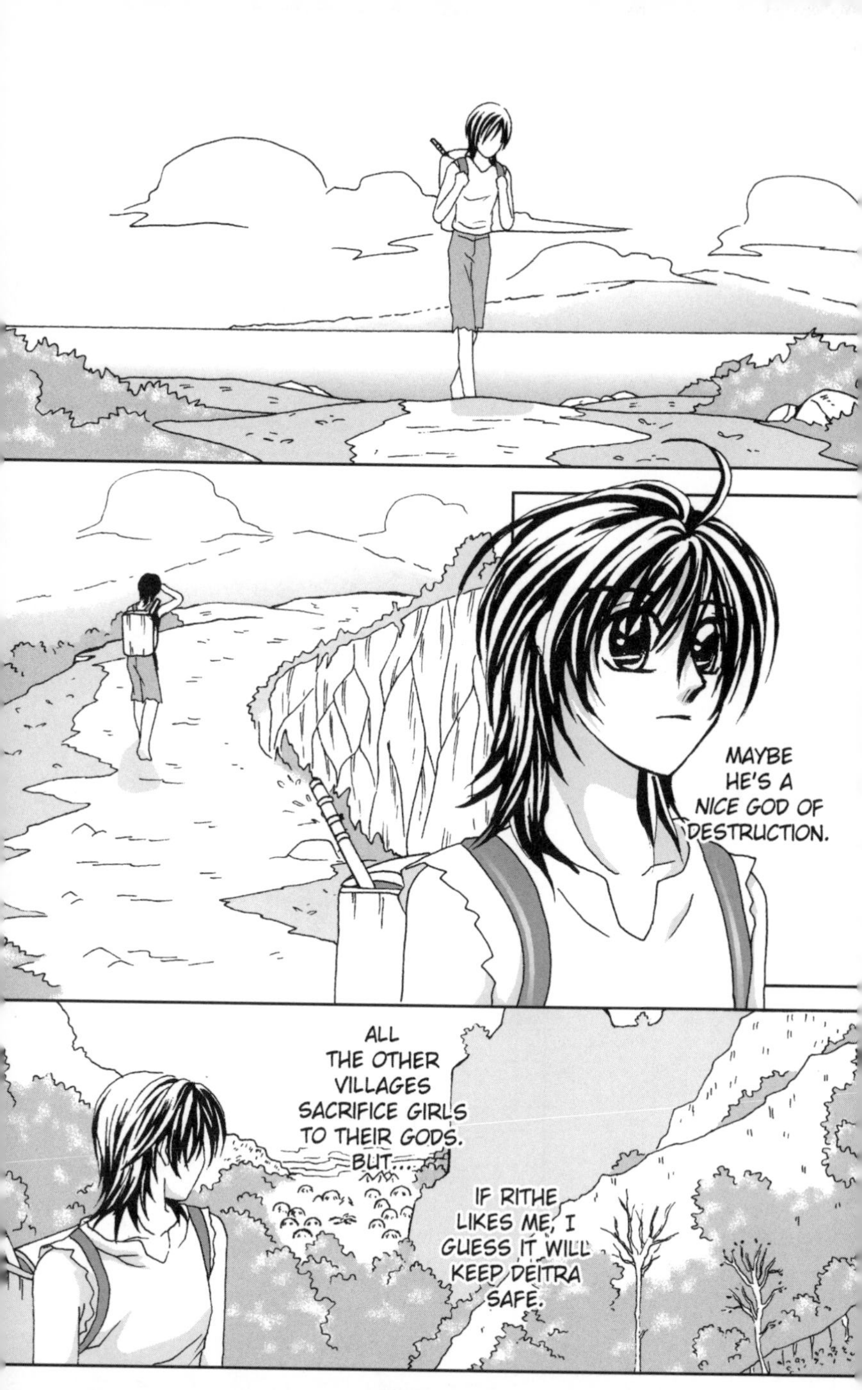
MAYBE HE'S A NICE GOD OF DESTRUCTION.
ALL THE OTHER VILLAGES SACRIFICE GIRLS TO THEIR GODS. BUT...
IF RITHE LIKES ME, I GUESS IT WILL KEEP DEITRA SAFE.

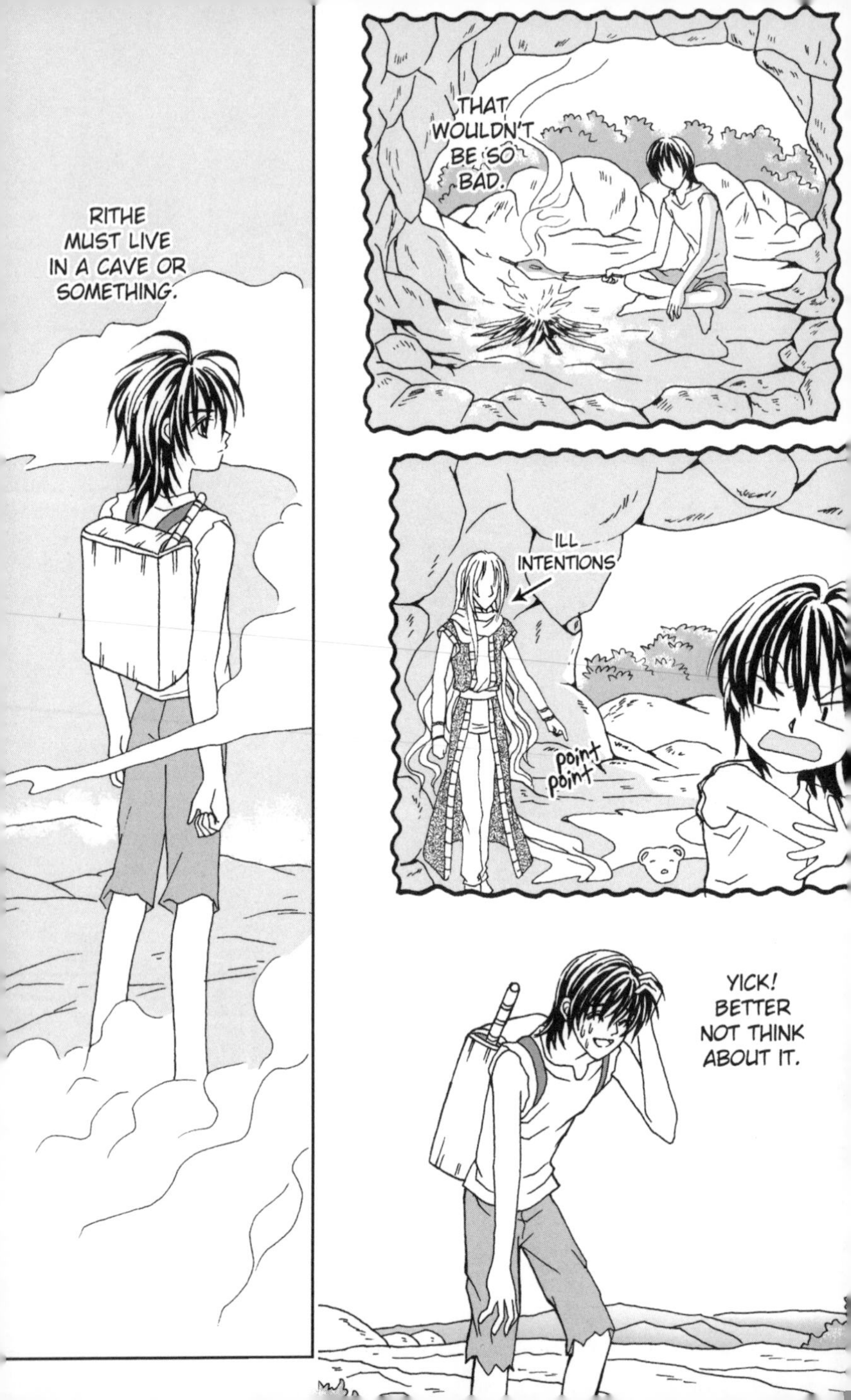
RITHE MUST LIVE IN A CAVE OR SOMETHING.
THAT WOULDN'T BE SO BAD.
ILL INTENTIONS
point point
YICK! BETTER NOT THINK ABOUT IT.

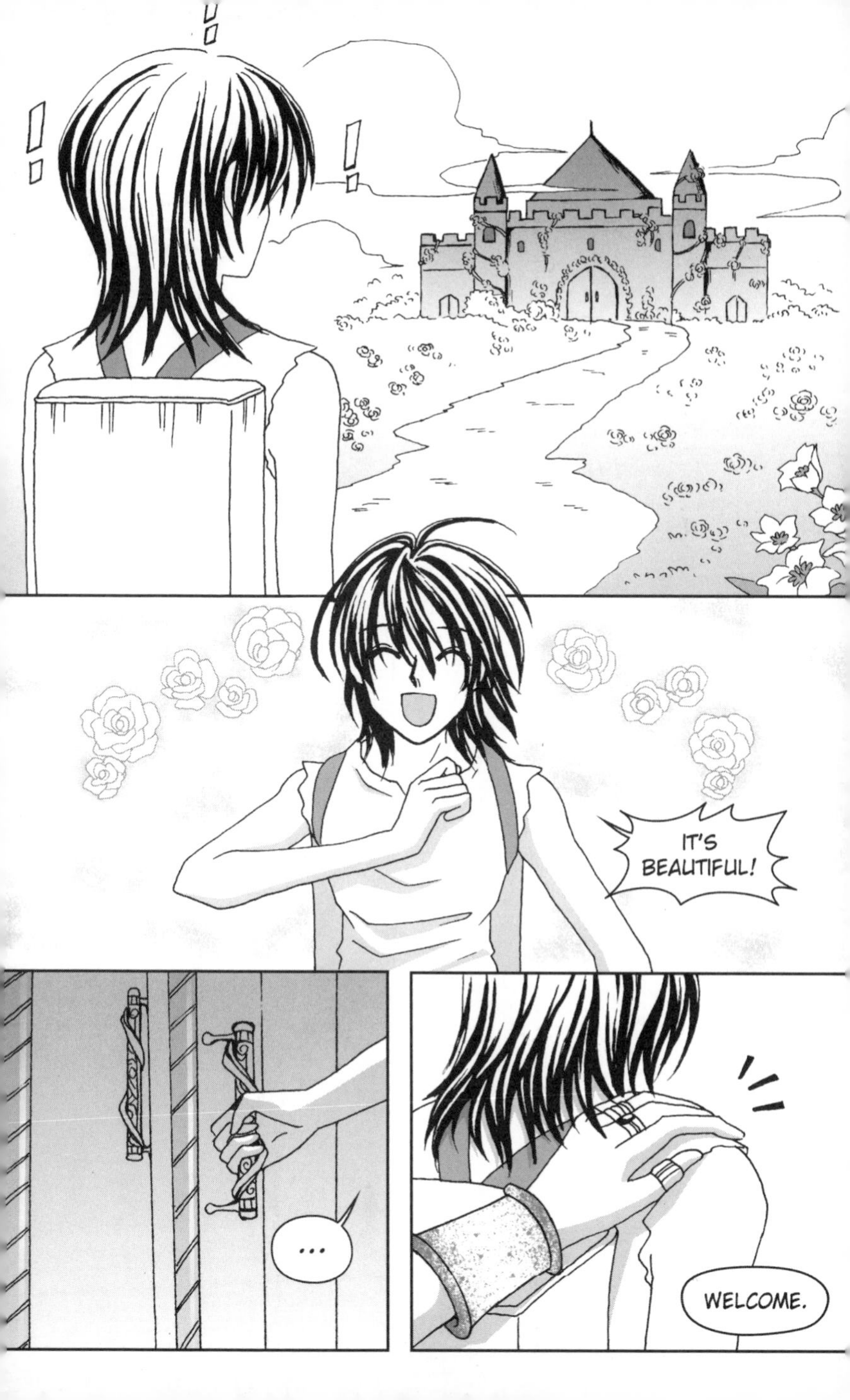

IT'S BEAUTIFUL!
WELCOME.
...

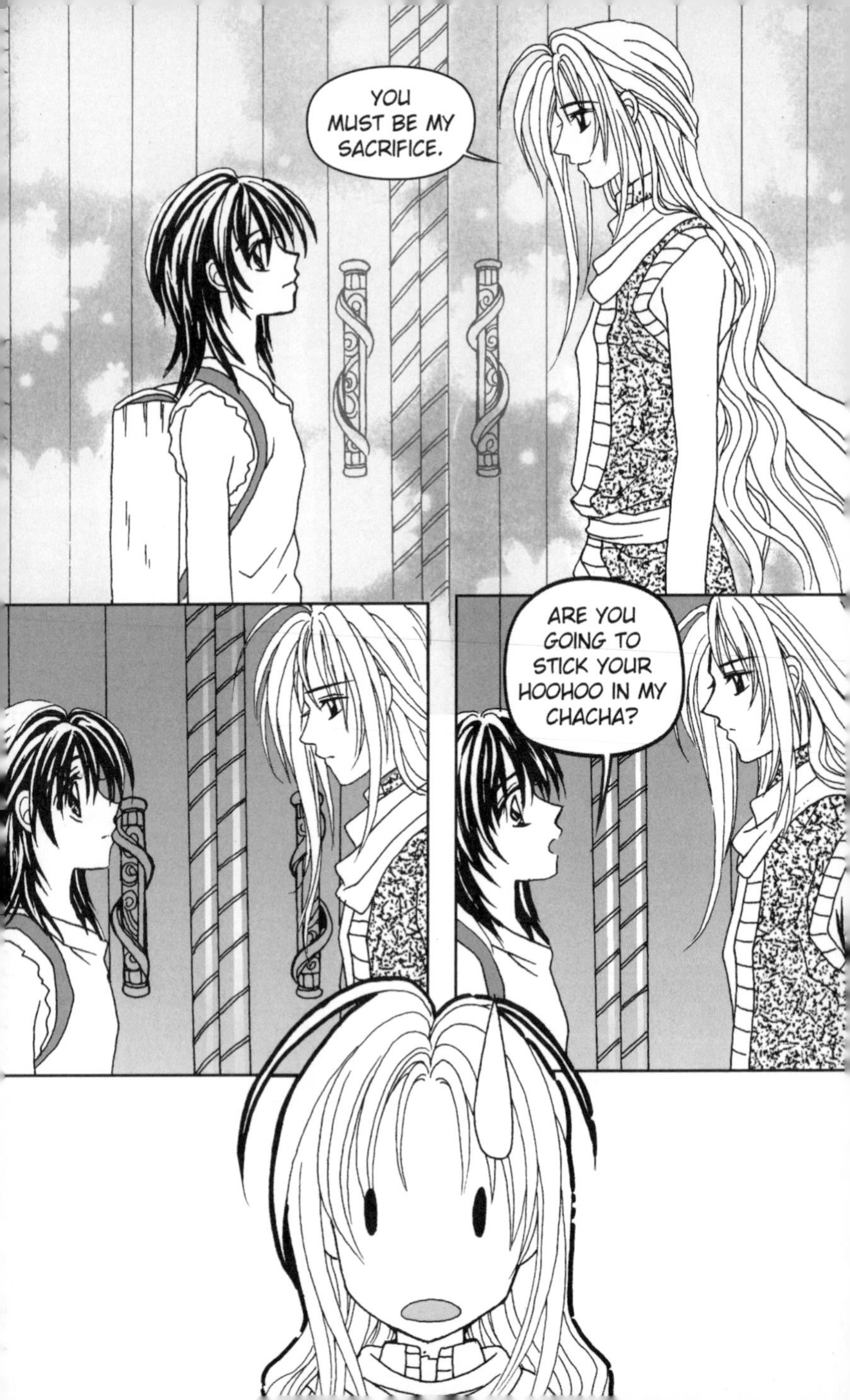
YOU MUST BE MY SACRIFICE.
ARE YOU GOING TO STICK YOUR HOOHOO IN MY CHACHA?

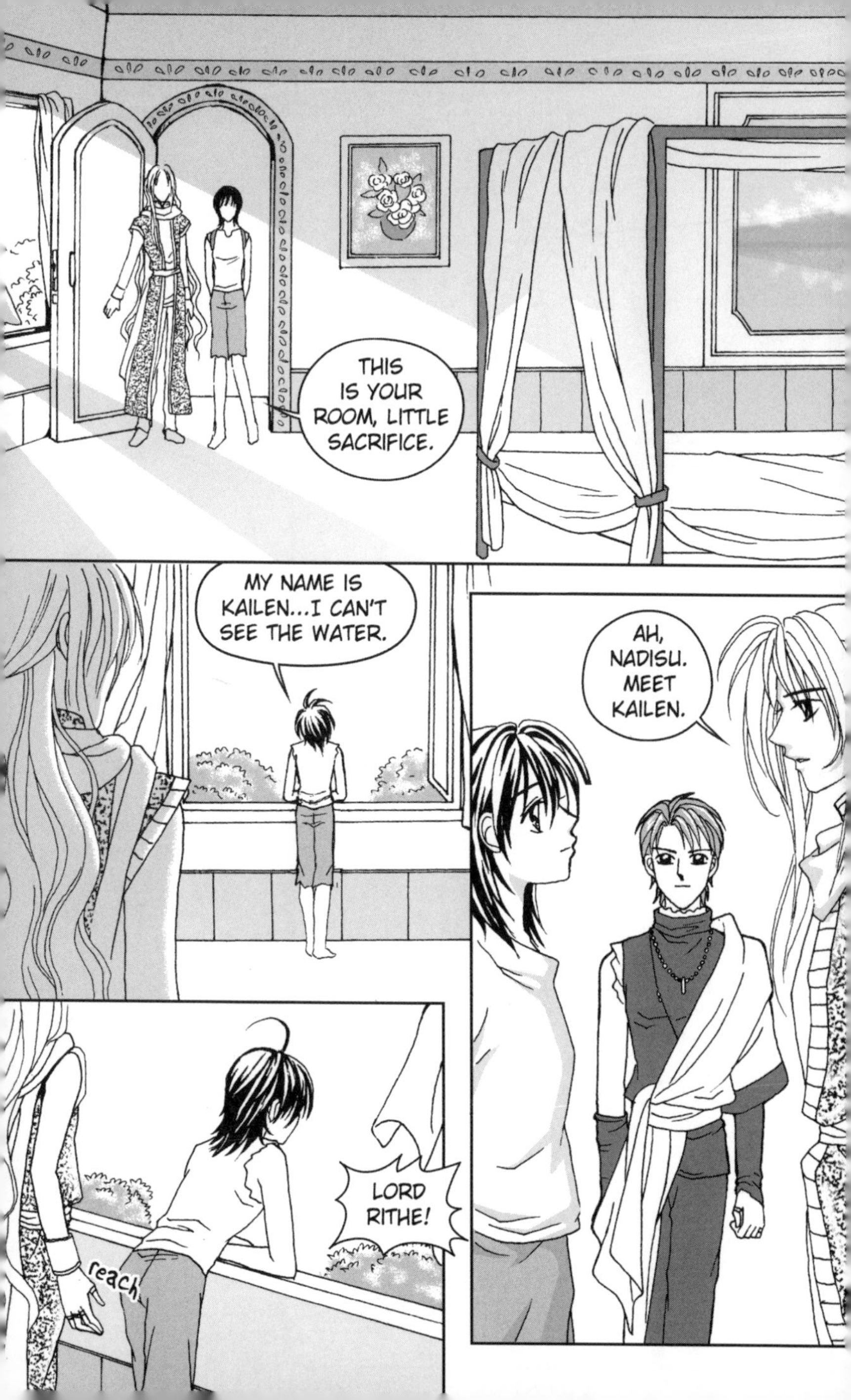
THIS IS YOUR ROOM, LITTLE SACRIFICE.
MY NAME IS KAILEN...I CAN'T SEE THE WATER.
reach
LORD RITHE!
AH, NADISU. MEET KAILEN.

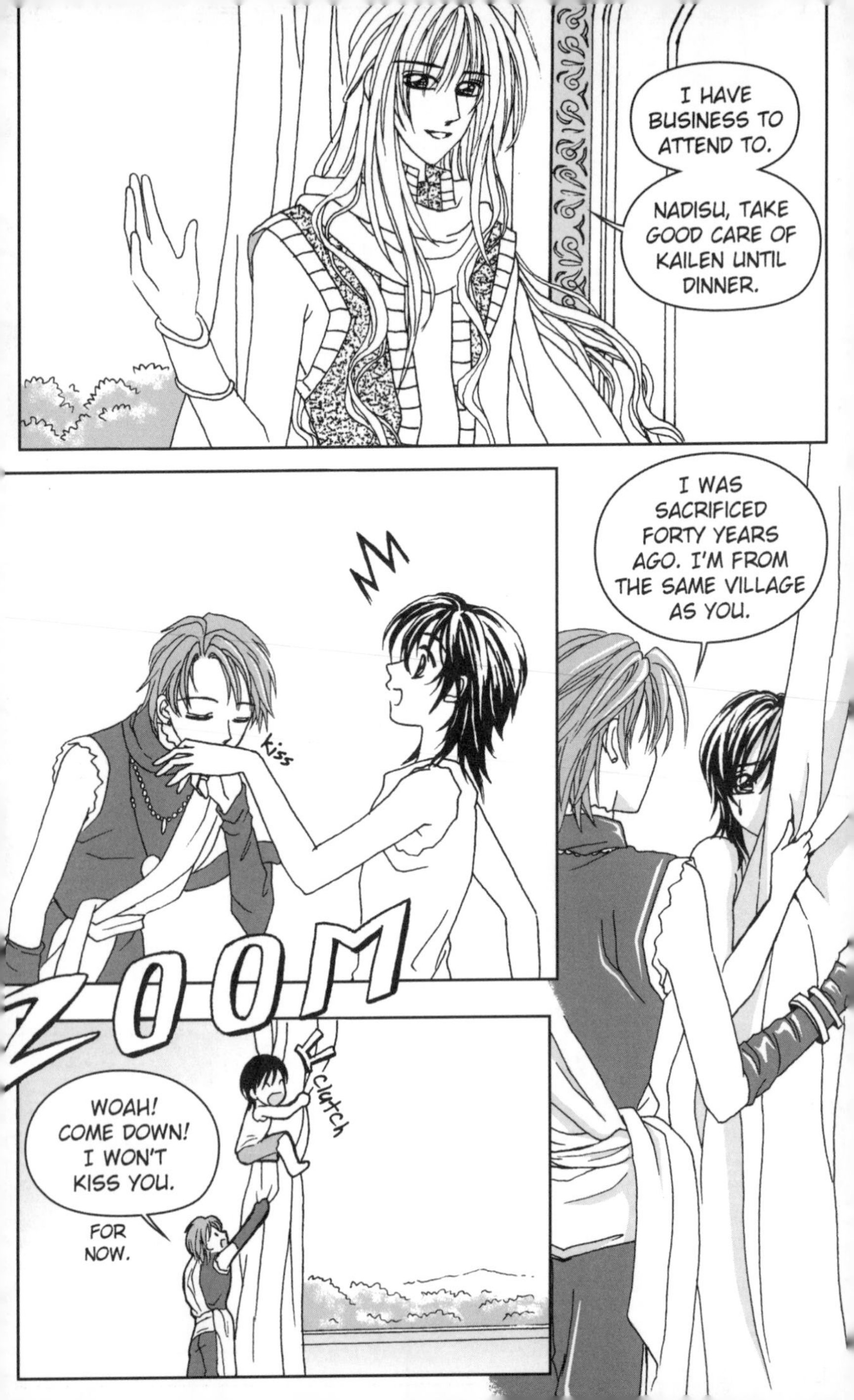
I HAVE BUSINESS TO ATTEND TO.
NADISU, TAKE GOOD CARE OF KAILEN UNTIL DINNER.
I WAS SACRIFICED FORTY YEARS AGO. I'M FROM THE SAME VILLAGE AS YOU.
kiss
ZOOM
clutch
WOAH! COME DOWN! I WON'T KISS YOU.
FOR NOW.

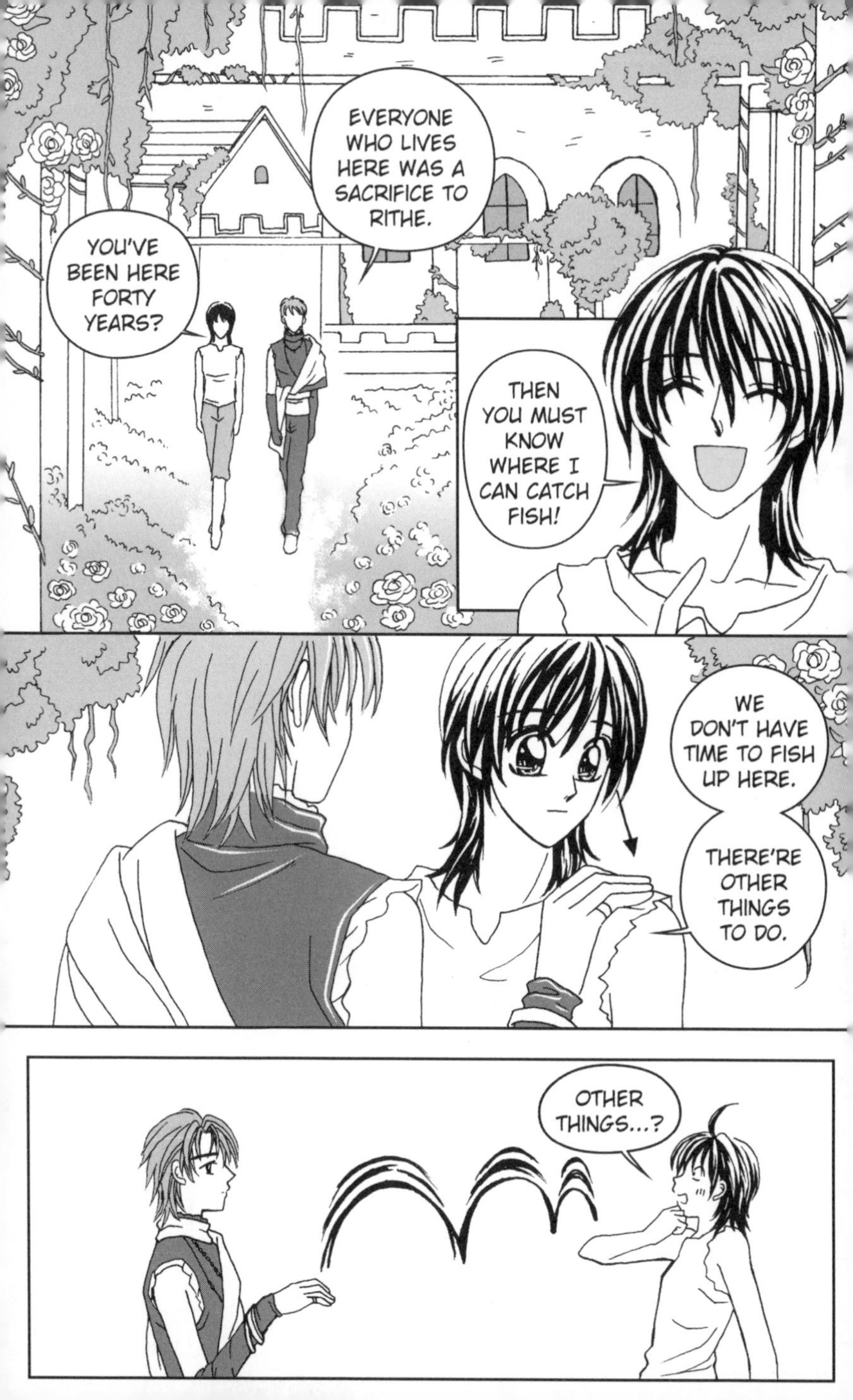
EVERYONE WHO LIVES HERE WAS A SACRIFICE TO RITHE.
YOU'VE BEEN HERE FORTY YEARS?
THEN YOU MUST KNOW WHERE I CAN CATCH FISH!
WE DON'T HAVE TIME TO FISH UP HERE.
THERE'RE OTHER THINGS TO DO.
OTHER THINGS...?

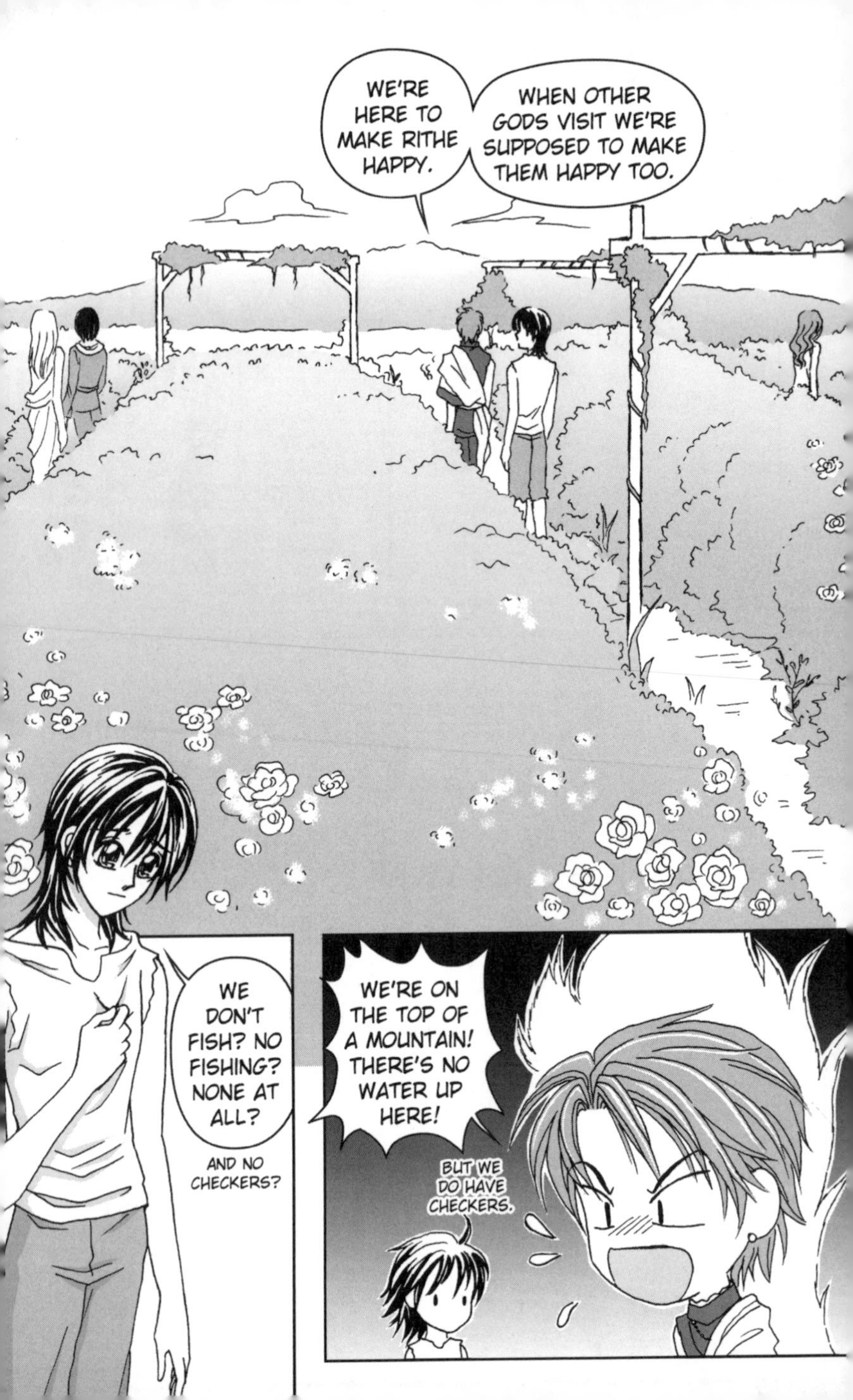
WE'RE HERE TO MAKE RITHE HAPPY.
WHEN OTHER GODS VISIT WE'RE SUPPOSED TO MAKE THEM HAPPY TOO.
WE DON'T FISH? NO FISHING? NONE AT ALL?
AND NO CHECKERS?
WE'RE ON THE TOP OF A MOUNTAIN! THERE'S NO WATER UP HERE!
BUT WE DO HAVE CHECKERS.

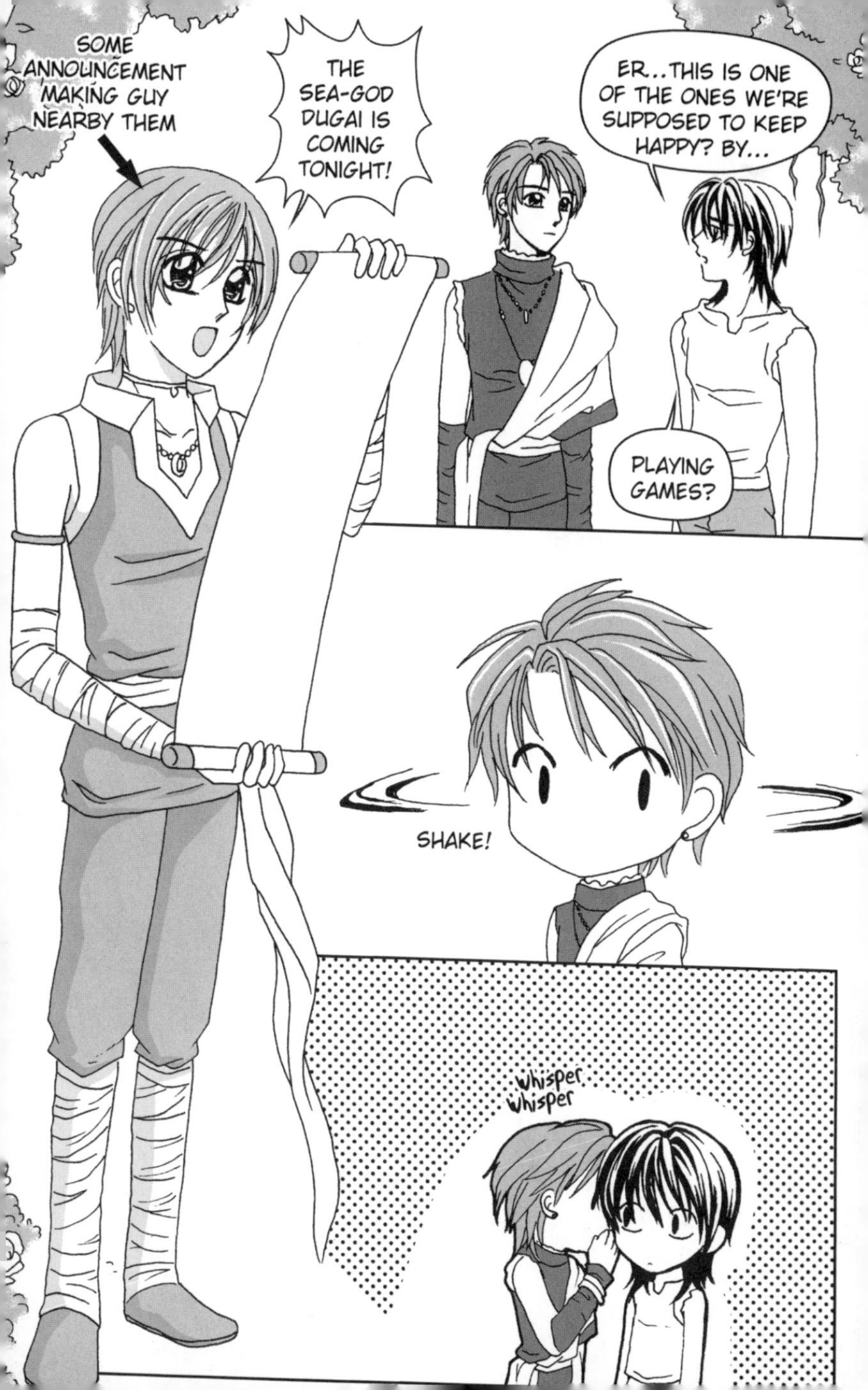

SOME ANNOUNCEMENT MAKING GUY NEARBY THEM
THE SEA-GOD DUGAI IS COMING TONIGHT!
ER...THIS IS ONE OF THE ONES WE'RE SUPPOSED TO KEEP HAPPY? BY...
PLAYING GAMES?
SHAKE!
whisper whisper

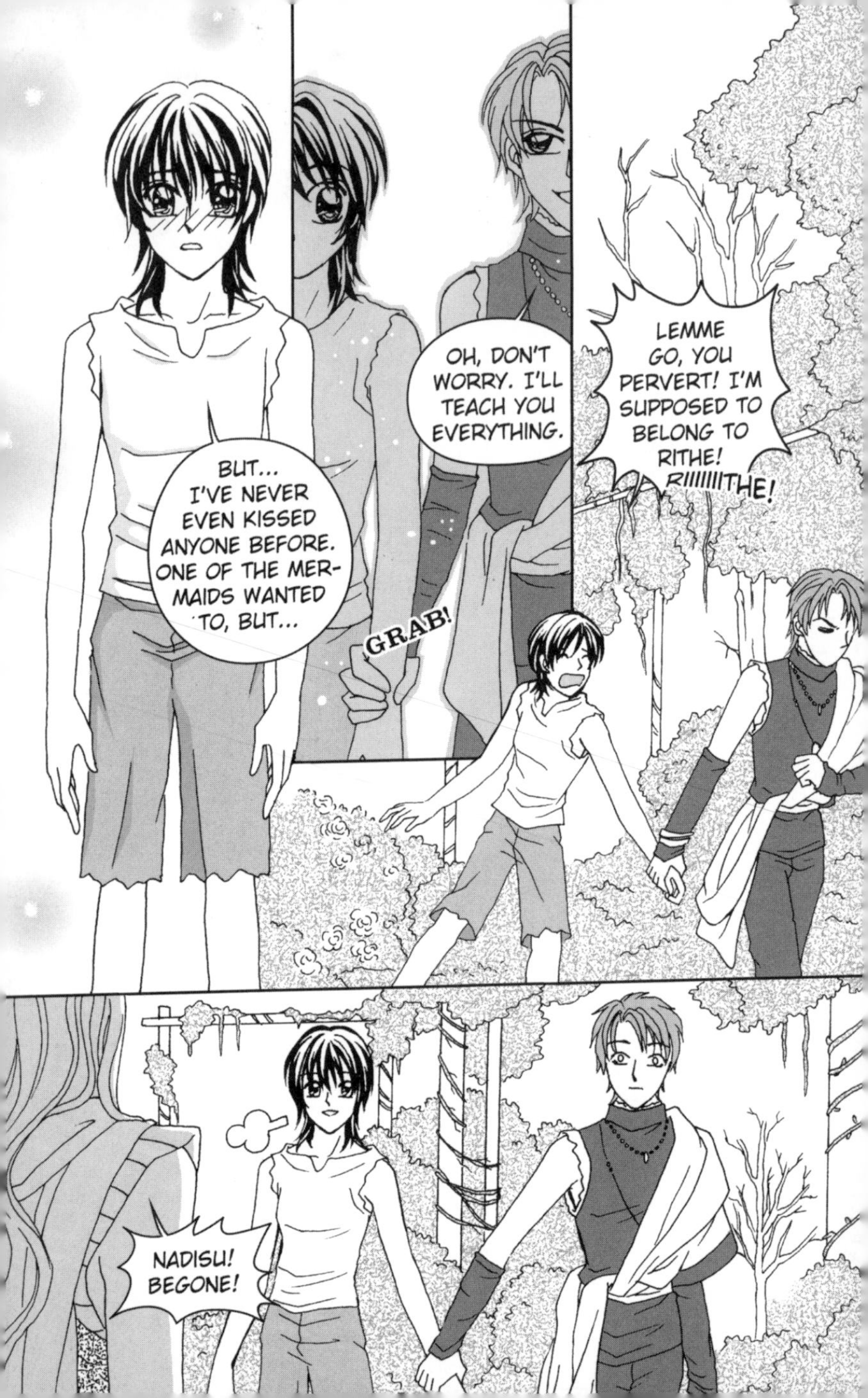

BUT... I'VE NEVER EVEN KISSED ANYONE BEFORE. ONE OF THE MER-MAIDS WANTED TO, BUT...
OH, DON'T WORRY. I'LL TEACH YOU EVERYTHING.
GRAB!
LEMME GO, YOU PERVERT! I'M SUPPOSED TO BELONG TO RITHE!
RIIIIIIITHE!
NADISU! BEGONE!

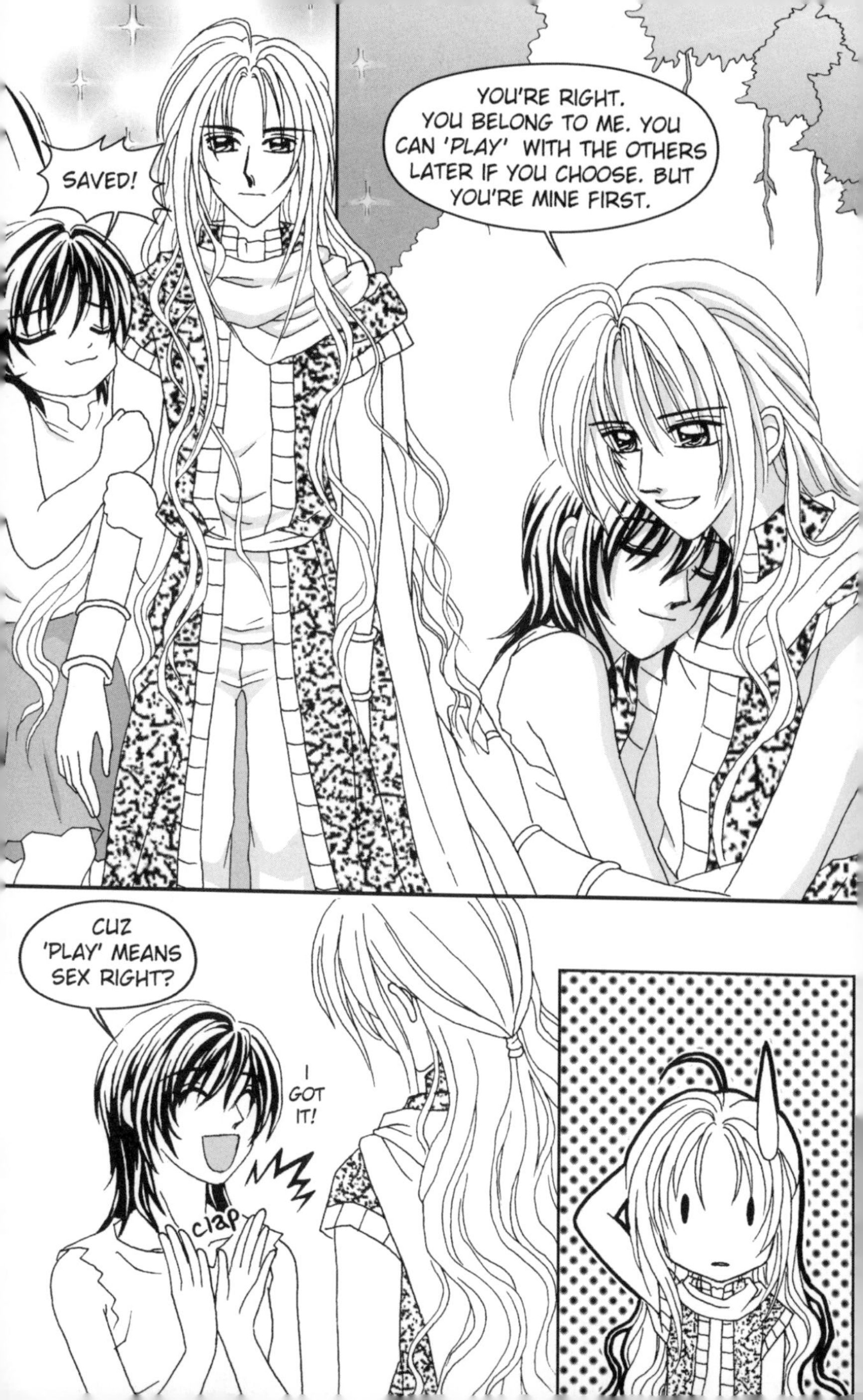
SAVED!
YOU'RE RIGHT. YOU BELONG TO ME. YOU CAN 'PLAY' WITH THE OTHERS LATER IF YOU CHOOSE. BUT YOU'RE MINE FIRST.
CUZ 'PLAY' MEANS SEX RIGHT?
I GOT IT!
clap

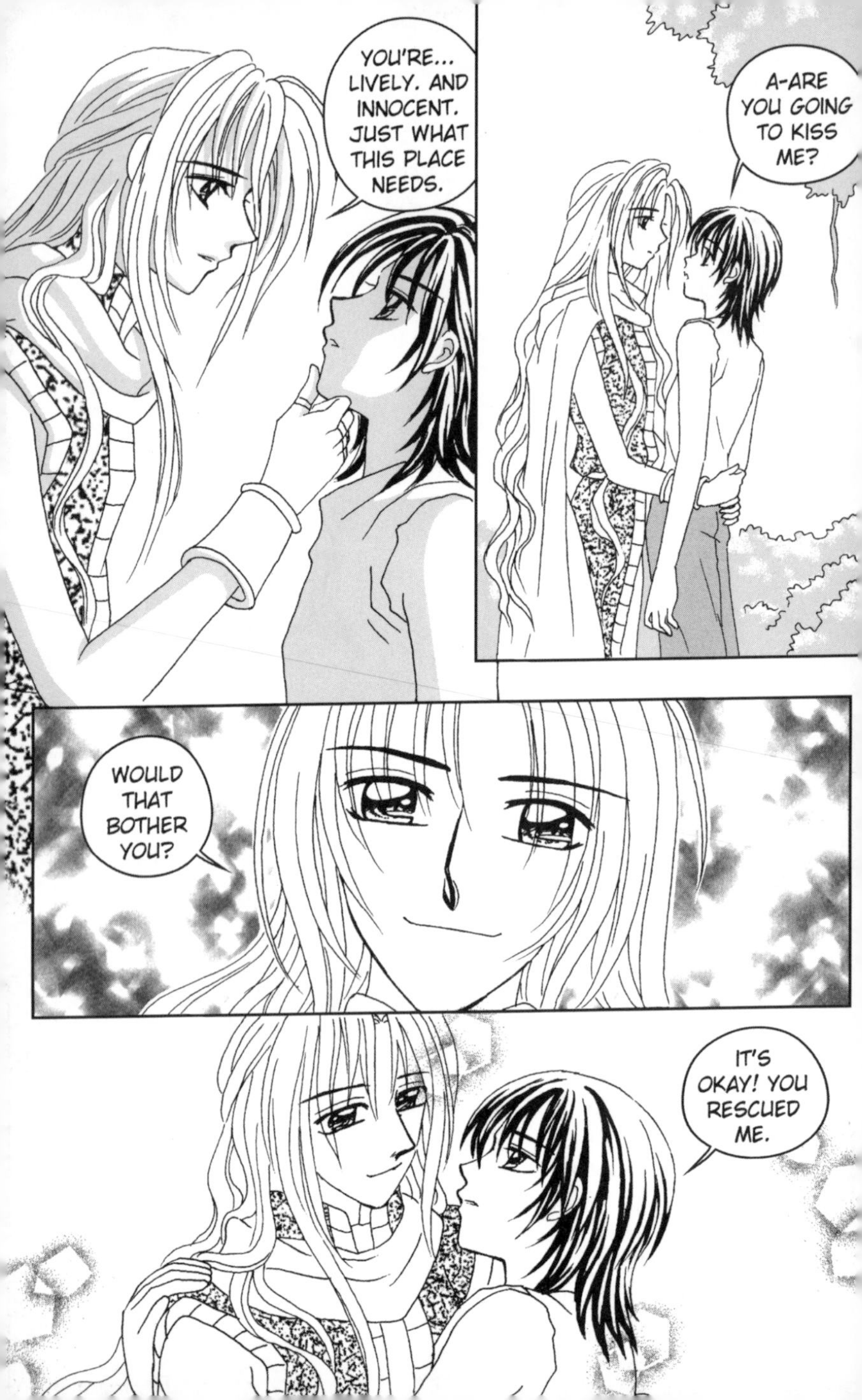
A-ARE YOU GOING TO KISS ME?
YOU'RE... LIVELY. AND INNOCENT. JUST WHAT THIS PLACE NEEDS.
WOULD THAT BOTHER YOU?
IT'S OKAY! YOU RESCUED ME.

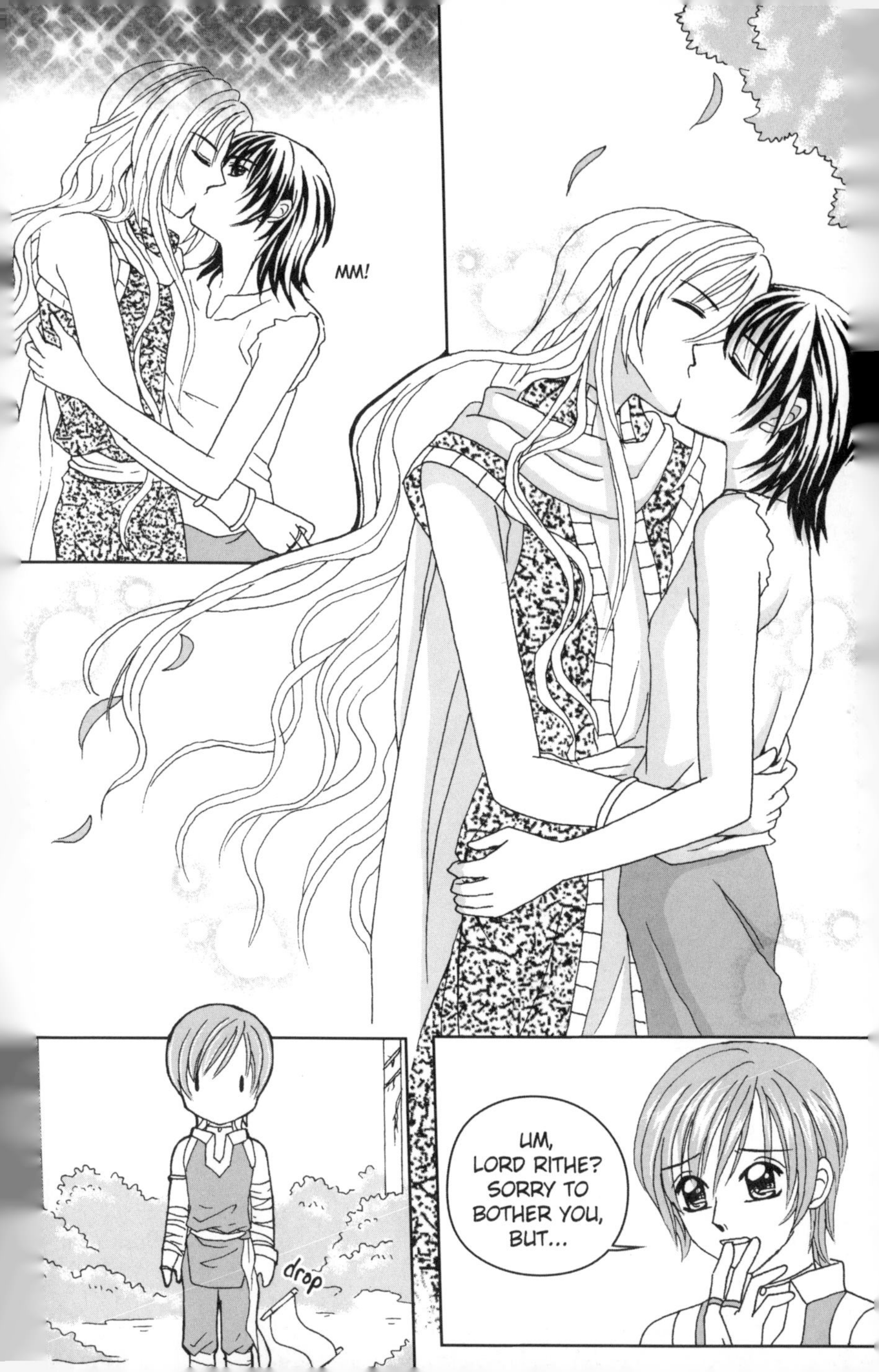
MM!
drop
UM, LORD RITHE? SORRY TO BOTHER YOU, BUT...

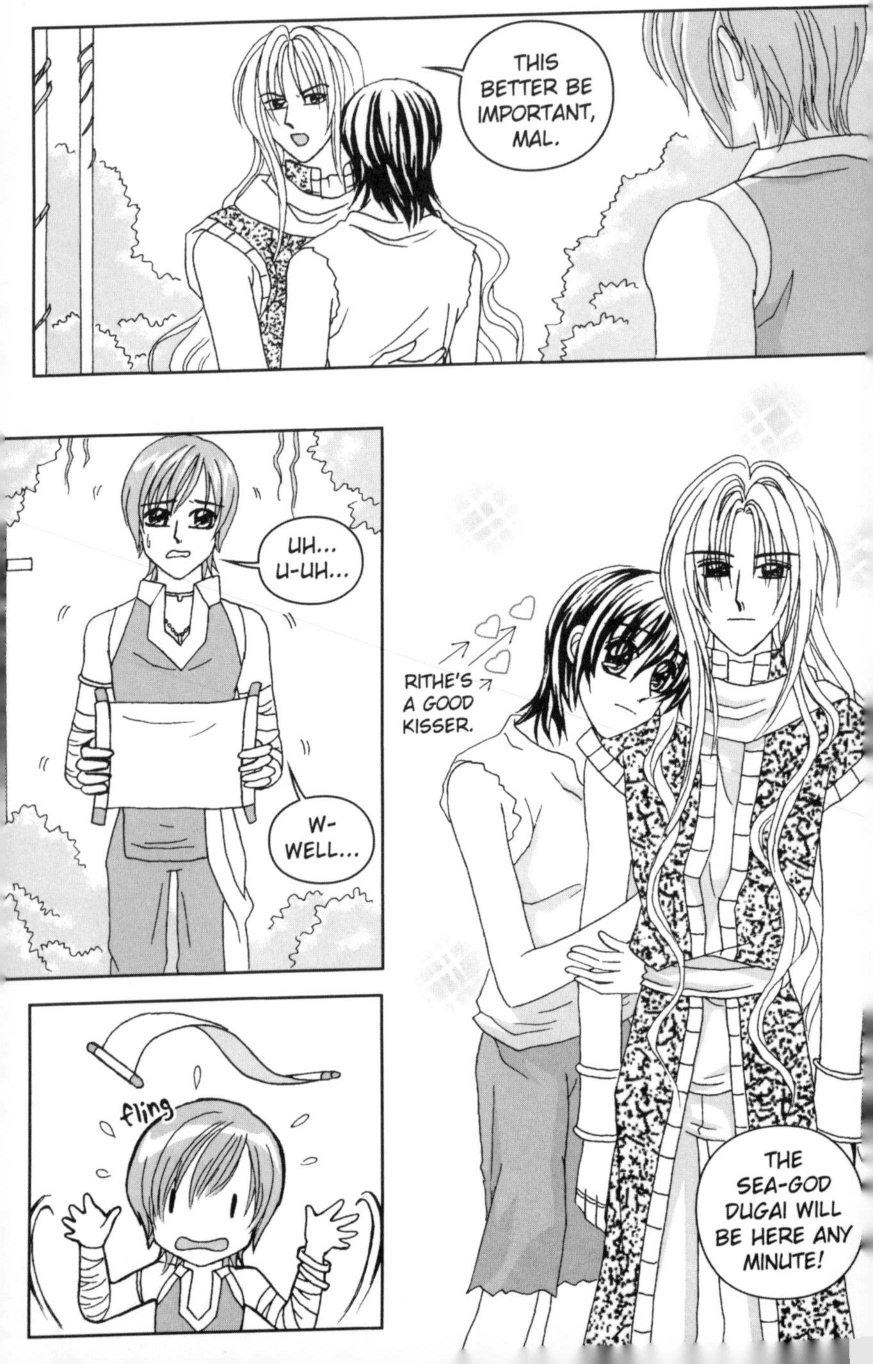
THIS BETTER BE IMPORTANT, MAL.
UH... U-UH...
W-WELL...
fling
RITHE'S A GOOD KISSER.
THE SEA-GOD DUGAI WILL BE HERE ANY MINUTE!

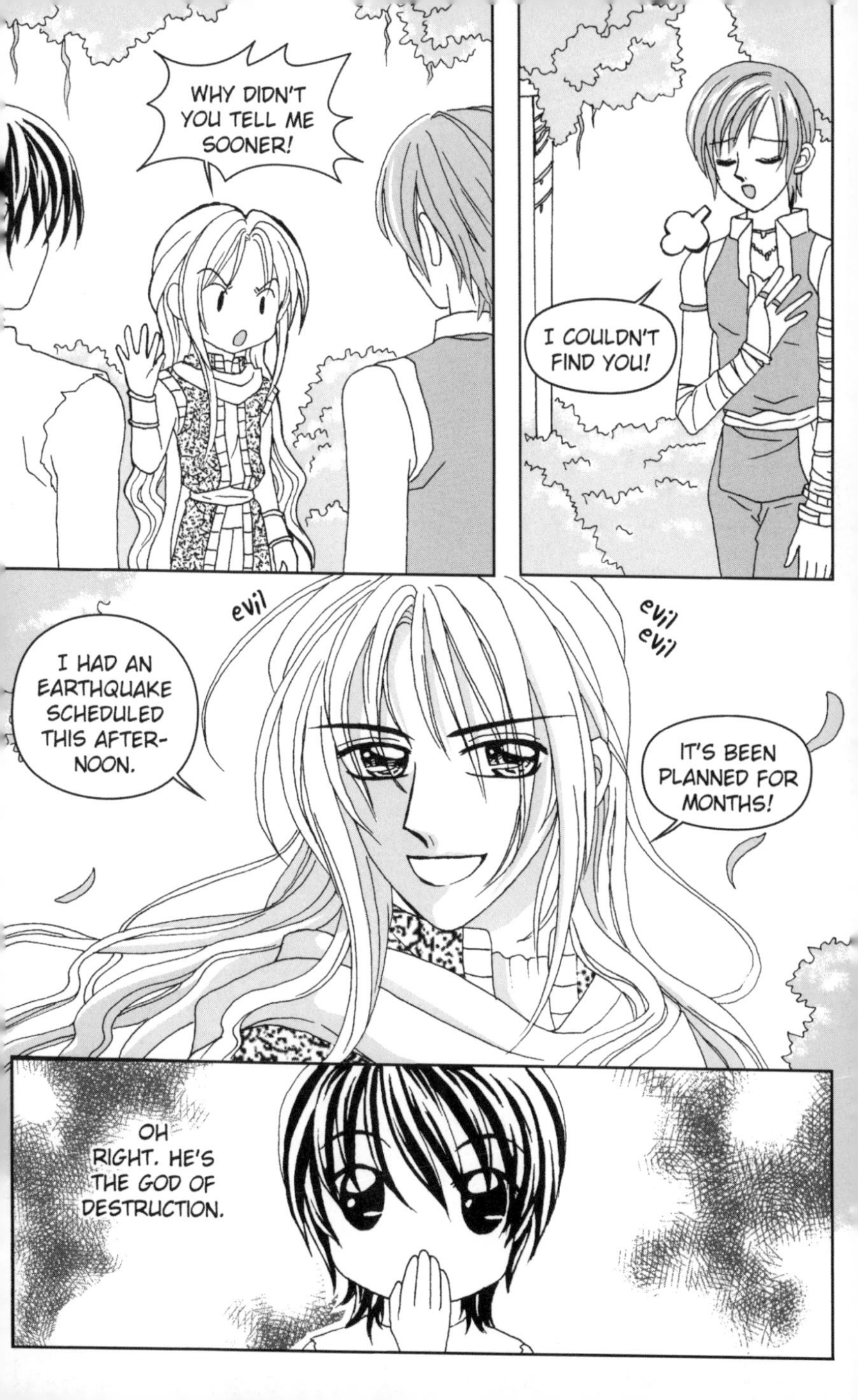
WHY DIDN'T YOU TELL ME SOONER!
I COULDN'T FIND YOU!
evil
evil
evil
I HAD AN EARTHQUAKE SCHEDULED THIS AFTER-NOON.
IT'S BEEN PLANNED FOR MONTHS!
OH RIGHT. HE'S THE GOD OF DESTRUCTION.

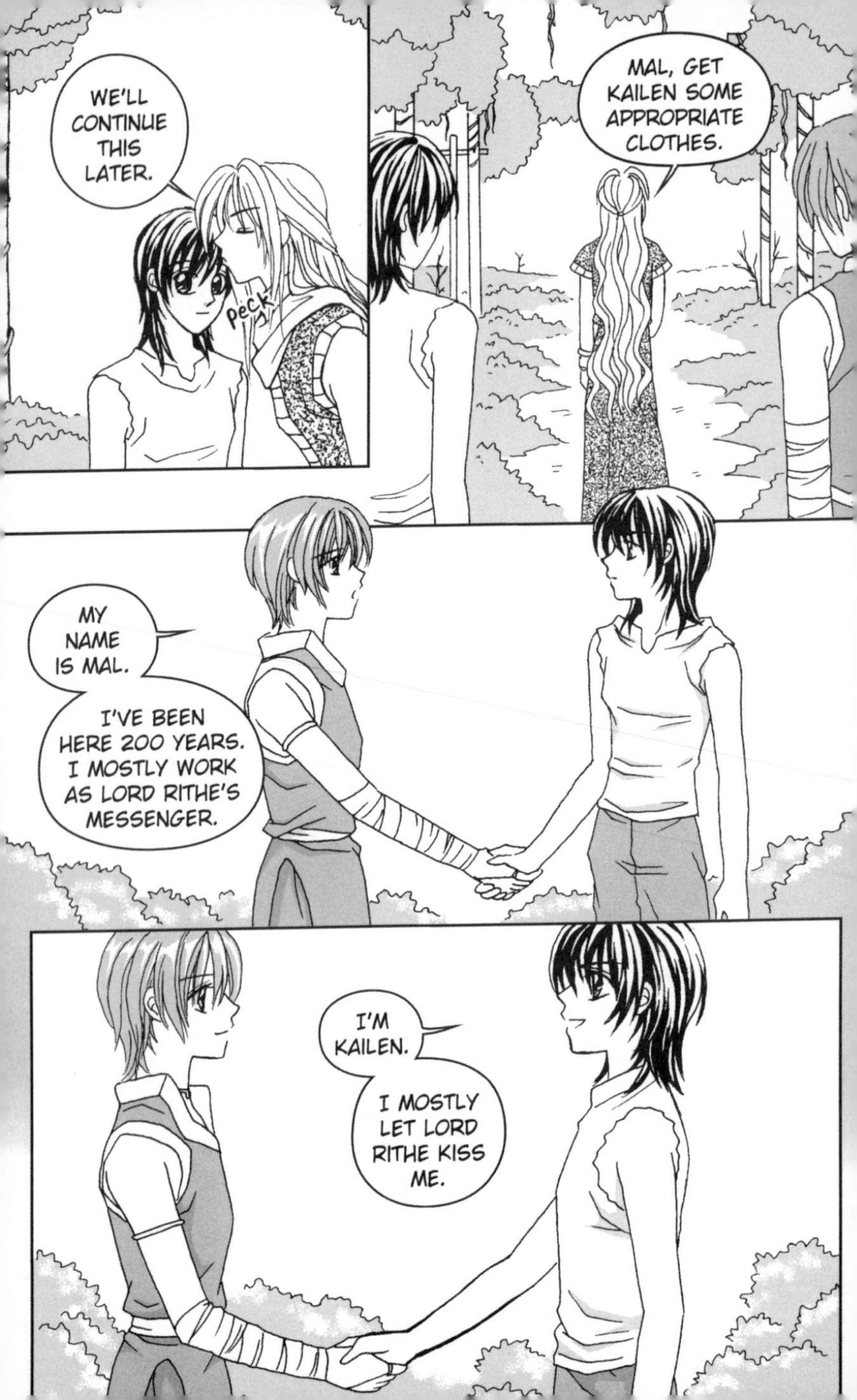
WE'LL CONTINUE THIS LATER.
peck
MAL, GET KAILEN SOME APPROPRIATE CLOTHES.
MY NAME IS MAL.
I'VE BEEN HERE 200 YEARS. I MOSTLY WORK AS LORD RITHE'S MESSENGER.
I'M KAILEN.
I MOSTLY LET LORD RITHE KISS ME.

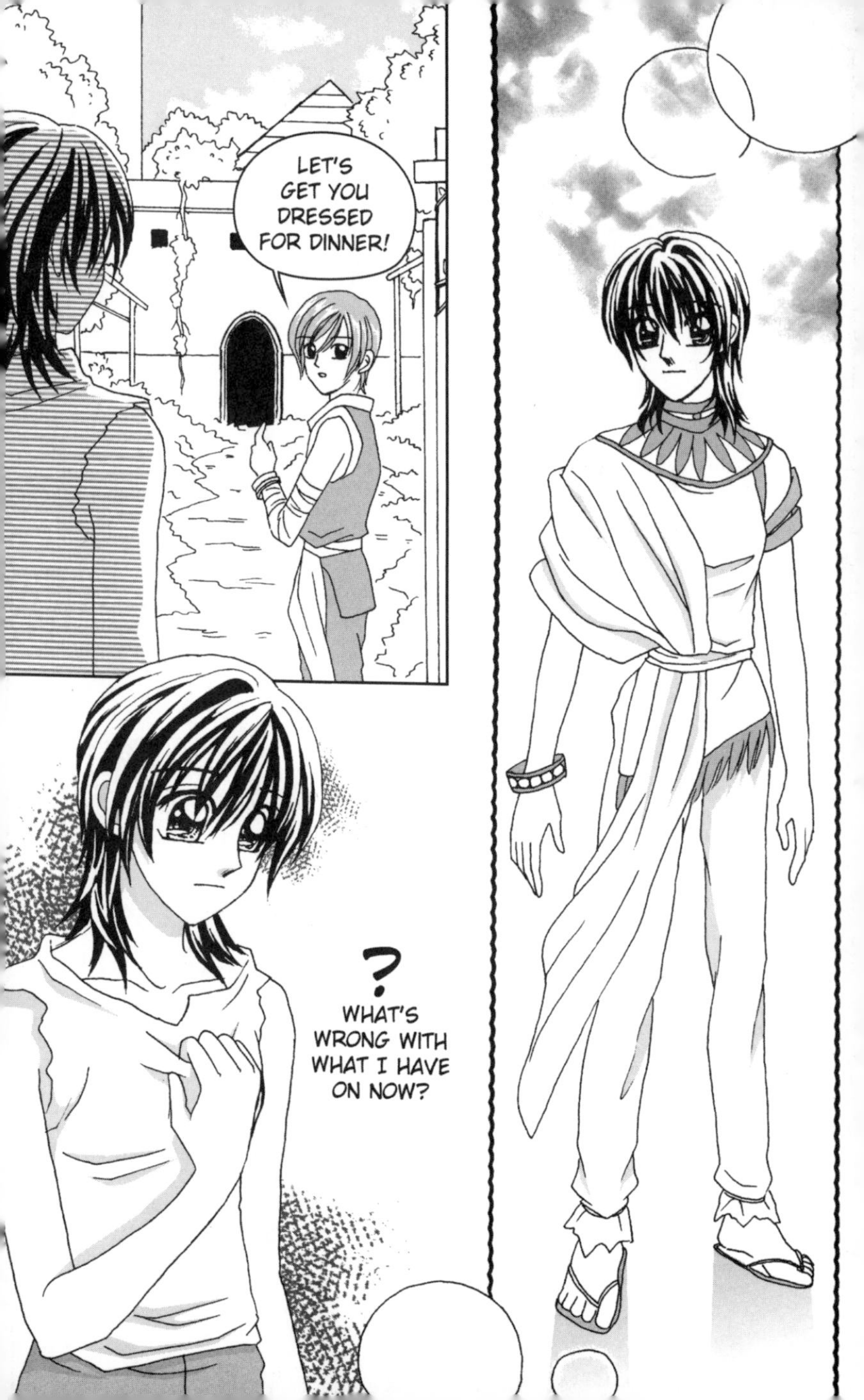
LET'S GET YOU DRESSED FOR DINNER!
WHAT'S WRONG WITH WHAT I HAVE ON NOW?

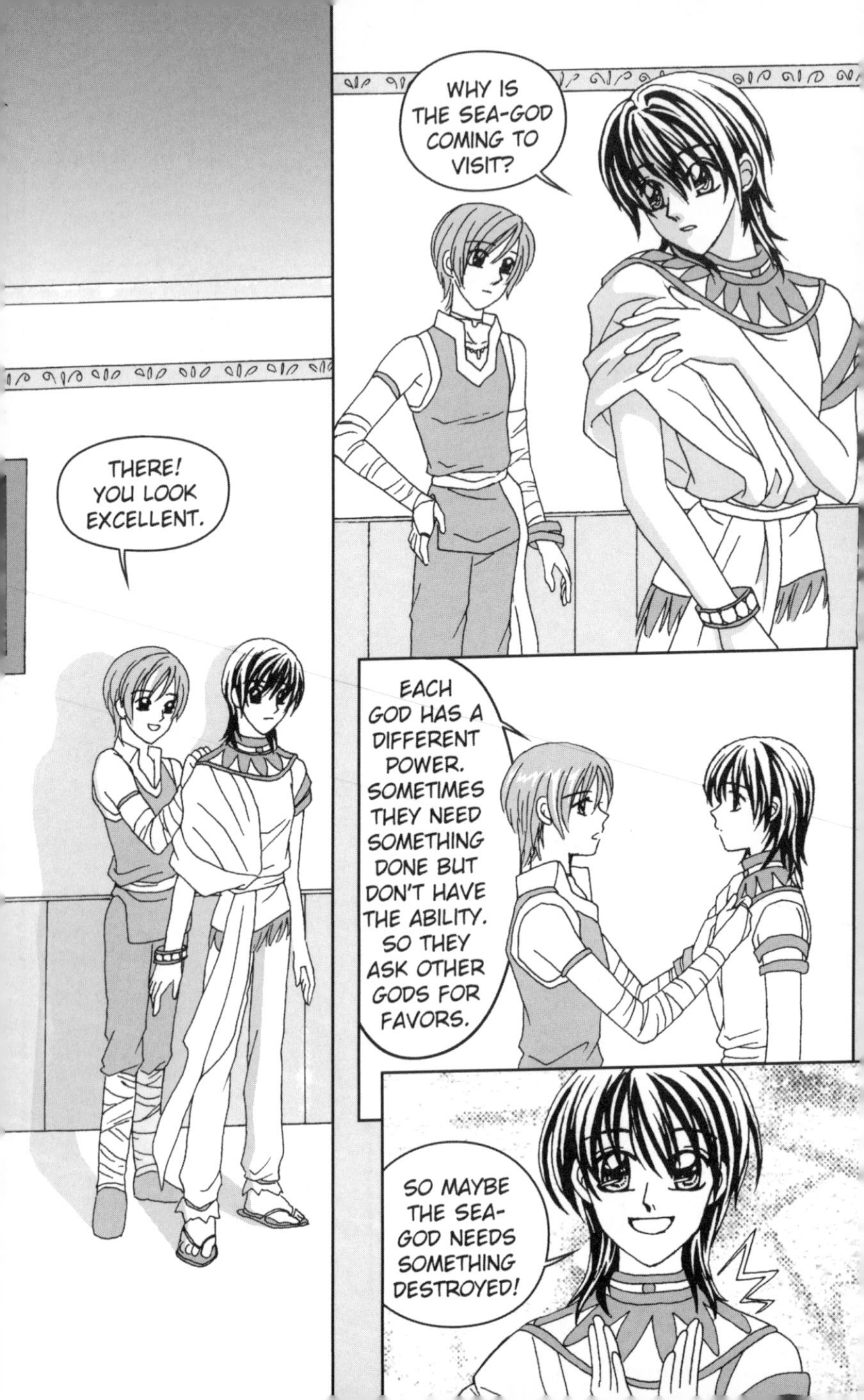

THERE! YOU LOOK EXCELLENT.
WHY IS THE SEA-GOD COMING TO VISIT?
EACH GOD HAS A DIFFERENT POWER. SOMETIMES THEY NEED SOMETHING DONE BUT DON'T HAVE THE ABILITY. SO THEY ASK OTHER GODS FOR FAVORS.
SO MAYBE THE SEA-GOD NEEDS SOMETHING DESTROYED!

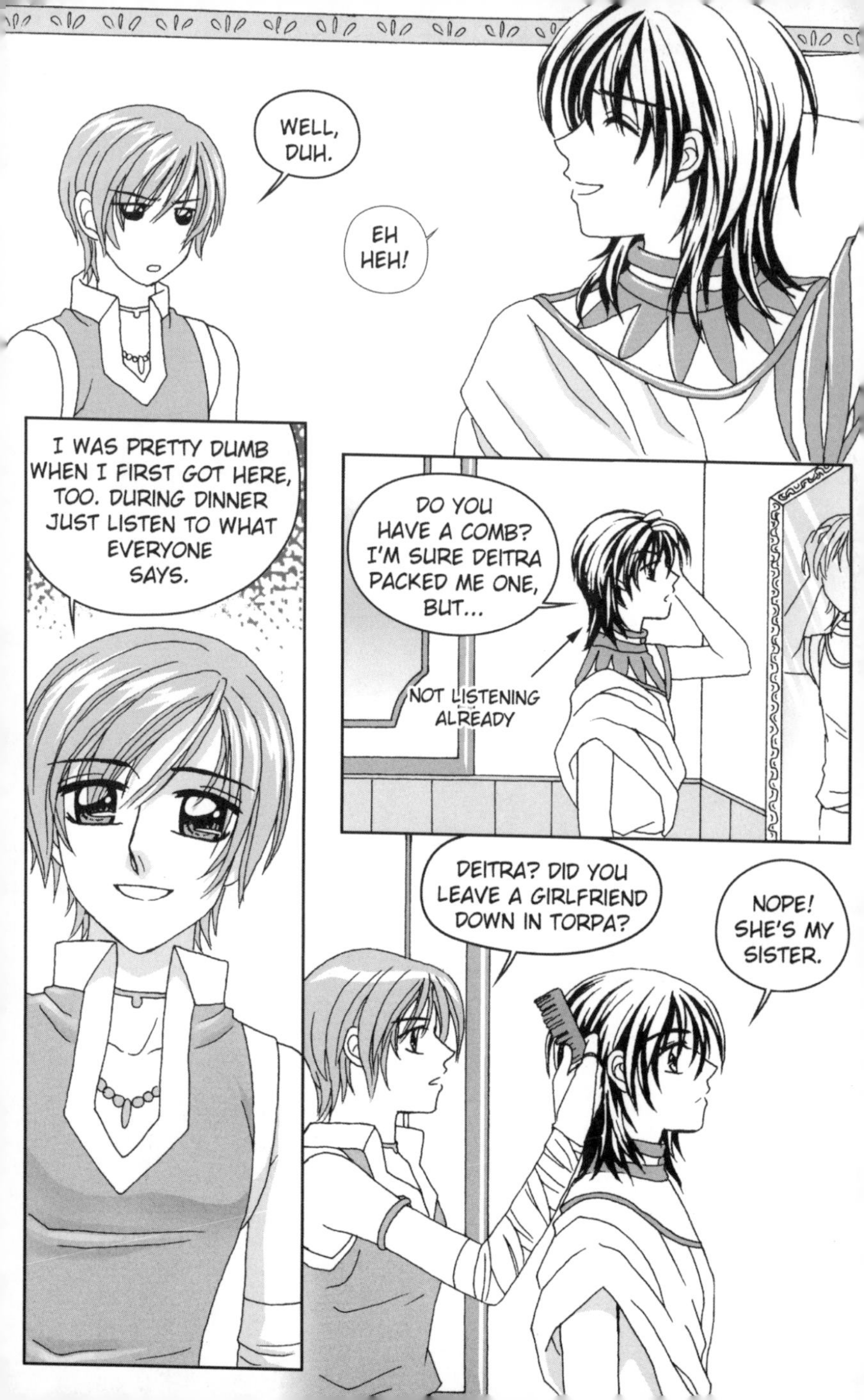
WELL, DUH.
EH HEH!
I WAS PRETTY DUMB WHEN I FIRST GOT HERE, TOO. DURING DINNER JUST LISTEN TO WHAT EVERYONE SAYS.
DO YOU HAVE A COMB? I'M SURE DEITRA PACKED ME ONE, BUT...
NOT LISTENING ALREADY
DEITRA? DID YOU LEAVE A GIRLFRIEND DOWN IN TORPA?
NOPE! SHE'S MY SISTER.

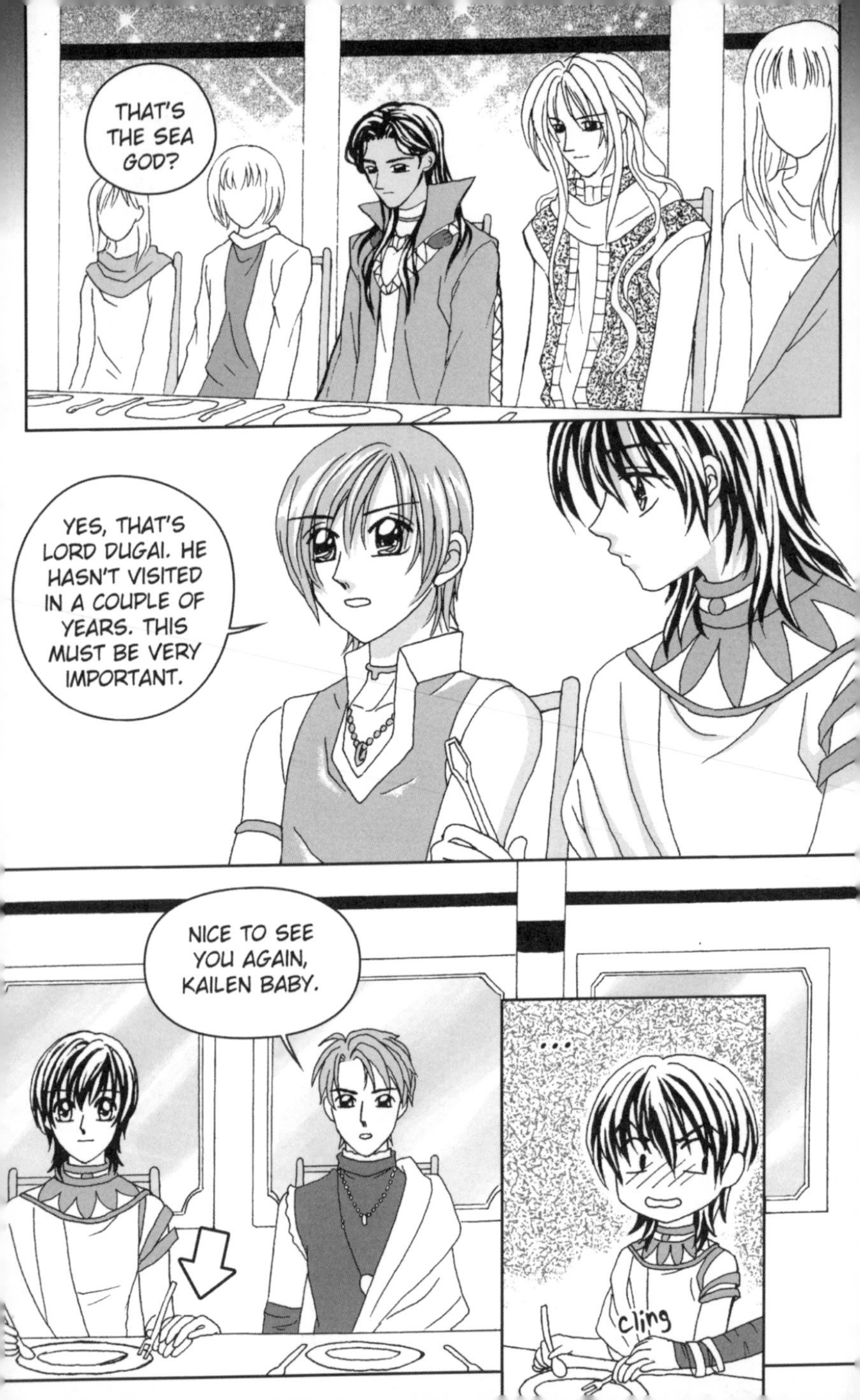
THAT'S THE SEA GOD?
YES, THAT'S LORD DUGAI. HE HASN'T VISITED IN A COUPLE OF YEARS. THIS MUST BE VERY IMPORTANT.
NICE TO SEE YOU AGAIN, KAILEN BABY.
...
cling

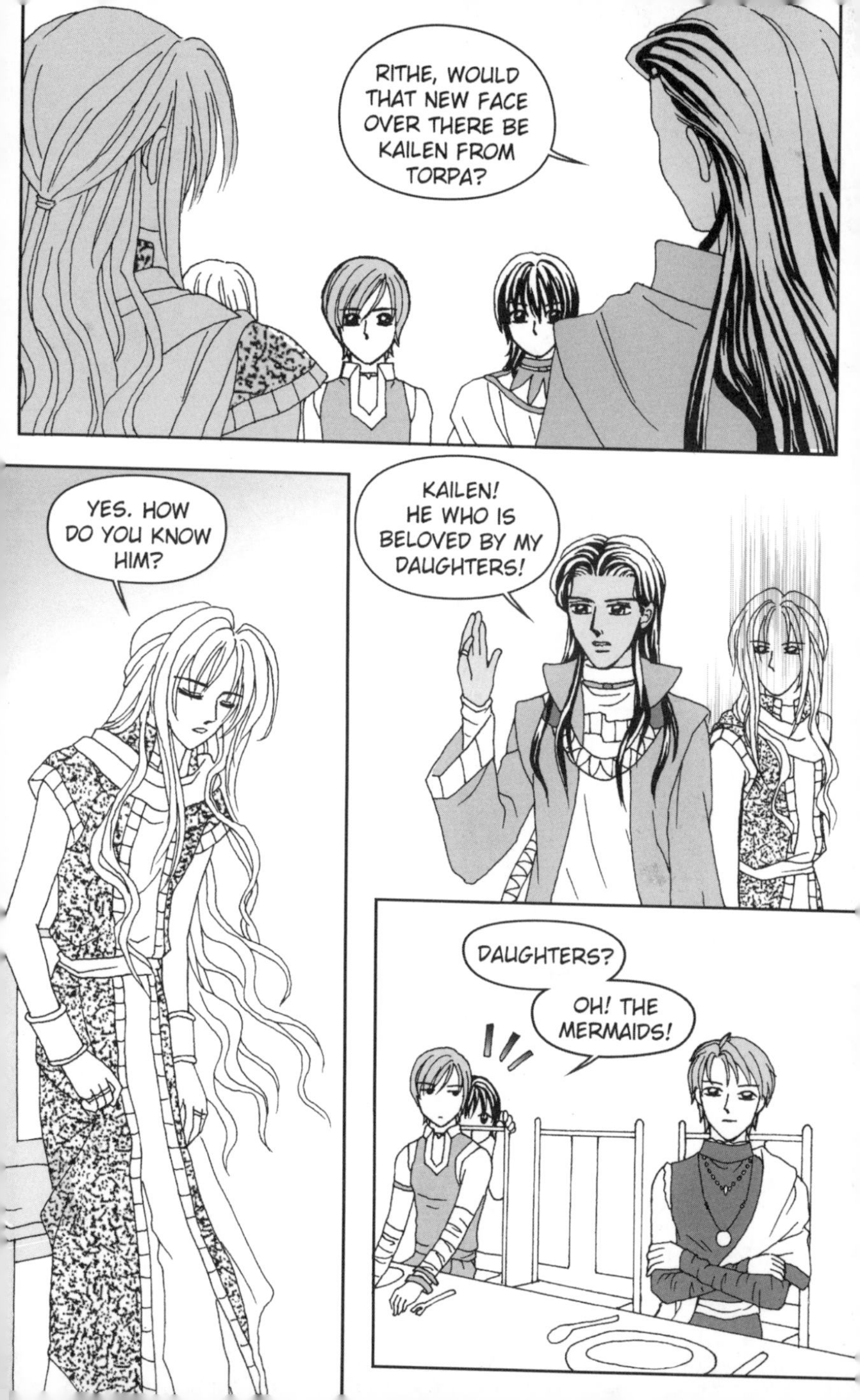
RITHE, WOULD THAT NEW FACE OVER THERE BE KAILEN FROM TORPA?
YES. HOW DO YOU KNOW HIM?
KAILEN! HE WHO IS BELOVED BY MY DAUGHTERS!
DAUGHTERS?
OH! THE MERMAIDS!

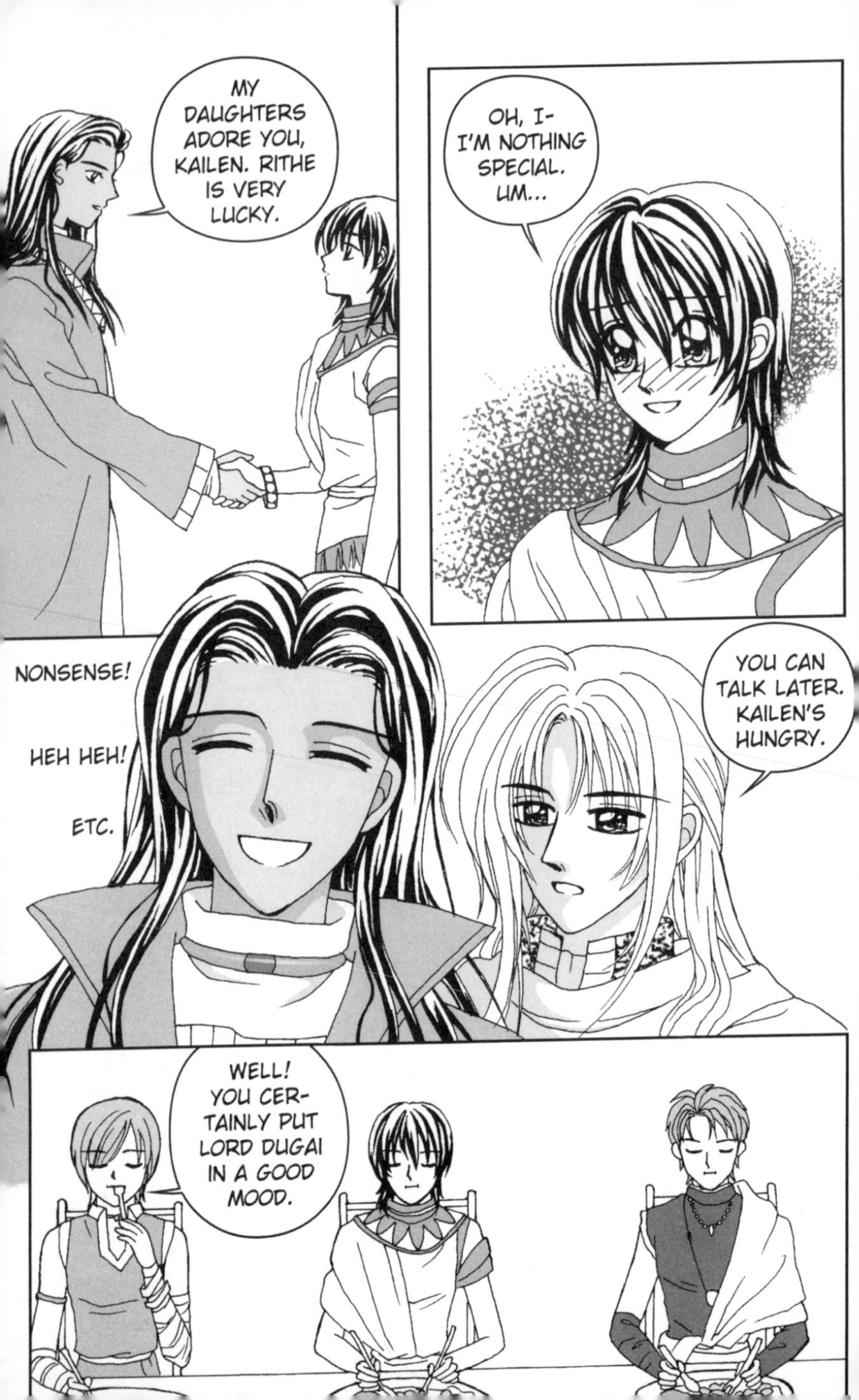
MY DAUGHTERS ADORE YOU, KAILEN. RITHE IS VERY LUCKY.
OH, I- I'M NOTHING SPECIAL. UM...
YOU CAN TALK LATER. KAILEN'S HUNGRY.
NONSENSE!
HEH HEH!
ETC.
WELL! YOU CER-TAINLY PUT LORD DUGAI IN A GOOD MOOD.

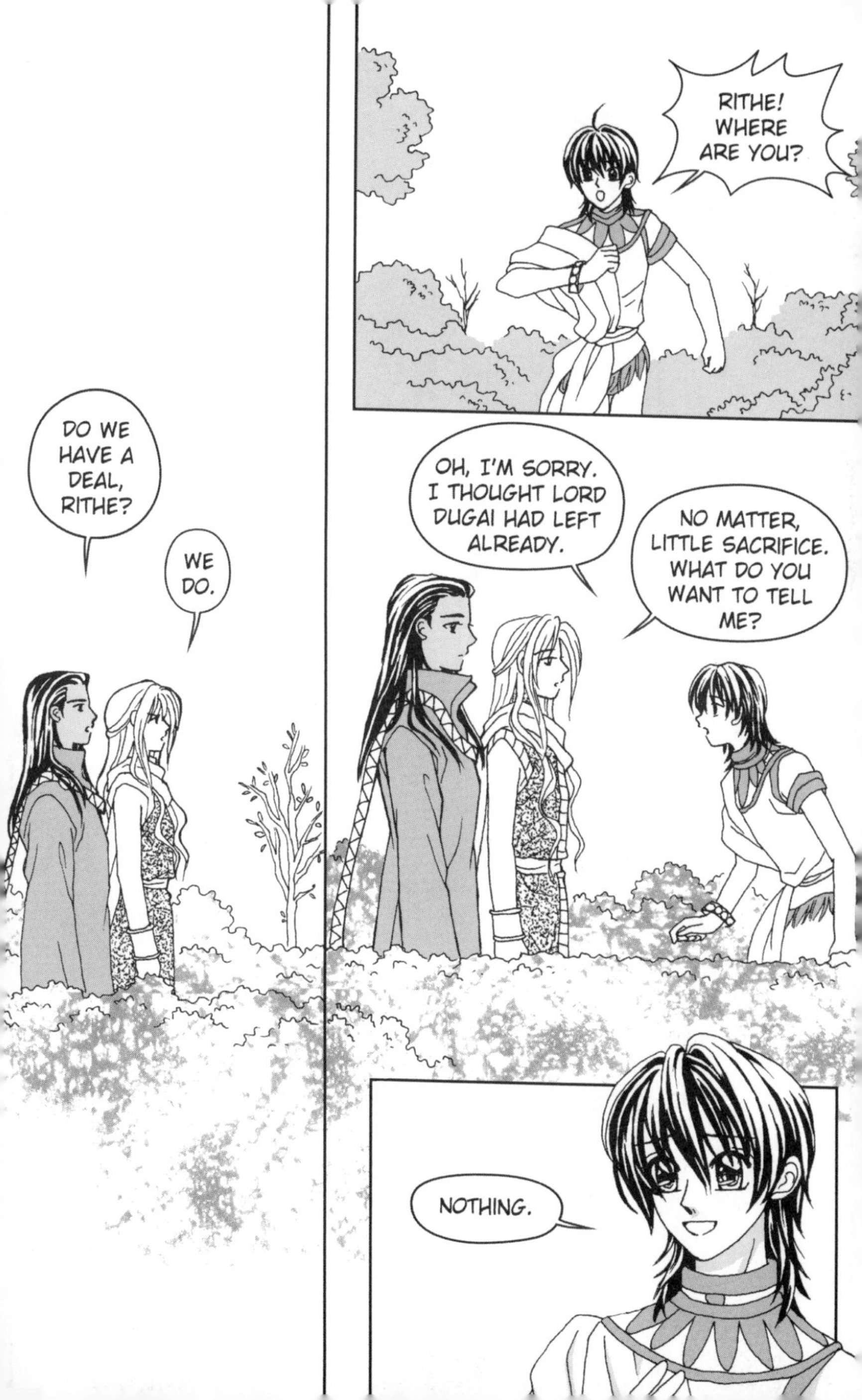

DO WE HAVE A DEAL, RITHE?
WE DO.
RITHE! WHERE ARE YOU?
OH, I'M SORRY. I THOUGHT LORD DUGAI HAD LEFT ALREADY.
NO MATTER, LITTLE SACRIFICE. WHAT DO YOU WANT TO TELL ME?
NOTHING.

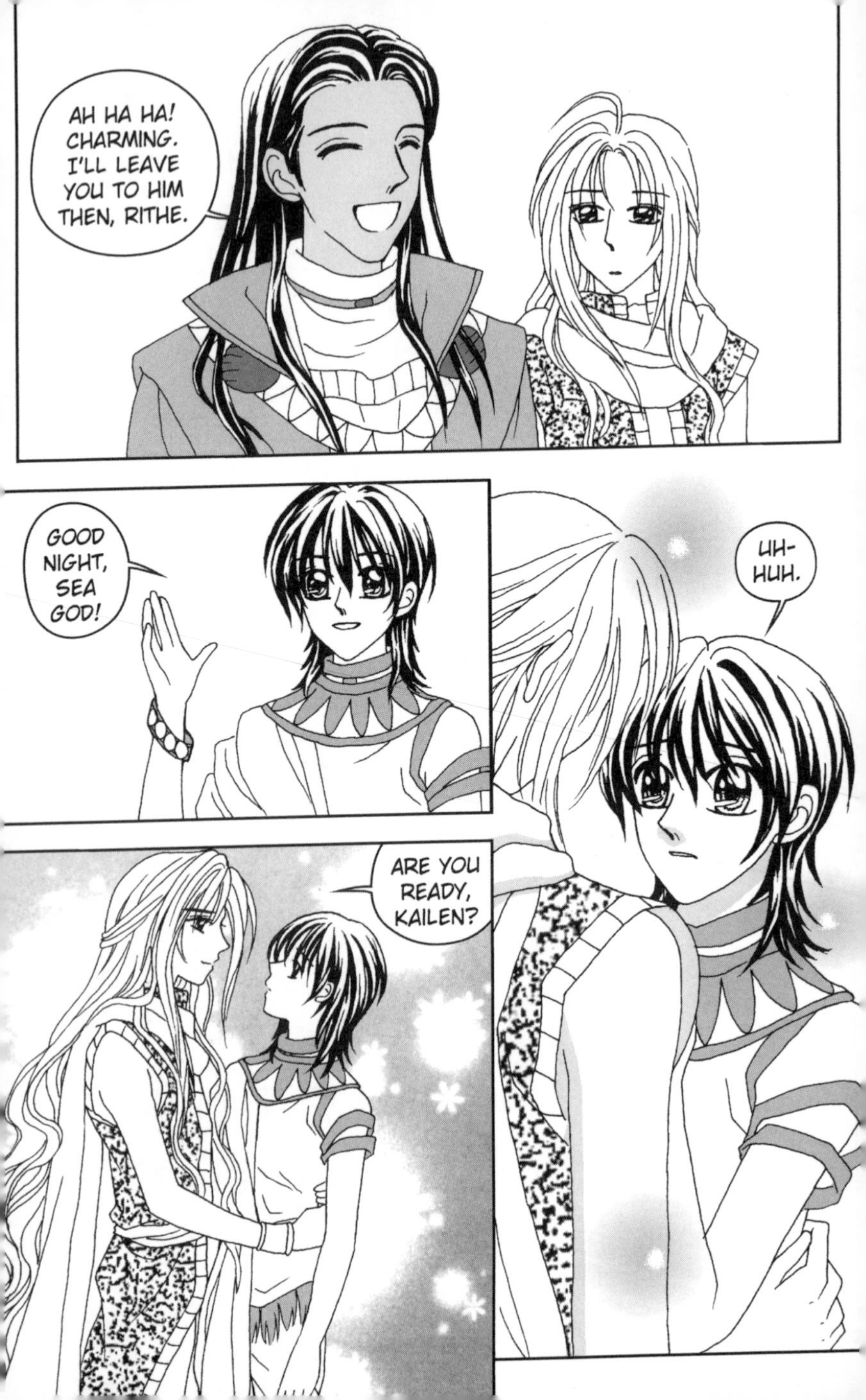
AH HA HA! CHARMING. I'LL LEAVE YOU TO HIM THEN, RITHE.
GOOD NIGHT, SEA GOD!
UH-HUH.
ARE YOU READY, KAILEN?

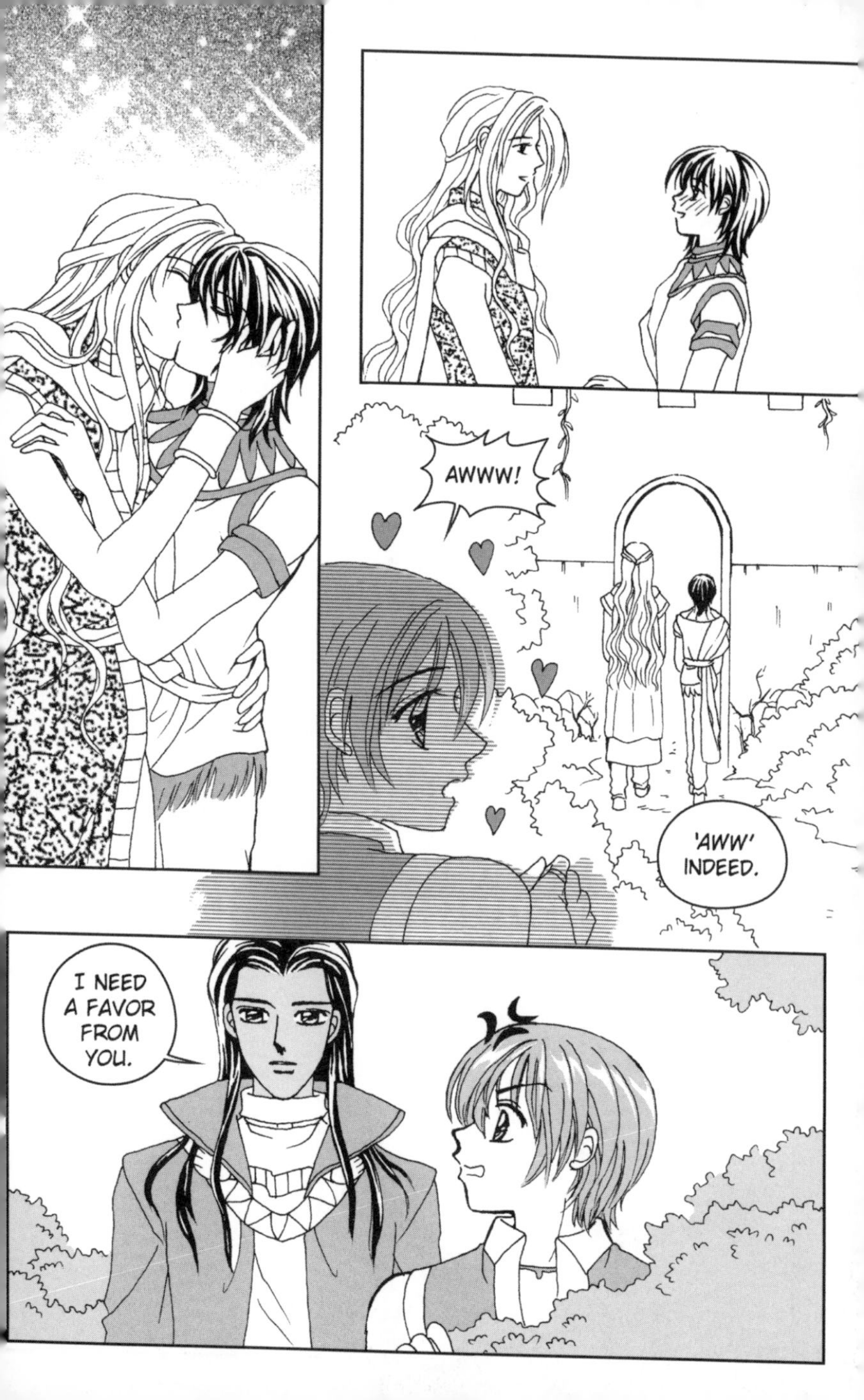
AWWW!
'AWW' INDEED.
I NEED A FAVOR FROM YOU.

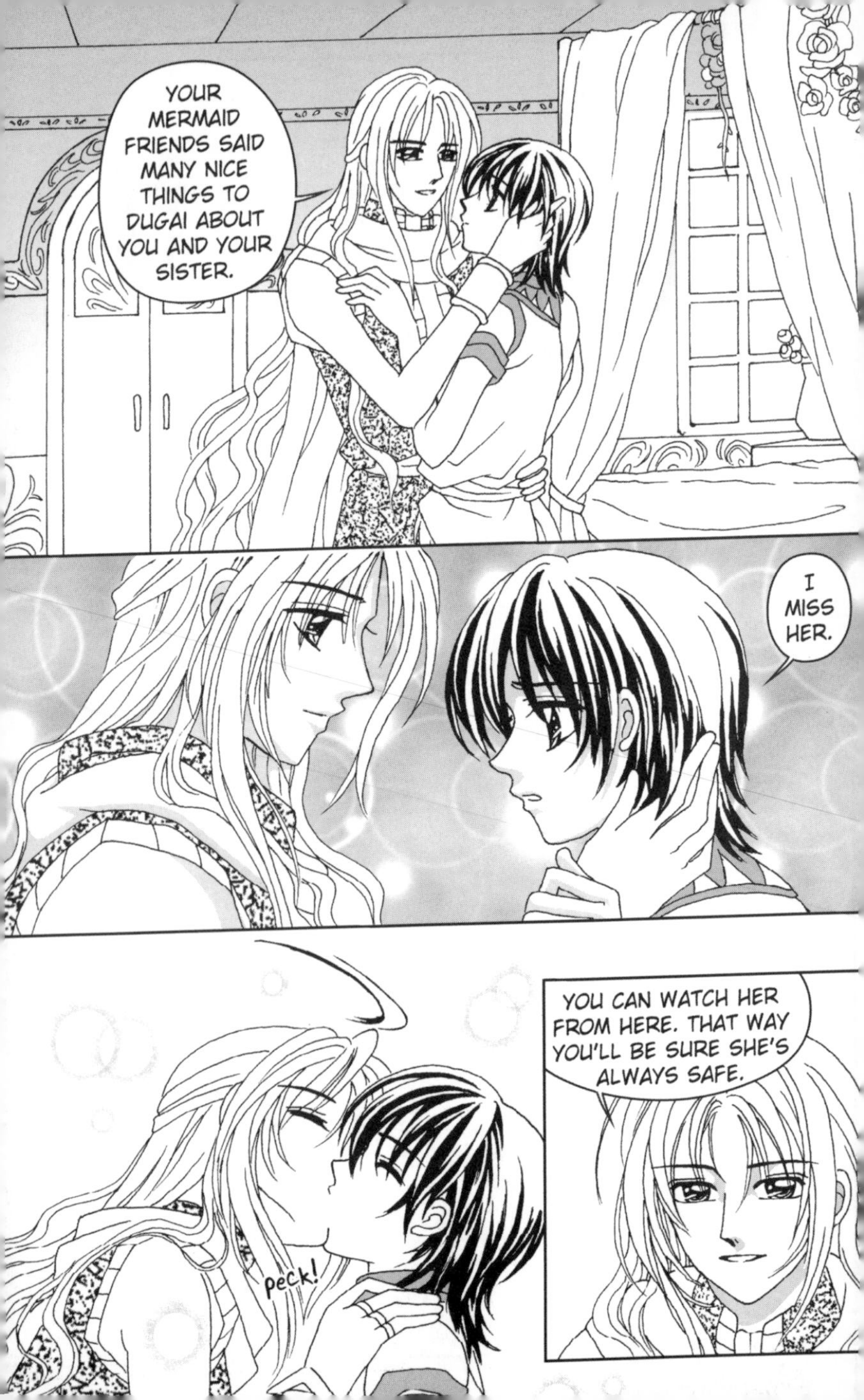
YOUR MERMAID FRIENDS SAID MANY NICE THINGS TO DUGAI ABOUT YOU AND YOUR SISTER.
I MISS HER.
YOU CAN WATCH HER FROM HERE. THAT WAY YOU'LL BE SURE SHE'S ALWAYS SAFE.
peck!

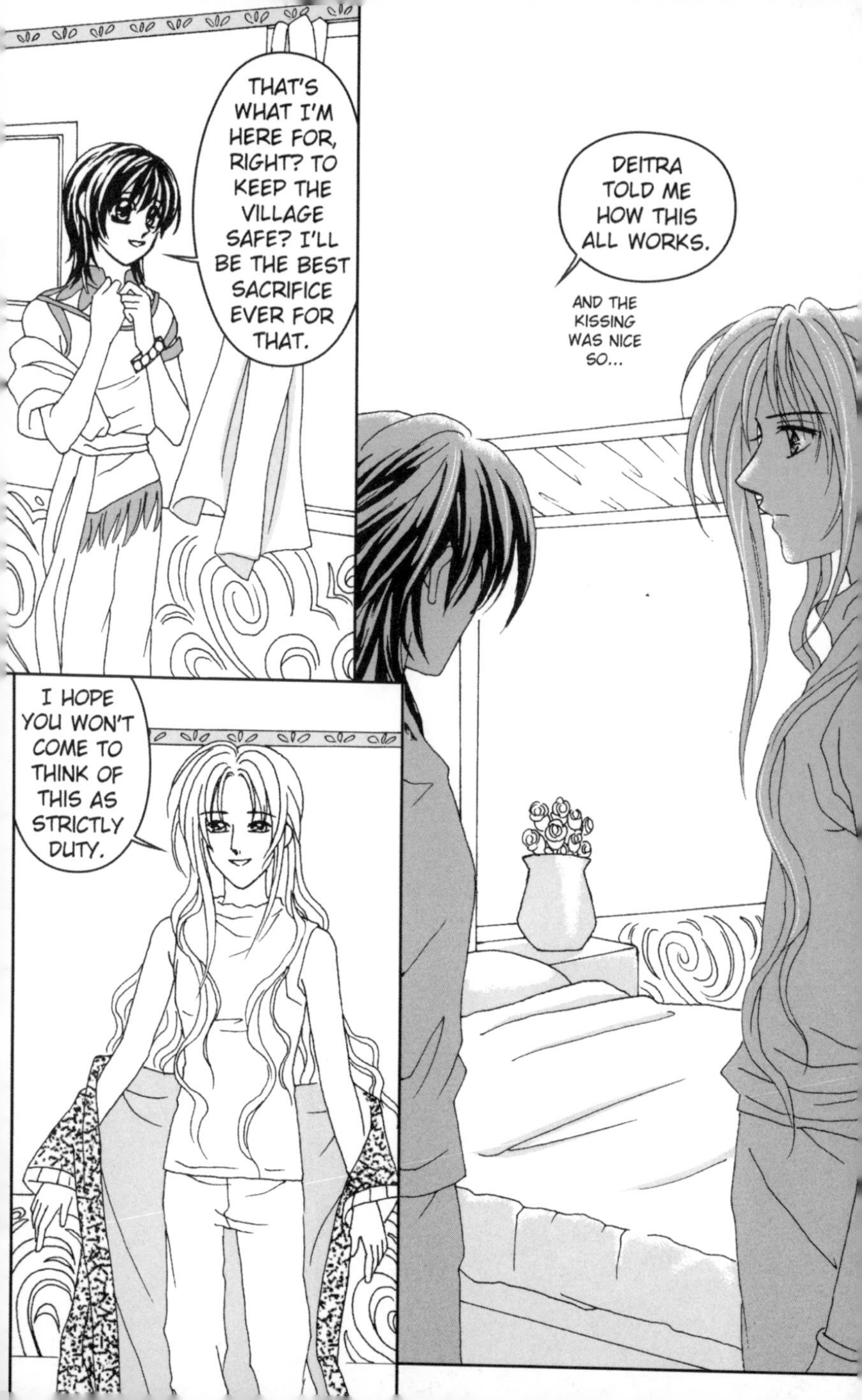
THAT'S WHAT I'M HERE FOR, RIGHT? TO KEEP THE VILLAGE SAFE? I'LL BE THE BEST SACRIFICE EVER FOR THAT.
DEITRA TOLD ME HOW THIS ALL WORKS.
AND THE KISSING WAS NICE SO...
I HOPE YOU WON'T COME TO THINK OF THIS AS STRICTLY DUTY.

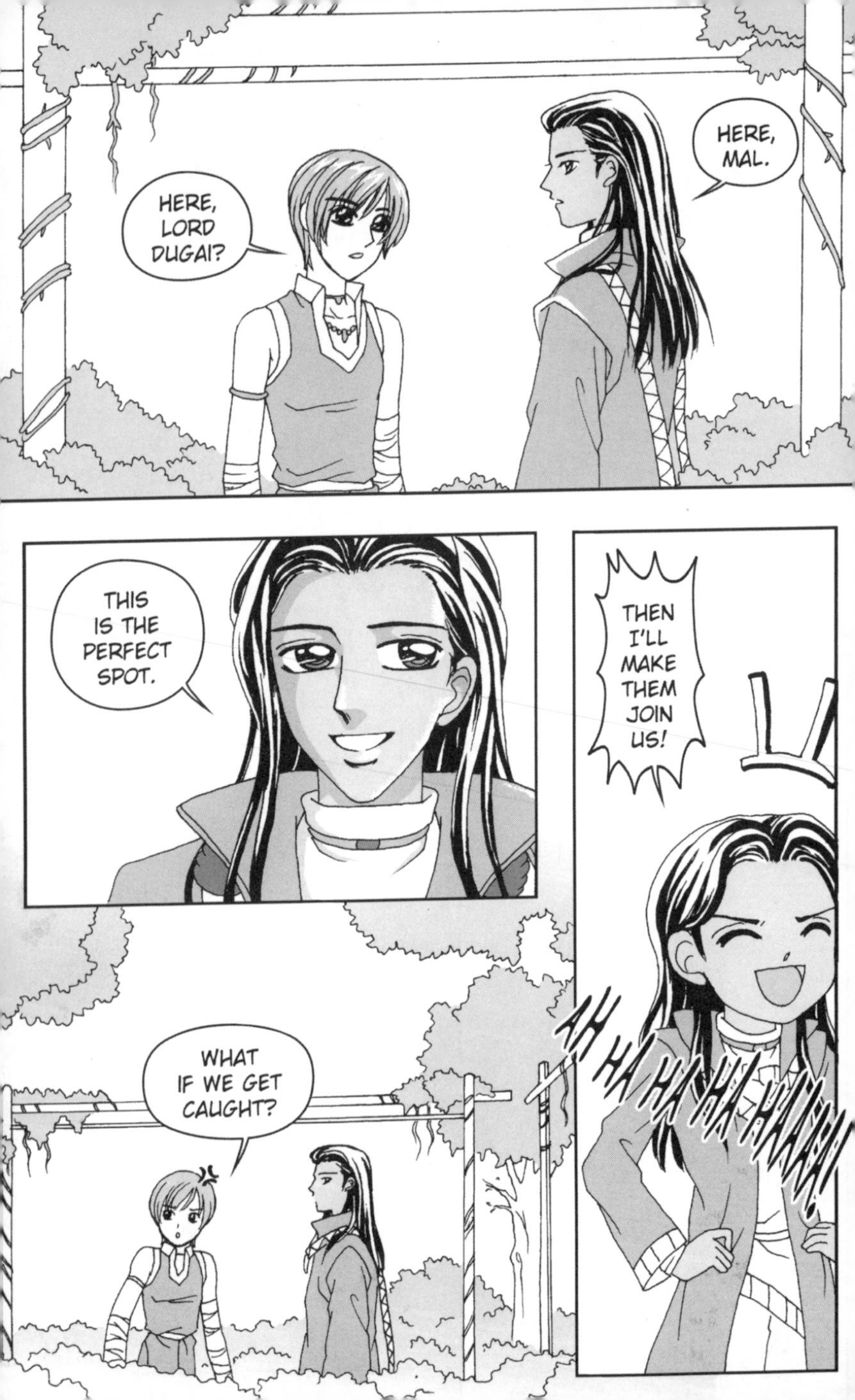
HERE, LORD DUGAI?
HERE, MAL.
THIS IS THE PERFECT SPOT.
WHAT IF WE GET CAUGHT?
THEN I'LL MAKE THEM JOIN US!
AH HA HA HA HA HAAA!

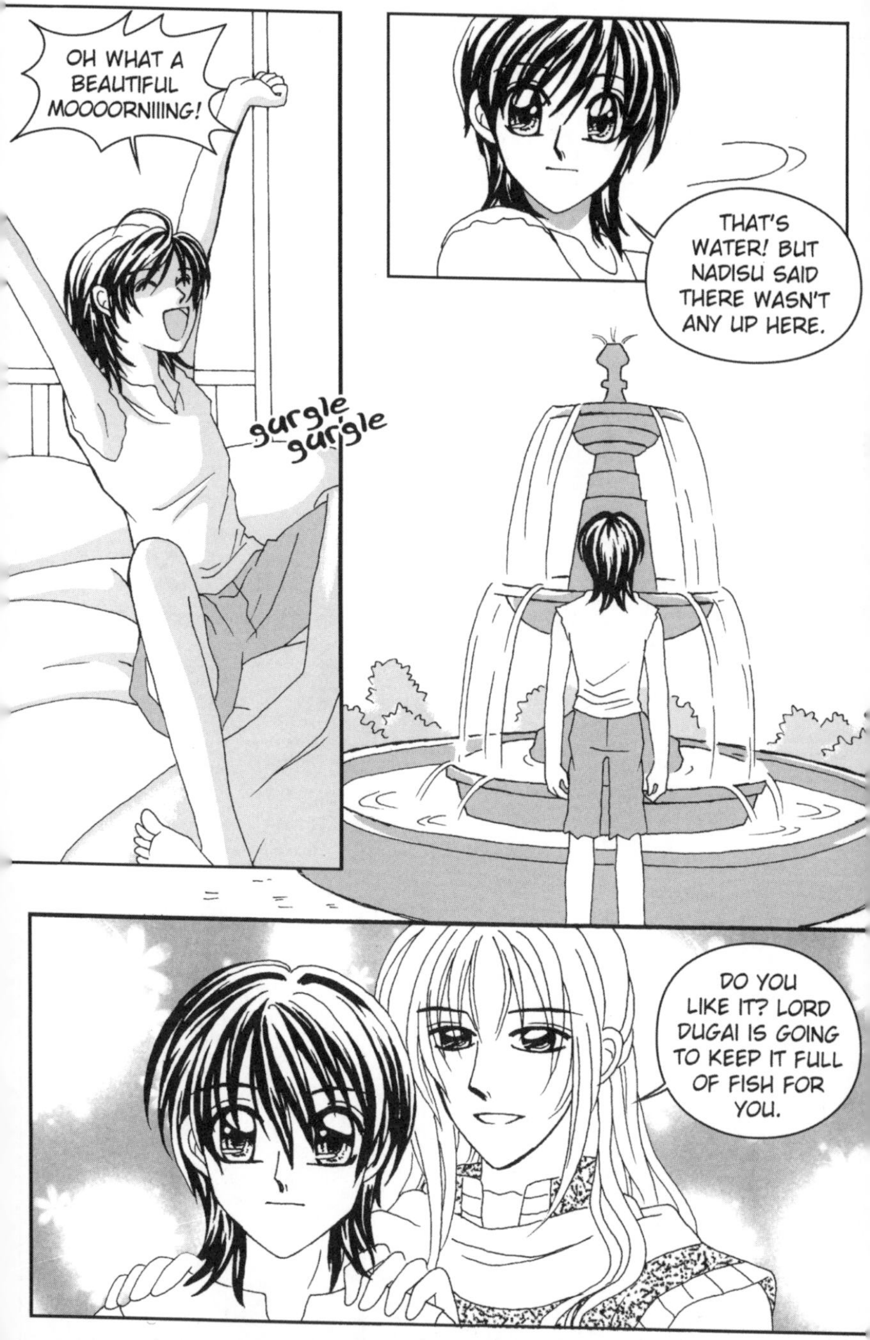
OH WHAT A BEAUTIFUL MOOOORNIIIING!
gurgle gurgle
THAT'S WATER! BUT NADISU SAID THERE WASN'T ANY UP HERE.
DO YOU LIKE IT? LORD DUGAI IS GOING TO KEEP IT FULL OF FISH FOR YOU.

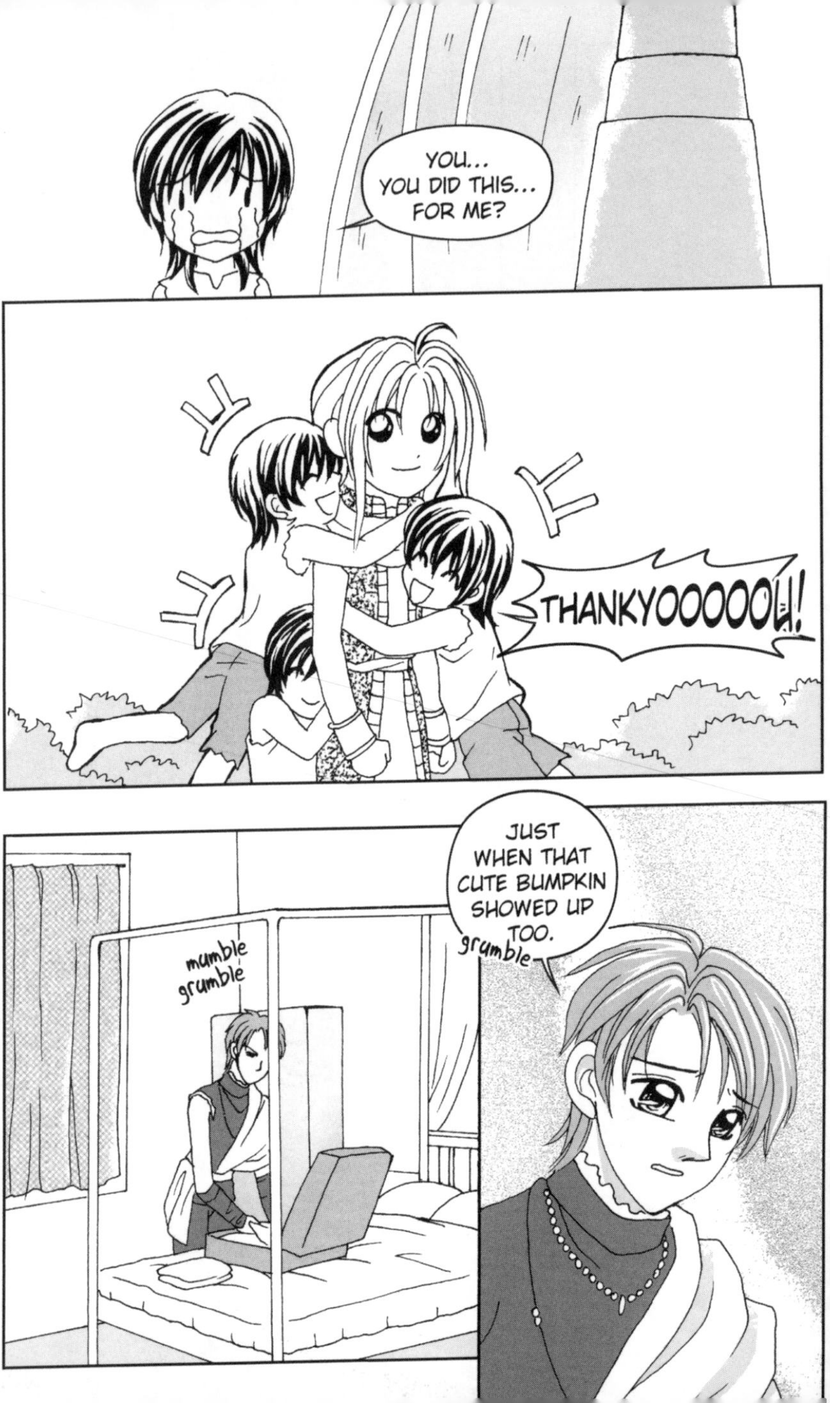
YOU...
YOU DID THIS...
FOR ME?
THANKYOOOOOOU!
JUST WHEN THAT CUTE BUMPKIN SHOWED UP TOO.
mumble grumble
grumble

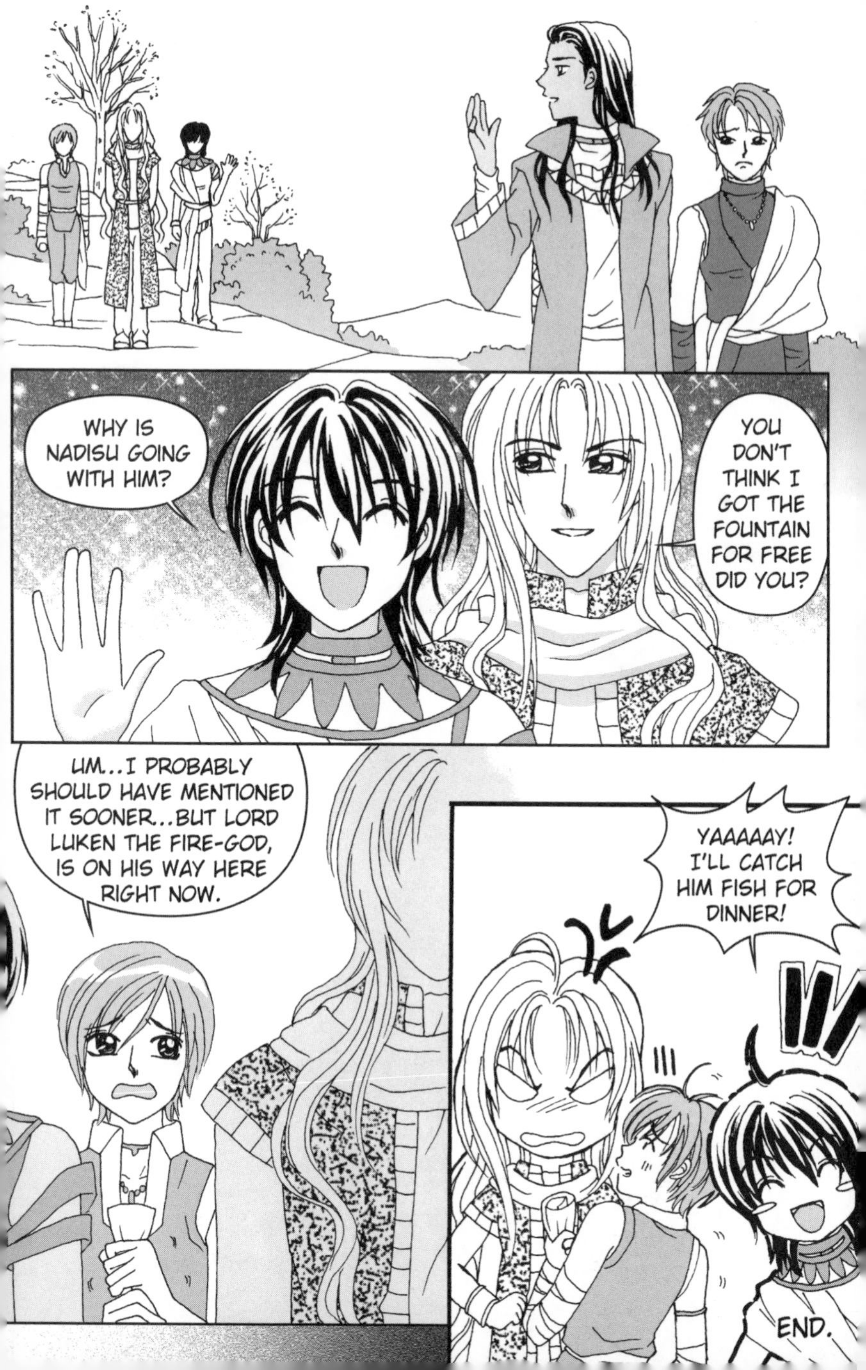
WHY IS NADISU GOING WITH HIM?
YOU DON'T THINK I GOT THE FOUNTAIN FOR FREE DID YOU?
UM...I PROBABLY SHOULD HAVE MENTIONED IT SOONER...BUT LORD LUKEN THE FIRE-GOD, IS ON HIS WAY HERE RIGHT NOW.
YAAAAAY! I'LL CATCH HIM FISH FOR DINNER!
END.

Coming Jan. 2007!

Zesty
by Margot Redding and Studio Kosaru

Smash hit Web Comic now in print! Flamboyant gay playboy Zesty sabotages his tycoon father's corrupt business schemes. Daddy joins with a secret sect to stop him. Dreamy sect agent Prince can't catch Zesty, but sure has captured his heart!

BY THE SAME ARTIST AS 'SMALL SACRIFICE'!

Coming Nov 2006!
Enjoy This Breif Preview!

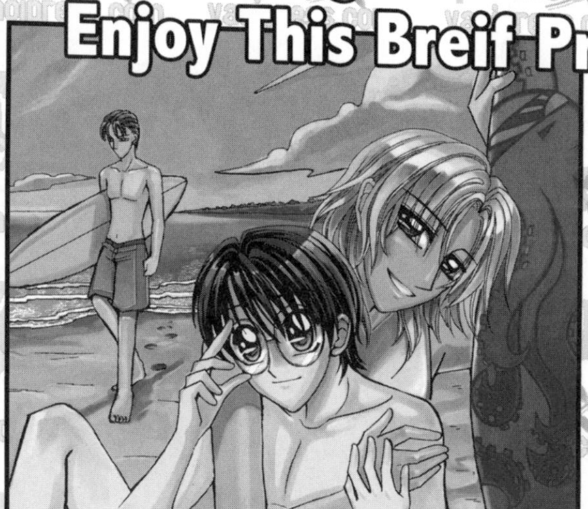
Surge
Kyle Green
Studio Kosaru

Surge

by Kyle Green and Studio Kosaru

Gorgeous surfer Shawn needs to pass a test or he'll flunk out of school. Luckily, the cute nerd Alan wants to learn how to surf so they strike a deal. Romantic sparks fly for the very mismatched couple, but Shawn's jealous ex warns Alan he's just being used.

FROM THE SAME ARTIST AS 'SMALL SACRIFICE'!

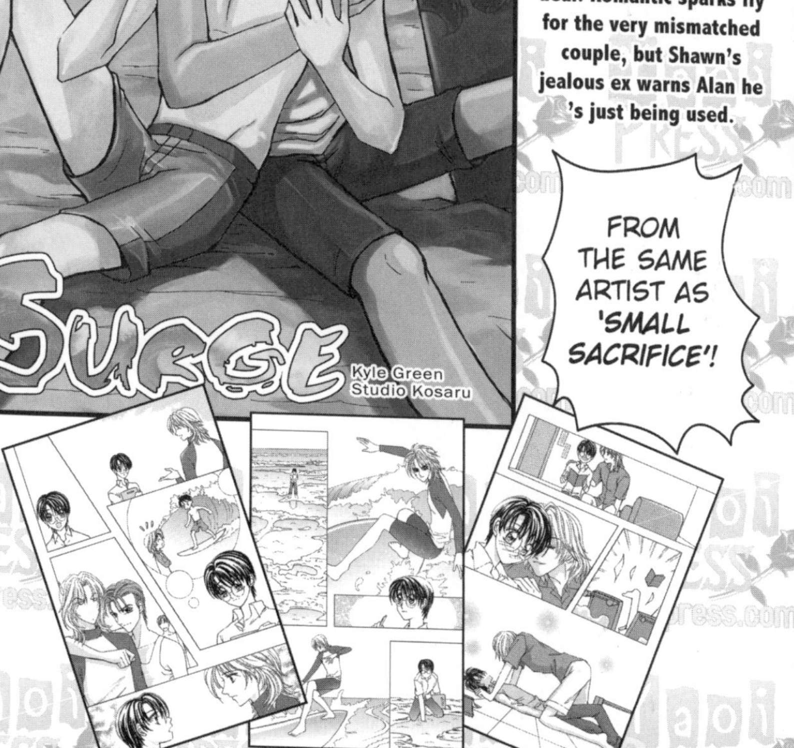

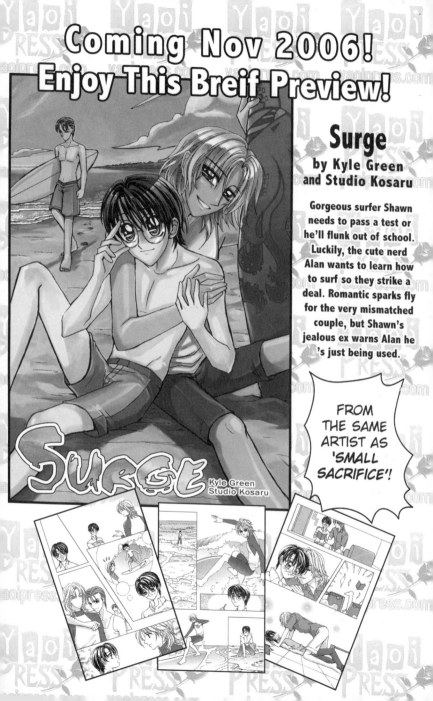

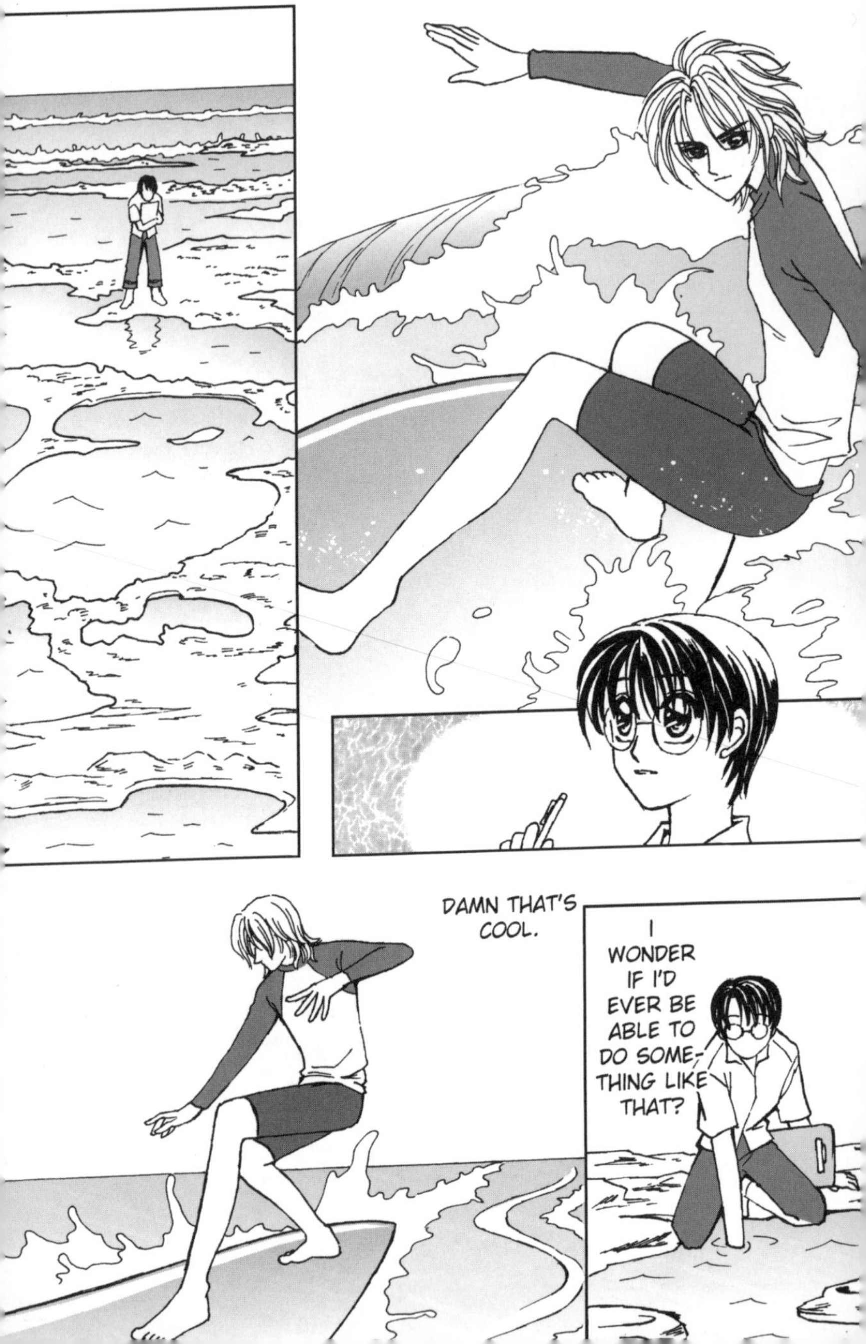
DAMN THAT'S COOL.
I WONDER IF I'D EVER BE ABLE TO DO SOME-THING LIKE THAT?

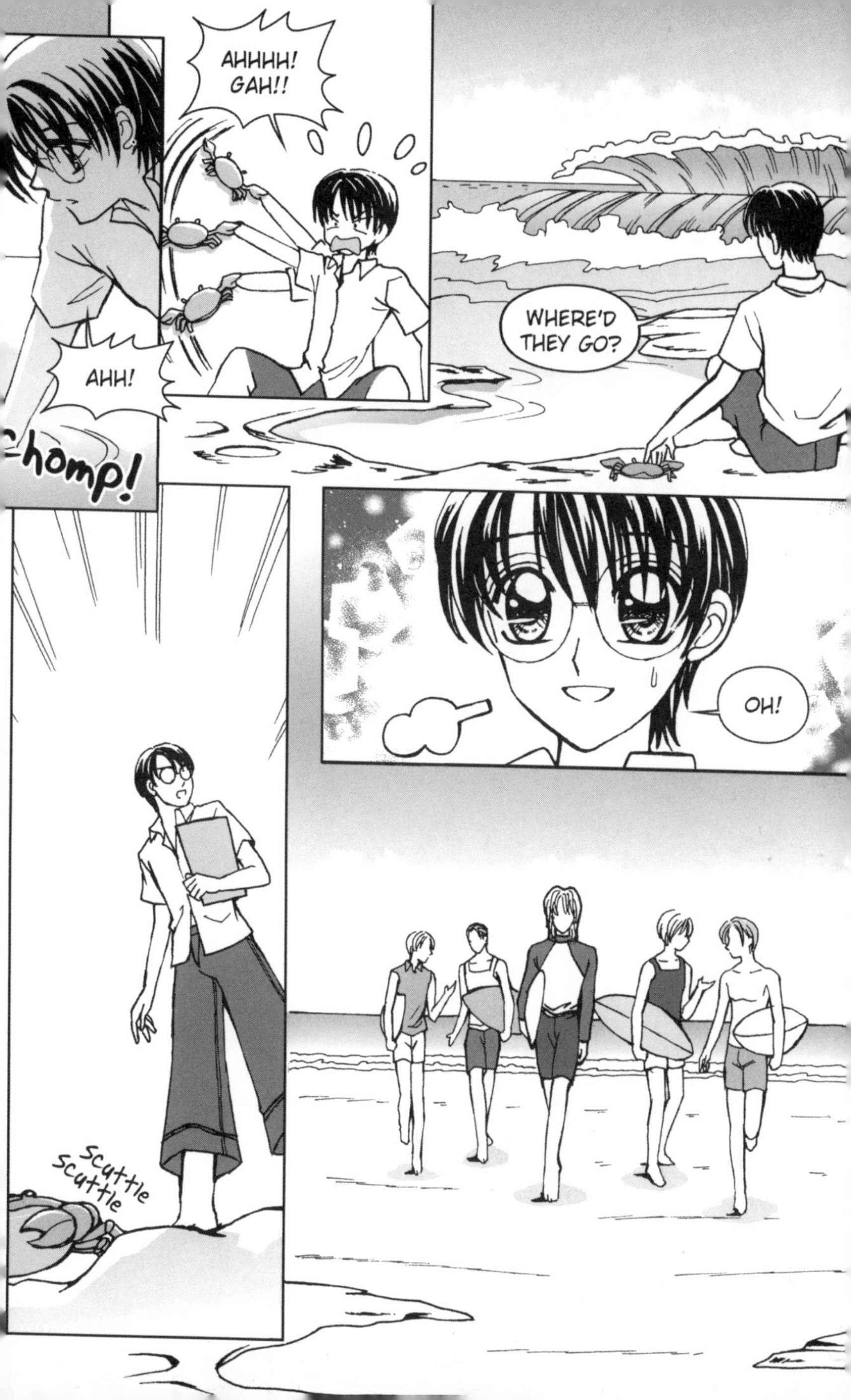
AHHHH! GAH!!
AHH!
Chomp!
WHERE'D THEY GO?
OH!
Scuttle scuttle

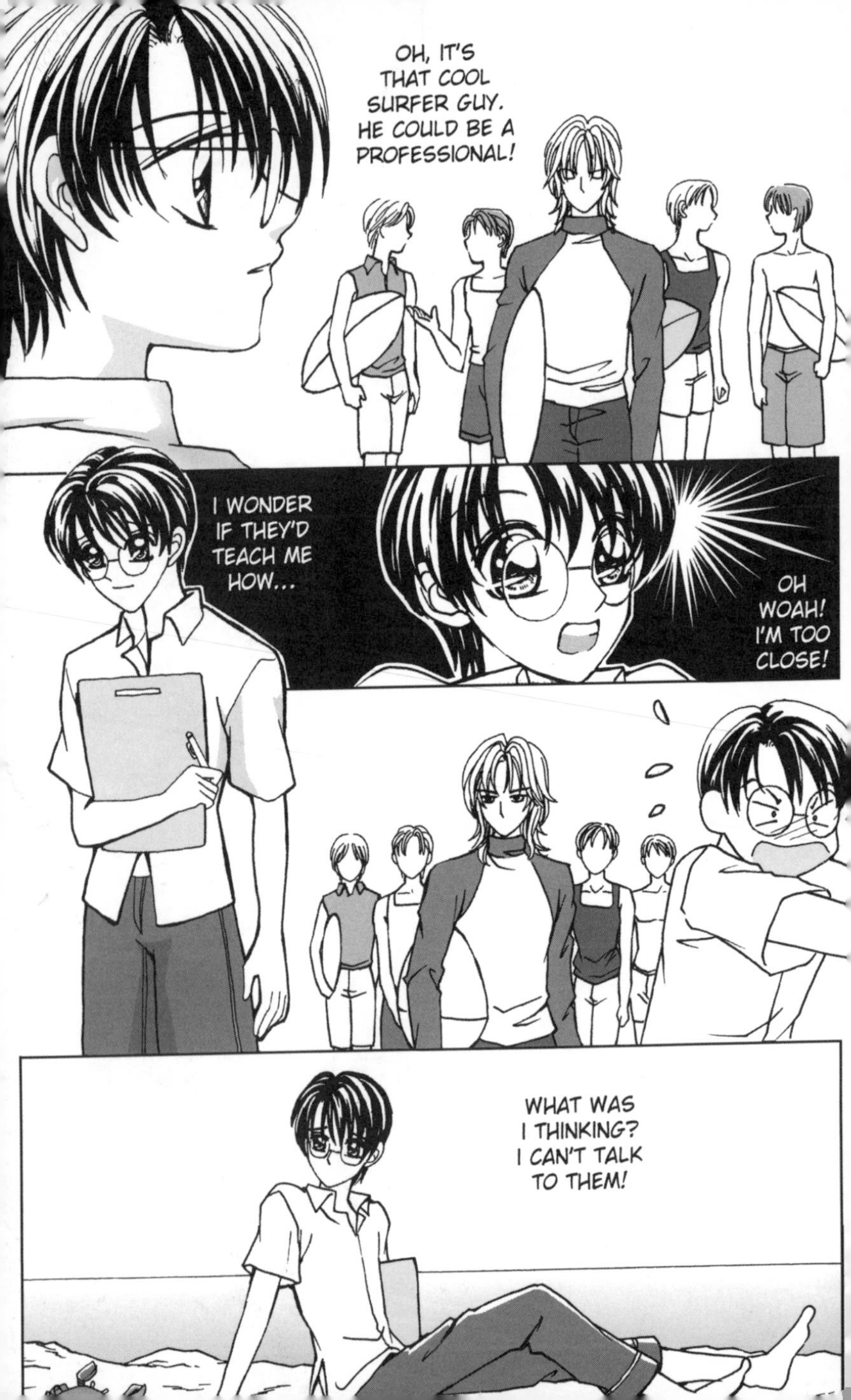
OH, IT'S THAT COOL SURFER GUY. HE COULD BE A PROFESSIONAL!
I WONDER IF THEY'D TEACH ME HOW...
OH WOAH! I'M TOO CLOSE!
WHAT WAS I THINKING? I CAN'T TALK TO THEM!

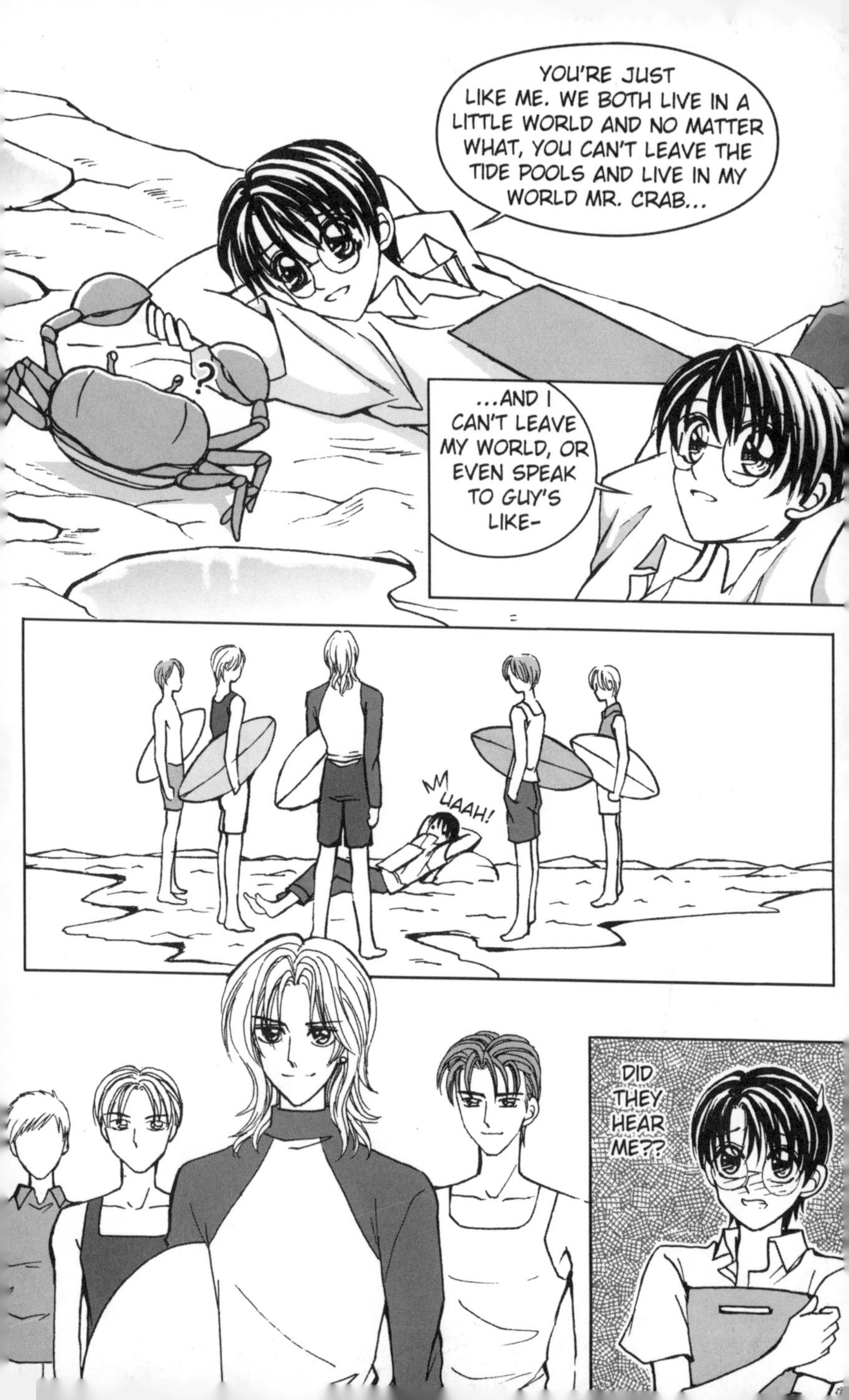
YOU'RE JUST LIKE ME. WE BOTH LIVE IN A LITTLE WORLD AND NO MATTER WHAT, YOU CAN'T LEAVE THE TIDE POOLS AND LIVE IN MY WORLD MR. CRAB...
?
...AND I CAN'T LEAVE MY WORLD, OR EVEN SPEAK TO GUY'S LIKE-
UAAH!
DID THEY HEAR ME??

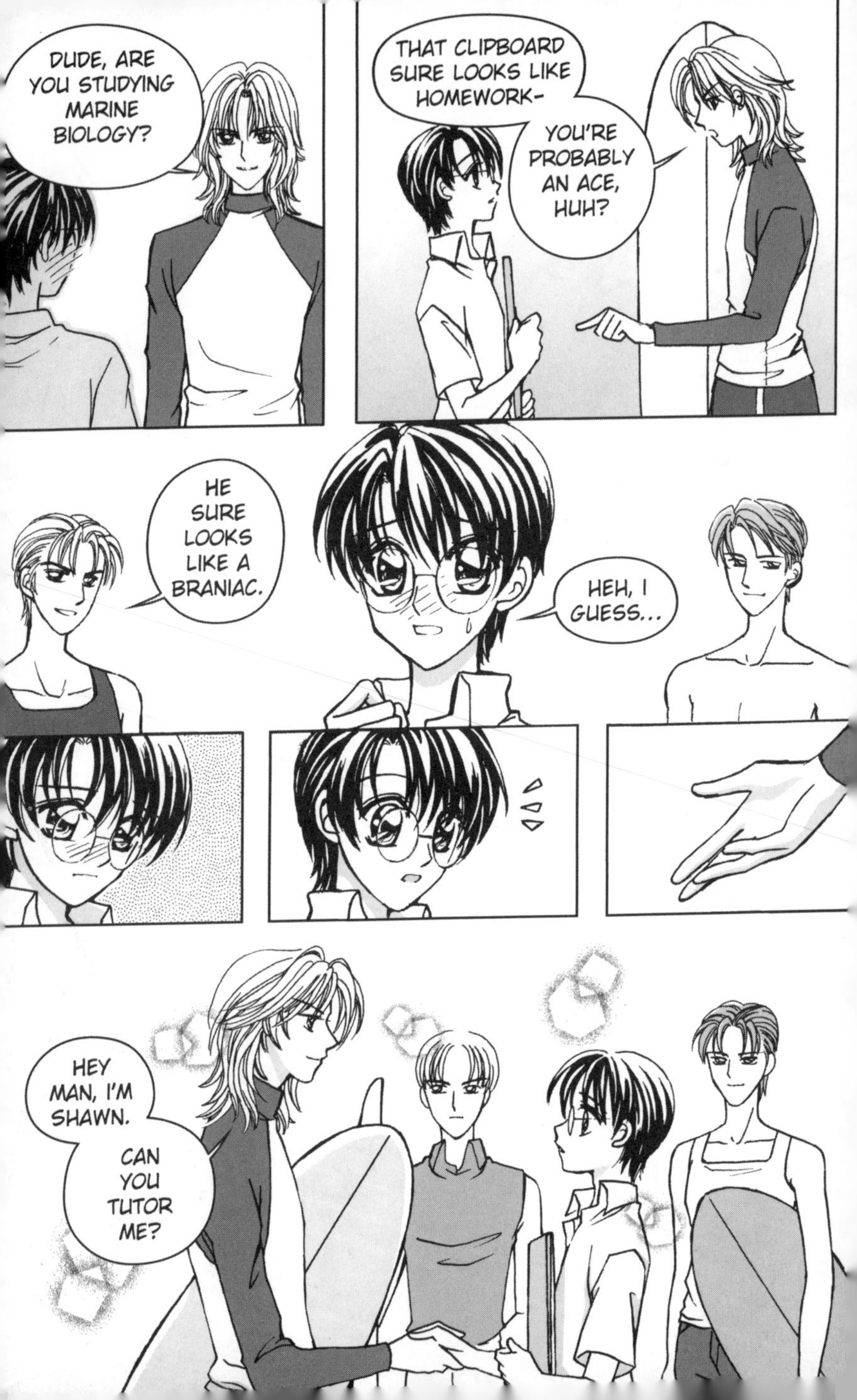
DUDE, ARE YOU STUDYING MARINE BIOLOGY?
THAT CLIPBOARD SURE LOOKS LIKE HOMEWORK-
YOU'RE PROBABLY AN ACE, HUH?
HE SURE LOOKS LIKE A BRANIAC.
HEH, I GUESS...
HEY MAN, I'M SHAWN.
CAN YOU TUTOR ME?

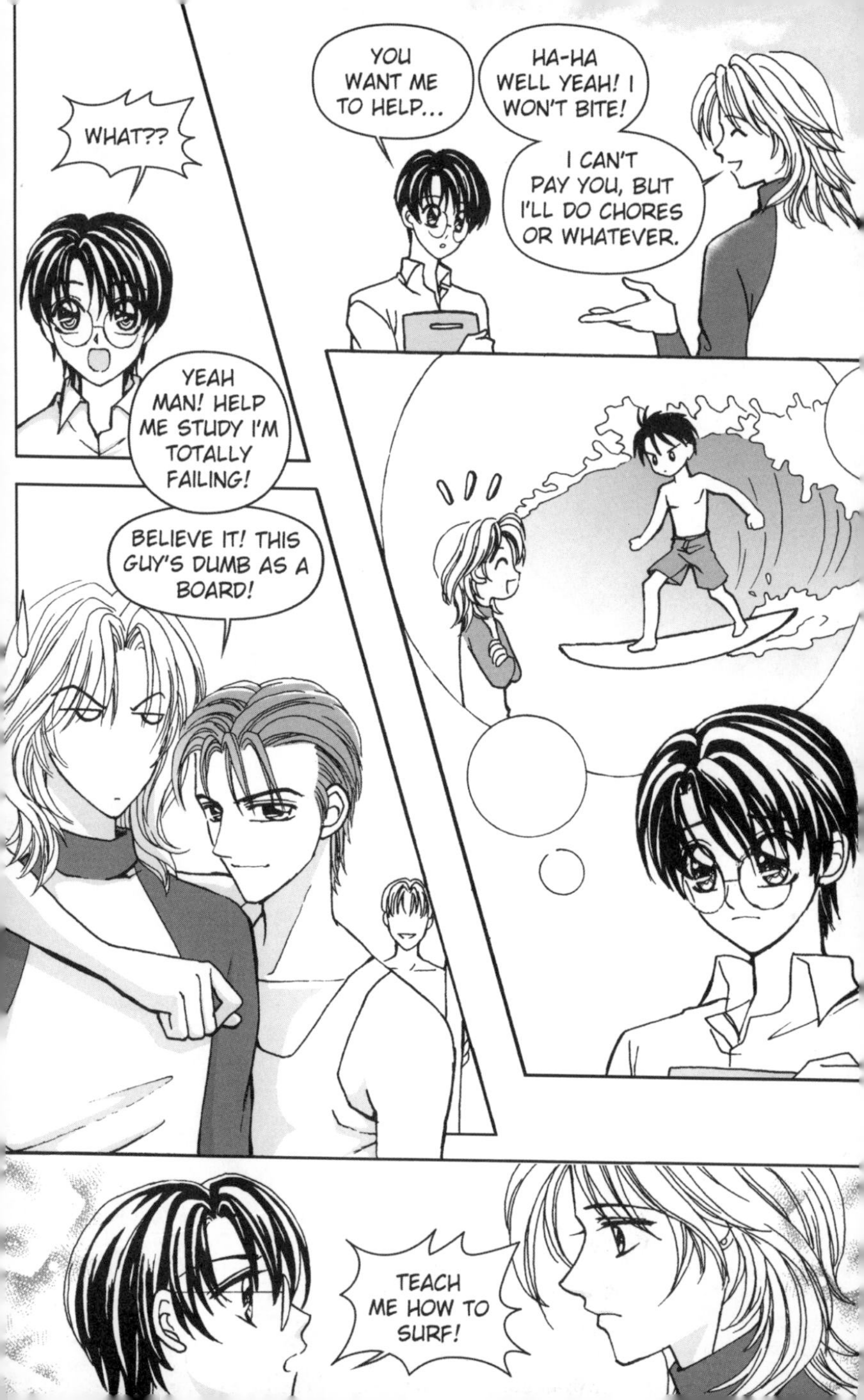
WHAT??
YOU WANT ME TO HELP...
HA-HA WELL YEAH! I WON'T BITE!
I CAN'T PAY YOU, BUT I'LL DO CHORES OR WHATEVER.
YEAH MAN! HELP ME STUDY I'M TOTALLY FAILING!
BELIEVE IT! THIS GUY'S DUMB AS A BOARD!
TEACH ME HOW TO SURF!

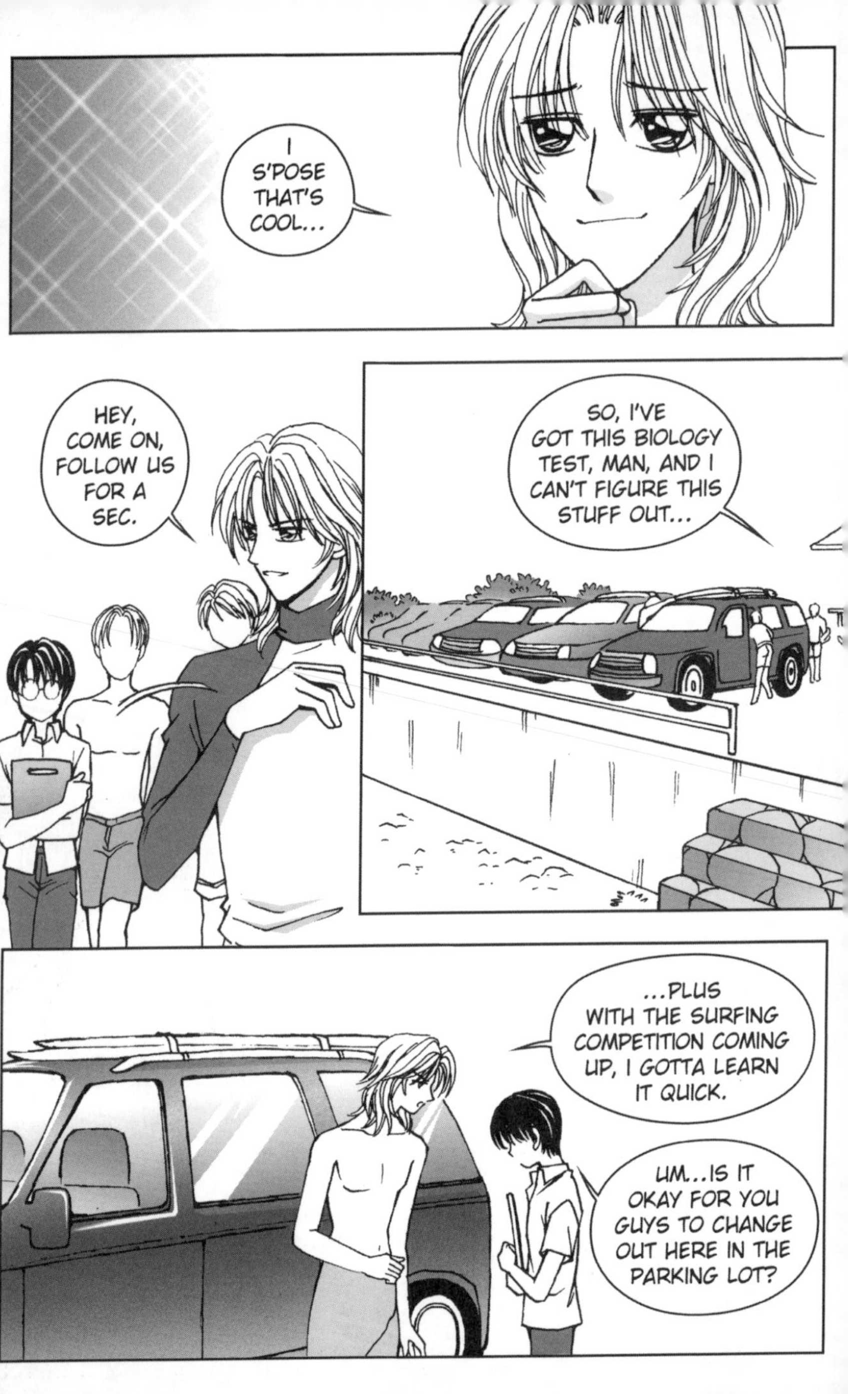
I S'POSE THAT'S COOL...
SO, I'VE GOT THIS BIOLOGY TEST, MAN, AND I CAN'T FIGURE THIS STUFF OUT...
HEY, COME ON, FOLLOW US FOR A SEC.
...PLUS WITH THE SURFING COMPETITION COMING UP, I GOTTA LEARN IT QUICK.
UM...IS IT OKAY FOR YOU GUYS TO CHANGE OUT HERE IN THE PARKING LOT?

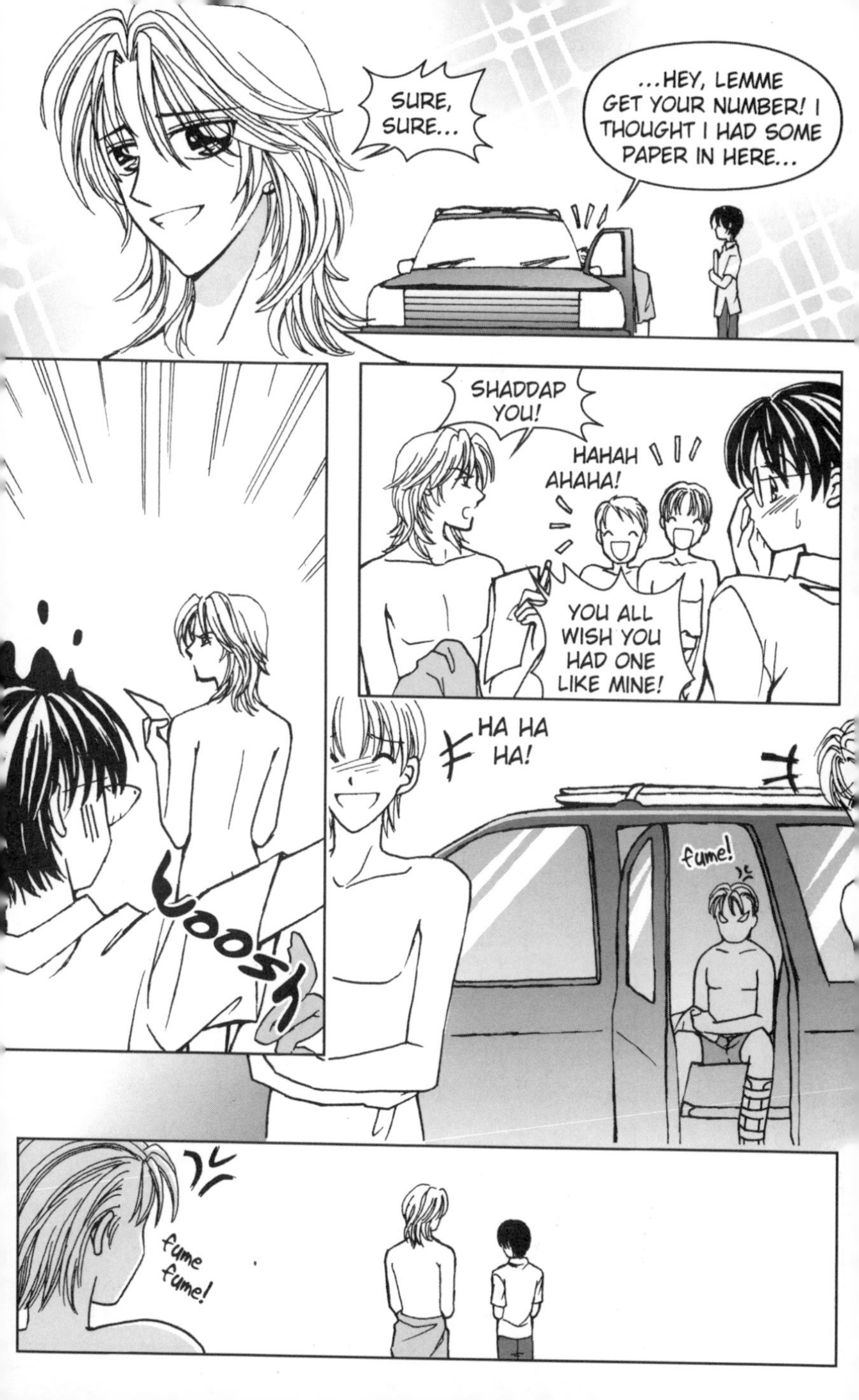
...HEY, LEMME GET YOUR NUMBER! I THOUGHT I HAD SOME PAPER IN HERE...
SURE, SURE...
SHADDAP YOU!
HAHAH AHAHA!
YOU ALL WISH YOU HAD ONE LIKE MINE!
WOOSH
HA HA HA!
fume!
fume fume!

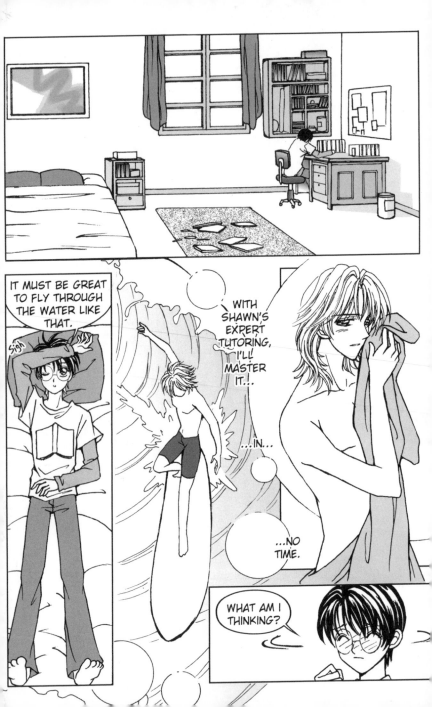

IT MUST BE GREAT TO FLY THROUGH THE WATER LIKE THAT.

Sigh

WITH SHAWN'S EXPERT TUTORING, I'LL MASTER IT...

...IN...

...NO TIME.

WHAT AM I THINKING?

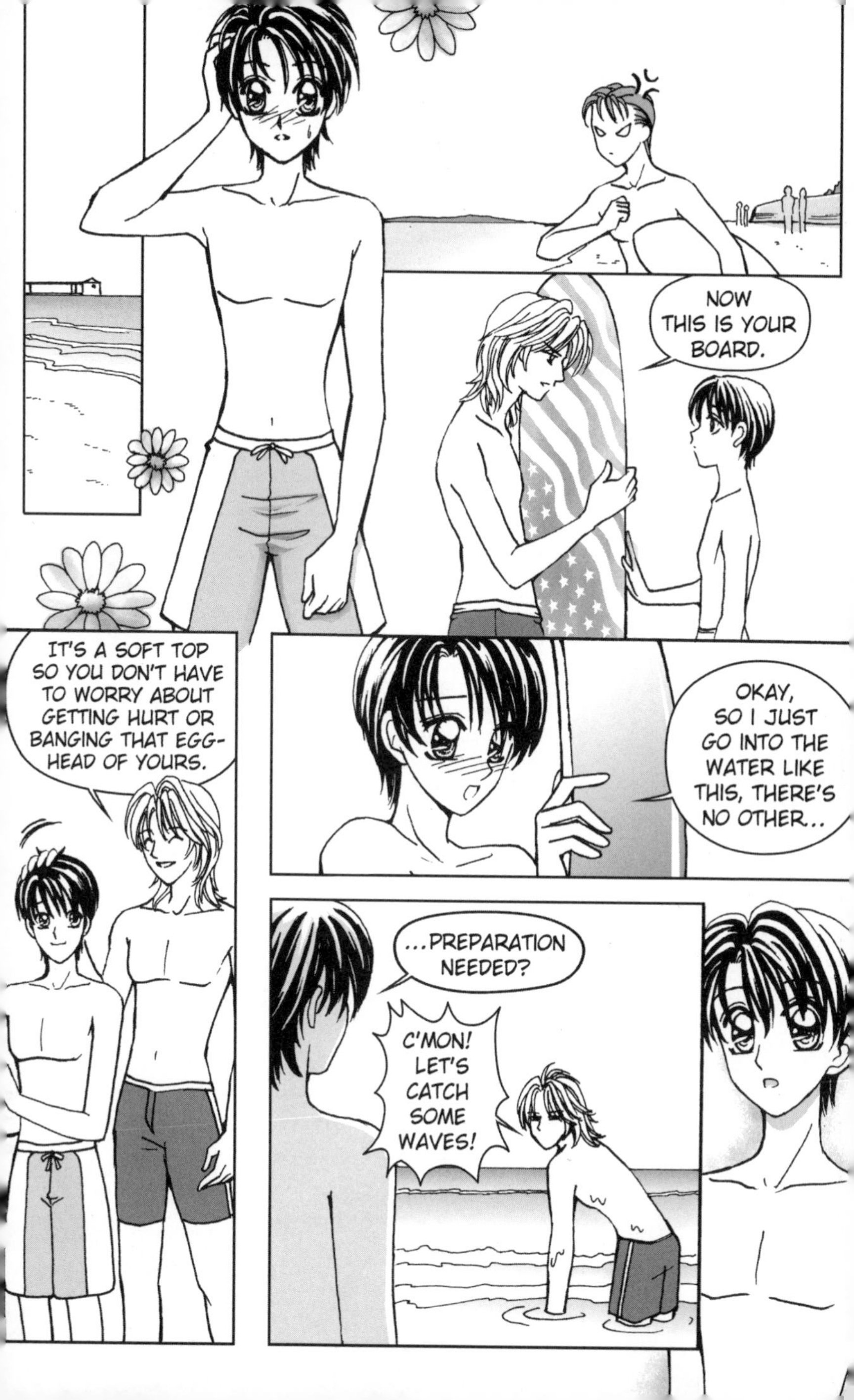
NOW THIS IS YOUR BOARD.
IT'S A SOFT TOP SO YOU DON'T HAVE TO WORRY ABOUT GETTING HURT OR BANGING THAT EGG-HEAD OF YOURS.
OKAY, SO I JUST GO INTO THE WATER LIKE THIS, THERE'S NO OTHER...
...PREPARATION NEEDED?
C'MON! LET'S CATCH SOME WAVES!

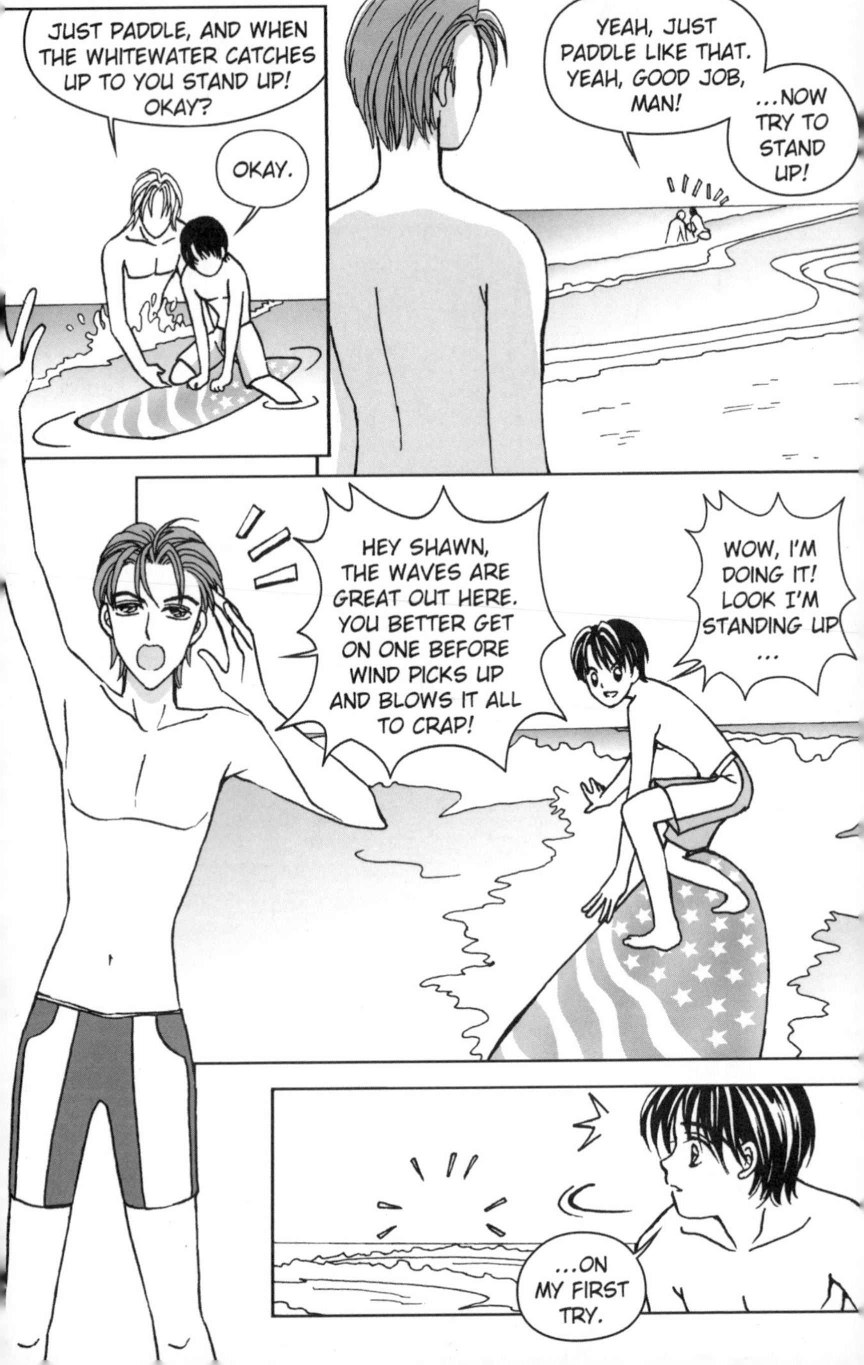
JUST PADDLE, AND WHEN THE WHITEWATER CATCHES UP TO YOU STAND UP! OKAY?
OKAY.
YEAH, JUST PADDLE LIKE THAT. YEAH, GOOD JOB, MAN!
...NOW TRY TO STAND UP!
HEY SHAWN, THE WAVES ARE GREAT OUT HERE. YOU BETTER GET ON ONE BEFORE WIND PICKS UP AND BLOWS IT ALL TO CRAP!
WOW, I'M DOING IT! LOOK I'M STANDING UP ...
...ON MY FIRST TRY.

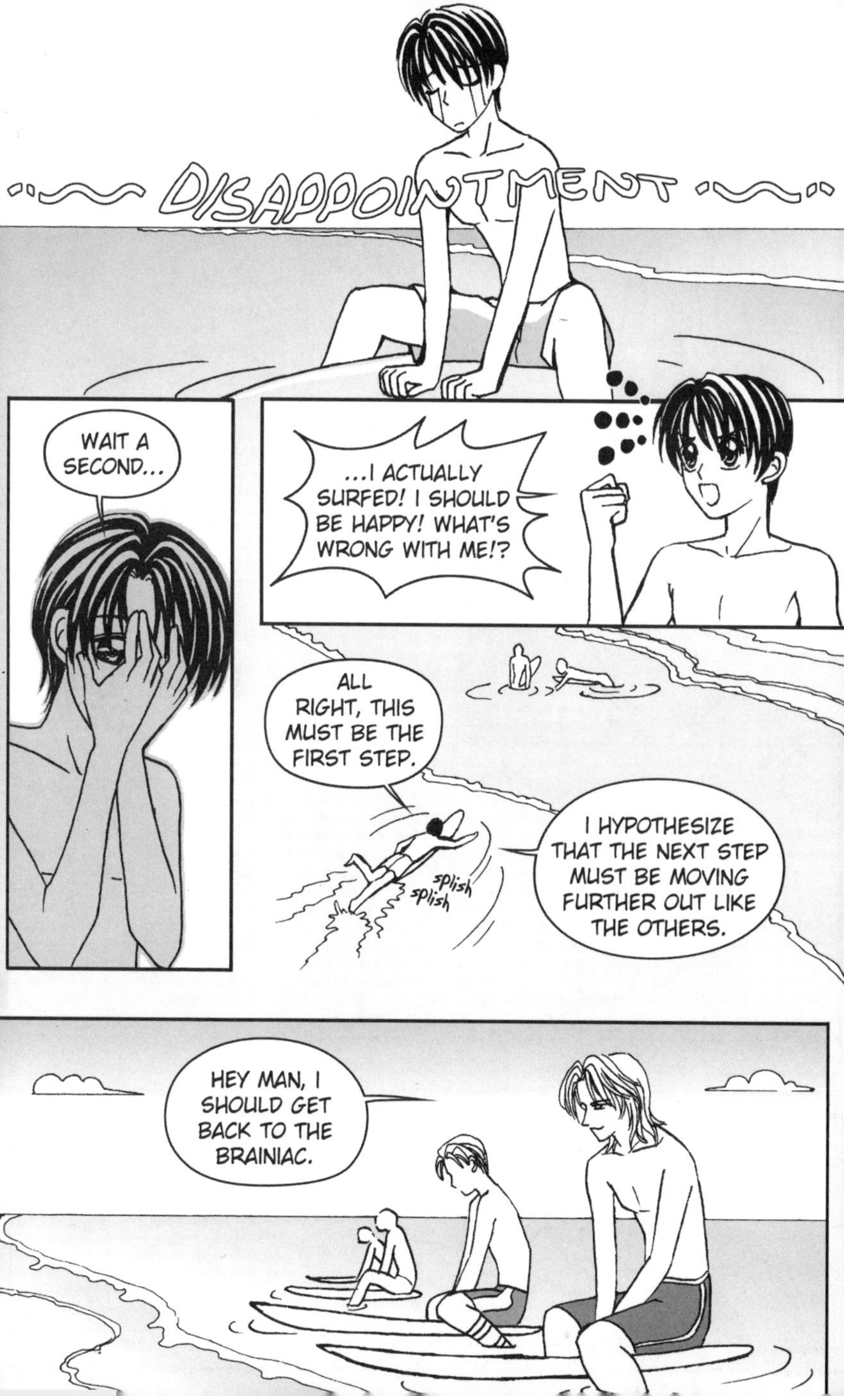
DISAPPOINTMENT
WAIT A SECOND...
...I ACTUALLY SURFED! I SHOULD BE HAPPY! WHAT'S WRONG WITH ME!?
ALL RIGHT, THIS MUST BE THE FIRST STEP.
I HYPOTHESIZE THAT THE NEXT STEP MUST BE MOVING FURTHER OUT LIKE THE OTHERS.
splish splish
HEY MAN, I SHOULD GET BACK TO THE BRAINIAC.

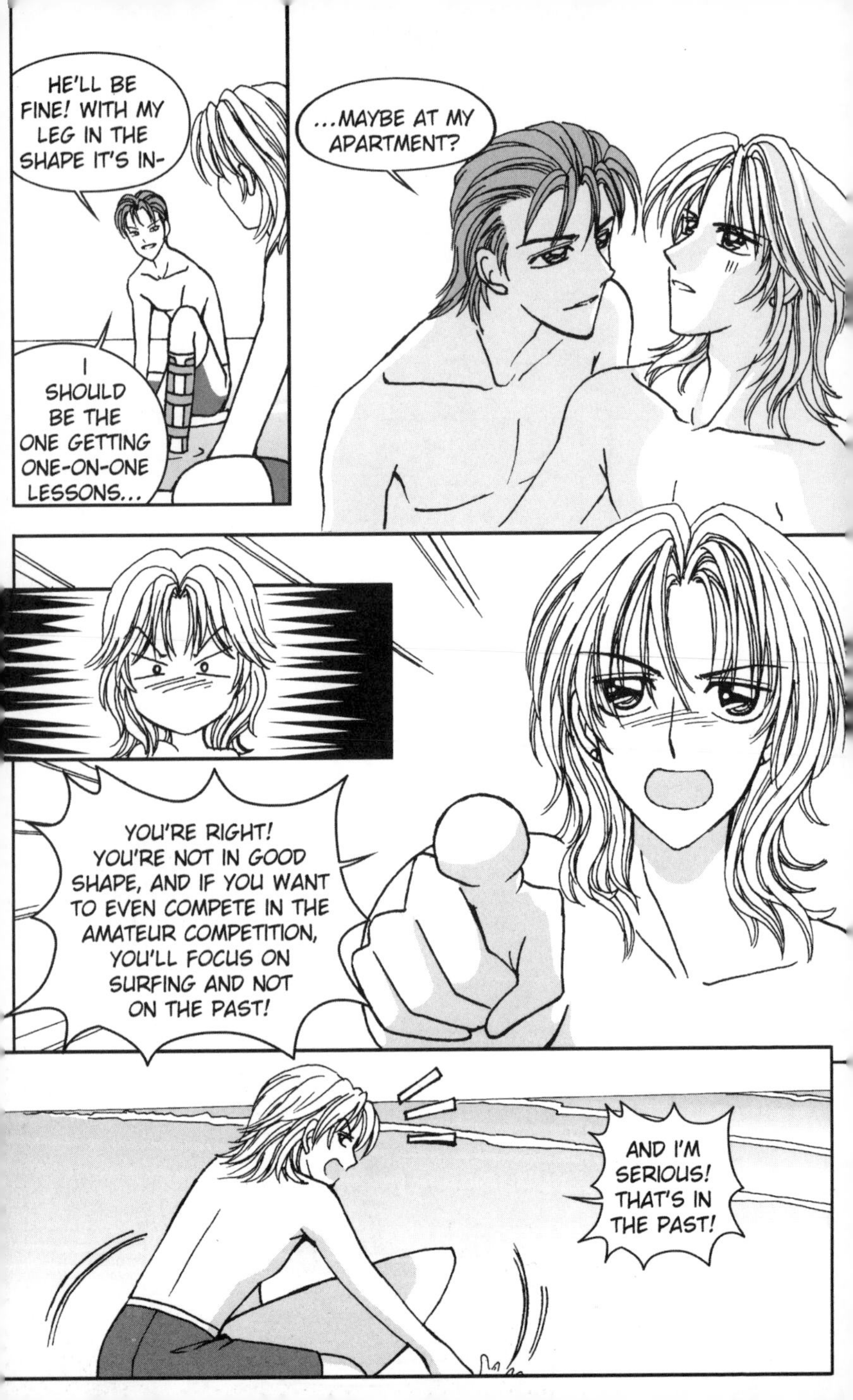
HE'LL BE FINE! WITH MY LEG IN THE SHAPE IT'S IN-
I SHOULD BE THE ONE GETTING ONE-ON-ONE LESSONS...
...MAYBE AT MY APARTMENT?
YOU'RE RIGHT! YOU'RE NOT IN GOOD SHAPE, AND IF YOU WANT TO EVEN COMPETE IN THE AMATEUR COMPETITION, YOU'LL FOCUS ON SURFING AND NOT ON THE PAST!
AND I'M SERIOUS! THAT'S IN THE PAST!

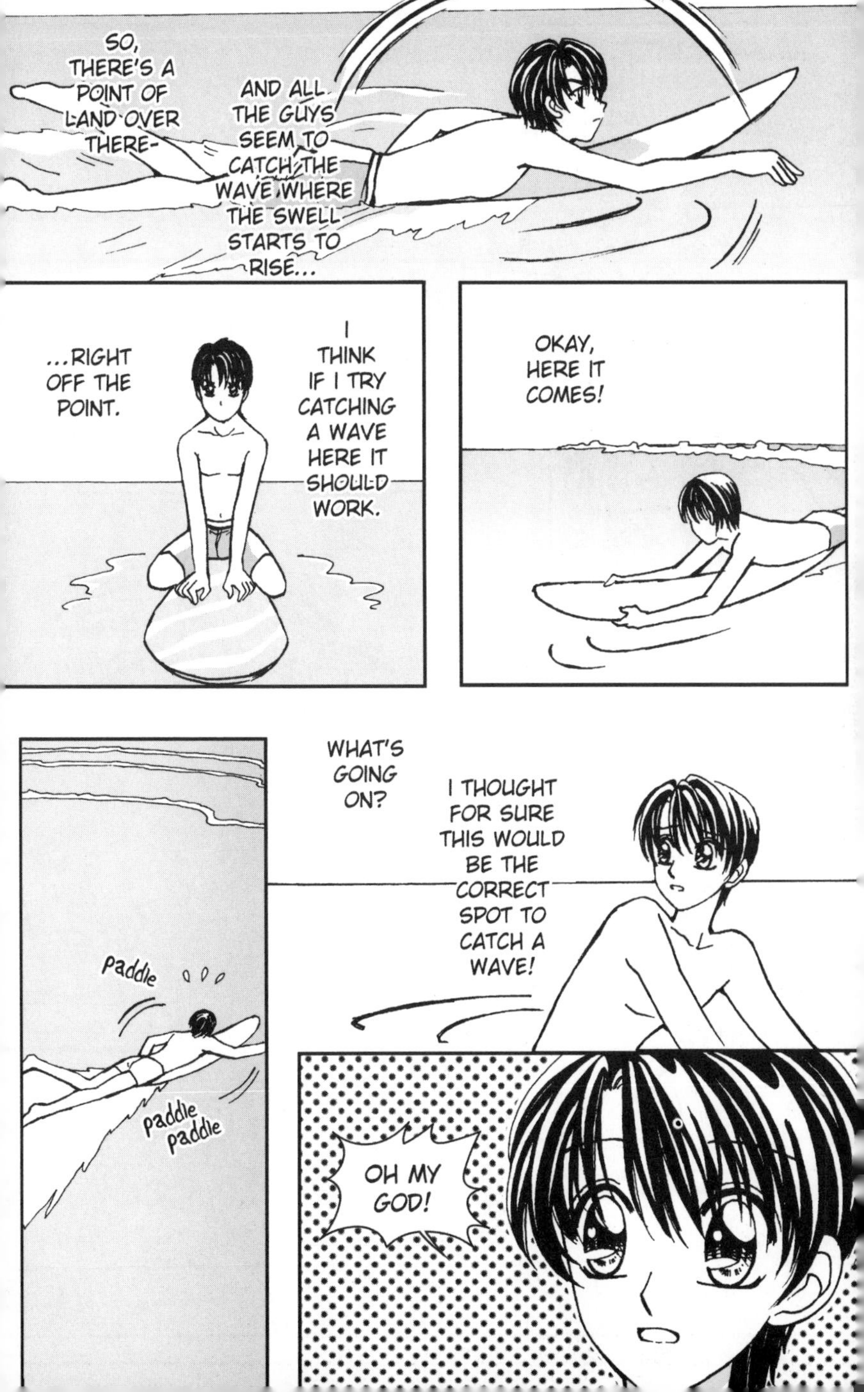
SO, THERE'S A POINT OF LAND OVER THERE-
AND ALL THE GUYS SEEM TO CATCH THE WAVE WHERE THE SWELL STARTS TO RISE...
...RIGHT OFF THE POINT.
I THINK IF I TRY CATCHING A WAVE HERE IT SHOULD WORK.
OKAY, HERE IT COMES!
WHAT'S GOING ON?
I THOUGHT FOR SURE THIS WOULD BE THE CORRECT SPOT TO CATCH A WAVE!
paddle
paddle paddle
OH MY GOD!

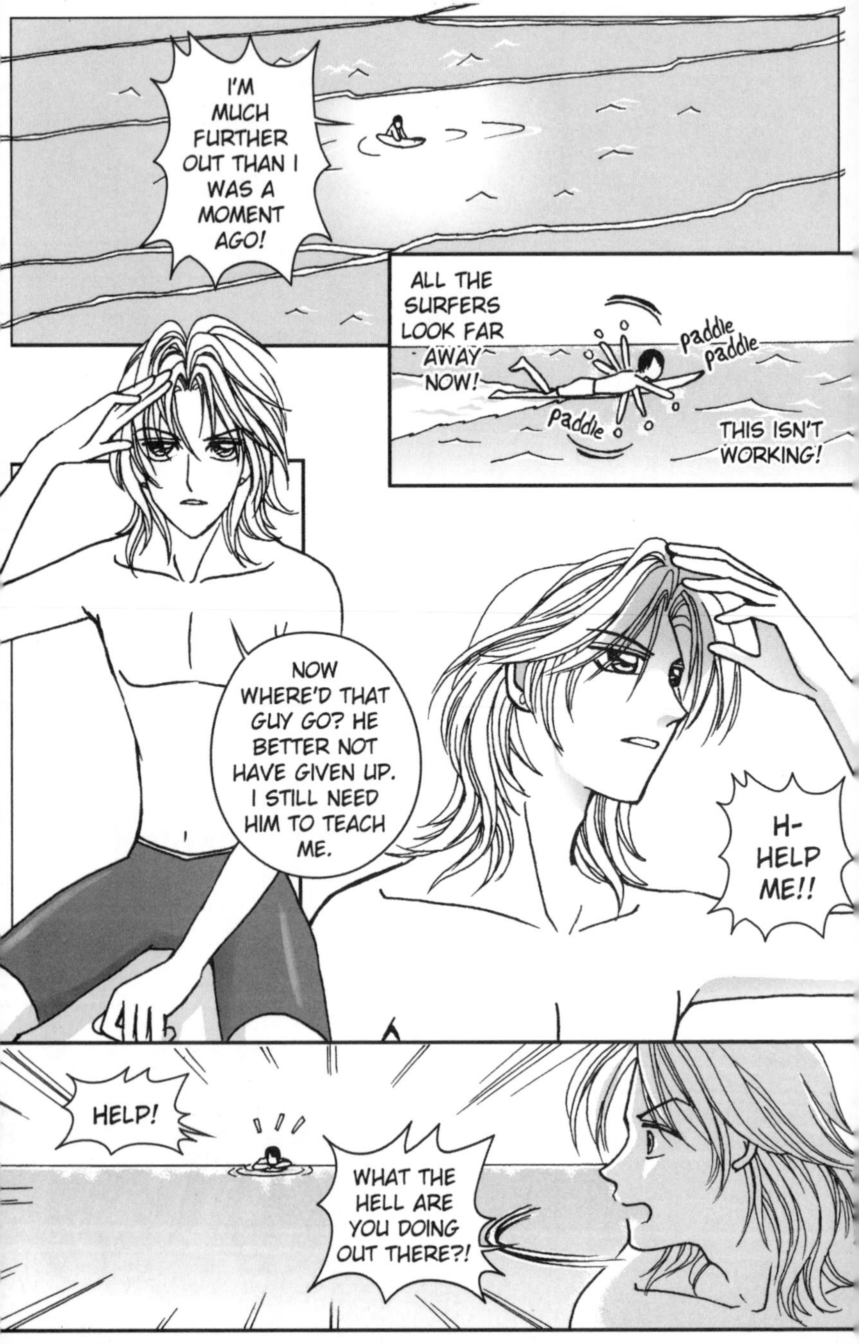
I'M MUCH FURTHER OUT THAN I WAS A MOMENT AGO!
ALL THE SURFERS LOOK FAR AWAY NOW!
paddle paddle
paddle
THIS ISN'T WORKING!
NOW WHERE'D THAT GUY GO? HE BETTER NOT HAVE GIVEN UP. I STILL NEED HIM TO TEACH ME.
H-HELP ME!!
HELP!
WHAT THE HELL ARE YOU DOING OUT THERE?!

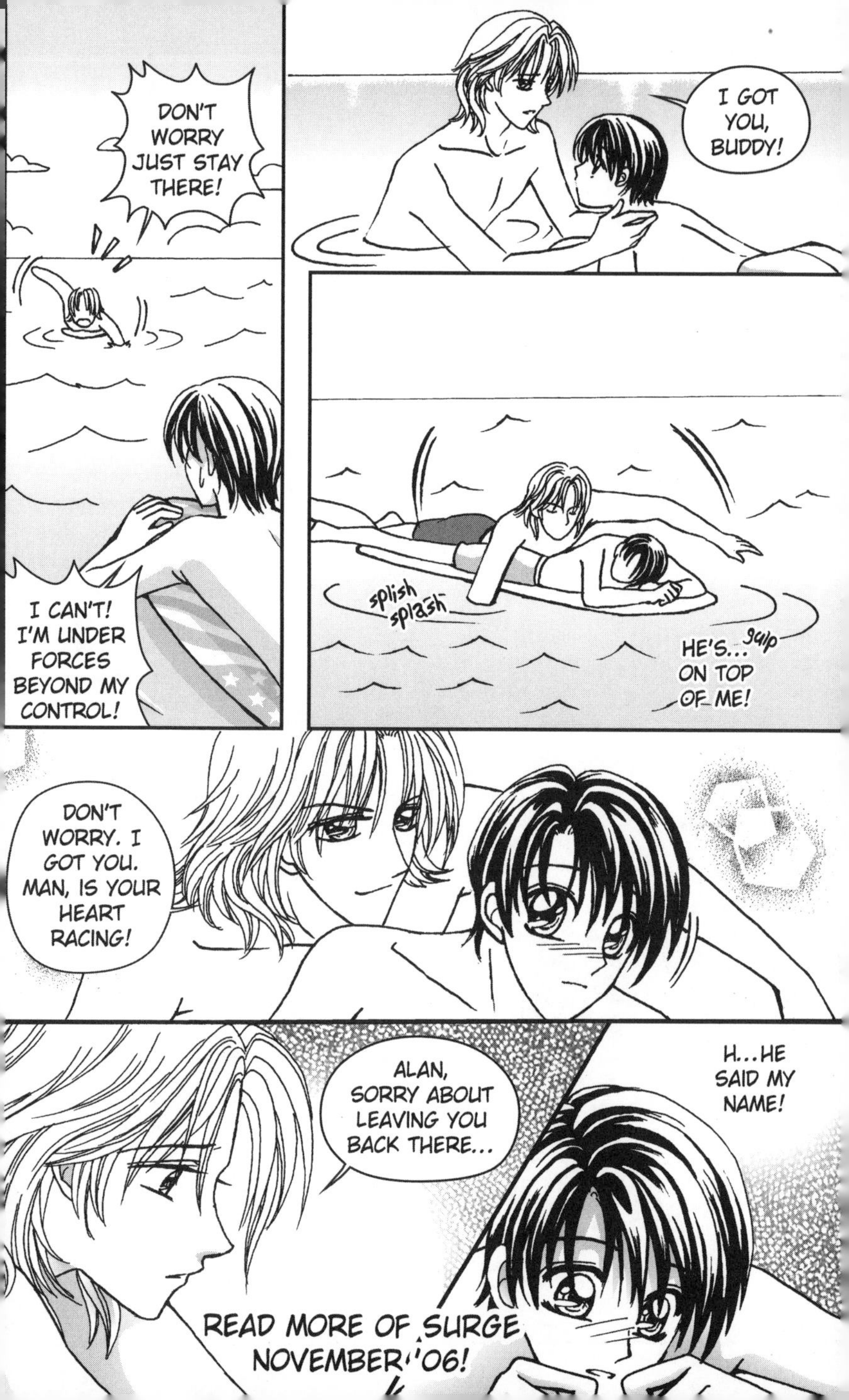
DON'T WORRY JUST STAY THERE!
I CAN'T! I'M UNDER FORCES BEYOND MY CONTROL!
I GOT YOU, BUDDY!
splish splash
HE'S... gulp ON TOP OF ME!
DON'T WORRY. I GOT YOU. MAN, IS YOUR HEART RACING!
ALAN, SORRY ABOUT LEAVING YOU BACK THERE...
H...HE SAID MY NAME!
READ MORE OF SURGE NOVEMBER '06!

Coming Feb. 2007!

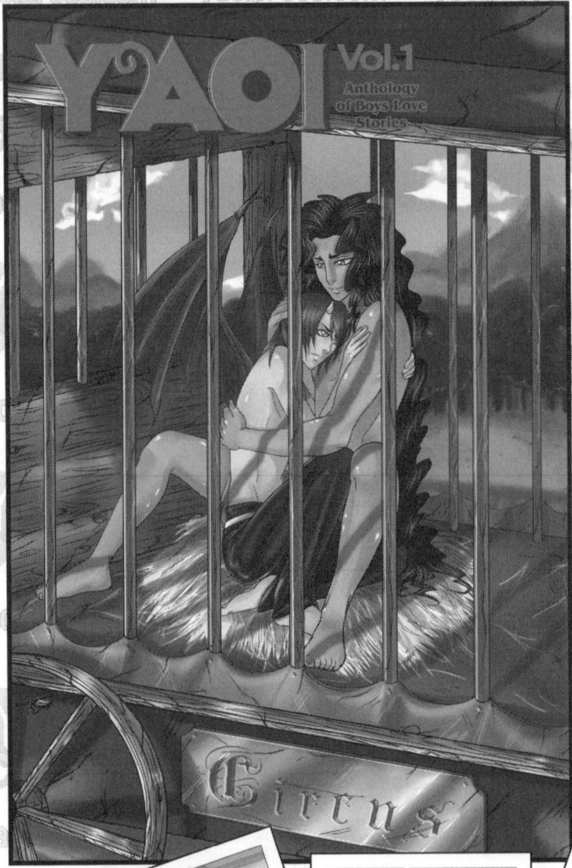
YAOI
Vol.1
Anthology of Boys Love Stories
Circus

Yaoi Vol.1

Various Artists

Yaoi anthology of three heart wrenching love stories. First theres romance between prisoners of a medieval circus, then between members of rival Tokyo gangs, and finally, between a cop and a young man who escapes two sadistic hillbilly captors.

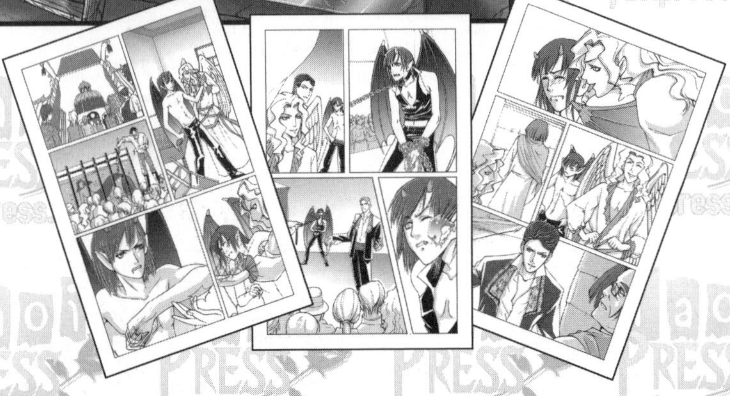

Available Now!

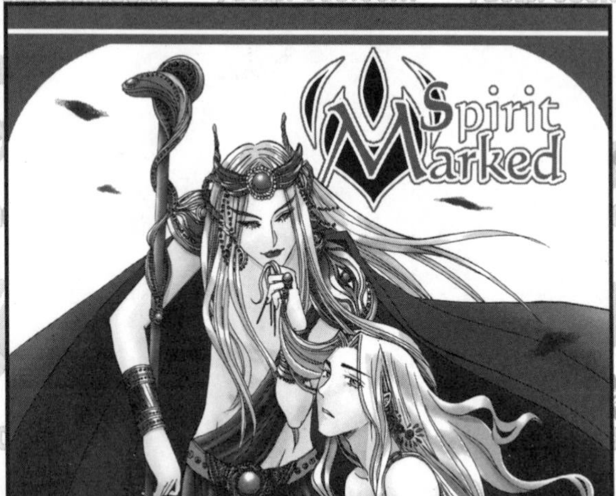
Spirit Marked
Art by Yishan Li
Story by Colter Hillman

Spirit Marked

by Yishan Li and Colter Hillman

The demon shogun murdered the emperor, and only his nephew Tatsuki escaped. Tatsuki becomes marked with power of the tiger spirit. He's joined by a second spirit-marked, the beautiful acrobat, Keo. He's sure he can avenge his emperor now, but the shogun crafts a seductive deception for him.

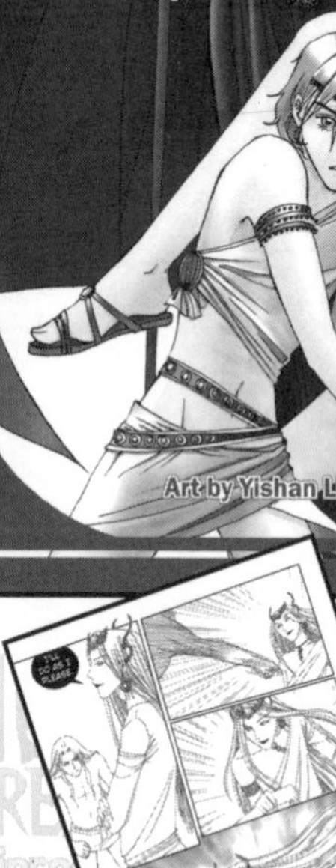
I'LL DO AS I PLEASE.

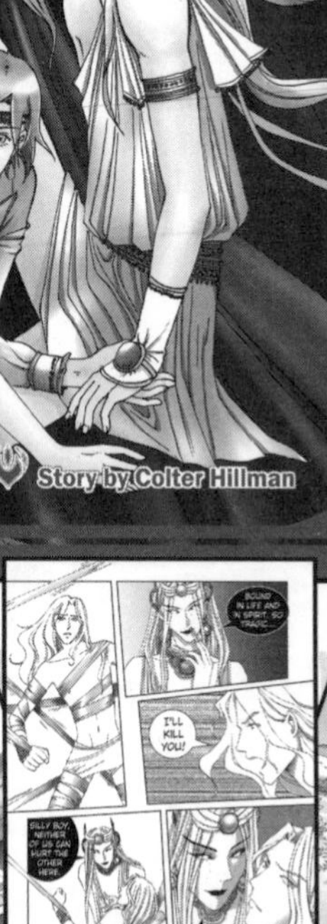
BOUND IN LIFE AND IN SPIRIT, SO TRAGIC...
I'LL KILL YOU!
SILLY BOY, NEITHER OF US CAN HURT THE OTHER HERE.
HURTING YOU...
...IS THE LAST THING I WANT TO DO.

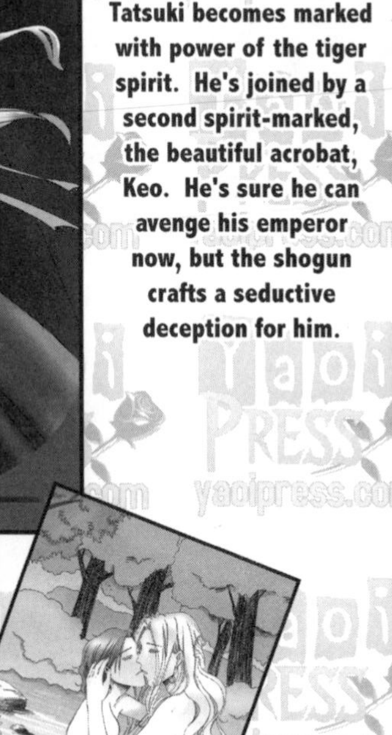